Pets Welcome! 2000

1

PETS WELCOME!

2000

The Animal Lovers' Holiday Guide

COLOUR SECTION

Please note all advertisers in this Colour section also have full display and classified entries under the relevant county in the main section of the Guide.

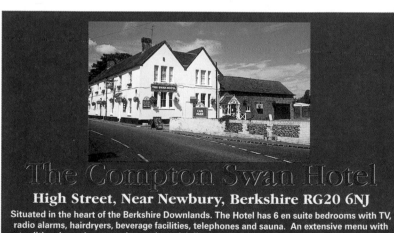

The Compton Swan Hotel

High Street, Near Newbury, Berkshire RG20 6NJ

Situated in the heart of the Berkshire Downlands. The Hotel has 6 en suite bedrooms with TV, radio alarms, hairdryers, beverage facilities, telephones and sauna. An extensive menu with traditional, exotic, vegetarian, and special diets catered for. Our home-cooked meals are a speciality. Downlands Healthy Eating Award winner. Large walled garden where we have *al fresco* eating; BBQs. Near the famous ancient Ridgeway National Trail and is an ideal base for walking, horse-riding, and golf. Stabling and horsebox available. Real Ales and Bar Meals available. Entry in CAMRA Good Beer Guide and Good Pub Guide. ETB.
A friendly reception by staff and our Jack Russell "Berkeley".

Phone **Garry Mitchell F.B.I.I.** on **01635 578269** Fax: **01635 578765**
Email: garry@comptonswan.freeserve.co.uk www.SmoothHound.co.uk/hotels/comptons.html

An age old hostelry...
...perched in cliff top gardens

Open in all seasons, in all weathers for every travellers needs with windows of ships timber, log fired rooms, gazing seawards above the lost harbours of Trevaunance.

Warm beds, cool ales, fine wines and appetising fayre with abundant seafood, home baked scones and scrumptious Cornish clotted cream.

We rate food very highly in our list of priorities as borne out by the fact that we employ three chefs! It might be the ample breakfast where the aromas of coffee and bacon merge to tempt the tastebuds; lifesavers at lunchtime, tempting, tasty and accompanied by whatsoever you fancy from the bar, or the romantic evening meal where a wide variety of fresh fish, meat and vegetarian dishes are produced, complemented by the hotel's extensive wine list, the whole experience enhanced by the attentive service, soft candlelight and the flickering firelight casting shadows and shapes over old beams and relaxed faces.

Trevaunance Point Hotel

Children are welcome to eat with parents but a special menu including a junior menu is available.

Trevaunance Cove St Agnes Cornwall TR5 0RZ

Telephone 01872 553235

Facsimile 01872 553874

Dalswinton
COUNTRY HOUSE HOTEL

A Victorian stone built Cornish house of character in a rural setting. Standing in 8 acres of secluded formal gardens and meadowland, the house overlooks the Vale of Lanherne and the village of St Mawgan with views to the sea at the dog friendly beach of Mawgan Porth. The Hotel is family run offering excellent food in a comfortable and friendly atmosphere. Please call 01637 860385 for more details and our colour brochure.

DINNER, BED AND BREAKFAST FROM £222.00 PER WEEK ● BED AND BREAKFAST FROM £144.00 PER WEEK ● SOLAR HEATED OUTDOOR SWIMMING POOL ● AMPLE CAR PARKING ● 8 ACRES OF PRIVATELY OWNED MEADOWLAND FOR DOG EXERCISE ● DOGS FREE OF CHARGE AND ALLOWED EVERYWHERE EXCEPT THE DINING ROOM ● TEA / COFFEE / COLOUR TV IN ALL ROOMS ● RESTAURANT AND BAR ● ONE FAMILY CHALET SELF CATERING/ROOM RATE ● OPEN ALL YEAR

STUART AND NICOLA BUSH,
DALSWINTON COUNTRY HOUSE HOTEL, ST MAWGAN-IN-PYDAR,
NEWQUAY, CORNWALL TR8 4EZ. TEL/FAX: (01637) 860385

White Lodge Hotel

Mawgan Porth Bay, Near Newquay, Cornwall TR8 4BN
Tel: St. Mawgan (STD 01637) 860512

GIVE YOURSELVES & YOUR DOGS A BREAK

at our family-run White Lodge Hotel overlooking beautiful
Mawgan Porth Bay, near Newquay, Cornwall

★ Dogs most welcome-
FREE OF CHARGE
★ Your dogs sleep with you in your
bedroom.
★ Direct access to sandy beach and
coastal path.
★ Dog loving proprietors with 17
years' experience in catering for
dog owners on holiday with their
dogs
★ ALL bedrooms with colour TV
with video and satellite channels,
tea/coffee makers, alarm clocks,
radios, intercoms, heaters etc.
★ Some en suite bedrooms
★ Fantastic sea views from most
rooms
★ Well-stocked residents' lounge
bar, dining room & sun patio with
outstanding sea views across the
bay.
★ Games room with pool table and
dart board etc.
★ Large free car park within hotel
grounds

SPECIAL 6 DAYS (5 NIGHTS) CHRISTMAS HOUSE PARTY **ONLY £235** *Full Board*	SPECIAL 6 DAYS (5 NIGHTS) NEW YEAR (HOGMANAY) BREAK **ONLY £205** *Half Board*	SPECIAL 6 DAYS (5 NIGHTS) BREAKS **ONLY** **£155-£170** *BB &* *Evening Meal*	WEEKLY TERMS **FROM £203-£225** FOR 5-COURSE EVENING DINNER, BED AND 4-COURSE BREAKFAST WITH CHOICE OF MENU

Phone 01637 860512 John or Diane Parry
for free colour brochure

ALL PRICES INCLUDE VAT AT 17½%

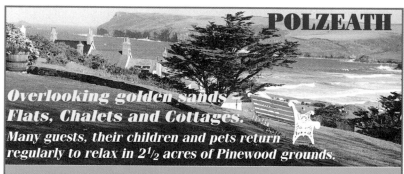
Please mention Pets Welcome! when enquiring

Derwent Manor

Portinscale, KESWICK, Cumbria, England, CA12 5RE

rwent Manor

ıry Lakeland Holiday Cottages and Apartments

This former gentleman's country residence now provides some of Lakeland's finest self-catering accommodation amid tranquil surroundings on the fringe of a picturesque village. Wander down to the shores of Lake Derwentwater through 16 acres of private, unspoilt meadows - a recognised conservation area, or stroll along footpaths and over the River into the market town of Keswick.

Our tastefully converted one or two bedroomed self-catering apartments and cottages are all superbly appointed and offer a uniquely high standard of facilities. Fully fitted feature kitchens (many with dishwashers), independent central heating, remote control teletext colour televisions with video player, CD player and direct dial telephone, whilst the bedrooms are complete with hairdryer, trouser press and radio alarms.

Your accommodation comes complete with welcoming tea tray, bouquet of fresh flowers, fruit basket, beds made and towels supplied. Even fresh milk in the fridge, and to be sure your holiday starts with a sparkle, a bottle of chilled Champagne.

But that's not all.

On your first evening with our compliments, you may have dinner at the adjacent award winning and highly commended Derwentwater Hotel. Likewise, breakfast on your departure morning is also included, and there is more, ample free parking, takeaway meal and grocery delivery service, and a special welcome for pets.

For that really special occasion try our Glaramara Cottage, which is tucked away in the corner of the grounds and enjoys king size, half tester bed making an ideal romantic hideaway.

Derwent Manor ...
an unrivalled location
with quality accommodation
and a range of
services and facilities
seldom matched.

Call us now for
our full colour brochure
on 017687 72211.

Holbeck Ghyll Lodge

Tel: 01484 684605
Fax: 01484 689051

Extremely comfortable traditional Lakeland stone lodge with enclosed garden at rear. Two twin bedded bedrooms. Dining/living room with open fire and sofa bed. Fully equipped oak fitted kitchen. Bathroom with bath and shower. Second toilet. Antique pine furniture throughout. House situated for local walks, lake and pubs. Secure covered way for bikes. Parking for three cars. Available Easter to end of October. Saturday change over.

**Mrs Kay, Holmdene,
Stoney Bank Road, Holmfirth HD7 2SL**

Tanglewood Caravan Park

CAUSEWAY HEAD, SILLOTH-ON-SOLWAY, CUMBRIA CA5 4PE

Tanglewood is a family-run park on the fringes of the Lake District National Park. It is tree-sheltered and situated one mile inland from the small port of Silloth on the Solway Firth, with a beautiful view of the Galloway Hills. Large modern holiday homes are available from March to October, with car parking beside each home. Fully equipped except for bed

linen, with end bedroom, central heating in bedrooms, electric lighting, hot and cold water, toilet, shower, gas fire, fridge and colour TV, all of which are included in the tariff. Touring pitches also available with electric hook-ups and water/drainage facilities, etc. Play area. Licensed lounge with adjoining children's play room. Pets welcome free but must be kept under control at all times. Full colour brochure available.

TEL: 016973 31253 ✓✓✓

Overwater Hall

**OVERWATER, near IREBY,
KESWICK, CUMBRIA CA5 1HH**

Tel & Fax: (017687) 76566

Elegant 18th century Country House Hotel in extensive grounds. AA award-winning restaurant. 4 poster Bedrooms for those special occasions. Peacefully secluded - the ideal location for a REAL break.

Dogs very welcome in your room. 18 acres of gardens for your dog to enjoy unleashed.
Special four night breaks available all year.

Available from most bookshops, the year 2000 edition of
The GOLF GUIDE covers details of every UK golf course –
well over 2500 entries – for holiday or business golf.
Hundreds of hotel entries offer convenient accommodation,
accompanying details of the courses – the 'pro', par score, length etc.
*Holiday Golf in Ireland, France, Portugal, Spain,
The USA and Thailand. In association with* **GOLF**
Including the Ryder Cup Report. MONTHLY

**£9.95 from bookshops or £10.50 including postage
(UK only) from FHG Publications,
Abbey Mill Business Centre, Paisley PA1 1TJ**

FHG

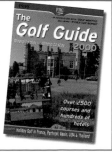

Welcome

Family Holiday Park
DAWLISH WARREN SOUTH DEVON

First rate facilities and friendly personal service provide the perfect family holiday!

★ Stylish Dolphin Club, Entertainment Centre with Kaleidoscope Disco

★ Superb Indoor Heated Neptune Tropicana Water Leisure Complex - four feature packed Pools, Solarium and Spectator Viewing area.

★ Childrens' Jolly Roger Club with Disco, Cinema and large Games Arcade

★ Short, level walk to safe sandy beach

★ Hire service with Computer Games
★ Pets Welcome (at small charge)

★ Caravans, Villas, Apartments & Bungalows - Accommodation to suit all tastes and pockets.

We are Here!

BRISTOL
M5
EXETER   A303
PLYMOUTH
Welcom

Situated in a picturesque part of Devon, only a short level walk to sandy dunes and wildlife areas. Only 15 minutes from the M5, a half hour or so drive from a host of attractions!

★
Cruisers Adult Cocktail Bar with Big Screen TV

★ Great value-for-money prices
★ Free electricity, linen, Colour TV
★ Welcome Movie Channel - great films for all the family
★ 3 Shops • Cafe • 2 Takeaways • Crazy Golf
★ Adventure Playground
★ Launderette

English Tourism Council
★★★★
HOLIDAY PARK

ROSE AWARD

Enquiries / Reservations 01626 862070

Please mention Pets Welcome! when enquiring

YOUR PET STAYS FREE

**Your pet is welcome to
stay FREE if you
return this advert
with your booking**

Commended

THE EXMOOR SANDPIPER INN

A fine old coaching Inn, reputedly dating in part from the 13th and 15th centuries. It is in a beautiful setting amidst rolling moors, high above Lynmouth on the coastal road with the dramatic backdrop of Exmoor. Let us spoil you on arrival with a **free cream tea** and then be shown up to a beautiful character bedroom with tea making, colour TV and bathroom en suite, designed for your every comfort. A warm bath then a 5-course dinner including smoked salmon, seafood platters with lobster, steaks and a delicious selection of sweets. Sit in the character bars and sample our real ales or watch the late film in your bedroom.

After a traditional English breakfast set off to discover the magic of Exmoor whether in the car or on foot, along Doone Valley following the River to the majestic Watersmeet, or further to the Valley of the Rocks and up over to Glenthorne and beyond to the Devon/Somerset Borders. We have 7 circular walks around the area and the Inn can provide a packed lunch.

Please write or ring for FREE colour brochure to:-

**The Exmoor Sandpiper Inn,
Countisbury, Lynmouth,
N.Devon EX35 6NE**

**Tel: 01598 741263
E-mail: exmoorsandpiper.demon.co.uk**

YOUR PET STAYS FREE

♛ ♛ ♛ ♛

Sandy Cove Hotel stands in 20 acres of cliff, coast and garden. The Hotel Restaurant overlooks the sea and cliffs with spectacular views of the bay. You will probably wonder how we can do it for the price when we offer a FIVE-COURSE MEAL including seafood platters with lobster, smoked salmon and steak. Every Saturday a Swedish Smorgasbord and Carvery carved by the Chef, and followed by dancing till late. Live entertainment weekly from Whitsun until September. All bedrooms have colour TV, telephone, teamaking and are en suite. The cocktail bar overlooks the bay and you have the use of the hotel's 80° heated indoor pool and recreation centre with sauna, sunbed, gym equipment and whirlpool, ALL FREE OF CHARGE.

Please return this advertisement to qualify for "Pets Stay Free" offer. Bargain Breaks and weekly rates available all year. Includes 5-course Evening Meal and coffee. Children – free accommodation. Please send for free brochure pack. Children under 5 years completely free, including meals.

Sandy Cove Hotel

Combe Martin Bay,
Devon EX34 9SR
Tel: (01271) 882243 & 882888

Indoor pool heated to 80°F with roll-back sides to enjoy the sun

"Easily the best choice of cottages in Devon..."

...and comfortably the best value you'll find anywhere !

Contact us now for a free copy of our guide to the 500 best value cottages around Devon's unspoilt National Trust Coast. Choose from Spring and Autumn breaks in delightful Exmoor farm cottages from only £89 to luxury beachside homes with swimming pools at over £890 per week in Summer.

All are regularly inspected and guaranteed to offer first class value.

North Devon Holiday Homes

19 Cross Street, Barnstaple EX31 1BD
Tel:(01271) 376322 (24 hrs) Fax:(01271) 346544
www.northdevonholidays.co.uk

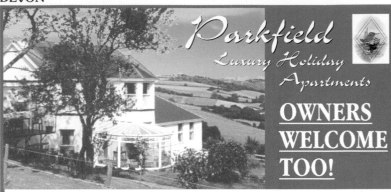
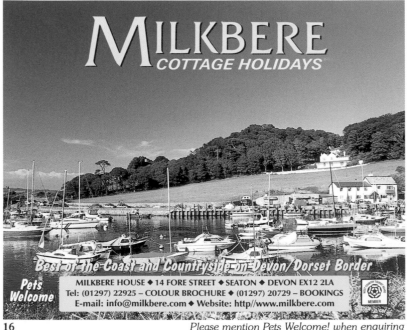

Flear Farm Cottages

Discover nine superb cottages set in 75 acres of a beautiful South Devon valley - just five miles from the sea. As well as peace and quiet, we offer a 40ft indoor heated swimming pool, sauna, all weather tennis court, large indoor and outdoor play areas.

Non-smokers only. Children and dogs welcome. Log fires and full central heating - perfect for off-season breaks

East Allington, Totnes, South Devon TQ9 7RF
E-mail: www.flearfarm.co.uk

'Phone (01548) 521227 or Fax (01548) 521600 For our Colour Brochure

---

PUBLISHER'S NOTE

While every effort is made to ensure accuracy, we regret that FHG Publications cannot accept responsibility for errors, omissions or misrepresentations in our entries or any consequences thereof. Prices in particular should be checked because we go to press early. We will follow up complaints but cannot act as arbiters or agents for either party.

THE LIMES HOTEL

A warm welcome awaits all dogs – and their owners – at the Limes Hotel, only a few hundred yards from wonderful coastal walks and surrounded by the unspoilt Purbeck Hills. En suite rooms with colour TV and hospitality trays. Pets come free!

• **Open All Year** • **Licensed Bar** • **Families Welcome** •
• **Bed and Breakfast** •

48 Park Road, Swanage, Dorset BH19 2AE
Tel: 01929 422664   Fax: 0870 0548794
e-mail: info@limeshotel.demon.co.uk
Website: www.limeshotel.demon.co.uk

Jersey Farm is family-run by the original owners still with the farm animals in the fields. We guarantee a relaxing time in this peaceful and scenic part of England

All Pets welcome Plenty of space to exercise pets

• **20 En suite Rooms including five Luxury Suites**
• **Renowned Carvery Restaurant open seven days**
• **Alternative Menu available**
• **Open all day for meals/drinks**
• **Conservatory with Games** • **Licensed Bar**
 • **Mini Breaks available**
HIGHLY COMMENDED   ★ ★ ★

Egon Ronay Recommended

Jersey Farm Hotel, Darlington Road,
Barnard Castle, Co. Durham DL12 8TA
Tel: 01833 638223 Fax: 01833 631988 Website: jerseyfarmhotel.enta.net

Other **FHG** holiday and accommodation guides

FHG Publications are available in most bookshops and larger newsagents but we will be happy to post you a copy direct if you have any difficulty. We will also post abroad but have to charge separately for post or freight.

The inclusive cost of posting and packing the guides in the UK is as follows:

£5.60

£5.00

£5.00

£5.60

£10.50

£4.20

£5.00

£4.20

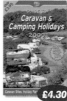
£4.30

£5.00

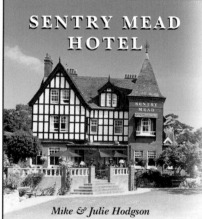
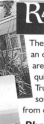

AN AWARD WINNING HOTEL
*....with style, elegance, set in tranquil surroundings
at affordable prices.*

CHASE LODGE HOTEL
10 PARK ROAD, HAMPTON WICK,
KINGSTON-UPON-THAMES KT1 4AS

Quality en suite bedrooms • Full English breakfast
• A la carte menu • Licensed bar • Wedding receptions
• Honeymoon suite • 20 minutes from Heathrow Airport

London Tourist Board ★★★ • Easy access to Kingston town centre and all major transport links

for business or pleasure... Reservations 020 8943 1862 Fax: 020 8943 9363

AA QQQQ Selected   Les Routiers   RAC Highly Acclaimed   All major credit cards accepted.

CROSSKEYS RIVERSIDE HOTEL
Tel: 01366 387777   ❦❦❦ *Commended*

Small family-run country hotel beside the River Wissey
in converted 17th century buildings, retaining the
original character. Oak beams. 3 rooms with 4-poster
bed. All en suite. Ideal for touring Norfolk and
the Cambridgeshire Fens, coast and countryside.

• *B&B- £30 per person* • *Extra nights- £27*
B&B tariff 10% reduction for all stays of 5 nights or over.

Bridge Street, Hilgay, Nr. Downham Market, Norfolk PE38 0LD

Fakenham Racecourse
Caravan & Camping Site
*The ideal choice for your Norfolk holiday
A country site. Near the sea*

Set in beautiful countryside and sheltered by tall conifers, the grounds and modern
facilities are excellently maintained. 120 pitches accommodating touring caravans,
motorcaravans and tents. Centrally heated lavatories and shower blocks. Disabled
facilities, Laundry rooms and mothercare unit. Site shop. Cable TV. Sports Centre
on site (golf, tennis, squash, meals and licensed bar).
Ideally located for visiting Norfolk's coastal resorts, stately homes, wildlife and
bird sanctuaries and many other attractions.

From £8.50 to £11.00 for 2 adults per night.   ✓✓✓✓ Tourist Board rating
Fakenham Racecourse Caravan & Camping Site, The Racecourse, Fakenham, Norfolk NR21 7NY
Tel: (01328) 862388 Fax: (01328) 855908

Carefree
HOLIDAYS

A warm welcome for you and your pets. Inexpensive, 'live-as-you-please' self-catering holidays in beautiful Norfolk. Chalets, Bungalows, Cottages and super Apartments near Great Yarmouth & Norfolk Broads.

SUPERB VALUE FOR THE MILLENNIUM

Booking Hotline
Tel: 01493 732176
All calls personally answered

Short breaks available all season from £55.

1st pet £5; 2nd pet Free

Main Season Prices

Chalets from £85 to £275

Bungalows & Cottages from £105 to £355

Seadell Holiday Park, Beach Rd, Hemsby: Fully Detached.

The Laurels - Superb Bungalows close to beach. Private car park.
The Jasmines - Lovely cottages. 100 yards to golden sandy beach.
Belle-Aire - Family chalets, clubhouse. Free Electric and Linen.
Seadell - Fully detached. Parking in front of chalet.
Winterton Valley - Chalets in pretty fishing village.
Fennside - Detached 3 bedroom bungalow. In residential Hemsby.

All accommodation is fully equipped for your holiday needs, including Free linen and entertainment at our club

1-6 The Laurels: Close to beach - Hemsby

1-9 The Jasmine Cottages: Close to sandy beach where you can take your pets, with access to lovely walks along Valley

For Free Colour Brochure:-

Write or phone to **Carefree Holidays, Chapel Briers, Yarmouth Road, Hemsby, Norfolk NR29 4NJ (Tel: 01493 732176)**
Find us on the internet: www.uktourism.com/nr-carefreeholidays

The HOSTE ARMS

Johansens 'Inn of the Year' 1996 ✦ *Egon Ronay 'Inn of the Year' 1996*

✦ *Good Hotel Guide Cesar Awards 1998 'Inn of the Year'*

✦ *Norfolk Dining Pub of the Year 1996 & 1999*

✦ *February 1999 – Voted by the Times as their second favourite Hotel in England, 27th favourite in the World*

✦ *June 1999 The Sunday Times 'Golden Pillow Award' for accommodation.*

✦ *Catey Award Winner 1999*

I have loved the North Norfolk coast since childhood and owning the Hoste is more than I could have wished for.

We now have 28 en suite bedrooms designed and returbished by my wife Jeanne. There are three air conditioned dining rooms serving an excellent and varied cuisine, as well as an outdoor restaurant in the gardens during summer. There is also an art gallery, conservatory and a beautiful 17th century bar, a favourite haunt for locals and visitors alike.

I have always adored dogs and have two black Labradors myself, Augustus and Sweep. Holkham and Brancaster beaches, both within three miles, provide wonderful lead free walking through sand and forest. Dogs are welcomed in all areas of the Hoste and insist on coming back time and time again.

I look forward to meeting you and your dogs at the Hoste.

Prices:
Bed and Breakfast, Doubles from £64.00 a night.
Amazing value Dinner, Bed and Breakfast rates,
selected months midweek.

The Hoste Arms Hotel, The Green, Burnham Market, Norfolk PE31 8HD
Tel: 01328 738777 • Fax: 01328 730103
E-mail: TheHosteArms@compuserve.com
Web: www.hostearms.co.uk

Pictures of pets required!

For our next edition of the unique guide **Pets Welcome!**, we would like to feature a series of pictures of readers', or advertisers', pets.

If you have a photo of your pet you would be willing to have included we would be grateful if you could forward it along with a brief note of the pet's name and any interesting anecdotes about them. Please remember to include your own name and address and let us know if you would like the pictures returned.

Everyone sending a photo can select a **FREE** copy of any of FHG's year 2000 guides from the list shown at the back of this book. If your picture is featured in the next issue we will also pay £10 – and if the photo proves suitable for use on the front cover of the guide we will pay £100.

We will be happy to receive prints, transparencies or pictures on disk or by e-mail to **fhg@ipc.co.uk**. Please let us know which of our guides you would prefer as your free gift.

All pictures should be forwarded by September 1st 2000 to be considered for inclusion in the 2001 edition of **Pets Welcome!**.

Send to: FHG Publications, Abbey Mill Business Centre, Seedhill, Paisley PA1 1TJ.

PUBLISHER'S NOTE

While every effort is made to ensure accuracy, we regret that FHG Publications cannot accept responsibility for errors, omissions or misrepresentations in our entries or any consequences thereof. Prices in particular should be checked because we go to press early. We will follow up complaints but cannot act as arbiters or agents for either party.

Please mention Pets Welcome! when enquiring

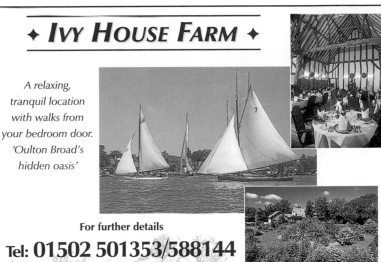

LITTLE HEMINGFOLD HOTEL

★ **Relax** and enjoy the friendly and tranquil atmosphere of our part 17th century and early Victorian farmhouse.

★ **Meander** through our 40 acres of farm and woodland with endless walks in the adjoining countryside.

★ **Treat** your pets to one of our ground-floor garden rooms, all en suite and some with log-burning stoves.

★ **Fish,** row and swim in our two-acre trout lake or take up a challenge on our grass tennis court.

Discounts for children and FREE accommodation for pets.
Weekly Dinner, Bed and Breakfast
from £52 per person per night.
Two day breaks from £56 per person per night.

Please ring or write to Paul and Allison Slater

LITTLE HEMINGFOLD HOTEL, TELHAM,
BATTLE, EAST SUSSEX TN33 0TT

Tel: 01424 774338 Fax: 01424 775351

"Which" Hotel Guide   ETC ◆◆◆   **RAC**

Cleavers Lyng

16th CENTURY COUNTRY HOTEL
Church Road, Herstmonceux
East Sussex BN27 1QJ

TEL: (01323) 833131
FAX: (01323) 833617

For excellent home cooking in traditional English style, comfort and informality, this small, family-run hotel in the heart of rural East Sussex is well recommended. Peacefully set in beautiful landscaped gardens extending to one-and-a-half acres featuring an ornamental rockpool. Adjacent to Herstmonceux Castle West Gate, the house dates from 1577 as its oak beams and inglenook fireplace bear witness. This is an ideal retreat for a quiet sojourn away from urban clamour. The castles at Pevensey, Scotney, Bodiam and Hever are all within easy reach, as are Battle Abbey, Kipling's House, Batemans, Michelham Priory and the seaside resorts of Eastbourne, Bexhill and Hastings. The bedrooms are fully en suite, and all have central heating and tea/coffee making facilities, some with separate sitting area with colour TV and direct dial telephones. On the ground floor there is an oak-beamed restaurant with a fully licensed lounge bar, cosy residents' lounge with television, and an outer hall with telephone and cloakrooms. Cleavers Lyng does not have any single rooms, however at certain times of the year, we offer a reduced single occupancy rate for double/twin bedroom. At Cleavers Lyng we observe a strictly non-smoking policy in our Restaurant and T.V. Lounge. Smoking is permitted in the Lounge Bar. Visa and Mastercard accepted.

Pets welcome. Peace, tranquillity and a warm welcome await you.
Special Attraction: Badger Watch. Room Rate from £30 pp, sharing Double/Twin rooms.

Red Hall

Great Broughton, Stokesley,
Near Middlesbrough, N. Yorkshire TS9 7ET
Tel: 01642 712300 Fax: 01642 714023
E-mail: NATHAN@MYTHRAL.DEMON.CO.UK

An elegant 17th Century Grade II Listed building offers the charm of the small country house. Our family-run business with spacious centrally heated en suite bedrooms provides personal service in a friendly convivial atmosphere. Join us in our lovely Queen Anne country house set in tranquil meadows and woodland at the foot of the rugged North York Moors National Park.   AA ◆◆◆◆

Rudding Holiday Park, Follifoot, Harrogate, HG3 1JH Telephone: 01423 870439 Fax: 01423 870859

Your gateway to the Yorkshire Dales

- Luxury Cottages, completely restored retaining many of their original features, 2-10 persons
- Timber Lodges situated in beautiful parkland, many overlooking a small lake, 2-6 persons
- Excellent accommodation of the highest standard • All are centrally heated and fully equipped

Facilities within the private country estate include:
- Heated swimming pool and paddling pool • Children's adventure playground • Licensed bar • Games room and bicycle hire
- 18 hole pay & play golf course plus floodlit driving range

Please send for free illustrated brochure:

Superior Holiday Cottages and Lodges in picturesque surroundings near Harrogate
E-mail: HPReception@Rudding-park.co.uk
Website: www.rudding-park.co.uk

ROSE AWARD UP TO HIGHLY COMMENDED

RUDDING holiday **PARK**

Family Holiday and Attractions Guides

Children Welcome!

The market leader for family holidays, especially for those with younger children and babies. For almost fifty years this colourful pocket guide has provided a rich selection of accommodation, attractions and resorts whose facilities are particularly suited to family holidays.

Full colour section including Good Beach Guide. Regional holiday information and things to do. With maps and special Readers' Offer Vouchers.

From FHG Publications

SCOTLAND'S
HOTELS OF DISTINCTION

For the *real* taste of Scotland

Corsemalzie House, Port William, Newton Stewart DG8 9RL
Corsemalzie is a country house hotel set in 40 acres of totally unspoiled and tranquil
environment. Food and service are under the personal supervision of the resident
proprietors and are complemented by a comprehensive wine list. The hotel specialises
in game fishing and has extensive private salmon/trout fishing rights on the rivers
Bladnoch and Tarff as well as trout fishing in a stocked loch. Rough shooting, duck
flighting and some driven pheasant shooting is available on the hotel's estate
Tel: 01988 860 254   **Fax:** 01988 860 213
Website: www.galloway.co.uk

STB ★★★ Hotel   AA ★★★

Mansfield House, Scotsburn Road, Tain, Ross-shire IV19 1PR
Built in the 1870s and recently refurbished, Mansfield House retains its original features
including pine paneling and ornate plaster ceilings. Rooms in the Victorian part of the
house have been furnished to deluxe standard with antique furniture and many
bathrooms have jacuzzis. It is perfectly situated for touring the Highlands, and has at
least eight excellent golf courses within 30 minutes. Food, served in our two restaurants,
is of the highest standard and draws extensively on fresh local seafood and game.

STB ★★★★ Hotel   AA ★★ ☺☺
Tel: 01862 892 052   **Fax:** 01862 892 260
Website: www.mansfield-house.co.uk   **E-mail:** mansfield@cali.co.uk

Kinloch Lodge, Sleat, Isle of Skye IV43 8QY
Kinloch dates back to the early 1600s and is very much the home of Lord and Lady
MacDonald. Two comfortable drawing rooms, with log fires, enjoy the most
spectacular views. The decor throughout is the choice of Lady MacDonald as is the
food in the dining room. Claire MacDonald is one of the greatest cooks and food
enthusiasts in Scotalnd – an award winning journalist and author of twelve best-
selling cookbooks. She produces delicious food using superb local ingredients
Tel: 01471 833 333/333 214   **Fax:** 01471 833 277
E-mail: kinloch@dial.pipex.com

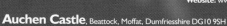

STB ★★★★ Hotel   AA ★★ ☺☺

Loch Melfort, Arduaine, by Oban, Argyll PA34 4XG
With its superb location on the beautiful West Coast and with Awards for Hospitality
from The AA and The Good Hotel Guide this is the perfect place for a relaxing holiday
or short break. Personally run by resident proprietors, the hotel offers comfortable
accommodation with stunning views down the Sound of Jura. Superb cuisine uses only
the best of fresh local produce including lobsters, oysters and scallops, complemented
by an excellent wine list.

STB ★★★★ Hotel   AA ★★★ ☺☺
Tel: 01852 200 233;   **Fax:** 01852 200 214
Website: www.loch.melfort.co.uk   **E-mail:** lmhotel@aol.com

Auchen Castle, Beattock, Moffat, Dumfriesshire DG10 9SH
An imposing 19th century mansion house set in 30 acres of beautifully maintained
gardens and woodland with its own private trout loch and panoramic views over the
Moffat Hills. The countryside of Robert Burns is full of history and romance and well
worth exploring. Ideal for golfing, walking and fishing and at the end of a busy day relax
and enjoy a wide range of malt whiskies in the bar before dining in our award winning
restaurant – a warm welcome is assured.
Tel: 01683 300 407   **Fax:** 01683 300 667

STB ★★★ Hotel   AA ★★★

PLEASE CALL US ON 0800 975 5975 FOR ASSISTANCE
WITH YOUR RESERVATION
OR VISIT OUR WEBSITE: www.scotlands-hotels.com

Please mention Pets Welcome! when enquiring

Forglen
COUNTRY COTTAGES

The Estate lies along the beautiful Deveron River and our traditional stone cottages nestle in individual seclusion. Visitors can explore one of the ancient baronies of Scotland. The sea is only nine miles away, and the market town of Turriff only two miles, with its golf course, swimming pool, etc. Places of interest including the Cairngorms, Aviemore, picturesque fishing villages and castles, all within easy reach on uncrowded roads. See our Highland cattle.

Terms: from £145 weekly. Special Winter lets. 10 cottages sleeping 6-9. Children and reasonable dogs welcome. STB Inspected.

For a brochure contact: **Mrs P. Bates, Holiday Cottages, Forglen Estate, Turriff, Aberdeenshire AB53 4JP**
Tel: 01888 562918/562518; Fax: 01888 562252

Raemoir House Hotel – Self-Catering Apartments

STB ★★★★

Raemoir House Hotel is part of an idyllic 3,500 acre estate, situated on Royal Deeside and within easy reach of Aberdeen. Within the grounds of the hotel the original coach house and stable buildings have been converted into four de luxe self-catering cottages with one, two or three bedrooms, sleeping up to 8 people. Full details available on request.

Raemoir House Hotel, Raemoir, Banchory, Kincardineshire AB31 4ED

COLOGIN FARM HOLIDAY CHALETS
Oban

All Scottish Glens have their secrets: let us share ours with you – and your pets !

- Tranquil country glen, just 3 miles from Oban
- Free fishing and dinghy use on our hill loch.
- Excellent walks for you and your dogs.
- Home-cooked food and licensed bar in our converted farm-yard byre.
- A safe haven for pets and children.
- A friendly, family run complex with a good range of facilities. **PETS WELCOME**

Our cosy holiday chalets, set on an old farm in a peaceful private glen, can sleep from two to six people in comfort. They all have private parking, central heating, colour TV and bed linen.

Call now for our colour brochure and find out more:

MRS LINDA BATTISON,
COLOGIN FARMHOUSE,
LERAGS GLEN, BY OBAN, ARGYLL PA34 4SE
Tel: Oban (01631) 564501 Fax: (01631) 566925
E-mail: cologin@oban.org.uk
STB ★ ★ Self Catering

Open all year round.
Rates from £140 to £390 per week.
Autumn Gold breaks and
mid-week deals also available.

Warmanbie Country House
Hotel & Restaurant

*Secluded country house, dogs very welcome and
allowed in rooms, river walks, scenic grounds.
Huge breakfasts, creative cooking, two four
poster bedrooms. Free fishing, golf nearby.*

**Annan, Dumfriesshire, DG12 5LL
Telephone 01461 204015.**

See our advert under Dumfries & Galloway

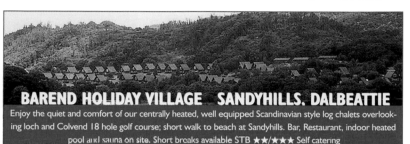

BAREND HOLIDAY VILLAGE   SANDYHILLS. DALBEATTIE

Enjoy the quiet and comfort of our centrally heated, well equipped Scandinavian style log chalets overlooking loch and Colvend 18 hole golf course; short walk to beach at Sandyhills. Bar, Restaurant, indoor heated pool and sauna on site. Short breaks available STB ★★/★★★ Self catering

Tel: 01387 780663; Fax: 01387 780283; www.barendholidayvillage.co.uk

Barnsoul Farm
**Irongray, Shawhead, Dumfries DG2 9SQ
Tel/Fax 01387 730249
Website: BarnsoulDG@aol.com**

*Barnsoul, one of Galloway's scenic working
farms. Birdwatching, walking, fishing on your
doorstep. Spot the dog awaits your arrival.*

Car/caravan £6-8		Open Easter-October
Car/tent £6-8		Map ref: E4
Tent £6		20 pitches 10acres

Annandale Arms Hotel
High Street, Moffat. DG10 9HF

*A warm welcome is offered at the Annandale Arms Hotel to dogs with
well-mannered and house-trained owners. There are all the comforts and
facilities that owners enjoy such as an excellent restaurant and a relaxing
panelled bar. The Hotel has a large private parking area at the rear full of
the most exquisite sniffs.*

**£64.00 per room
for Dogs travelling
with two owners**

Tel: 01683-220013

**£40.00 per room
for Dogs travelling
with one owner**

Dinwoodie Lodge

Country House Hotel
Near Lockerbie, Dumfriesshire DG11 2SL
Tel: 01576 470289

Grade B Listed small country house hotel in South-west Scotland. Caravan Park and Holiday Cottages adjacent. Fishing, golf, shooting available in area. Ideal centre for touring Borders, Galloway; Edinburgh and Glasgow approximately 70 miles. Seven bedrooms, three with private facilities including a room for disabled guests. All rooms have colour television and tea/coffee facilities. Full central heating. Breakfast, Lunches, Bar Meals, Licensed Bar, Separate Pool Room and Darts Board. Children and pets welcome

---

Hunter Holiday Cottages
Rosewell, Edinburgh

Hunter Holiday Cottages offer a range of cottages in beautiful countryside only eight miles from Edinburgh city centre. These superior cottages are recently renovated, have all modern facilities and sleep six to eight plus. They provide the ideal base for the perfect Scottish holiday from their location in Midlothian's historic countryside. There is easy access to Scotland's capital and the major routes to the rest of Scotland. For more information visit our website. Also B&B, £20-£25 per night

Contact Duncan Hunter   Tel: 0131 448 0888   Fax: 0131 440 2082
E-mail: hunter@holidaycottages.demon.co.uk   Website: www.holidaycottages.demon.co.uk

---

Kylesku Lodges, Kylesku, Sutherland IV27 4HW
Tel/Fax: 01971 502003

Escape to Kylesku and discover one of Britain's last remaining areas of true wilderness. Situated amidst the rugged scenery of West Sutherland our self-catering holiday lodges are set in a secluded location with extensive views over Loch A'Chairn Bhain and the surrounding mountains. Kylesku is ideally located for touring the North West Highland coastal route and our lodges are a convenient centre for bird watching, hill walking and fishing.
OPEN: March – October. £180 – £450 per week. Phone for further details and a colour brochure

---

NOTE

All the information in this book is given in good faith in the belief that it is correct. However, the publishers cannot guarantee the facts given in these pages, neither are they responsible for changes in policy, ownership or terms that may take place after the date of going to press. Readers should always satisfy themselves that the facilities they require are available and that the terms, if quoted, still apply.

FOR THE MUTUAL GUIDANCE OF GUEST AND HOST

Every year literally thousands of holidays, short breaks and overnight stops are arranged through our guides, the vast majority without any problems at all. In a handful of cases, however, difficulties do arise about bookings, which often could have been prevented from the outset.

It is important to remember that when accommodation has been booked, both parties – guests and hosts – have entered into a form of contract. We hope that the following points will provide helpful guidance.

GUESTS: When enquiring about accommodation, be as precise as possible. Give exact dates, numbers in your party and the ages of any children. State the number and type of rooms wanted and also what catering you require – bed and breakfast, full board etc. Make sure that the position about evening meals is clear – and about pets, reductions for children or any other special points.

Read our reviews carefully to ensure that the proprietors you are going to contact can supply what you want. Ask for a letter confirming all arrangements, if possible.

If you have to cancel, do so as soon as possible. Proprietors do have the right to retain deposits and under certain circumstances to charge for cancelled holidays if adequate notice is not given and they cannot re-let the accommodation.

HOSTS: Give details about your facilities and about any special conditions. Explain your deposit system clearly and arrangements for cancellations, charges etc. and whether or not your terms include VAT.

If for any reason you are unable to fulfil an agreed booking without adequate notice, you may be under an obligation to arrange suitable alternative accommodation or to make some form of compensation.

While every effort is made to ensure accuracy, we regret that FHG Publications cannot accept responsibility for errors, omissions or misrepresentations in our entries or any consequences thereof. Prices in particular should be checked because we go to press early. We will follow up complaints but cannot act as arbiters or agents for either party.

DON'T DELAY, SEND, PHONE OR FAX FOR FREE COLOUR BROCHURE.

TYGLYN HOLIDAY ESTATE

CILIAU AERON, NEAR LAMPETER, CEREDIGION, WALES SA48 8DD TEL & FAX: 01570 470684

FOR THE MORE ACTIVE HOLIDAYMAKER

- horseriding
- golf
- tennis
- bowls
- walking
- swimming
- ten-pin bowling
- cycling
- quad-biking

a number of leisure centres are all within easy reach.

A chance to spend a relaxing time amidst beautiful, unspoilt Welsh countryside yet within easy reach of the renowned coastal towns and beaches of New Quay and Aberystwyth with the nearest being the picturesque Aberaeron.

The bungalows are set within seventeen acres of the awe-inspiring Aeron Valley which is home to some magnificent wildlife with Buzzards, Kestrels and the re-established Red Kites being a main attraction, with fishing available on the River Aeron which runs through the estate.

The bungalows are semi-detached self-catering, ideal for four people but will cater for six, with two bedrooms, lounge, kitchen and bathroom. Bed linen and Electricity are included.

Your evenings can be spent happily at the adjacent Tyglyn Aeron Hotel, whose bars and restaurants are available to all our visitors.

Don't forget your dogs are always welcome with a nine acre field for their exercise and freedom.

Short breaks available on request.

Please mention Pets Welcome! when enquiring

LOCHMEYLER FARM

Tel: 01348 837724
Fax: 01348 837622

Mrs Morfydd Jones
Llandeloy,
Pen-y-Cwm,
Near Solva,
St. Davids,
Pembrokeshire
SA62 6LL

A warm welcome awaits you at Lochmeyler, a 220 acre dairy farm in the centre of the St David's Peninsula. It is an ideal location for exploring the beauty of the coast and countryside.

There are 16 bedrooms, eight of them in the adjacent cottage suites. All are en-suite, non-smoking, luxury rooms with colour TV, video and refreshment facilities. Optional evening dinner with choice of menu including vegetarian. Children are welcome and there is a children's play area. Dogs free. Kennel facilities are free for owners wishing to leave their dogs during the day. Well behaved

dogs can sleep in bedrooms providing they have their own bedding on the floor.

Open all year. Credit cards accepted. Colour brochure on request.

 RAC
◆◆◆◆◆ FARM GOLD

DAILY RATES
Bed & Breakfast per person per night • min £20 - max £25
Optional evening dinner £12.50
Children half price sharing family room.

Other FHG Holiday and Attractions Guides

SELF-CATERING HOLIDAYS

One of the best and perhaps the widest selection of self-catering accommodation, covering the whole of the UK. Established 30 years, and with over 1,000 entries it is firmly established as the market-leader for self-catering holiday choices throughout Britain.

From modern apartment complexes to hidden forest cabins, there is a holiday to suit every need. There is also a large selection of caravan holidays. The guide has proved popular with families and couples who enjoy the freedom of a direct-booked self catering holiday.

CARAVAN & CAMPING HOLIDAYS

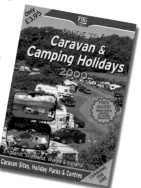

This handy sized guide is one of our most popular titles and has been a best-seller for over 20 years. This guide covers every type of caravan and camping facility with user-friendly symbols to show grading of standards and facilities. As a longtime best-seller our Guide to Caravan & Camping Holidays continues to offer advertisers low cost year-long exposure to the largest single category of holiday-maker throughout the UK.

BRITAIN'S BEST HOLIDAYS

An extremely popular and inexpensive quick reference guide for all kinds of holiday opportunities throughout Britain. The extensive range of holidays is split into four main categories – Board (hotels, guest houses, farms, bed & breakfast, etc); Self-Catering (houses, cottages, flats, chalets); Caravans (solus sites, parks and camping sites); Activity holidays (camping, golfing, sporting holidays) This guide is very user-friendly with self-explanatory symbols to show services and amenities. It is most popular amongst families and those looking for the easiest route to making a direct booking.

Guides available from most bookshops and larger newsagents. or direct from
FHG Publications Ltd. Abbey Mill Business Centre, Seedhill, Paisley PA1 1TJ
Prices (inc. post and packing), Caravan & Camping £4.30
Britains Best Holidays £4.20 and Self Catering Holidays £5.00

Other FHG Holiday and Attractions Guides

Recommended
Country Hotels
of Britain

A quality selection of country hotels and country houses which offer the best of traditional hospitality and comfort.

This is a guide for those who appreciate good living with the high standards of food, wine, accommodation and service which that entails.

Mainly independent, with a resident proprietor. and often historic or with unique character, these hotels are ideal for quiet holidays in pampered surroundings.

Quick reference sections for Hotels with Leisure and Hotels with Conference Facilities

Recommended
Wayside & Country Inns
of Britain

This guide lists a large selection of inns, pubs and small hotels in every part of the country, all offering the same high-quality service, accommodation and, especially, cuisine as many of the bigger hotels, yet managing to retain that sense of history and the warm, friendly atmosphere for which the traditional inn is renowned. With separate supplements for Pet-Friendly and Family-Friendly Pubs to ensure that every member of the party receives a warm welcome when they stop for refreshment, the guide is an invaluable and informative source.

Please mention Pets Welcome! when enquiring

PETS
WELCOME!

2000

The Animal Lovers' Holiday Guide

with Special Supplements

Kennels & Catteries
Holidays with Horses
Pet Friendly Pubs

FHG Publications
Paisley

39th Edition © IPC Magazines Ltd 2000
ISBN 1 85055 305 X

Cover design: Oliver Dunster, Link House Magazines
Cover Pictures: Images Colour Library
Imagebank/IPN
RETNA/IPN
Photodisk/IPN

Cartography by GEO Projects, Reading

Maps are based on Ordnance Survey Maps with the permission
of the Controller of Her Majesty's Stationery Office,
Crown Copyright reserved.

Typeset by FHG Publications Ltd, Paisley.
Printed and bound in Great Britain by Guernsey Press, Guernsey.

Distribution. Book Trade: WLM, Unit 11, Newmarket Court, Newmarket Drive, Derby
DE24 8NW
(Tel: 01332 573737. Fax: 01332 573399).
News Trade: Market Force (UK) Ltd, 247 Tottenham Court Road, London WlP 0AU
(Tel: 020 7261 6809; Fax: 020 7261 7227).

Published by FHG Publications Ltd., Abbey Mill Business Centre,
Seedhill, Paisley PA1 ITJ (Tel: 0141-887 0428 Fax: 0141-889 7204).
e-mail: fhg@ipc.co.uk

Pets Welcome is a Link House publication, published by
IPC Country & Leisure Media Ltd, part of IPC Magazines Group of Companies.

All the advertisers in PETS WELCOME! have an entry in the appropriate classified
section and each classified entry may carry one or more of the following symbols:

ᕯ This symbol indicates that pets are welcome free of charge.

£ The £ indicates that a charge is made for pets. We quote the amount where
possible, either per night or per week.

pw! This symbol shows that the establishment has some special provision for pets;
perhaps an exercise facility or some special feeding or accommodation
arrangements.

⌂ Indicates separate pets accommodation.

PLEASE NOTE that all the advertisers in PETS WELCOME! extend a welcome to pets
and their owners but they may attach conditions. The interests of other guests have to
be considered and it is usually assumed that pets will be well trained, obedient and under
the control of their owner.

CONTENTS

ENGLAND

SCOTLAND

WALES

PETS WELCOME!
2000

Any dog owner who has endured that enthusiastic 'welcome home' lick will surely agree that our pets miss us when we are away from home, even for a short time, and it goes without saying that we miss them too. It's not surprising therefore that most of us like to include the family pet in our holiday plans whenever possible, and this is why Pets Welcome, with its varied choice of holiday accommodation, is so popular. Demand for the 1999 issue has remained high, and this new edition for the year 2000 has an even bigger colour section, as well as more holiday choices in the main section of the book - lots of old favourites and new prospects to offer a warm welcome.

As usual we include a small selection of Kennels and Catteries as an extra option, plus a section of accommodation contacts for Horses, with or without owners, and travelling perhaps for Shows or Trials. Pet-Friendly Pubs is now an established feature, and who knows what other pet-related topics will be useful in future.

Some proprietors offer fuller facilities for pets than others, and in the classified entry which we give each advertiser we try to indicate by symbols whether or not there are any special facilities and if additional charges are involved. However, we suggest that you raise any queries or particular requirements when you make enquiries and bookings.

Most of our entries are of long standing and are tried and tested favourites with animal lovers. However as publishers we do not inspect the accommodation advertised in *Pets Welcome!* and an entry does not imply our recommendation. If you have any problems or complaints, please raise them on the spot with the owner or his representative in the first place. We will follow up complaints if necessary, but we regret that we cannot act as intermediaries nor can we accept responsibility for details of accommodation and/or services described here. Happily, serious complaints are few.

Finally, if you have to cancel or postpone a holiday booking, please give as much notice as possible. This courtesy will be appreciated and it could save later difficulties.

Some useful hints for safe travel appear on page 71 and we would be more than happy to receive readers own suggestions. Please also let us know if you have had any unusual or humorous experiences with your pet on holiday. This always makes interesting reading! And we hope that you will mention Pets Welcome when you make your holiday inquiries or bookings.

Anne Cuthbertson, Editor

A magical miniature world of make-believe depicting rural England in the 1930's. "A little piece of history that is forever England."

Open:
10am to 5pm daily 19th February to 31st October.

Directions:
Junction 16 M25, Junction 2 M40.

FHG PUBLICATIONS, ABBEY MILL BUSINESS CENTRE, PAISLEY PA1 1TJ

A working steam museum with a very large collection of steam locomotives, carriages and wagons. Steam train rides, extensive miniature railway; refreshments, picnic areas, gift shop.

Open:
11am to 5pm
Sundays April to October
Also Wednesdays July/August

Directions:
off A41 Aylesbury-Bicester road at Waddesdon

FHG PUBLICATIONS, ABBEY MILL BUSINESS CENTRE, PAISLEY PA1 1TJ

Visit the rescued donkeys, feed and groom them; donkey picnics. Assault course, bouncy castle.

Open:
one week before Easter to end October
10am to 5pm daily.
Winter hours by arrangement.

Directions:
follow brown and white signs from A39

FHG PUBLICATIONS, ABBEY MILL BUSINESS CENTRE, PAISLEY PA1 1TJ

World's finest steamboat collection and premier all-weather attraction. Swallows and Amazons exhibition, model boat pond, tea shop, souvenir shop. Free guided tours.

Open:
10am to 5pm 3rd weekend in March to last weekend October

Directions:
on A592 between Windermere and Bowness-on-Windermere

FHG PUBLICATIONS, ABBEY MILL BUSINESS CENTRE, PAISLEY PA1 1TJ

An underground wonderland of stalactites, stalagmites, rocks, minerals and fossils. Home of the unique Blue John stone – see the largest single piece ever found. Suitable for all ages.

Open:
March to October opens 9.30am,
November to February opens 10am.
Enquire for last tour of day and closed days.

Directions:
½ mile west of Castleton on A6187 (old A625)

FHG PUBLICATIONS, ABBEY MILL BUSINESS CENTRE, PAISLEY PA1 1TJ

*"England for Excellence" award-winning
rural attraction combining traditional
rural crafts with hilarious novelties
such as sheep racing and duck trialling.
Indoor adventure zone for adults and
children.*

Open:

daily all year, 10am to 6pm

Directions:

on A39 North Devon link road, two
miles west of Bideford Bridge

---

*Award-winning centre sited on
Plymouth's famous Hoe telling the
story of the city, from the epic voyages
of Drake, Cook and the Mayflower
Pilgrims to the devastation of the Blitz.
A must for all the family*

Open:

daily all year except Christmas Day
(Smeaton's Tower closed October to Easter)

Directions:

follow signs from Plymouth City Centre
to the Hoe and seafront

---

*Britain's best preserved lead
mining site – and a great day out
for all the family, with lots to see
and do. Underground Experience –
Park Level Mine now open.*

Open:

April 1st to October 31st
10.30am to 5pm daily

Directions:

alongside A689, midway between Stanhope
and Alston in the heart of the North Pennines.

---

*On three floors of a Listed Victorian
warehouse telling 200 years of
inland waterway history.
• Historic boats • Painted boat gallery
• Blacksmith • Archive film
• Hands-on displays
"A great day out"*

Open:

10am to 5pm Closed Christmas Day

Directions:

Junction 11A or 12 off M5 – follow brown signs
for Historic Docks. Railway and bus station
10 minute walk. Free coach parking.

---

*The museum of everyday life in
Roman Britain. An award-winning
museum with re-created Roman
rooms, hands-on discovery areas,
AV, and some of the best mosaics
outside the Mediterranean*

Open:

Monday to Saturday 10am-5.30pm
Sunday 2pm-5.30pm

Directions:

St Alban's

Europe's finest collection of tigers, including Siberian, Royal Bengal, White and rare Chinese. Other big cats include leopard, black panther and jaguar; also collection of endangered primates.

Open:
Easter to end October 10am to 5pm
Phone for winter opening hours.

Directions:
on B3329 road (Sandown to Bembridge), along seafront towards the White Cliff

---

Over 3500 years of history vividly brought to life. Visit the hands-on 'Roman Encounters' and step into the 1940's Dover Street in 'Our Finest Hours'. New: The Dover Bronze Age Boat Gallery

Open:
April to October 10am to 5pm
November to March 10am to 3pm

Directions:
signposted from M2/A2 and M20/A20; brown/white signs on entering Dover

---

Enjoy a marvellous day out: feed the animals, tractor ride, indoor adventure play area, nature trail. Indoor and outdoor picnic areas, tea room, fine food and gift shop. Disabled access.

Open:
daily 10.30am to 5pm. Closed between Christmas and New Year's Day.

Directions:
M6 Junction 35; on B6254 at Arkholme, towards Kirkby Lonsdale.

The world's largest collection of Grand Prix racing cars – over 130 exhibits within five halls, including McLaren Formula One cars.

Open:
daily 10am to 5pm (last admission 4pm). Closed Christmas/New Year.

Directions:
2 miles from M1 (J23a/24) and M42/A42; to north-west via A50.

All-weather museum of science and working life. Loads of "hands-on" science fun indoors and out.

Open:
May to August 10am to 6pm
September to April 10am to 5pm
Closed 25/26 December

Directions:
10 minutes from Junction 22 M1 or Junction 13 M42/A42.

Large wildlife park with Reptile Land, Tropical House, Insectarium, Birds of Prey Centre, farm animals, wallaby enclosure, llamas; adventure playground, tea room and gift shop.

Open:
daily from 10am
April to end October

Directions:
off A17 at Long Sutton

Lions, snow leopards, chimpanzees, penguins, reptiles, aquarium and lots more, set amidst landscaped gardens. Gift shop, cafe and picnic areas.

Open:
all year round from 10am

Directions:
on the coast 16 miles north of Liverpool; follow the brown and white tourist signs

---

Come to the world's greatest medieval adventure and enter our world of mystery and merriment. Jump on the magical 'Travel Back in Time' and ride in search of Robin.

Open:
daily 10am to 6pm
(last admission 4.30pm)

Directions:
near Nottingham Castle in city centre – follow brown tourist signs

---

The largest motor museum in the UK providing a unique insight into the history of the motor vehicle. Something for all ages to educate and entertain. Full catering and picnic area.

Open:
9.30 am to 5.30pm daily
(until 6.30pm in summer)

Directions:
Sparkford

---

* Britain's most spectacular caves
* Traditional paper-making
* Penny Arcade
* Magical Mirror Maze *

Open:
Summer 10am to 5pm; Winter 10.30am to 4.30pm. Closed 17-25 Dec

Directions:
from M5 J22 follow brown-and-white signs via A38 and A371. Two miles from Wells.

The world's largest display of Royal Doulton figures past and present. Video theatre, demonstration room, museum, restaurant and shop. Factory Tours by prior booking weekdays only.

Open:
Monday to Saturday 9.30am to 5pm
Sundays 10.30am to 4.30pm
Closed Christmas week

Directions:
from M6 Junction 15/16; follow A500 to junction with A527. Signposted.

The story of the people and horses involved in racing from its royal origins to Lester Piggott, Frankie Dettori and other modern heroes. Millennnium Exhibition – The Essential Horse.

Open:
Easter to end October: Tuesdays to Saturdays; also Bank Holiday Mondays and Mondays in July and August.

Directions:
on High Street next to Jockey Club

18-hole American Adventure Golf set in ⅓ acre landscaped surroundings. Played on different levels including water features.

Open:
April until end October
10am until dusk

Directions:
on the seafront ¼ mile east of Eastbourne Pier.

Suitable for all ages. All-weather attractions include: Planet Earth and Dinosaur Museum, fabulous Botanical Garden, Living Rain Forest, indoor Oriental Garden, Newhaven Miniature Railway, Pleasure Gardens, Water Gardens, gift shops, Garden Centre, licensed Coffee Shop.

Open:
all year, except Christmas Day and Boxing Day.

Directions:
signposted off A26 and A259

---

100 acres of parkland, home to hundreds of duck, geese, swans and flamingos. Discovery centre, cafe, gift shop; play area.

Open:
every day except Christmas Day

Directions:
signposted from A19, A195, A1231 and A182

FHG

READERS'
OFFER
2000

HATTON COUNTRY WORLD FARM PARK

Dark Lane, Hatton, Near Warwick, Warwickshire CV35 8XA

Tel: 01926 843411

Admit TWO for the price of one into Farm Park
(not valid Bank Holidays). Admission into Shopping Village free.

valid during 2000

NOT TO BE USED IN CONJUNCTION WITH ANY OTHER OFFER

FHG

READERS'
OFFER
2000

LONGLEAT

Warminster, Wiltshire BA12 7NW

Tel: 01985 844400

£1 off Longleat Passport tickets, up to a max. of 6 per voucher

valid April to October 2000

NOT TO BE USED IN CONJUNCTION WITH ANY OTHER OFFER

FHG

READERS'
OFFER
2000

Embsay & Bolton Abbey Steam Railway

Bolton Abbey Station, Skipton, N. Yorkshire BD23 6AF

Tel: 01756 710614

One adult travels FREE when accompanied by a full fare paying adult
(does not include Special Event days)

valid during 2000

NOT TO BE USED IN CONJUNCTION WITH ANY OTHER OFFER

FHG

READERS'
OFFER
2000

Yorkshire Dales Falconry and Conservation Centre

Crows Nest, Giggleswick, Settle, North Yorkshire LA2 8AS

Tel: 01729 822832

One FREE adult admission with every full-paying adult

valid 1/4 to 30/9/2000 (not Bank Holidays)

NOT TO BE USED IN CONJUNCTION WITH ANY OTHER OFFER

FHG

READERS'
OFFER
2000

Staintondale Shire Horse Farm

Staintondale, Scarborough, North Yorkshire YO13 0EY

Tel: 01723 870458

10% discount

valid during 2000 season

NOT TO BE USED IN CONJUNCTION WITH ANY OTHER OFFER

A totally unique blend of shopping and leisure. Hatton Farm Park has farm animals, pets' corner, nature trail, farming and falconry displays. Hatton Rural Craft and Shopping Village has the UK's biggest craft centre, discount shops, antiques, cafe/bar and soft play area. Free parking.

Open:

daily 10am to 5pm.
Closed Christmas Day and Boxing Day

Directions:

5 minutes from J15 M40, A46 towards Coventry, then just off A4177 Warwick to Solihull road

---

Longleat is probably best known for its Safari Park where your family can view the famous lions, tigers, wolves, giraffes, zebras and many more magnificent animals. Also Parrot Show, Pets' Corner, Mirror Maze, feeding sea lions on the Safari Boats, the 'World's Longest Hedge Maze' and Longleat House

Open:

April to October 10am to 6pm (all attractions);
rest of year House open 10am to 4pm
(except Christmas Day)

Directions:

just off the A362 between
Warminster and Frome

Steam train operated over a 4½ mile line from Bolton Abbey Station to Embsay Station. Many family events including Thomas the Tank Engine take place during major Bank Holidays.

Open:

steam trains run every Sunday throughout the
year and up to 5 days a week in summer.
11am to 4.15pm

Directions:

Embsay Station signposted from the A59 Skipton
by-pass; Bolton Abbey Station signposted from
the A59 at Bolton Abbey.

Award-winning bird of prey centre featuring free-flying demonstrations daily. 30 species on permanent display including the largest bird of prey in the world – the Andean Condor. Children's adventure playground. Tea-room and gift shop.

Open:

daily 10am to 5pm

Directions:

just outside Settle on the A65
Skipton to Kendal road.

Daily shows and demonstrations with our Shire horses, Shetland ponies, and Palomino horse (Western style). Fun and photo time; children can brush and groom the Shetland ponies.

Open:

from Spring Bank Holiday to mid-September
Tues/Wed/Fri/Sun – 10.30am to 4.30pm
(plus Bank Holiday Mondays)

Directions:

Off A171 between Scarborough and Whitby

28-acre theme park with over 100 nursery rhyme characters, set in beautifully landscaped gardens. Shop and restaurant on site.

Open:
1st March to 31st Oct:daily 10am-6pm
1st Nov to end Feb: Sat/Sun only 11am-4pm

Directions:
6 miles west of Aberdeen off B9077

A fascinating collection of Clyde maritime displays, memorabilia, stunning archive film and entertaining hands-on activities on board a unique three-masted schooner

Open:
daily 10am to 6pm April to September, 10am to 5pm October to March

Directions:
at Inveraray on the A83

Working farm with visitor centre showing rare breeds, deer herds, ranger-led activities and walks. Bird of prey displays and tuition. Corporate activities. Shop and cafe.

Open:
Daily: May-August 10am to 5.30pm; Sept/Oct 11am to 4.30pm

Directions:
5 miles south of Jedburgh on A68

STB award-winning museum designed to stimulate interest and wonder in the fascinating subjects of gems, crystals and mineralogy. Exciting audio-visual display.

Open:
Open daily Easter to 30th November; Dec/Jan/Feb – weekends only.

Directions:
7 miles from Newton Stewart, 11 miles from Gatehouse of Fleet; just off A75 Carlisle to Stranraer road.

Motor cars from 1896, motorcycles from 1902, commercial vehicles from 1919, cycles from 1880, British WWII military vehicles, ephemera, period advertising etc

Open:
daily October to Easter 10am to 5pm; Easter to October 10am to 6pm. Closed Christmas Day and New Year's Day

Directions:
off A198 near Aberlady. two miles from A1

Visitor Centre with Exhibition Room, factory tours, factory shop (children must be able to wear safety glasses provided), Crystal Shop, gift shop, coffee shop. Facilities for disabled visitors.

Open:
Visitor Centre open daily; Factory Tours weekdays (9am-3.30pm) all year, plus weekends (11am-2.30pm) April to September.

Directions:
10 miles south of Edinburgh on the A701 Peebles road; signposted a few miles from the city centre

---

Scotland's award-winning aquarium where you can enjoy a spectacular diver's eye view of our marine environment through the world's longest underwater safari. New 'Amazing Amphibians' display, behind the scenes tours. An unforgettable adventure whatever the weather

Open:
daily except Christmas Day and New Year's Day

Directions:
from Edinburgh follow signs for Forth Road Bridge, then signs through North Queensferry. From North, follow signs through Inverkeithing and North Queensferry.

Highland croft open to visitors for "hands-on" experience with over 35 different breeds of farm animals – "stroke the goats and scratch the pigs". Farm information centre and old farm implements. For all ages, cloud or shine!

Open:
daily mid-May to third week in September 10am to 5pm

Directions:
on A835 15 miles north of Ullapool

Beneath the heather and high in the glen, the secrets of the ancient Highlander live on. Experience through live performance the energy of the myths and legends which have governed the people here for centuries past.

Open:
daily April to October 10am to 4.30pm

Directions:
just off A82 opposite Ballachulish village, 15 mins south of Fort William

---

200-year old conservation village with award-winning Visitor Centre, set in beautiful countryside

Open:
daily all year round 11am to 5pm

Directions:
one mile south of Lanark; well signposted from all major routes

*Nine rooms in a Georgian house
filled with items illustrating
the happier times of family life
over the past 150 years.
Joyful nostalgia unlimited.*

Open:
March to end October

Directions:
opposite Beaumaris Castle

---

*Visit Wales' top Butterfly House,
with Bird House, Snake House,
Ant Avenue, Creepy Crawly
Cavern, shop, cafe,
adventure playground,
picnic area, nature trail etc.*

Open:
March to end October 10am to 5pm daily;
November/December 11am to 3pm.

Directions:
follow brown-and-white signs when
crossing to Anglesey; 1½ miles from Bridge

---

*Walk through the Rabbit Hole to the
colourful scenes of Lewis Carroll's
classic story set in beautiful
life-size displays. Recorded
commentaries and transcripts
available in several languages*

Open:
10am to 5pm daily Easter to end October;
closed Sundays November to Easter

Directions:
situated just off the main street,
250 yards from coach and rail stations

---

*A unique theme attraction presenting
the history and culture of the Celts.
Audio-visual exhibition, displays of
Welsh and Celtic history, soft play
area, tea room and gift shop.
Events throughout the year.*

Open:
10am to 6pm daily (last admission
to exhibitions 4.40pm

Directions:
in restored mansion just south of clock
tower in town centre; car park just off
Aberystwyth road

---

*A unique underground tour of a real coal
mine. The miners and engineers who
maintain the pit also act as guides. They will
lend you a helmet and lamp and take you
down the 90m shaft in the pit cage to walk
through the underground roadways.
Children must be 5 years or over
to go underground.*

Open:
March to November. Underground
tours 10am to 3.30pm
(ring for details)

Directions:
Junction 26 off M4

TAKING YOUR PET ON HOLIDAY

There are several common sense rules which make travelling with pets more enjoyable and less stressful for the animal and owner.

The first question to ask is, do I need to travel in the heat of the day? Often it is a lot easier to travel at early morning or even through the night when the roads are quieter and children and animals are more likely to be asleep in the back rather than requiring constant attention. It also means that the problems associated with travelling on a warm day can be eliminated.

No matter what time you travel you should make regular stops on a long journey, as much to refresh the humans as exercise the animals. Remember to carry a bottle of water for your pet, even on relatively cool journeys an animal can become dehydrated. Remember that air conditioning is not as effective in the boot area as it is in the main body of the car. Also include an easily accessible towel to allow you to dry the dog after stopping on a rainy day.

For safety your pet should always be restrained, either in a proper car cage or behind a dog guard. In the event of an accident it is not only rear seat passengers which might be thrown forward onto the driver.

Many dogs like to put their heads out of windows but this should be restricted in particular in narrow country lanes where hedges or tree branches can prove a danger.

Try to provide sun screens to prevent the animal being subjected to direct sunlight through the windows. This can very quickly build up heat to an uncomfortable level. NEVER leave your pet alone in the car when shopping or stopping for a break. The sun can move position quickly and a sheltered spot can rapidly change becoming a death trap for the animal.

A pleasant place to break a journey is a pet friendly pub where both you and your pet will be made welcome. At the back of this guide you will see a list of a variety of inns where you can relax with a meal or a drink.

George Pratt, General Manager

DIPLOMA WINNERS 1999

*Each year we award a small number of diplomas to holiday proprietors
whose services have been specially commended by our readers.
The following were our FHG Diploma Winners for 1999.*

ENGLAND

Mr & Mrs Haskell, Borwick Lodge, Outgate, Hawkshead, Cumbria LA22
0PU (015394 36332)

Mrs Val Sunter, Higher House Farm, Oxenholme Lane, Natland, Kendal,
Cumbria LA9 7QH (015395 61177)

Mrs Ellis, Efford Cottage Guest House, Milford Road, Everton, Lymington,
Hampshire SO41 0JD (015906 42315)

Mrs Melanie Smith, Capernwray House, Capernwray, Via Carnforth,
Lancashire LA6 1AE (01524 732363)

Mrs D. Cole, Hillcrest House, Barrasford, Hexham, Northumberland
NE48 4BY (01434 681426)

Mrs J. Hartsilver, Perhams Farm, Templecombe, Somerset BA8 0NE (01963
371123)

SCOTLAND

Mr Ewan, Glen Lyon Lodge, Nairn, Nairnshire IV12 4RH (01667 452780)

Mr Sutton, Linnhe Caravan and Camping Park, Corpach, Fort William,
Inverness-shire PH33 7NL (01397 772376)

WALES

Mrs Hazel Davies, Caebetran Farm, Felinfach, Brecon, Powys LD3 0UL
(01874 754460)

Mrs Bronwen Prosser, Upper Genffordd Guest House, Talgarth, Brecon,
Powys LD3 0EN (01874 711360)

BERKSHIRE

The Compton Swan Hotel, High Street, Near Newbury, Berkshire RG20 6NJ

In the Berkshire Downlands, the Hotel has 5 en suite bedrooms, TV, beverages and telephones. An extensive menu with traditional, exotic, vegetarian and special diets catered for. Home-cooked meals a speciality. Downlands Healthy Eating Award winner. Walled garden where we have *al fresco* eating; BBQs. Near the Ridgeway National Trail, an ideal base for walking, horse-riding and golf, Stabling and horsebox. Real Ales, Bar Meals available. CAMRA Good Beer Guide and Good Pub Guide. ETB.

Phone Garry Mitchell F.B.I.I. on 01635 578269   Fax: 01635 578765

See also Colour Advertisement on page 2

Compton

Village 5 miles/7Km west of Streatley where Georgian houses are one of the notable sights on the banks of the Thames.

COMPTON SWAN HOTEL, HIGH STREET, COMPTON, NEAR NEWBURY RG20 6NJ (01635 578269; Fax: 01635 578765). Situated in the heart of the Berkshire Downlands; 5 rooms en suite with TV, beverage facilities and telephones. Extensive menu with special diets catered for. Large walled garden. [🐾]

BUCKINGHAMSHIRE

THE PLOUGH Hyde Heath, Near Amersham,
Buckinghamshire HP6 5RW Tel: 01494 783163

In a tranquil position on the gentle slopes of the Chiltern Hills, this homely inn is a leisurely drive from the urban hassle of Greater London. Just the place to recharge the batteries through the medium of excellent refreshment and good company. Varied selection of home-cooked dishes on offer at lunchtime and in the evening. CAMRA.

Amersham

Attractive small town featuring Georgian houses, gabled and timbered inns and cobbled courtyards leading to thatched cottages.

THE PLOUGH, HYDE HEATH, NEAR AMERSHAM, BUCKINGHAMSHIRE HP6 5RW (01494 783163). Situated in the Chiltern Hills, and just the place to recharge the batteries with excellent refreshment and good company. Home-cooked dishes lunchtime and evenings.

SYMBOLS

🐾   Indicates that pets are welcome free of charge.

£   Indicates that a charge is made for pets: nightly or weekly.

pw!   Shows some special provision for pets; exercise facility, feeding or accommodation arrangement.

⌂   Indicates separate pets accommodation.

Ely

Magnificent Norman Cathedral dating from 1083. Ideal base for touring the fen country of East Anglia.

JANE LATIMER, 52 WATERSIDE, ELY CB7 4AZ (01353 667570). Listed eighteenth century family home overlooking River Ouse in medieval cathedral city of Ely – Gateway to the Fens. One double en suite and one double with shared facilities. Tea/coffee and colour TV in each room. Open all year. Dogs welcome. Totally non-smoking. [🐕]

MRS C. H. BENNETT, STOCKYARD FARM, WISBECH ROAD, WELNEY PE14 9RQ (01354 610433). Comfortable converted farmhouse, rurally situated between Ely and Wisbech. Conservatory breakfast room, TV lounge. Free range produce. Miles of riverside walks. No smoking. B&B £13–£20. [🐕 pw!]

Huntingdon

Town on River Ouse, 15 miles north-west of Cambridge. Famous for its medieval bridge and links with Oliver Cromwell.

ELEPHANT & CASTLE FREEHOUSE & MOTEL, THE GREEN, WOOD WALTON, HUNTINGDON PE17 5YN (01487 773337; Fax: 01487 773553) Enjoy a break in this village location set amidst wildlife and nature reserves. All motel flatlets are en suite, have TV, tea/coffee making facilities and are on the ground floor. Pets welcome in the motel complex. [🐕]

CHESHIRE

Balterley Green Farm

Deans Lane, Balterley, Near Crewe CW2 5QJ
Tel: 01270 820214 🐾🐾 COMMENDED

Jo and Pete Hollins offer guests a friendly welcome to their home on a 145-acre dairy farm in quiet and peaceful surroundings. Situated on the Cheshire/Staffordshire border within easy reach of Junction 16 on the M6. Pets' corner and pony rides for young children. Within easy reach of Chester, Alton Towers and the Potteries. One family room en suite, one single & one twin (suitable for disabled). Bed and Breakfast from £19pp. Caravans and tents welcome.

THE EATON HOTEL   CITY ROAD, CHESTER CH1 3AE

AA ★★   TEL: 01244 320840; FAX: 01244 320850

The Eaton Hotel is the perfect location for sightseeing in Chester. Not only is it convenient for the River Dee, Roman Walls and main shopping areas, all of which are only a few minutes' walk away, but also its canalside position makes walking your dog the pleasure it should be. All this, complemented by good food and a very friendly atmosphere makes the Eaton Hotel the obvious choice for your stay in Chester. Secure parking on the premises.

Balterley

Small village two miles west of Audley.

MR & MRS HOLLINS, BALTERLEY GREEN FARM, DEANS LANE, BALTERLEY, NEAR CREWE CW2 5QJ (01270 820214). 2 Crowns Commended. 145-acre dairy farm in quiet and peaceful surroundings. Within easy reach of Junction 16 on the M6. Bed and Breakfast from £19pp. Caravans and tents welcome. [pw! Pets £1 per night]

Chester

Former Roman city on the River Dee, with well-preserved walls and beautiful 14th century Cathedral. Liverpool 25 miles.

THE EATON HOTEL, CITY ROAD, CHESTER CH1 3AE (01244 320840; Fax: 01244 320850). In a perfect central location. All rooms have bath or shower, colour TV, radio, telephone, hairdryers and tea making facilities. [🐕]

Macclesfield

Old silk town nestling beween the tranquil farmland of the Cheshire Plain and the dramatic rugged hills of the Peak District National Park and Buxton.

MOORHAYES HOUSE HOTEL, MANCHESTER ROAD, TYTHERINGTON, MACCLESFIELD SK10 2JJ. Comfortable accommodation, mostly en suite, tea and coffee making facilities, colour TVs. Ample parking, hearty breakfast, friendly atmosphere. Dogs welcome - enclosed garden, river walk nearby, dog food available. ETC ◆◆◆. Ring HELEN WOOD on 01625 433228. [pw! 🐕]
E–mail: helen@moorhayeshouse.freeserve.co.uk

CORNWALL

CLASSY COTTAGES
POLPERRO TO FOWEY

ETB up to 🏠🏠🏠🏠🏠 Highly Commended

We are the proud owners of 3 SUPERB coastal cottage locations
Our cottages are of the highest standard

★ Dishwashers, microwaves & washing machines
★ Telephone and Fax available

★ Open fires and heating
★ Cleaning/maid services

WE HAVE FARM PETS FOR OUR VISITORS TO ENJOY

★ Daily feeding of farm pets
★ We are animal lovers.

You are very welcome to arrange to bring your pets

Shark Fishing

INDOOR PRIVATE POOL 85°F
Sauna, Spa & Solarium

 Golf courses

Please contact FIONA and MARTIN NICOLLE on 07000 423000

Coombe Mill

ETB ♟♟♟♟
and ♟♟♟♟♟

A picturesque hamlet of secluded cottages and quiet riverside lodges set amidst an idyllic 30 acre private estate.

Cottages to sleep 2-6/7 with four posters and log burners. Lodges for 2-5, each with its own verandah.

Farm animals and wildlife in abundance. Special morning tractor run for children to feed the animals.

Trout and Carp fishing lakes, private river fishing. Grocery and home cooking to order.

Beaches, coastal walking, rugged moorland nearby. Indoor pool 5 minutes.

Open All Year.

PETS VERY WELCOME

St Breward, Bodmin Cornwall PL30 4LZ

Tel: 01208 850344

Internet: www.coombemill.com

FREE and REDUCED RATE Holiday Visits!
Don't miss our Readers' Offer Vouchers
on pages 53 to 70

"Halwyn"

For a brochure contact John and Sally Clarke,
"Halwyn", Manaccan, Helston, Cornwall. TR12 6ER
Telephone: 01326 280359
E-Mail: John-Sally@freezone.co.uk

Halwyn is a Cornish Farmstead, nestling in a lovely valley on the unspoilt Lizard Peninsula, designated an Area Of Outstanding Natural Beauty. Our cosy, well-equipped cottages offer the peace and tranquillity of lovely waterside gardens, rich with wildlife, an indoor pool, sauna and solarium. Halwyn is close to spectacular coastal and inland walks, sandy coves and beaches, sailing on the Helford, both sea and fresh-water fishing, diving off the Manacles, surfing, galleries, good village pubs and restaurants, tropical gardens, pasties and cream teas! Well-behaved dogs welcome. Short breaks out of season.

GORRAN HAVEN   NEAR MEVAGISSEY

Self catering apartments sleeping 2-6. Beautiful rural area. 600 yards from sandy beach and harbour. Colour TV, cooker, microwave, fridge freezer. Secluded garden. Private parking. Open all year. Registered with both English and Cornwall Tourist Boards. Pets welcome. Near the Lost Gardens of Heligan.
Ken and Sally Pike, Tregillan, Trewollock Lane, Gorran Haven PL26 6NT (01726 842452)

CORNWALL
ST IVES BAY
HOLIDAY PARK

CHALETS CARAVANS AND CAMPING
with private access to a huge sandy beach. With a large indoor pool and two clubs on the Park. Phone us NOW on the toll free number below for your FREE colour brochure.

right on the beach!

Call our 24 hr BROCHURE LINE on 0800 317713

Country *Caradon* Cottages

Luxury cottages in the heart of the Cornish countryside. Ideal centre for exploring Devon and Cornwall, coast and moor. Central heating and log burners for cosy off-season breaks

Every comfort for you and your pets.
Celia Hutchinson, Caradon Country Cottages
East Taphouse, Near Liskeard, Cornwall PL14 4NH
Telephone & Fax: 01579 320355

Cutkive Wood Holiday Lodges

St. Ive, Liskeard PL14 3ND
Tel: 01579 362216

Six cedarwood chalets in 41 acres own Bluebell Woods with nature trails. Dogs welcome. Pets corner. Children welcome to help milk goats, feed poultry etc. Three hole practice golf course. Present owner retired PGA professional golfer. Tuition available. Ideal touring. From £95 to £340 per week April to October.

See also Colour Advertisement on page 7

CORNWALL *Lizard Peninsula, Looe*

89

Secluded country cottages set in idyllic grounds of historic estate in the enchanting Looe Valley. Each has its own charming garden with a further third of an acre of manicured lawn. They are individually furnished with antiques and country furnishings. Although steeped in character, we offer all modern conveniences such as washer dryers, dishwashers, microwaves, linen, colour TV, video, personal telephones and much more. Open log fires and inclusive heating for warm cosy breaks off season. Guests and dogs are welcome to walk or stroll in the immediate parkland and grounds. Countryside and

coastal walking all nearby. Looe 1½ miles with beaches and excellent restaurants. Delicious home-cooked meals service delivered to your door.

For details contact: **Mrs E.M. Chapman, Trenant Lodge, Sandplace, Looe, Cornwall PL13 1PH**
Tel: 01503 263639/262241
e-mail: Liz@holiday-cottage2.demon.co.uk
For on-line Colour Brochure: www.holiday-cottage2.demon.co.uk

---

Valleybrook Peakswater, Lansallos, Looe PL13 2QE

Dogs and their owners are welcome at our family-run small holiday complex of pine lodges and caravans, set in a peaceful country valley 2 miles inland from Polperro. It is a quiet site with no club-house or swimming pool. The centrally-heated double-glazed lodges sleep 6. Open all year. Short breaks available.

For free brochure Tel: 01503 220493

LOOE BAY
A Very Special Place!

A ward winning Holiday Park in an area of outstanding natural beauty and close to superb, sandy beaches.

 01392 447447 **WESTSTAR** *Holiday Parks*

Licensed family run hotel. Dogs most welcome, sleeping in your room free of charge. Panoramic views across the village and Mawgan Porth Bay. Golfing breaks, short breaks, mid-week bookings. Weekly rates from £182 – £206 BB&EM

SeaVista Hotel

Mawgan Porth, near Newquay TR8 4AL
Tel: 01637 860276
Phone Margaret or David for free brochure.

See also Colour Advertisement on page 7

**Readers are requested to mention this guidebook
when seeking accommodation
(and please enclose a stamped addressed envelope).**

White Lodge Hotel

Mawgan Porth Bay, Near Newquay, Cornwall TR8 4BN
Tel: St. Mawgan (STD 01637) 860512

GIVE YOURSELVES & YOUR DOGS A BREAK

at our family-run White Lodge Hotel overlooking beautiful
Mawgan Porth Bay, near Newquay, Cornwall

* Dogs most welcome-
  FREE OF CHARGE
* Your dogs sleep with you in your
  bedroom.
* Direct access to sandy beach and
  coastal path.
* Dog loving proprietors with 17
  years' experience in catering for
  dog owners on holiday with their
  dogs
* ALL bedrooms with colour TV
  with video and satellite channels,
  tea/coffee makers, alarm clocks,
  radios, intercoms, heaters etc.
* Some en suite bedrooms
* Fantastic sea views from most
  rooms.
* Well-stocked residents' lounge bar,
  dining room & sun patio with
  outstanding sea views across the
  bay.
* Games room with pool table and
  dart board etc.
* Large free car park within hotel
  grounds

SPECIAL 6 DAYS (5 NIGHTS) CHRISTMAS HOUSE PARTY **ONLY £235** *Full Board*	SPECIAL 6 DAYS (5 NIGHTS) NEW YEAR (HOGMANAY) BREAK **ONLY £205** *Half Board*	SPECIAL 6 DAYS (5 NIGHTS) BREAKS **ONLY £155-£170** *BB&EM*	WEEKLY TERMS **FROM £203-£225** FOR 5-COURSE EVENING DINNER, BED AND 4-COURSE BREAKFAST WITH CHOICE OF MENU

Phone 01637 860512 John or Diane Parry
for free colour brochure

ALL PRICES INCLUDE
VAT AT 17$\frac{1}{2}$%

See also Colour Advertisement on page 5

CORNWALL *Portreath, Portscatho, Praa Sands, Redruth, Ruanhighlanes, Ruthern Valley*

Friesian Valley Cottages
Mawla, Redruth, Cornwall TR16 5DW
Telephone: 01209 890901
Atlantic coast, between Newquay and St Ives. Superb luxury cottages. Sleep 2 to 6. Peaceful rural hamlet. 2 miles beaches and National Trust coastal footpath. Launderette, games room, bar. Ample parking. Colour brochure.

See also Colour Advertisement on page 8

Trewince Manor
Portscatho, Near Truro TR2 5ET
Peter and Liz Heywood invite you to take your self-catering or touring holiday at their Georgian Manor House Estate in this undiscovered and peaceful corner of Cornwall.
Luxury lodges, cedarwood cabins, cottage and manor house apartments available. Spectacular sea views; our own quay and moorings.
• Relaxing lounge bar and restaurant • Shop • Launderette • Games rooms
• Superb walking and sailing • Abundance of wildlife • DOGS WELCOME
Please write or telephone for further information.
FREEPHONE 0800 0190289   E-mail: bookings@trewince.com.uk

Jasmine and Two Ways, Praa Sands, Near Penzance
Well appointed bungalows. One chalet-bungalow sleeps 9+ in 4 bedrooms. Lovely peaceful countryside with very large garden, not overlooked. 2 miles inland. One three bedroomed, sleeps 6+, sea views with large garden. Both fully equipped. Dogs very welcome.
**MRS JANE LAITY, CHYRASE FARM, GOLDSITHNEY, PENZANCE TR20 9JD
TEL: 01736 763301**

In The Countryside Near The Sea
Perfect for pets and owners. Unlimited trails to explore and near 'Dogs Allowed Beaches'. Also Shop, Children's Play area, Launderette, Bar and Games Room

GLOBE VALE HOLIDAY PARK
CARAVANS • TOURERS • TENTS
Radnor • Redruth • Cornwall • TR16 4BH • Tel: 01209 891183

Polsue Manor
AA ◆◆◆◆
Ruanhighlanes, Near St Mawes, Cornwall TR2 5LU
Tranquil secluded Manor House in 8 acres. En suite bedrooms. Close to sandy coves, Coastal Paths, country walks and National Trust Gardens. Pets very welcome. Dog exercise area.
Tel: 01872 501270; Fax: 01872 501177 for brochure

Ruthern Valley, Cornwall.
Beautiful rural site in the heart of Cornwall. No Bar, No Bingo, No Disco. Centrally based for fine beaches, walking etc. Self-catering lodges, bungalows and holiday caravans for up to six people. Pets very welcome. Lovely local walks direct from the site.
Colour Brochure: Alex and Alison Dawson 01208 831395

Visit the FHG website
www.holidayguides.com
for details of the wide choice of accommodation featured in the full range of FHG titles

98

Rosemundy House Hotel

St Agnes, Cornwall
TR5 0UF

ETB
Commended

Rosemundy House Hotel is an elegant Queen Anne residence set in its own informal garden and woodland, sheltered and secluded, in the pretty, unspoilt village of St Agnes, within easy reach of the spectacular North Cornish coast with its magnificent sandy beaches.

Rosemundy offers the perfect combination for a holiday with your pet. Our comfortable bedrooms have their own individual charm and all are centrally heated and provided with colour TV and tea and coffee making facilities. Our 45ft heated swimming pool, games room, badminton court, putting and croquet lawn are here for your pleasure.

There is much to do and much to see in beautiful Cornwall. There are magnificent walks along cliff tops, historic houses and gardens to visit, and many quaint fishing villages with their stone-built harbours to explore.

From only £200 per week for dinner, bed and breakfast in April to £300 in August.

Why not come and see for yourself? Write or phone for your full colour brochure and tariff.

Tel: (01872) 552101; Fax: (01872) 554000

GREY ROCKS

PENSTRAZE IRISH WOLFHOUNDS, TRURO, CORNWALL TR4 8PE
TEL/FAX: 01872 560231 E-MAIL: PWELLSIW@GLOBALNET.CO.UK

Bed and Full Old Fashioned English Breakfast ● *Open all year
Central heating* ● *Own large car park*

*Pam and Reg Wells welcome you to their small 100-year-old former
farmhouse set in half-an-acre of garden in the lovely Cornish countryside.
Ideally situated for touring the whole of Cornwall, south coast 10 miles, north
coast five miles and the quaint city of Truro four miles. The two attractive*

*double bedrooms have country views,
wash basins, colour TV, courtesy trays
and jug kettles. Reduction for children
under 10 years in small room with bunk
beds. Dogs welcome free. Large kennel
with run available if required. There are
many lovely walks for dogs, nearby and
throughout Cornwall. Please write or
telephone for brochure and terms*

CLASSIC COTTAGES, HELSTON, CORNWALL TR13 8NA (01326 565555).
Choose your cottage from 400 of the finest coastal and country cottages
throughout the West Country. Many welcome pets.

CORNISH TRADITIONAL COTTAGES. A fine selection of self-catering and similar
cottages on both coasts of Cornwall and on Scilly. Pets welcome in many cottages. Free colour brochure from: CORNISH TRADITIONAL COTTAGES,
BLISLAND, BODMIN PL30 4HS (01208 821666; Fax: 01208 821766).

FARM AND COTTAGE HOLIDAYS (01237 479698). 400 superb cottages in
coastal and rural locations in Cornwall, Devon and Somerset.
Website: www.farmcott.co.uk

HOLIDAY HOMES & COTTAGES S.W, 365A TORQUAY ROAD, PAIGNTON TQ3
2BT (01803 663650; Fax: 01803 664037). Hundreds of Self-Catering Holiday
Cottages, Houses, Bungalows, Apartments, Chalets and Caravans in Devon and
Cornwall. Please write or phone for free colour brochure. [🐕]
E–mail: holcotts@aol.com

SYMBOLS

🐕   Indicates that pets are welcome free of charge.

£   Indicates that a charge is made for pets: nightly or weekly.

pw!   Shows some special provision for pets; exercise facility, feeding or accommodation arrangement.

⌂   Indicates separate pets accommodation.

POWELLS COTTAGE HOLIDAYS, HIGH STREET, SAUNDERSFOOT, PEM-BROKESHIRE SA69 9EJ. Many of our top quality holiday properties accept pets. Cottages in Devon, Cornwall, Cotswolds, Pembrokeshire and Heart of England. For colour brochure FREEPHONE 0800 378771 (24 hours).

WELCOME COTTAGE HOLIDAYS. Quality Cottages in wonderful locations at welcoming low prices. Pets, linen and fuel mostly included. PHONE FOR FREE 2000 FULL COLOUR BROCHURE 01756 702201.

Bodmin

Quaint county town of Cornwall, standing steeply on the edge of Bodmin moor. Pretty market town and touring centre. Plymouth 31 miles, Newquay 20, Wadebridge 7.

COOMBE MILL, ST BREWARD, BODMIN PL30 4LZ (01208 850344; Fax: 01208 850344). A picturesque private hamlet of cottages and quiet riverside lodges. 30 acres of glorious grounds. Carp and Trout lakes and private river fishing. Four-posters, log burners, grocery and home cooking to order. ETC 4/5 keys to Highly Commended. Pets very welcome.[First Pet £17.50 per week, others £5 per week] Website: www.coombemill.com

PENROSE BURDEN, ST BREWARD, BODMIN PL30 4LZ (01208 850277 & 617). Holiday Care Award Winning Cottages featured on TV. Open all year. Outstanding views over wooded valley. Free Salmon and Trout fishing. Daily meal service. Superb walking area. Dogs welcome, wheelchair accessible.[Pets £15 per week]

MRS JOAN HARRISON, WILBURY, SUNNYBANKS LANE, FLETCHERS BRIDGE, BODMIN PL30 4AN (01208 74001). Spacious house, centrally situated. Three double bedrooms. Optional evening meal. The surrounding area is breathtakingly beautiful, especially in springtime. Short walks from the house will take you to some of the county's best beauty spots like Cardinham Woods which is ideal for dog walking. B&B £15, BB&EM £21. [🐕]

Boscastle

Picturesque village in tiny harbour, with rocky beach, some sand, and fine scenery. Tintagel 4 miles.

Boscastle/Crackington-Haven area. Modern bungalow sleeping 2–6, heating; microwave; ETB 🏠🏠🏠 Approved. Near sandy beaches, cliff and valley walks. Beautiful scenery, walking distance local store and Inn. Just off A39 and central to most tourist attractions. Spring and Autumn £90-£200 per week. Pets welcome. MRS PROUT (01840 250289). [🐕]

THE WELLINGTON HOTEL, THE HARBOUR, BOSCASTLE (01840 250202). Historic 16th-century coaching inn by Elizabethan harbour and National Trust countryside. Fine Anglo-French restaurant, specialising in regional cuisine and seafood. Freehouse with real ales, pub grub, open fires and beams. 10 acres of private woodland walks. [🐕]
E–mail: vtobutt@enterprise.net
Website: www.enterprise.net/wellington-hotel

Bude

Popular seaside resort overlooking a wide bay of golden sand and flanked by spectacular cliffs. Ideal for surfing; sea water swimming pool for safe bathing.

Two cottages in an area of outstanding natural beauty. Sleep 6 and 8. 100 yards from unspoilt beach. Open all year. Pets and children welcome. APPLY – MR AND MRS H. CUMMINS, MINESHOP, CRACKINGTON HAVEN, BUDE EX23 0NR (01840 230338). [£9 per pet per week.]

MORNISH HOLIDAY APARTMENTS, SUMMERLEAZE CRESCENT, BUDE. EX23 8HJ (Tel & Fax: 01288 352972). ♈♈♈♈ HIGHLY COMMENDED. Two luxury fully en suite bedroomed holiday apartments each enjoying panoramic views of the seashore and coastline. Pets by arrangement. Brochure on request. [🐾]

STAMFORD HILL HOTEL, STRATTON, NEAR BUDE EX23 9AY (01288 352709). Elegant Georgian manor, 5 mins from beaches, 15 en suite rooms, all with colour TV, tea/coffee makers. Heated pool, tennis court, badminton etc. Ideal for golf, fishing, walking. 3 Crowns Commended. [£2 per night.]

Cawsand

Quaint fishing village with bathing beach; sand at low tide. Ideal for watersports. Plymouth (car ferry) 11 miles, (foot ferry) 3.

MR AND MRS A. FIDLER, RAME BARTON, RAME, CAWSAND PL10 1LG (01752 822789). Two self contained holiday flats in old farmhouse on the beautiful Rame peninsula. Lovely coastline, beaches, country park. Children and pets welcome.

WRINGFORD DOWN HOTEL, CAWSAND PL10 1LE (01752 822287). Old Cornish farmhouse with fully licensed bar. Set in four acres just outside Kingsand and Cawsand. B&B from £20. Write or phone for brochure. [🐾]

Crackington Haven

Small coastal village in North Cornwall set amidst fine cliff scenery. Small sandy beach. Launceston 18 miles, Bude 10, Camelford 10.

HENTERVENE PINE LODGE CARAVAN AND CAMPING PARK, CRACKINGTON HAVEN, NEAR BUDE EX23 0LF (01840 230365, Fax: 01840 230514). 1½ miles unspoilt sandy beach. Area of outstanding natural beauty. Luxury caravans to let. First-class facilities for families and pets. Caravans for sale. Open all year. AA 3 Pennants. Short breaks. Camping £3.60 pppn, child Half 4-14 years.[Pets £15 per week, £1 per night camping]

5 beautiful cottages in lovely rural setting 5 miles from Crackington Haven. Log fires, every comfort, furnished and equipped to a very high standard. Dogs welcome by arrangement. Open all year. From £125 per week. Cornwall Tourist Board Inspected. APPLY: JANE AND KEITH BERRY, TRENANNICK COTTAGES, TRENANNICK, WARBSTOW, LAUNCESTON PL15 8RP (01566 781443). [Pets £10 per stay]

Crafthole

Village near sea at Portwrinkle. Fine views over Whitsand Bay and River Lynner. Golf course nearby. Torpoint 6 miles.

THE LISCAWN INN, CRAFTHOLE, NEAR TORPOINT PL11 3BD (01503 230863). Charming, family-run 14th century Hotel. Close to Coastal Path in the forgotten corner of Cornwall. En suite accommodation; bar meals available; cask ales a speciality. Open all year. Self-catering available from Spring 2000. [🐕]

Cusgarne

CUSGARNE (NEAR TRURO), JOYCE AND GEORGE CLENCH, SAFFRON MEADOW, CUSGARNE, TRURO TR4 8RW (01872 863171). A cosy single storey clean detached dwelling within grounds of Saffron Meadow, in a quiet hamlet. Secluded and surrounded by wooded pastureland. Central to Truro, Falmouth and North Coast. £110 to £220 per week. [pw! 🐕]

Delabole

Village two miles west of Camelford.

JOHN AND SUE THEOBALD, TOLCARNE, TREBARWITH ROAD, DELABOLE PL33 9DB. Quiet, comfortable guesthouse in beautiful North Cornwall close to coast path, beaches and surfing. Private bathroom, TV lounge. Kennel and covered run for pets left home during the day. Woodturning courses available. Ample parking. For free brochure call 01840 213558. [pw! 🐕]

Falmouth

Well-known port and resort on Fal estuary, ideal for boating, sailing and fishing; safe bathing from sandy beaches. Of interest is Pendennis Castle (16th century). Newquay 26, Penzance 26, Truro 11.

PETER WATSON, CREEKSIDE HOLIDAY HOUSES, RESTRONGUET, FALMOUTH TR11 5ST (Tel & Fax: 01326 372722). Peaceful, picturesque waters edge hamlet. Boating facilities. Use of boat. Own quay, beach. Spacious houses sleep 4/8. Secluded gardens. Near Pandora Inn. Friday bookings. Dogs welcome. [£10 per week]

Ideally situated for touring Cornwall. First floor flat with 3 bedrooms, lounge with colour TV, kitchen/diner; bathroom, shower room with toilet. Hot water, electricity, bed linen incl. Garden. Open all year. MRS B. NEWING, GLENGARTH, BURNTHOUSE, ST GLUVIAS, PENRYN TR10 9AS (01872 863209). [🐕]

HOLIDAY BUNGALOW ~ FALMOUTH. Magnificent river, sea, countryside views. Spacious detached bungalow and gardens. Shower room. bathroom and seperate WC. Sleeps two to six plus cot. Garage and parking. From £100 to £475 per week including unlimited electricity and hot water. Booking Office: CREATION ACCOMMODATION, 96 MARKET STREET, PENRYN TR10 8BH (Tel: 0800 298 65 65 (Voice/Minicom) Fax: 01326 375088)
E-mail: Falmouth@Encompasstravel.com

Self-catering bungalow sleeps 6. Walking distance of harbour and town, One and a half miles from coast. Dogs welcome. Low Season: £160 to £205; High Season: £240 to £350. Apply MRS J.A. SIMMONS, 215A PERRY STREET, BILLERICAY, ESSEX CM12 0NZ (01277 654425). [Pets £5 weekly.]

Fowey

Historic town, now a busy harbour. Regatta and Carnival Week in August.

CLASSY COTTAGES – Three superb coastal cottage locations between Polperro and Fowey. Willy Wilcox cottage is just 11 feet from beach over smugglers' cave. Log fires, dishwashers, washing machines etc. Indoor Private Swimming Pool. Contact FIONA & MARTIN NICOLLE (01720 423000). [Pets £12 per week]

OLD FERRY INN, BODINNICK-BY-FOWEY PL23 1LX (01726 870237 Fax: 01726 870116). Family-run Inn, ideal for many varied walks. Excellent à la carte restaurant; bar meals available. Comfortable bedrooms with colour TV and tea/coffee. B&B from £20pppn. [Pets £2 per night]

Gillan

Village on coast, eight miles east of Helston.

Family-run Cornish farmstead, converted into self-catering holiday cottages set in two acres of beautiful gardens, indoor heated swimming pool, sauna and solarium. For brochure contact: JOHN AND SALLY CLARKE, "HALWYN", MANACCAN, HELSTON, CORNWALL. TR12 6ER (01326 280359) [Pets £15 per week]. E–mail: John-Sally@freezone.co.uk

Gorran Haven

Coastal village, 3 miles from Mevagissey.

MS M.R. BULLED, MENAGWINS, GORRAN, ST AUSTELL PL26 6HP (01726 843517). Traditional cottage, sleeps five. Linen, towels, electricity supplied. Beach one mile. pets welcome. large garden. Central for touring/walking. Near coastal footpath. [🐕]

Self catering apartments sleeping 2–6. Beautiful rural area, 600 yards from sandy beach and harbour. Near the Lost Gardens of Heligan. Colour TV, cooker, microwave, fridge freezer. Secluded garden, private parking. Open all year. Registered with both English and Cornwall Tourist Boards. KEN AND SALLY PIKE, TREGILLAN, TREWOLLOCK LANE, GORRAN HAVEN PL26 6NT (01726 842452). [Pets £14 per week]

Hayle

Resort, shopping centre and seaport with excellent sands and dunes. Helston 10 miles, Redruth 10, Penzance 8, Cambourne 5.

MR A. JAMES, ST IVES BAY HOLIDAY PARK, 73 LOGGANS ROAD, UPTON TOWANS, HAYLE TR27 5BH (24hr Brochure Line 0800 317713). Park in sand dunes adjoining huge sandy beach. Choice of bars, free entertainment. Chalets, Caravan and Camping. Large indoor pool. [Pets £14 per week.]

Helston

Ancient Stannary town and excellent touring centre, noted for the annual "Furry Dance". Nearby is Loe Pool, separated from the sea by a bar. Truro 17 miles, St Ives 15, Redruth 11.

GREYSTONES GUEST HOUSE, 40 WEST END, PORTHLEVEN, HELSTON TR13 9JL (Tel & Fax: 01326 565583). Picturesque fishing village, ideal for touring. Dogs/children welcome. Overlooking sea, near harbour, beaches, shops, pubs and restaurants. tea and coffee facilities, colour TV. From £15.00 pppn. [🐾]

Liskeard

Pleasant market town and good centre for exploring East Cornwall. Bodmin Moor and the quaint fishing villages of Looe and Polperro are near at hand. Plymouth 19 miles, St Austell 19, Launceston 16, Fowey (via ferry) 15, Bodmin 13, Looe 9.

SUE JEWELL, BOTURNELL FARM COTTAGES, ST PINNOCK, LISKEARD PL14 4QS (Tel: 01579 320880; Fax: 01579 320375). Cosy character stone cottages set in 25 acres of fields and woodland between Looe and Bodmin. Linen, microwave, electricity included. Well equipped. Pets welcome free. [🐾]

CELIA HUTCHINSON, CARADON COUNTRY COTTAGES, EAST TAPHOUSE, NEAR LISKEARD, CORNWALL PL14 4NH (TEL & Fax: 01579 320355). Luxury cottages in the heart of the Cornish countryside. Ideal centre for exploring Devon and Cornwall, coast and moor. Central heating and log burners for cosy off-season breaks. [pw! Pets £10 per week]

MRS E. COLES, CUTKIVE WOOD HOLIDAY LODGES, ST. IVE, LISKEARD PL14 3ND (01579 362216). Self-catering chalets in 41 acres of woodland. 2/3 bedrooms; fully equipped inc. linen, colour TV, fridge, cooker and microwave. Pets corner for children. Dogs welcome. [🐾 pw!]

MRS V.M. NORTHCOTT, "PENDOWER", EAST TAPHOUSE, LISKEARD PL14 4NH (01579 320332). All comforts. Open all year. Main road, Good food. Moderate terms. Ground floor suite available. Central for Cornwall. [🐾]

Gorgeous old world country cottages dating back to 15th century. Open all year. Log fires, antiques and lovely country furnishings, fresh linen, flowers and all comforts of home. Heated pool, meals service, private garden, plenty of country walks. A paradise for dogs and their owners. O. SLAUGHTER, TREFANNY HILL, DULOE, LISKEARD PL14 4QF (01503 220622).

MRS STEPHANIE ROWE, TREGONDALE FARM, MENHENIOT, LISKEARD PL14 3RG (Tel & Fax: 01579 342407). Delightful character cottage. Warm and cosy in winter, barbecue on the patio in summer. Play tennis or fish. Explore the woodland farm trail or many beautiful walks. [🐾 One pet free.]

TRESARRAN COTTAGES, HERODSFOOT, NEAR LISKEARD PL14 4QX (01579 320147). 4 cosy cottages in idyllic setting. Excellent walks through woodland, 6 miles from Looe/Polperro. Beamed ceilings, log fires, perfect for dogs and their owners. [Pets £10 per week]

Idyllic 18th century country cottages for romantics and animal lovers. Looe 3 miles. Wonderful walks from your gate. Cottages warm and cosy in winter. Personal attention and colour brochure from: B. WRIGHT, TREWORGEY COTTAGES, DULOE, LISKEARD PL14 4PP (01503 262730).

Lizard

The most southerly point in England, with fine coastal scenery and secluded coves. Sandy beach at Housel Bay. Truro 28 miles, Heiston 11.

MULLION HOLIDAY PARK. A very special place! Situated in an area of outstanding natural beauty close to glorious sandy beaches. ◆◆◆◆. Phone WESTSTAR HOLIDAY PARK on 01326 240000.

Looe

Twin towns linked by a bridge over the River Looe. Capital of the shark fishing industry; nearby Monkey Sanctuary is well worth a visit.

MRS KEILTHY, CARDWEN FARM, PELYNT, LOOE PL13 2LU (Tel & Fax: 01503 220213). Cardwen is a 17th century Grade II Listed Farmhouse set in three acres of notable gardens with a stream and pond. We have two en suite double bedrooms and one twin room, all overlooking the garden and surrounding fields. [🐾]

CLASSY COTTAGES – Three superb coastal cottage locations between Polperro and Fowey. Willy Wilcox cottage is just 11 feet from beach over smugglers' cave. Log fires, dishwashers, washing machines etc. Indoor Private Swimming Pool. Contact FIONA & MARTIN NICOLLE (01720 423000). [Pets £12 per week].

HENDRA FARM COTTAGES, PELYNT, LOOE PL13 2LU (Tel & Fax: 01503 220701). Three quality cottages peacefully set in 250 acres of beautiful countryside on working farm. A hidden retreat only four miles Looe, Polperro, Coastal Path and coves. Excellent locality for walking. Cottages sleep 2 to 5 persons. Heating, electricity and bed linen included in price. ⛺⛺⛺ Highly Commended. [Pets £5 per week],
E–mail: Roderick.J.Farrelly@farmline.com

LOOE VALLEY TOURING PARK, LOOE, CORNWALL. (01503 262425). Tour and Explore the Looe Valley. Set in glorious countryside, Looe Valley is ideally situated for touring beautiful South East Cornwall. Close to beautiful, safe, sandy beaches, secluded coves and picturesque villages.

MRS ANN BRUMPTON, TALEHAY HOLIDAY COTTAGES, PELYNT NR LOOE PL13 2LT (Tel&Fax: 01503 220252). Cosy, traditional cottages set in four acres of unspoilt countryside offering peace and tranquillity Breathtaking coastal and country walks. An ideal location for dogs and their owners. C.T.B. approved. [🐕]
E–mail: pr.brumpton@ukonline.co.uk
Website: www.cornwallexplore.co.uk/talehay

TALLAND BARTON CARAVAN PARK, TALLAND BAY, LOOE PL13 2JA (01503 272715). Fully equipped two and three bedroom caravans. Direct access to coastal path and beach. Shop, clubroom, laundry, play area and swimming pool. Pets welcome. Short Breaks off-season. [Pets £20.00 per week.]

LOOE. Five miles along the coast from Looe at Polperro 250 yards harbour, holiday cottages sleeping 2, 4, 6 or 8. Spectacularly situated either overlooking Harbour, fabulous outlook, 15 miles sea views and terraced gardens giving Mediterranean setting or nicely positioned by river in old part of village. Gardens, private parking, 2 minutes shops, beach, quay, NT cliff walks. Well-furnished, colour TV. Open all year. Competitive rates. Children Welcome. Pets welcome free of charge. Ring or write NOW. GRAHAM WRIGHT, THE MILL, POLPERRO, CORNWALL PL13 2RP (01579 344080). [🐕]

Gorgeous old world country cottages dating back to 15th century. Open all year. Log fires, antiques and lovely country furnishings, fresh linen, flowers and all comforts of home. Heated pool, meals service, private garden, plenty of country walks. A paradise for dogs and their owners. O. SLAUGHTER, TREFANNY HILL, DULOE, LISKEARD PL14 4QF (01503 220622).

TRELAWNE LODGE, LOOE. Delightful detached period lodge. Lovely secluded wooded gardens. Summer house. Barbecue. Woodland and coastal walks. Beaches one mile. Comfortably furnished, well equipped. Two bedrooms. Sleeps five. ENQUIRIES: BARTERS OLD FARMHOUSE, NORTH WHILBOROUGH, NEWTON ABBOT TQ12 5LP (Tel: 01803 873213; Fax: 01803 875096) [Pets £7 per week]
E–mail: holcot@eclipse.co.uk

JOHN & NANCY JOLLIFF, TREMAINE GREEN, PELYNT, NEAR LOOE PL13 2LS (01503 220333). Dogs love our cosy and comfortable character cottages, Cornish countryside and coastal walks. Accompanying humans also welcome if well-behaved. Send for our free colour brochure. [Pets £16.00 per week.]

TRENANT PARK COTTAGES. Four delightful cottages sleep from 2 to 7 persons. Each has spacious lounge with colour TV, fully equipped kitchen, private garden. Ample room to relax. APPLY: MRS E. CHAPMAN, TRENANT LODGE, SANDPLACE, LOOE PL13 1PH (01503 263639/262241). [Pets £12.50 per week.]
E–mail: Liz@holiday-cottage2.demon.co.uk
Website: www.holiday-cottage2.demon.co.uk

VALLEYBROOK, PEAKSWATER, LANSALLOS, LOOE, CORNWALL. PL13 2QE (01503 220493). Self-catering quality pine lodges and caravans in peaceful setting near Polperro. Open all year. Short breaks. Phone for brochure. Dogs £1.50 per day.

LOOE BAY. A very special place! Award Winning Holiday Park situated in an area of outstanding natural beauty close to glorious sandy beaches. ◆◆◆◆. Phone WESTSTAR HOLIDAY PARKS on 01392 447447.

Mawgan Porth

Modern village on small sandy bay. Good surfing. Inland stretches the beautiful Vale of Lanherne. Rock formation of Bedruthan Steps is nearby. Newquay 6 miles west.

THE MALMAR HOTEL, TRENANCE, MAWGAN PORTH, CORNWALL TR8 4DA (01637 860324). Small licensed Hotel. Close to beach and coastal path. Two good golf courses nearby. Good English cooking. Rooms with tea-making facilities, most en suite. [🐕]

SEAVISTA HOTEL, MAWGAN PORTH, NEAR NEWQUAY TR8 4AL (01637 860276). Licensed family run hotel, nine bedrooms all with shower, washbasins, colour TV, tea/coffee facilities. Car park, residents' lounge, TV lounge, pool table, darts and garden. [🐕]

WHITE LODGE HOTEL, MAWGAN PORTH BAY, NEAR NEWQUAY TR8 4BN (01637 860512). Give yourselves and your dogs a quality holiday break at this family-run hotel overlooking beautiful Mawgan Porth Bay. Bedrooms en suite, all rooms with washbasins, shaver points, heaters etc. Lounge bar, games room, sun patio, dining room. Car park. 17 years experience. Phone for free brochure. [🐕 pw!]

Mousehole

Picturesque fishing village with sand and shingle beach. Penzance 3 miles.

At the entrance to an unspoilt fishing village are four fully equipped S/C flats. Two with full sea view. All bedding and towels provided. Colour TV. Open all year from £80.00 per week. Special out of season short break terms. MR A.G. WRIGHT, 100 WENSLEY ROAD, WOODTHORPE, NOTTINGHAM NG5 4JU (Tel and Fax: 0115 963 9279 or 01736 731563). [🐕]

Mullion

Village 5 miles south of Helston; much of surrounding area owned by National Trust.

MRS JANET STANLAND, MEAVER FARM, MULLION TR12 7DN (Tel: 01326 240128; Fax: 01326 240011). Luxury B&B in 300-year-old farmhouse. Quiet valley on Lizard Peninsula. All rooms have private/en suite bathrooms. Acre fenced field for exercising run-away humans!

RIDGEBACK LODGE HOTEL & RESTAURANT, MULLION TR12 7DH (01326 241300). Overlooking Predannock Downs; dogs welcome on beach October to March. En suite available; all bedrooms with colour TV. Restaurant and bar serving local fish/meat. Short Breaks available. Open all year. [Pets £2 per night, £7 per week.]

Newquay

Popular family holiday resort surrounded by miles of golden beaches. Semi-tropical gardens, zoo and museum. Ideal for exploring all of Cornwall.

GOLDEN BAY HOTEL, PENTIRE, NEWQUAY TR7 1PD (01637 873318). ETC ◆◆◆. Affordable quality hotel. Overlooking Fistral beach with the Gannel River and National Trust countryside at the rear. All rooms private facilities, some deluxe four poster rooms. Lovely coastal and countryside walks, also close to golf. B&B £18-£30 E.M. optional. [🐾]

PARADISE BEACH HOTEL, WATERGATE BAY, NEWQUAY TR8 4AB (01637 860273). Superb location 200 yards from beach (dogs allowed); beautiful cliff walks. En suite rooms; sauna, solarium. Excellent choice meals. Licensed. [🐾] Website: http://freespace.virgin.net/paradise_beach.hotel/

CY & BARBARA MOORE, THE RANCH HOUSE, TRENCREEK NEWQUAY, CORNWALL. TR8 4NN (01637 875419). Detached Bungalow, quiet area, lovely gardens, panoramic views. Easy parking. Bed and Breakfast April to October £16-£20. No smoking. Also two bedroom self-catering Chalet, fully equipped £225 - £350 per week. [Pets £2 per night]

ROSEMERE HOTEL, WATERGATE BAY, NEWQUAY TR8 4AB (01637 860 238). Family-run hotel overlooking the beautiful Watergate Beach and Coastal Footpath. 38 en suite rooms, many with sea views. Heated outdoor pool. Dogs welcome to sleep in your room. [🐾]

WHITE LODGE HOTEL, MAWGAN PORTH BAY, NEAR NEWQUAY TR8 4BN (01637 860512). Give yourselves and your dogs a quality holiday break at this family-run hotel overlooking beautiful Mawgan Porth Bay. Bedrooms en suite, all rooms with washbasins, shaver points, heaters etc. Lounge bar, games room, sun patio, dining room. Car park. 16 years experience. Phone for free brochure. [🐾 pw!]

TRETHIGGEY TOURING PARK, QUINTRELL DOWNS, NEWQUAY TR8 4LG (01637 877672). Open 1st March to 2nd January. Toilets / hot showers / disabled toilet / shaver points / hairdryers / dishwashing facilities / launderette / shop / freezer packs / telephone / chemical toilet disposal point / electric hook-ups /games room / TV/off-licence. Touring caravans to let. ✓✓✓✓. [Pets £1.20 p.n.]

Otterham Station

Village 4 miles east of Boscastle.

JOHN AND ANGIE LAPHAM, SEA VIEW FARM, OTTERHAM STATION, CAMELFORD PL32 9SW (01840 261355). Comfy guest house in 10 acres, beaches nearby. Walking, fishing, riding, Bodmin Moor 3 miles. Rooms, tea/coffee, H&C, B&B, EM optional. Dogs welcome free. [pw! 🐾]

Padstow

Bright little resort with pretty harbour on Camel estuary. Extensive sands. Nearby is Elizabethan Prideaux Place. Newquay 15 miles, Wadebridge 8.

RAINTREE HOUSE HOLIDAYS, WHISTLERS, TREYARNON BAY, PADSTOW PL28 8JR (01841 520228; Fax:01841 520130). We have a varied selection of accommodation. Small or large, houses and apartments, some by the sea. All in easy reach of our lovely beaches. Please write or phone for brochure. [🐾]

Penzance

Well-known resort and port for Scilly Isles, with sand and shingle beaches. Truro 27 miles, Helston 13, Land's End 10, St Ives 8.

GLENCREE PRIVATE HOTEL, 2 MENNAYE ROAD, PENZANCE TR18 4NG (01736 362026). Just off seafront with comfortable friendly atmosphere. Spacious rooms with colour TV and tea-making. Most rooms are en suite, some with good sea views. Unrestricted parking. Good home cooking. All well-behaved pets welcome and their owners too! WCTB 2 Crowns. B&B from £18 nightly, £108 weekly. [🐾]

TRENGWAINTON HOLIDAY COTTAGES. Luxury granite cottages set in the lovely West Cornwall countryside. Beautifully furnished, centrally heated and fully equipped, sleeping 4 - 8. Dogs welcome at some of the cottages. Brochure from: THE ESTATE OFFICE, CHYANDOUR, PENZANCE TR18 3LW (01736 363021; Fax: 01736 368142). [Pets £10 per week (each)]

Polperro

Picturesque and quaint little fishing village and harbour. Of interest is the "House of the Props". Fowey 9 miles, Looe 5.

CLASSY COTTAGES – Three superb coastal cottage locations between Polperro and Fowey. Willy Wilcox cottage is just 11 feet from beach over smugglers' cave. Log fires, dishwashers, washing machines etc. Indoor Private Swimming Pool. Contact FIONA & MARTIN NICOLLE (01720 423000). [Pets £12 per week].

GREAT KELLOW BARNS. Beautifully converted barn sleeps 4/5. Private garden. Log burning stove. Also available, well appointed six berth caravan on small farm site. Apply ANNIE BURKMAR (01503 272707). [Pets £10 per week.]

GREAT KELLOW FARM, POLPERRO. Feel at ease with your pets. Two clean, comfortable, fully equipped four to six berth caravans. Rural situation, sea view, country/coastal walks nearby. Ring Jane Wilkinson on 01503 272138 for brochure.

POLPERRO. Five miles along the coast from Looe at Polperro 250 yards harbour, holiday cottages sleeping 2, 4, 6 or 8. Spectacularly situated either overlooking Harbour, fabulous outlook, 15 miles sea views and terraced gardens giving Mediterranean setting or nicely positioned by river in old part of village. Gardens, private parking, 2 minutes shops, beach, quay, NT cliff walks. Well-furnished, colour TV. Open all year. Competitive rates. Children Welcome. Pets welcome free of charge. Ring or write NOW. GRAHAM WRIGHT, THE MILL, POLPERRO, CORNWALL PL13 2RP (01579 344080). [🐕]

Polzeath

Small, friendly resort on cliffs near Padstow. Fine sands, good bathing, surfing. Sheltered by Pentire Head to the north. Wadebridge 8 miles.

D. & L. SHARPE, PINEWOOD FLATS, POLZEATH PL27 6TQ (01208 862269). Flats, Chalets and Cottage. Table Tennis, launderette, baby-sitting. Superb touring centre. [🐕]

Port Gaverne

Hamlet on east sid of Port Isaac, near Camel Estuary.

CHIMNEYS, PORT GAVERNE, PORT ISAAC PL29 3SQ (Tel & Fax: 01208 880254). A charming 18th century cottage only 10 metres from beach. Four bedrooms, two bathrooms, lounge, dining room and kitchen. Good size garden. Brochure from Mrs. Holmes. [🐕]

Port Isaac

Attractive fishing village with harbour. Much of the attractive coastline is protected by the National Trust. Camelford 9 miles, Wadebridge 9.

PORT GAVERNE HOTEL, NEAR PORT ISAAC PL29 3SQ (01208 880244; Fax: 01208 880151). Comfortably renovated character cottages, sleep 2/6, fully equipped, no meters, all inclusive price. ♛♛♛♛ Commended. Convenient for the Port Gaverne Hotel (4 Crowns). Open all year. [Pets £3 per night (hotel)].

SYMBOLS
🐕   Indicates that pets are welcome free of charge.
£   Indicates that a charge is made for pets: nightly or weekly.
pw!   Shows some special provision for pets; exercise facility, feeding or accommodation arrangement.
⌂   Indicates separate pets accommodation.

Homes from home around our peaceful courtyard garden 100 yds from sea in bygone fishing hamlet. Each sleeps six and has full CH, fridge-freezer, washer-dryer, dishwasher, microwave, video. £160 (February) £600 (August) weekly. Daily rates off-season. Resident owners APPLY:- CAROLE & MALCOLM LEE, GULLROCK, PORT GAVERNE, PORT ISAAC PL29 3SQ (01208 880106).[🐾]

LONG CROSS HOTEL & VICTORIAN GARDENS, TRELIGHTS, PORT ISAAC PL29 3TF (01208 880243). Set in magnificent public gardens with tavern in the grounds. Pets' corner. Perfect base for touring. Excellent food served all day. Bargain Spring/Autumn Breaks. [Pets £1.50 per night.]

Portreath

Coastal village 4 miles north west of Redruth.

Charming elegantly furnished self catering cottages between Newquay and St Ives. Sleep 2 to 6. Fully equipped including linen. 2 miles to sandy beaches. Laundry and pool room plus bar. Ample parking. Colour brochure – FRIESIAN VALLEY COTTAGES, MAWLA, CORNWALL TR16 5DW (01209 890901) [🐾]

Portscatho

Tiny cliff-top resort on Roseland Peninsula overlooking beach of rocks and sand. Harbour and splendid views. Falmouth 5 miles.

PETER AND LIZ HEYWOOD, TREWINCE MANOR, PORTSCATHO, NEAR TRURO TR2 5ET (FREEPHONE 0800 0190289). Georgian Manor house estate with luxury lodges, cedarwood cabins, cottage, manor house apartment. Lounge bar and restaurant; launderette. Superb walking and sailing. Dogs welcome. [pw! Pets £20 per week]
E–mail: bookings@trewince.com.uk

Praa Sands

Magnificent stretch of sands and dunes. Nearby is picturesque Prussia Cove. Penzance 7 ½ miles, Helston 6.

Well appointed Bungalows. One chalet bungalow sleeps 9+ in 4 bedrooms. Lovely peaceful countryside with large garden not overlooked. 2 miles inland. One 3 bedroomed sleeps 6+. Sea views with large garden. Both fully equipped. Dogs very welcome. APPLY – MRS J. LAITY, CHYRASE FARM, GOLDSITHNEY, PENZANCE TR20 9JD (01736 763301). [Pets £14 per week]

FLAT 1, 19 TRELOARTHA ROAD, PRAA SANDS, PENZANCE. Sleeps 4. Ground floor self-contained flat with enclosed garden and garage. Warm, roomy, comfortable and fully equipped. Located close to sandy beach; good touring centre. Coastal path walks nearby. Children and pets welcome. Available all year; Short Breaks in Winter. Weekly terms from £80. Contact: MRS A.G. HOLLAND, BLUE BURROW COTTAGE, PERRANUTHNOE, PENZANCE TR20 9NF (01736 711108).

Redruth

Market town 8 miles west of Truro.

GLOBE VALE HOLIDAY PARK, RADNOR, REDRUTH TR16 4BH (01209 891183). "In the Countryside, near the Sea." Perfect for pets and owners, with unlimited trails to explore and near "Dogs Allowed" beaches. Shop, play area, launderette, bar and games room. Caravans, tourers and tents welcome. [Pets £7.50 per week]

Ruanhighlanes

Picturesque hamlet convenient for Veryan and Philleigh. Beautiful surrounding countryside.

POLSUE MANOR, RUANHIGHLANES, NEAR ST. MAWES TR2 5LU (Tel: 01872 501270; Fax: 01872 501177). Tranquil secluded manor house in 8 acres. En suite bedrooms. Close to sandy coves, coastal paths and country walks. Pets very welcome. AA ◆◆◆◆. [Pets £3.50 per night]

Ruthernbridge

Hamlet four miles west of Bodmin.

RUTHERN VALLEY HOLIDAY PARK, CORNWALL. Beautiful rural site in the heart of Cornwall. No Bar, No Bingo, No Disco. Self-catering lodges, bungalows and holiday caravans for up to six people. Colour Brochure: ALEX AND ALISON DAWSON (01208 831395). [Pets £25 per holiday]

St Agnes

Patchwork of fields dotted with remains of local mining industry. Watch for grey seals swimming off St. Agnes Head.

CHIVERTON PARK, NEAR ST AGNES (01872 560667). Quiet, spacious park for caravan and touring holidays. Magnificent walks, short drives to superb beaches. Children's play area, games room; laundry and shop. Brochure.

THE DRIFTWOOD SPARS HOTEL, TREVAUNANCE COVE, ST AGNES TR5 0RT (01872 552428/553323). Take a deep breath of Cornish fresh air at this comfortable Hotel ideally situated for a perfect seaside holiday. Wonderful food, traditional Cornish home cooking. Children and pets welcome. [Pets £1.50 per night]

PENKERRIS, PENWINNICK ROAD, ST. AGNES TR5 0PA (01872 552262). Enchanting Edwardian licensed residence. AA, RAC Listed. Les Routiers recommended. Lounge with TV, video, piano, and log fires in winter. Open all year. ETC ◆◆. [🐾 One dog free]

ROSEMUNDY HOUSE HOTEL, ST AGNES TR5 0UF (Tel: 01872 552101; Fax: 01872 554000). An elegant Queen Anne residence set in 4 acres of informal garden and woodland. Swimming pool, games room, croquet, putting. Good food, friendly atmosphere. Half board from £190. Send or telephone for colour brochure.[Pets £10 per week]

SUNHOLME HOTEL, GOONVREA ROAD, ST AGNES TR5 0NW (01872 552318). Enjoy some of the finest views in the South West. Ideal for touring; cliff walks and beaches. Good food and service. All bedrooms en suite. Write or phone for brochure. [Pets £1.50 per night.]

MARC WATTS, TREVAUNANCE POINT HOTEL, ST AGNES TR5 0RZ (01872 553235; Fax: 01872 553874). Old world clifftop Hotel, ships timbered rooms, sea views, candlelight cuisine. Sea-food specialities. Open all year. Winter breaks. [🐴 pw!]

St Austell

Old Cornish town and china clay centre with small port at Charlestown (11/2 miles). Excellent touring centre. Newquay 16 miles, Truro 14, Bodmin 12, Fowey 9, Mevagissey 6.

BOSINVER HOLIDAY COTTAGES. Individual cottages and lodges in peaceful garden surroundings. Close to major holiday attractions. Short walk to shop and pub. Phone 01726 72128 for brochure. [Pets £15 per week].
E–mail: Bosinver@Holidays2000.freeserve.co.uk
Website: www.cornwall-cottages-holidays.co.uk

ST MARGARET'S PARK HOLIDAY BUNGALOWS, POLGOOTH, ST AUSTELL PL26 7AX (01726 74283; Fax: 01726 71680). Family-run timber Bungalows in sunny wooded valley. Village Inn, shop, golf 500 yards. Children and pets welcome. From £95 per week. [pw! £20 per week.]

St Breward

Village south of Camelford in North Cornwall.

DARRYNANE COTTAGES, DARRYNANE, ST BREWARD PL30 4LZ (Tel & Fax: 01208 850885). Absolutely fabulous detached cottages. Set in private gardens. Unique moorland valley setting. Waterfalls, woods, river Wood-burning stoves, four-poster bed. Excellent walking. Camel Trail close by. 🏠🏠🏠🏠 Commended.
E–mail: alegna@eclipse.co.uk
Website: www.chycor.co.uk/cottages/darrynane

St Ives

Picturesque resort, popular with artists, with cobbled streets and intriguing little shops. Wide stretches of sand.

CARLYON GUEST HOUSE, 18 THE TERRACE, ST IVES TR26 3BP (01736 795317). Warm, friendly atmosphere with good English cooking. All bedrooms with TV and tea/coffee facilities; most with showers. Bed and Breakfast, with Evening Meal optional.

MYRTWEDHEN. HELLESVEOR, ST. IVES. Lovely cottage. Colour TV, central heating, automatic washing machine (a cot and high chair can be provided on request). Available all year round for full weeks in the summer or off-peak breaks of any length. We are very happy to have children and dogs stay. Prices from £210 to £420 (including linen and heating) dependent on season. Details from: MRS P. H. SEABROOK, 30 NEWCOMBE STREET, MARKET HARBOROUGH. LEICESTERSHIRE LEI6 9PB (01858 463723).
E–mail: LarkForge@courtyard9.freeserve.co.uk

SANDBANK HOLIDAYS, ST IVES BAY, HAYLE (01736 752594). High quality Apartments and Bungalows for 2-6 persons. Heated, Colour TV, Microwave etc. Open all year. Short Breaks and weekly rates. Dogs welcome. [Pets £15 p.w]

St Mawgan

Delightful village in a wooded river valley. Ancient church has fine carvings.

DALSWINTON COUNTRY HOUSE HOTEL, ST MAWGAN, NEAR NEWQUAY TR8 4EZ (01637 860385). Old Cornish house standing in nine and a half acres of secluded grounds. All rooms en suite, colour TV, tea/coffee facilities. Solar heated outdoor swimming pool. Restaurant and bar. Out-of-season breaks. [🐕]

Sennen

Situated east of Land's End.

HOMEFIELDS LICENSED GUEST HOUSE, SENNEN, NEAR PENZANCE, CORNWALL TR19 7AD (01736 871418). A small and friendly place to stay. Near Lands End. All rooms have TV, heating, tea/coffee. En suite rooms, sea views, four posters. Prices from £12.50 - £19.00. Pets Welcome.

Tintagel

Attractively situated amidst fine cliff scenery; small rocky beach. Famous for associations with King Arthur, whose ruined castle on Tintagel Head is of interest. Bude 19 miles, Camelford 6.

BOSSINEY FARM CARAVAN AND CAMPING PARK, TINTAGEL PL34 0AY (01840 770481). BGHP ★★★★. Family-run park. 19 luxury letting vans; fully serviced, H&C with shower, room heater, TV. On the coast at Tintagel. Colour brochure available. [🐕]

FHG PUBLICATIONS LIMITED publish a large range of well-known accommodation guides. We will be happy to send you details or you can use the order form at the back of this book.

THE PENALLICK HOTEL, TREKNOW, TINTAGEL PL34 0EJ (01840 770296). Small, homely licensed hotel, magnificent cliff top position and walks. All rooms colour TV, tea-makers; en suite/sea views. Ground floor rooms available. Open all year. Regret no children under 12 years.[🐾]
E–mail: penallick@yahoo.com

PENPETHY HOLIDAY COTTAGES, set in large sheltered courtyard with ample parking. Peaceful, relaxing location, ideal for exploring coast, moors. Phone for brochure/tariff 01840 213903.

SANDY AND DAVE WILSON, SALUTATIONS, ATLANTIC ROAD, TINTAGEL PL34 0DE (01840 770287). Comfortable, well-equipped, centrally heated cottages sleeping two. Ideal for touring, walking and relaxing. Close to coastal path and village amenities. Private parking. Pets Free. [🐾]

MRS LYNDA SPRING, TRETHEVY MANOR, TINTAGEL, CORNWALL PL34 0BG (Tel/Fax: 01840 770636). Two comfortable, well-equipped, self-contained cottages adjoining historical 12th Century Manor House. One-and-a-half miles from Tintagel. Sandy beaches, spectacular coastal and country walks. [🐾]

NICK LEEDS, WILLAPARK MANOR HOTEL, BOSSINEY, TINTAGEL PL34 0BA (01840 770782). Beautiful character house amidst 14 acres and only minutes from the beach. All en suite rooms. Children and pets welcome. Open all year. SAE for brochure. ETC ★★. [🐾]

Torpoint

Busy and pleasant little town on the Hamoaze facing Devonport from and to which runs a car ferry. Plymouth (via ferry) 3 miles.

WHITSAND BAY HOTEL, PORTWRINKLE, BY TORPOINT, PLYMOUTH PL11 3BU (01503 230276; Fax: 01503 230297). Magnificent Country Manor Hotel on cliff top at edge of beach. Own 18 hole golf course, indoor heated swimming pool. Family-sized en suite rooms. AA/RAC ★★, Three Crowns. [Pets £3.50 per night, £24.50 per week] ,
Website: www.cornish-golf-hotels.co.uk ,
E–mail: earlehotels.btconnect.com

Truro

Pleasant cathedral city. An excellent touring centre with both north and south coasts within easy reach. There are numerous creeks to explore and boat trips may be made across the estuary to Falmouth. Penzance 27 miles, Bodmin 25, Helston 17, St. Austell 14, Falmouth 11, Redruth 8.

PAM AND REG WELLS, GREY ROCKS, PENSTRAZE IRISH WOLFHOUNDS, TRURO TR4 8PE (Tel & Fax: 01872 560231). Ideal base for touring Cornwall. We have three letting bedrooms – two doubles with washbasins and one small bunkbed room for children. Own car park. Bed and Breakfast £16.50 per person. Reductions for children sharing. [🐾]
E–mail: pwellsiw@globalnet.co.uk

MRS TRESEDER, MARCORRIE HOTEL, 20 FALMOUTH ROAD, TRURO TR1 2HX (01872 277374 or Fax: 01872 241666). Victorian town house, five minutes' walk from city centre. Ideal touring base. All rooms en suite with central heating, colour TV, telephone, tea-making facilities. Ample parking. Major credit cards accepted. Open all year. Bed and Breakfast from £23.25 pppn sharing twin/double room. 3 Crowns Commended. AA QQQQ. [Pets £2.50 per night]

Wadebridge

Town on River Camel, 6 miles north-west of Bodmin.

Farm cottages with superb views of Camel Valley. Ideal for walking, cycling, beaches and touring all Cornwall and North Devon. These fully equipped cottages have log fires, private gardens and parking. Electricity and linen included. Personally supervised, sleep two to seven plus cot. ETC ♦♦♦♦ Commended. Dogs by arrangement. MRS SUE ZAMARIA, COLESENT COTTAGES, ST TUDY, WADEBRIDGE, CORNWALL PL30 4QX (Tel/Fax: 01208 850112). [**]**

Key to Tourist Board Ratings

 The Crown Scheme

The English Tourism Council (formerly the English Tourist Board) has joined with the **AA** and **RAC** to create a new, easily understood quality rating for serviced accommodation.

Hotels will receive a grading ranging from **one to five STARS (★)**. Other serviced accommodation such as **guest houses** and **B&B establishments** will be graded from **one to five DIAMONDS (♦)**. These ratings represent Quality, Service and Hospitality not just facilities.

NB. Some properties had not been assessed at the time of going to press and in these cases the publishers have included the old CROWN gradings.

The Key Scheme

The Key Scheme covering self-catering in cottages, bungalows, flats, houseboats, houses, chalets, etc remains unchanged. The classification from **One to Five KEYS** indicates the range of facilities and equipment. Higher quality standards are indicated by the terms APPROVED, COMMENDED, HIGHLY COMMENDED AND DE LUXE.

NOTE

All the information in this book is given in good faith in the belief that it is correct. However, the publishers cannot guarantee the facts given in these pages, neither are they responsible for changes in policy, ownership or terms that may take place after the date of going to press. Readers should always satisfy themselves that the facilities they require are available and that the terms, if quoted, still apply.

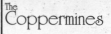

The **Coppermines**
& Coniston Cottages

*Unique Lakeland cottages for 2 –
27 of quality and character in
stunning mountain scenery. Log
fires, exposed beams.
Pets welcome!*
Tel: 015394 41765 (24hrs)
www.coppermines.co.uk

Mobile: 07721 584488

See also Colour Advertisement on page 8

Mrs D.A. Hall, Dow Crag House, Coniston LA21 8AT

Two chalet bungalows to let, sleeping 2/6. One mile from Coniston village on A593. First bungalow has sittingroom, kitchen/diningroom, 3 bedrooms sleeping 6; bathroom, separate toilet. Second bungalow comprises livingroom/kitchen, three bedrooms sleeping 5 and shower room. No linen. Set in private garden with direct access to to the Fells and Hills. Freedom, yet safe for children. Pets welcomed by arrangement. Mountain walks, boating, fishing, tennis and bowls in village. Available March till November. SAE please.   **Telephone 015394 41558**

THE BURNMOOR INN

Boot, Eskdale, Cumbria. CA19 1TG

Resident proprietors:
Harry and Paddington Berger

Situated in this stunning valley close to amazing walks, including Scafell, Harter and Gable to name but a few. Both you and your hounds can enjoy en suite luxury in one of our nine bedrooms, all with tea and coffee making facilities and comfortable furnishings. We offer good food in both restaurant and bar where you can enjoy one of our real ales (CAMRA Guide) and discuss your next day's assault. Dogs welcome to lie by the fire in the bar. We do not make a charge for well behaved dogs. Also available two-bed cottage. Call for a brochure.

**Tel: 019467 23224 Fax: 019467 23337
e-mail: enquiries@burnmoor.co.uk**

PLEASE MENTION THIS GUIDE WHEN YOU WRITE

OR PHONE TO ENQUIRE ABOUT ACCOMMODATION.

IF YOU ARE WRITING, A STAMPED,

ADDRESSED ENVELOPE IS ALWAYS APPRECIATED.

MRS. J. HALL: 01946 723319

Get away from it all on our lovely Lakeland Farm. Traditionalists love the stone cottages, - or how about a beautiful modern pine lodge? All fully fitted and equipped of course, - even including dishwashers. Couples will love the peace and tranquillity, and walking the dog couldn't be easier, for Eskdale is walking country - riverside, valley or high fell, you choose!

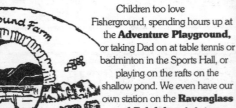

Children too love Fisherground, spending hours up at the **Adventure Playground,** or taking Dad on at table tennis or badminton in the Sports Hall, or playing on the rafts on the shallow pond. We even have our own station on the **Ravenglass and Eskdale miniature railway.** Pets Welcome; Colour brochure on request.
Tel: 01946 723319
ETB ♛♛♛ Commended

FISHERGROUND FARM   ESKDALE   CUMBRIA

Prospect House Hotel   Proprietor: Bill Lambert
Kents Bank Road, Grange-over-Sands, Cumbria LA11 7DJ   Tel: (015395) 32116
A warm welcome awaits you at Prospect House. Seven bedrooms, six with private facilities, all have TV, radio, tea/coffee making. Noted for our cuisine using fresh produce – no junk food. Car parking, Residents' bar. Our best advertisement is the many return visits we receive each year. Independently inspected to local authority approved criteria. Bed & breakfast from £23.50, Dinner (served at 7pm) £11.50.   **Please phone for brochure and full tariff.**

This beautiful late Georgian vicarage was built in 1803, but now has all the comforts of modern life. It is set in five acres of informal gardens and woodland, home to deer, red squirrels and an extraordinary variety of birds. The Old Vicarage is truly a place to unwind and forget for a while the stress of day to day life

Witherslack, near Grange-Over-Sands LA11 6RS
Tel: 015395 52381; Fax: 015395 52373;
E-mail: hotel@old-vic.demon.co.uk

Near to the Lakes, far from the crowds **The Old Vicarage**

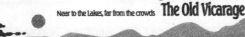

FHG PUBLICATIONS LIMITED publish a large range of well-known accommodation guides. We will be happy to send you details or you can use the order form at the back of this book.

FREE and REDUCED RATE Holiday Visits!
Don't miss our Readers' Offer Vouchers
on pages 53 to 70

Readers are requested to mention this guidebook
when seeking accommodation
(and please enclose a stamped addressed envelope).

Overlooking Lake Windermere

* ENJOY 3 NIGHTS DB&B FROM £99 *
☆ Elegant Georgian Mansion ☆ Roaring Log Fires
☆ All rooms en suite
(many with four-poster and jacuzzi bath)
☆ Exclusive Leisure Facilities
Indoor Pool, Steam Room, Gym and Spa
☆ Pets Welcome Free of Charge

To receive our brochure and tariff please telephone
015395 31222
Newby Bridge Hotel, Newby Bridge, Near Ulverston, Cumbria LA12 8NA

Lisco Farm ~ Penrith

Lisco has beautiful views of Saddleback and the Fells and provides a good base for touring Lakeland. Comfortable accommodation offered in one double and two en suite family rooms, all with tea/coffee making facilities and washbasins. Bathroom with shower. Lounge and separate dining room. Outside accommodation available for dogs if required.

Mrs Mary Teasdale, Lisco Farm, Troutbeck, Penrith CA11 0SY Tel: 017687 79645

Tastefully converted 18th century barn in peaceful surroundings with magnificent views, offering a warm welcome and Aga-cooked meals. Open all year. Accommodation is available in two bedrooms with en suite shower/toilet, comfortable beds, colour TV and tea/coffee making facilities. Full English breakfast is provided and freshly home cooked dinner is available if required. B&B from £17 per person; Dinner £12 per person. *Mrs Marion Barritt Tel: 017684 83492*

PENRUDDOCK, PENRITH CA11 0QU

♀♀♀♀ **SECLUDED COTTAGES with Leisure Fishing**
Commended   Crossfield Cottages, Kirkoswald, Penrith, Cumbria CA10 1EU
24 hour Brochure line: 01768 898711 (manned most Saturdays)

Tranquil quality cottages overlooking lake amid Lakeland's beautiful Eden Valley countryside, only 30 minutes' drive from Ullswater, North Pennines, Hadrian's Wall and Scottish Borders. Good coarse fishing at hand. Various cottages sleep 2—10, well equipped and maintained. **No silly rules.**

Westmorland Hotel

AA ★★★ ETC ★★★ RAC ★★★ AA ✪
Highly Commended
Orton Penrith Cumbria CA10 3SB

Somewhere to rest, to unwind and recharge the batteries and as a base to explore the Lakes, Dales and Pennines with excellent facilities and award-winning cuisine. Pets are very welcome.

015396 24351

All pets free of charge at **Tanglewood Caravan Park**
CAUSEWAY HEAD, SILLOTH-ON-SOLWAY, CUMBRIA CA5 4PE

Friendly, quiet tree-sheltered site just a mile inland from beautiful coastline and this charming harbour town. Friendly pub/club with adjacent children's games room. Large clean modern holiday homes for hire, electric hook-ups available

"The ideal holiday for you and your pet" Write or phone for colour brochure TEL: 016973 31253

See also Colour Advertisement on page 11

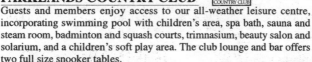

CUMBRIAN COTTAGES. 280 Luxury cottages and apartments throughout the Lake District and Cumbria. Many properties make pets welcome. All ETB inspected. For FREE Brochure and telephone bookings – 01228 599950 (24hrs). [Pets £15 per week]
Website: www.cumbrian-cottages.co.uk

DALES HOLIDAY COTTAGES offer a choice of over 400 superb, self catering, holiday properties in beautiful rural and coastal locations from Bronte, Herriot and Heartbeat country to Yorkshire's Coastline. Cosy cottages to country houses, many open all year. For FREE Brochure contact Dales Holiday Cottages, Carleton Business Park, Skipton BD23 2DG (01756 799821/790919).
E–mail: enq@dalesholcot.com

WELCOME COTTAGE HOLIDAYS. Quality Cottages in wonderful locations at welcoming low prices. Pets, linen and fuel mostly included. PHONE FOR FREE 2000 FULL COLOUR BROCHURE 01756 702208.
Website: www.recommended-cottages.co.uk

Allonby

Small coastal resort with sand and shingle beach, 5 miles from Maryport across Allonby Bay.

EAST HOUSE GUEST HOUSE, ALLONBY, MARYPORT CA15 6PQ (01900 881264 or 881276). Overlooking Solway Firth, two minutes sea. Central Lakes. Riding, tennis, golf near. Bed & Breakfast from £12 nightly, en suite Bed and Breakfast £15 nightly; EM, Bed and Breakfast £15 nightly, £95 weekly; en suite EM, Bed and Breakfast £18 nightly, £110 weekly. [🐕]

Alston

Small market town 16 miles north-east of Penrith.

MRS CLARE LE MARIE, BROWNSIDE HOUSE, LEADGATE, ALSTON CA9 3EL (01434 382169 / 382100). A warm welcome awaits you in the unspoilt North Pennines. Country situation, superb views, large fenced garden for "walkies". Sitting room with log fire and TV.

LOWBYER MANOR COUNTRY HOUSE HOTEL, ALSTON CA9 3JX (01434 381230). Former Jacobite manor house provides friendly, comfortable accommodation, all en suite. A la carte menu with vegetarian choices. Special autumn/winter/spring breaks.

Ambleside

Popular centre for exploring Lake District at northern end of Lake Windermere. Picturesque Stock Ghyll waterfall nearby, lovely walks. Associations with Wordsworth. Penrith 30 miles, Keswick 17, Windermere 5.

BRANTFELL HOUSE, ROTHAY ROAD, AMBLESIDE LA22 0EE (015394 32239). Chris and Jane welcome you with your well-behaved owners. Great "walkies" and breakfasts. Free sausage per dog each day. En suite rooms, parking; non-smoking. Leisure Club Membership for your owner! Telephone for information. 2 Crowns Commended.

GREENHOWE CARAVAN PARK, GREAT LANGDALE, AMBLESIDE LA22 9JU (015394 37231; Fax: 015394 37464; Freephone: 0800 0688837). Permanent Caravan Park with Self Contained Holiday Accommodation. An ideal centre for Climbing, Fell Walking, Riding, Swimming, Water Skiing or just a lazy holiday. Winners of the Rose Award 1983-2000. Grading "Very Good". [Pets £3 per night, £15 per week]

IVY HOUSE, HAWKSHEAD, NEAR AMBLESIDE LA22 0HS (FREEPHONE 0800 0563533). ETC ◆◆◆◆. Family-run listed Georgian hotel. 11 en suite bedrooms with colour TV and equipped with hot drinks trays. No charge for dogs. Children most welcome. Write or telephone David or Jane Vaughan for brochure. [🐾]
Website: www.ivyhousehotel.com

KIRKSTONE FOOT HOTEL, KIRKSTONE PASS ROAD, AMBLESIDE LA22 9EH (015394 32232; Fax: 015394 32805). Country house hotel with luxury self-catering Cottages and Apartments sleeping 2/7. Set in peaceful and secluded grounds. Adjoining lovely Lakeland fells, great for walking. Special winter breaks. [pw! Pets £2.70 per night.]

NEAR AMBLESIDE, CENTRAL LAKE DISTRICT (Tel & Fax: 01539 729799 (first), or 01539 431176 (second)). Set in one-and-a-half acres of mature garden with superb views of the mountains. Open fire in the lounge. Solid fuel range in the kitchen. In the heart of the country but near a busy attractive centre with shops, pubs and restaurants. [Pets £5 per week]

NEW DUNGEON GHYLL HOTEL, GREAT LANGDALE, AMBLESIDE LA22 9JY (015394 37213; Fax: 015394 37666). Situated at head of famed Langdale Valley. Breathtaking views and friendly, relaxed atmosphere. All bedrooms en suite, colour TV and tea/coffee making facilities. Johansens. 3 Crowns Highly Commended [🐾]

SKELWITH BRIDGE HOTEL NEAR AMBLESIDE, CUMBRIA LA22 9NJ (015394 32115 Fax: 015394 34254) Traditional seventeenth century Lakeland Inn. Well appointed en suite bedrooms with colour TV, radio, tea and coffee facilities, direct-dial telephone and hairdryer. Two private lounges, sun terrace and gardens. Children welcome. AA/ RAC ★★★.[Pets £3 per night, £21 per week]
E–mail: Skelwithbr@aol.com

SMALLWOOD HOUSE HOTEL COMPSTON ROAD, AMBLESIDE LA22 9DJ (015394 32330) 3 Crowns Commended. Dogs recommend us, they love the walks from here. Their owners love the rooms and the informality and enjoy their dinners. Car park. Residential licence. [🐾]
E–mail: enq@smallwoodhotel.co.uk
Website: www.smallwoodhotel.co.uk

GABLES HOTEL, AMBLESIDE (015394 332272). Friendly atmosphere; pretty, en suite rooms. Car parking. Special breaks available.

THE OLD VICARAGE, VICARAGE ROAD, AMBLESIDE LA22 9DH (015394 33364). "Rest awhile in style." Tranquil wooded grounds in heart of village. Car Park. All rooms en suite. Kettle, clock/radio, TV, hairdryer. Special breaks available. Friendly service where your pets are welcome. Phone Ian or Helen Burt.

WANSLEA GUEST HOUSE, LAKE ROAD, AMBLESIDE LA22 0DB (015394 33884). ETC ◆◆◆◆. Spacious family-run guest house with walks beginning at the door. Comfortable rooms, mostly en suite. Licensed lounge. B&B from £17.50; Evening Meal available to party bookings. Non-Smoking. Pets welcome by arrangement. [Pets £1 per night.]
E–mail: wanslea.guesthouse@virgin.net

Appleby

Pleasant touring centre on River Eden, between Pennines and Lake District. Castle and Moot Hall of historic interest. Trout fishing, swimming pool, tennis, bowls. Kendal 24 miles, Penrith 13.

APPLEBY MANOR COUNTRY HOUSE HOTEL, ROMAN ROAD, APPLEBY-IN-WESTMORLAND CA16 6JB (017683 51571; Fax: 017683 52888). Enjoy the comfort of Cumbria's award-winning Country House Hotel with superb meals, relaxing lounges, indoor leisure club and breathtaking scenery all around. Phone for a full colour brochure and interactive CD-ROM. [🐾 pw!]

THE GATE HOTEL, BONGATE, APPLEBY CA16 6LH (017683 52688). Family-run business, close to town centre shops, castle and swimming pool. Traditional log fire. Warm and friendly service all year round. En suite rooms. Enclosed garden and play area. Pets welcome by arrangement. Specialising in Thai food we also offer conventional English food. Licensed.

SYMBOLS	
🐾	Indicates that pets are welcome free of charge.
£	Indicates that a charge is made for pets: nightly or weekly.
pw!	Shows some special provision for pets; exercise facility, feeding or accommodation arrangement.
⌂	Indicates separate pets accommodation.

Bassenthwaite

Village on Bassenthwaite Lake with traces of Norse and Roman settlements.

SKIDDAW VIEW HOLIDAY PARK, BOTHEL, NEAR BASSENTHWAITE CA5 2JG (016973 20919). Quality self-catering cottages and holiday caravans. Pets come free. Northern Lake District, near market towns of Cockermouth and Keswick. Full weeks from £89 to £325, Short Breaks £99, prices include fuel (no meters). Brochure on request.

Borrowdale

Scenic valley of River Derwent, splendid walking and climbing country.

MARY MOUNT HOTEL, BORROWDALE, NEAR KESWICK CA12 5UU (017687 77223). Set in 4½ acres of gardens and woodlands on the shores of Derwentwater. 2½ miles from Keswick in picturesque Borrowdale. Superb walking and touring. All rooms en suite with colour TV and tea/coffee making facilities. Licensed. Brochure on request. 3 Crowns Commended. [🐕]

STAKIS LODORE SWISS HOTEL, BORROWDALE, NEAR KESWICK CA12 5UX (017687 77285; Fax: 017687 77343). Luxury Hotel with fabulous views overlooking Derwentwater and fells. Facilities include 75 bedrooms, restaurant and lounge, bar and leisure club. 4 Crowns Highly Commended. [Pets £2 per night.]

Buttermere

Between lake of same name and Crummock Water. Magnificent scenery. Of special note is Sour Milk Ghyll waterfall and steep and impressive Honister Pass. Keswick 15 miles, Cockermouth 10.

BRIDGE HOTEL, BUTTERMERE CA13 9UZ (017687 70252; Fax: 017687 70215). 22 bedrooms, all with private bathrooms; four-posters available. Daily freshly prepared menus, large selection wines; real ales. Superb walking and fishing. Dogs welcome. Self catering apartments available. [Pets £4 per night]

Carlisle

Important Border city and former Roman station on River Eden. Castle is of historic interest, also Tullie House Museum and Art Gallery. Good sports facilities inc. football and racecourse. Kendal 45 miles, Dumfries 33, Penrith 18.

DALSTON HALL CARAVAN PARK, DALSTON HALL, DALSTON, NEAR CARLISLE CA5 7JX (01228 710165). ✓✓✓ Exit 42 off M6, follow signs for Dalston. Small family-run park set in peaceful surroundings. Electric hook-ups, shops, playground, launderette, fly-fishing, nine-hole golf course. [pw!🐕]

GRAHAM ARMS HOTEL, ENGLISH STREET, LONGTOWN, CARLISLE CA6 5SE (01228 791213; Fax: 01228 792830). 14 bedrooms, most en suite, including four-poster and family rooms, all with tea/coffee facilities, TV and radio. Secure courtyard locked overnight. Pets welcome with well-behaved owners. RAC ★★. [🐕]
Website: www.cumbria.com/hotel

In an undiscovered corner of Cumbria two lovely cottages with 320 tranquil acres of flora and fauna to explore (maps provided). Use of swimming pool from May to September. Central for Hadrian's Wall and Gretna Green. ♥♥♥♥ Highly Commended. Apply: MRS J. JAMES, MIDTODHILLS FARM, ROADHEAD, CARLISLE CA6 6PF (016977 48213). [Pets £10.00 per week.]

NEWPALLYARDS, HETHERSGILL, CARLISLE CA6 6HZ (01228 577308). ♥♥♥♥ Highly Commended/3 Crowns Highly Commended. Relax and see beautiful North Cumbria and the Borders. Self-catering accommodation in one Bungalow, 3/4 bedrooms; two lovely Cottages on farm. Also Bed and Breakfast or Half Board – en suite rooms. [🐾]
E–mail: info@newpallyards.freeserve.co.uk
Website: www.newpallyards.freeserve.co.uk

Cockermouth

Market town and popular touring centre for Lake District and quiet Cumbrian coast. On Rivers Derwent and Cocker. Penrith 30 miles, Carlisle 26, Whitehaven 14, Keswick 12.

MRS B. WOODWARD, TODDELL FARM, BRANDLINGILL, COCKERMOUTH CA13 0RB (01900 828423). Unique family suite in barn conversion in 17th century farmhouse set in seven acres, en suite with own entrance. Also at www.lake-district.com [Pets £2 per night]

Coniston

Village 6 miles south-west of Ambleside, dominated by Old Man of Coniston (2635ft).

THE COPPERMINES AND CONISTON COTTAGES. Unique Lakeland cottages for 2 – 27 of quality and character in stunning mountain scenery. Log fires, exposed beams. Up to ♥♥♥♥ Highly Commended. Pets welcome! (Tel: 015394 41765 (24hrs); Mobile: 07721 584488) [Pets £20 per week]
Website: www.coppermines.co.uk

MRS ANNE HALL, DOW CRAG HOUSE, CONISTON LA21 8AT (015394 41558). Two chalet bungalows to let, sleeping two/six. Quiet location. Superb views across lake. Surrounded by gardens, farm fields. Well equipped. Owner maintained. [🐾]

LAKELAND HOUSE, TILBERTHWAITE AVENUE, CONISTON LA21 8ED (015394 41303). Family-run, in village centre; friendly atmosphere. Excellent walking. Hearty English, vegetarian or Continental breakfasts. Groups welcome. B&B from £16pp. One Crown Approved. [Pets £5 per stay]

 FHG FHG PUBLICATIONS
publish a large range of well-known accommodation guides. We will be happy to send you details or you can use the order form at the back of this book.

Elterwater

Village of green slate houses overlooked by stunning peaks of the Langdale Pikes.

THE BRITANNIA INN, ELTERWATER, AMBLESIDE LA22 9HP (015394 37210; FAX: 015394 37311) The very picture of a traditional inn, the Britania overlooks the green in the delightful village of Elterwater in the heart of the Lake District. Home cooked bar meals are served in cosy bars with oak beams and log fires. 3 Crowns Commended.

Eskdale

Lakeless valley, noted for waterfalls and ascended by a light-gauge railway. Tremendous views, Roman fort. Keswick 35 miles, Broughton-in-Furness 10 miles.

THE BURNMOOR INN, BOOT, ESKDALE, CUMBRIA. CA19 1TG (019467 23224 Fax: 019467-23337). Dogs welcome to lie by the fire in the bar. We do not make a charge for well behaved dogs. Also available two-bed cottage. Call for a brochure. [🐕]

MRS J. P . HALL, FISHERGROUND FARM, ESKDALE CA19 1TF (01946 723319). Self-catering to suit everyone. Scandinavian Pine Lodges and Cottages – on a delightful traditional farm. Adventure playground. Sports Hall and games room. Pets' and children's paradise. Brochures available. ETC ♛♛♛ Commended. [🐕]

Grange-Over-Sands

Quiet resort at the north of Morecambe Bay, convenient centre for Lake District. Fine gardens; golf, boating, fishing, tennis and bowls. Lancaster 25 miles, Windermere 16.

HAMPSFELL HOUSE HOTEL, HAMPSFELL ROAD, GRANGE-OVER-SANDS LA11 6BG (015395 32567). 3 Crowns Commended, AA★★. Peaceful country house hotel is set in two acres of mature woodland. The fell is ideal for walking dogs. All rooms en suite with colour TV and tea/coffee making facilities. Excellent food and wines. Ample safe parking. [🐕]

MR BILL LAMBERT, PROSPECT HOUSE, KENTS BANK ROAD, GRANGE-OVER-SANDS LA11 7DJ (015395 32116). A warm welcome awaits you at Prospect House. En suite rooms with TV, radio and tea/coffee making facilities. Residents' bar. Excellent food using fresh produce. B&B from £23.50; dinner £11.50. Our best advert is the many return visits we receive. [🐕]

THE OLD VICARAGE, WITHERSLACK, NEAR GRANGE-OVER-SANDS LA11 6RS (Tel: 015395 52381; Fax: 015395 52373) Beautiful late Georgian vicarage set in five acres of informal gardens and woodland, home to deer, red squirrels and an extraordinary variety of birds. The Old Vicarage is truly a place to unwind and forget for a while the stress of day to day life. [Pets £3 per night] E–mail: hotel@old-vic.demon.co.uk

Grasmere

Village famous for Wordsworth associations; the poet lived in Dove Cottage (preserved as it was), and is buried in the churchyard. Museum has manuscripts and relics.

ASH COTTAGE, RED LION SQUARE, GRASMERE LA22 9SP (015394 35224). Centrally located guest house with comfortable en suite bedrooms. Licensed. residents' lounge. Quality British Cuisine served in an informal atmosphere with guests returning year after year. Pleasant award winning garden. Private car parking. [Pets £1 per night]

GRASMERE HOTEL, GRASMERE, NEAR AMBLESIDE LA22 9TA (015394 35277). 12-bedroomed licensed Hotel set in the centre of the Lakes. Ideal for walking or sightseeing. All rooms have en suite facilities, TV etc. Gourmet food and interesting wines. [🐾]

Greystoke

Pretty village 6 miles from Penrith, 11 from Keswick. Famous for it's fine old church, racehorses and heated outdoor swimming pool.

SMITHY COTTAGE, JOHNBY, NEAR GREYSTOKE, CUMBRIA CA11 0UU (017684 83564). Pretty cottage, warm, cosy and very well-equipped One double, one twin and cot. Small garden with furniture. Open all year. Short Breaks available November – March. Dogs Welcome. [1st dog free, Extra dogs £2 per night each]

Hawkshead

Quaint village in Lake District between Coniston Water and Windermere. The 16th century Church and Grammar School, which Wordsworth attended, are of interest. Ambleside 5 miles

BETTY FOLD GUEST HOUSE, HAWKSHEAD HILL, AMBLESIDE LA22 0PS (015394 36611). Self-catering Flat and Cottage. Set in peaceful and spacious grounds. Ideal for the walker and dog. Open all year. 🏠🏠🏠 Commended and Approved respectively. [Pets £2 per night.]

Ireby

Quiet Cumbrian village between the fells and the sea. Good centre for the northern Lake District. Cockermouth 11 miles, Bassenthwaite 6.

WOODLANDS COUNTRY HOUSE AND COTTAGE, IREBY CA5 1EX (016973 71791). In private wooded grounds four miles from Bassenthwaite, ideal for Lakes and Borders. All bedrooms en suite with tea making facilities. Residential licence. B&B from £28.00. ETC ◆◆◆◆. [Pets £2 per night, £10 per week.]
E–mail:hj@woodlnd.u-net.com
Website: www.woodlnd.u-net.com

Kendal

Market town and popular centre for touring the Lake District. Of historic interest is the Norman castle, birthplace of Catherine Parr. Penrith 25 miles, Lancaster 22, Ambleside 13.

MRS HELEN JONES, PRIMROSE COTTAGE, ORTON ROAD, TEBAY CA10 3TL (015396 24791). Excellent rural location for North Lakes and Yorkshire Dales. Superb facilities include jacuzzi bath and four-poster bed. Pets welcome, very friendly. One acre garden. Self-contained ground floor flat available. ETC ◆◆◆◆. [🐾]

ANNE TAYLOR, RUSSELL FARM, BURTON-IN-KENDAL, CARNFORTH, LANCS. LA6 1NN (01524 781334). Bed, Breakfast & Evening Meal offered. Ideal centre for touring Lakes and Yorkshire Dales. Good food, friendly atmosphere on working dairy farm. Modernised farmhouse. Guests' own lounge. [🐾]

Keswick

Famous Lake District resort at north end of Derwentwater with Pencil Museum and Cars of the Stars Motor Museum. Carlisle 30 miles, Ambleside 17, Cockermouth 12.

CHAUCER HOUSE HOTEL, DERWENTWATER PLACE, KESWICK CA12 4DR (Tel: 017687 72318/73223; Fax: 017687 75551). A Victorian Town House Hotel, quietly situated with efficient friendly service and an excellent reputation for cuisine. Ideal for a relaxing short break or a longer holiday with your pet. Self-catering also available. [Pets £5 per night]
E–mail: enquiries@chaucer-house.demon.co.uk
Website: www.chaucer-house.co.uk

JIM & MARGARET CORRIGAN, CHERRY TREES GUEST HOUSE, 16 ESKIN STREET, KESWICK CA12 4DQ (017687 71048). All bedrooms have colour TV, direct dial telephones, clock/radio alarms and tea/coffee facilities. Our double, twin and family rooms are all en suite. Try the Leisure Pool in the town, Keswick's 18-hole golf course, bowls and tennis. ETC ◆◆◆. [🐾]

CRAGSIDE GUEST HOUSE, 39 Blencathra Street, Keswick CA12 4HX (017687 73344). AA ◆◆◆. Quiet, comfortable guest house close to the centre of Keswick. All rooms tastefully decorated, centrally heated and have clock radio, colour TV and tea/coffee making facilities. En suite available. [🐾]

LUXURY LAKELAND HOLIDAY COTTAGES AND APARTMENTS. Tastefully appointed one or two bedroom self-catering apartments and cottages set amid tranquil surroundings on the fringe of a picturesque village. Full colour brochure on request. DERWENT MANOR, PORTINSCALE, KESWICK CA12 5RE (017687 72211).
E–mail: derwentwater.hotel @dial.pipex.com
Website: http://ds.dial.pipex.com/derwentwater.hotel/

CUMBRIA

HARNEY PEAK, PORTINSCALE, NEAR KESWICK. We offer you the best in S/C accommodation in our spacious, well equipped apartments in the quiet village of Portinscale. Glorious lake views. Ideal for couples or families. Apply: MR & MRS SMITH, THE LEATHES HEAD HOTEL, BORROWDALE, CUMBRIA CA12 5UY (017687 77247). [Pets £10 per week.]

MRS J.M. ALMOND, IRTON HOUSE FARM, ISEL, COCKERMOUTH, NEAR KESWICK CA13 9ST (017687 76380). Farm location with superb views over lake and mountains. Sleeps 2/6. Wheelchair accessible. Apartments for two designed with wheelchairs in mind and caravans for two/six (not accessible). [Pets £15 per week]

Warm, comfortable homes in Keswick and beautiful Borrowdale, welcoming your dog. inspected and quality graded. LAKELAND COTTAGE HOLIDAYS, KESWICK CA12 5ES (9017687 71071; Fax: 017687 75036).
E–mail: info@lakelandcottages.co.uk
Website: lakelandcottages.co.uk

DERWENTWATER MARINA, PORTINSCALE, KESWICK CA12 5RF – Lakeside Studio Apartments. Self catering apartments sleep 2 plus child with superb views over the lake and fells. Includes colour TV, heating and bed linen. Tel: 017687 72912 for brochure. [🐕]

LOW BRIERY RIVERSIDE HOLIDAY VILLAGE, KESWICK CA12 4RN (017687 72044). Cottages, flats, lodges and caravans; superb amenities and leisure facilities. On eastern outskirts of Keswick. [Pets £10 per week]
Website: www.keswick.uk.com

THE MIDDLE RUDDINGS HOTEL, BRAITHWAITE, KESWICK. CA12 5RY (017687 78436; Fax: 017687 78438). Set in wooded grounds overlooking Skiddaw, offering quality en suite accommodation and Table d'Hôte cuisine. Ideally placed for walking. Very well behaved dogs welcome. RAC ★★★. AA ★★. Four Crowns.

JOHN & JEAN MITCHELL, 35 MAIN STREET, KESWICK (Tel & Fax: 017687 72790; Home Tel No: 016973 20220). Luxurious Lakeland flats and cottages located in one of Keswick's most desirable areas. All gas central heating. Some with two bathrooms (one en suite). From £99 weekly. [🐕]

ORCHARD HOUSE, APPLETHWAITE, NEAR KESWICK. A perfect place for dogs and children, with a secure paddock, quiet lanes and hundreds of walks, yet with the delights of Keswick and Lake Derwentwater just over a mile away. Sleeps up to 12. Booking and Brochure telephone 01946 723319. [🐕]

OVERWATER HALL, OVERWATER, NEAR IREBY, KESWICK CA5 1HH (017687 76566). Elegant Country House Hotel in spacious grounds. Dogs very welcome in your room. Any 4 nights from £180 per person, inclusive of Dinner, Room and Breakfast. Mini breaks also available all year. Award winning restaurant. [🐕]

VAL BRADLEY, RICKERBY GRANGE, PORTINSCALE, KESWICK CA12 5RH (017687 72344). Delightfully situated in quiet village. Licensed. Imaginative home-cooked food, attractively served. Open all year. [Pets £2 per night, £10 per week]

A traditional 17th-century farmhouse, one acre grounds with lovely garden. Ideal for numerous walks. Good home cooking. Pets and children welcome. Open February to November. ETC ◆◆◆. ROY BUTCHER, THORNTHWAITE HALL, THORNTHWAITE, NEAR KESWICK CA12 5SA (017687 78424; Fax: 017687 78122). [🐕]
Website: www.swanhotel.org.uk

COLIN AND JOY HARRISON, SWAN HOTEL, THORNTHWAITE, KESWICK CA12 5SQ (017687 78256). Family run 17th century former coaching inn. Excellent restaurant and bar food. Summer Prices, B&B £27; DBB £40; 3 nights DBB £118. Winter breaks, Nov-Mar from £20 pppn. Pets welcome. [£1.75 per night]

ROYAL OAK HOTEL, ROSTHWAITE, KESWICK CA12 5XB (017687 77214). Traditional Lakeland hotel with friendly atmosphere. Home cooking, cosy bar, comfortable lounge and some riverside rooms. Winter and Summer discount rates. Brochure and Tariff available. ETC ★ Hotel. [🐕],
Website: www.SmoothHound.co.uk/hotels/royal02.html

THWAITE HOWE HOTEL, THORNTHWAITE, NEAR KESWICK CA12 5SA (Tel: 017687 78281; Fax: 017687 78529). Small friendly country house hotel specialising in delicious home cooking and fine wines. Eight en suite bedrooms. Residents lounge and bar. Well behaved dogs welcome. Non-smoking rooms. ETC ★★. [Pets £3 per night.]

THRELKELD VILLAGE (KESWICK 4 MILES). Tourist Board ♛♛♛♛ Commended. Delightful Bungalows. Sleep 4/6. All amenities, fridge, electric cooker, central heating, colour TV, telephone. Laundry room. Own grounds with ample parking. £190 minimum to £450 maximum. Bargain breaks low season. Children and pets welcome. APPLY – MRS F. WALKER, THE PARK, RICKERBY, CARLISLE CA3 9AA (01228 524848). [pw! 🐕]

Kirkby Lonsdale

Small town on River Lune, 14 miles north-east of Lancaster. Of interest – the motte and bailey castle, mid 19th century Market House and the 16th century Abbots Hall.

MRS P. BAINBRIDGE, TOSSBECK FARM, MIDDLETON, KIRKBY LONSDALE, VIA CARNFORTH, LANCS LA6 2LZ (015242 76214). Tourist Board Listed. A warm welcome awaits you at Tossbeck, a 17h century listed farmhouse, situated in the unspoilt Lune Valley. One en suite and one with private facilities, both with televisions and drink making facilities. Bed and Breakfast from £16.50. No–smoking. [🐕]

NOTE

All the information in this book is given in good faith in the belief that it is correct. However, the publishers cannot guarantee the facts given in these pages, neither are they responsible for changes in policy, ownership or terms that may take place after the date of going to press. Readers should always satisfy themselves that the facilities they require are available and that the terms, if quoted, still apply.

Kirkby in Furness

Small coastal village (A595). 10 minutes to Ulverston, Lakes within easy reach. Ideal base for walking and touring.

MRS C. DOWLE, 1 FRIARS GROUND, KIRKBY-IN-FURNESS LA17 7YB (01229 889601). "Sunset Cottage." Self catering 17th century two-bedroom character cottage with garden. Panoramic views over sea/mountains; Coniston/ Windermere 20 minutes. Terms from £115. Open all year. [🐾]

Kirkby Stephen (near Mallerstang)

5 miles south on B6259 Kirkby Stephen to Hawes road.

COCKLAKE HOUSE, MALLERSTANG CA17 4JT (017683 72080). Charming, High Pennine Country House B&B in unique position above Pendragon Castle in Upper Mallerstang Dale offering good food and exceptional comfort to a small number of guests. Two double rooms with large private bathrooms. Three acres riverside grounds. Dogs welcome.

MRS S. CANNON, COLDBECK COTTAGE, RAVENSTONEDALE, KIRKBY STEPHEN, CUMBRIA CA17 4LW (Tel & Fax: 015396 23230). Accessible Grade 2. Accommodation for six, plus cot. Centrally heated. Ground floor bedroom suitable for wheelchair users. Two-acre garden. The country pub opposite provides inexpensive meals. [🐾]
E–mail: david.cannon@coldbeck.demon.co.uk

Kirkoswald

Village in the Cumbrian hills, lying north west of the Lake District. Ideal for touring. Penrith 7 miles.

SECLUDED COTTAGES WITH PRIVATE FISHING, KIRKOSWALD CA10 1EU (24 hr brochure line 01768 898711 manned most Saturdays). Escape to quality cottages, clean, well equipped and well maintained. Centrally located for Lakes, Pennines, Hadrian's Wall, Borderland. Enjoy the Good Life in comfort. Pets' paradise. Bookings/enquiries 01768 896275. [pw! £2 per pet per night].

Little Langdale

Hamlet 2 miles west of Skelwith Bridge. To west is Little Langdale Tarn, a small lake.

HIGHFOLD COTTAGE, LITTLE LANGDALE. A cosy, comfortable cottage, ideally situated for walking and touring. Superb mountain views. Sleeps 5. ♔♔♔ Commended. Personally maintained. Pets welcome. Weekly £180 - £310. MRS C.E. BLAIR, 8 THE GLEBE, CHAPEL STILE, AMBLESIDE LA22 9JT (015394 37686). [🐾]

Lorton

Village 4 miles south east of Cockermouth.

NEW HOUSE FARM, LORTON, COCKERMOUTH CA13 9UU (Tel & Fax: 01900 85404). New House Farm has 15 acres of fields, woods, streams and ponds which guests and dogs can wander around. Comfortable en suite accommodation and fine traditional food. Off season breaks. AA ◆◆◆◆◆. [🛏]

Loweswater

Hamlet at end of Lake Loweswater (owned by National Trust). Beautiful hilly scenery.

LOWESWATER HOLIDAY COTTAGES, LOWESWATER, COCKERMOUTH CA13 9UX (01900 85232). Nestling among the magnificent Loweswater/Buttermere fells, our luxury cottages are available all year. They have open fires, colour TV, central heating, a four poster and gardens. Colour Brochure. [Pets £15 per week]

Lowick

Delightful small village in Lake District National Park, 3 miles from Coniston Water and ideal for exploring the Southern and Western Lakes.

MRS JENNY WICKENS, GARTH ROW, LOWICK GREEN, ULVERSTON LA12 8EB (01229 885633). Traditional cottage standing alone amidst farmland and common. Quality accommodation, good food, excellent walking, no smoking. Ideal for children and pets. B&B from £16.00. Brochure. [🛏]

Mungrisdale

Small village ideal for touring. Keswick 8 miles.

NEAR HOWE FARM HOTEL AND COTTAGES, MUNGRISDALE, PENRITH CA11 0SH (Tel or Fax: 017687 79678). Quiet, away from it all. Within easy reach of Lakes walking. Good food. Bar, log fire in cold weather. 5 Bedrooms en suite. B&B from £18, En suite £22. [Pets – Hotel £1 per day, in Cottages £10 per week.]

THE MILL INN, MUNGRISDALE, NEAR PENRITH CA11 0XR (Tel and Fax: 017687 79632). Historic 16th century coaching inn set in peaceful village, on the doorstep of some of the best walking in the Lake District. Quality en suite accommodation. Families and pets welcome. ETC ◆◆◆. [Pets £2.50 per night].

SYMBOLS
🛏   Indicates that pets are welcome free of charge.
£   Indicates that a charge is made for pets: nightly or weekly.
pw!   Shows some special provision for pets; exercise facility, feeding or accommodation arrangement.
▢   Indicates separate pets accommodation.

Near Sawrey

This beautiful village on the west side of Windermere has many old cottages set among trees and beautiful gardens with flowers. The world-famous writer Beatrix Potter lived at Hill Top Farm. A ferry travels across the lake to Hawkshead (2 miles), Far Sawrey ½ mile.

SAWREY HOUSE COUNTRY HOTEL, NEAR SAWREY, HAWKSHEAD LA22 0LF (015394 36387; Fax: 015394 36010). Elegant family-run hotel in three acres of peaceful gardens with magnificent views across Esthwaite Water. Excellent food, warm friendly atmosphere. Lounge, separate bar. Children and pets welcome. ETC/RAC/AA ◆◆◆◆◆. [Pets £3 per night.]
Website: www.sawrey-house.com

Newby Bridge

Village at southern end of Lake Windermere, 8 miles from Ulverston.

NEWBY BRIDGE HOTEL, NEAR ULVERSTON LA12 8NA (015395 31222). Overlooking Lake Windermere. 3 night breaks from £99 per person Dinner, Bed and Breakfast. All rooms en suite with two movie channels. Bar and restaurant. [🐾]

Penrith

Market town and centre for touring Lake District. Of interest are 14th century castle, Gloucester Arms (1477) and Tudor House. Excellent sporting facilities. Windermere 27 miles, Keswick 18.

MRS MARY TEASDALE, LISCO FARM, TROUTBECK, PENRITH CA11 0SY (017687 79645). Comfortable accommodation offered in one double and two en suite family rooms, all with tea/coffee making facilities and washbasins. Outside accommodation available for dogs if required. A good base for touring Lakeland.

MRS MARION BARRITT, LOW GARTH GUEST HOUSE, PENRUDDOCK, PENRITH CA11 0QU (017684 83492). Tastefully converted 18th century barn in peaceful surroundings with magnificent views, offering a warm welcome and Aga-cooked meals. En suite facilities. [🐾]

SECLUDED COTTAGES WITH PRIVATE FISHING, KIRKOSWALD CA10 1EU (24 hr brochure line 01768 898711, manned most Saturdays). Escape to quality cottages, clean, well equipped and well maintained. Centrally located for Lakes, Pennines, Hadrian's Wall, Borderland. Enjoy the Good Life in comfort. Pets' paradise. Bookings/enquiries 01768 896275. [pw! £2 per pet per night].

WESTMORLAND HOTEL, ORTON, PENRITH CA10 3SB (015396 24351; Fax: 015396 24354). Situated in the Lune Gorge with panoramic views of the Cumbrian Fells. 53 spacious en suite bedrooms. Impressive restaurant menu. First class service. AA ★★★ & Rosette, RAC ★★★, Four Crowns Highly Commended. Pets welcome.

Silloth

Solway Firth resort with harbour and fine sandy beach. Mountain views. Golf, fishing. Penrith 33 miles, Carlisle 23, Cockermouth 17.

MR AND MRS G.E. BOWMAN, TANGLEWOOD CARAVAN PARK, CAUSEWAY HEAD, SILLOTH CA5 4PE (016973 31253). Friendly country site, excellent toilet and laundry facilities. Tourers welcome or hire a luxury caravan. Telephone or send stamp for colour brochure. [🐴]

Thurstonfield

Village west of Carlisle. Ideal for visits to the Lake District and Southern Scotland

THE TRANQUIL OTTER, LAKESHORE LODGES AND FLY FISHING, THUR-STONEFIELD CA5 6HB (01228 576661; Fax: 01228 576662). Peaceful, quiet and off-the-beaten-track beauty spot in North Cumbria. Six comfortable lakeside lodges, each with verandah and own boat. Set in 50 acres of private nature reserve. [Pets £20 per booking]

Troutbeck

Village north of Lake Windermere. Church has east window by Burne-Jones.

HOLBECK GHYLL LODGE, TROUTBECK. Lakeland stone lodge. Two twin bedded bedrooms. Dining/living room with open fire and sofa bed. Secure covered way for bikes. Parking for three cars. Available Easter to end of October. Saturday change over. ETC ♙♙♙♙ Highly Commended. MRS KAYE, HOLMDENE, STONEY BANK ROAD, HOLMFIRTH HD7 2SL (Tel: 01484 684605; Fax: 01484 689051). [🐴]

ROSE COTTAGE AND ROSE BARN, MRS ANNE KELLY, 1 ROBIN LANE, TROUT-BECK, WINDERMERE LA23 1PF (015394 32780). 18th century cottage and barn with gardens and beautiful views over the Troutbeck Valley with lovely walks from the door. Warm and cosy. Two good food pubs nearby. ETC ♙♙♙♙ Commended.
E–mail: skelly@hotmail.com

Ullswater

Lake stretching for seven miles with attractive Lakeside walks.

MR & MRS BURNETT, (FELL VIEW HOLIDAYS), FELL VIEW, GLENRIDDING, PENRITH CA11 0PJ (Tel & Fax: 017684 82342; Evenings 01768 867420) Comfortable, well-equipped cottage/apartments, sleep 2-6, in quiet, beautiful surroundings, all with lovely views. Use of gardens/grounds. Ideal walking base. Up to ♙♙♙ Highly Commended. [pw! 🐴]

GOOSEMIRE COTTAGES, NORTH LODGE, LONGTAIL HILL, BOWNESS LA23 3JD (015394 47477). 20 Lakeland cottages & barn conversions sleeping 2 /8, with gardens. Set on, or very near to Lake Ullswater or Haweswater, also in the peaceful Eden Valley. Walks from doorstep. Pets at no extra charge. [🐾]
Website: www.goosemirecottages.co.uk,
E–mail: goosemirecottages@virgin.net

Windermere

Famous resort on lake of same name, the largest in England. Magnificent scenery. Car ferry from Bowness, one mile distant. Kendal 9 miles.

APPLEGARTH HOTEL, COLLEGE ROAD, WINDERMERE LA23 1BU (015394 43206; Fax: 015394 46636). An elegant Victorian mansion house with lovely gardens. Individually designed bedrooms and four-poster rooms. All rooms with private facilities, most with Lake and Fell views. Lounge bar and car park. Ideally situated for shops, restaurants, walking and touring. Warm welcome with excellent food. 3 Crowns. Dogs Welcome. [🐾]

BURNSIDE HOTEL, KENDAL ROAD, BOWNESS ON WINDERMERE LA23 3EP (015394 42211). The Lake District's Complete Resort, set in mature gardens overlooking Lake Windermere. Pets welcome. Choose either luxurious hotel or one of our self-catering cottages and relax in our on-site leisure club. FREEPHONE 0800 220688 for bookings. [Pets £11.75 per week (cottages only)]
E–mail: stay@burnsidehotel.com
Website: www.burnsidehotel.com

DENE CREST GUEST HOUSE, WOODLAND ROAD, WINDERMERE LA23 2AE (015394 44979). Comfortable, tastefully furnished Guesthouse. All rooms en suite, colour TV, central heating, tea/coffee making. Open all year. Short Break terms available. Pets Welcome. [pw!, Pets £3 per stay]

GREENRIGGS GUEST HOUSE, 8 UPPER OAK STREET, WINDERMERE LA23 2LB (Tel & Fax: 015394 42265). ETC ◆◆◆ Small, family-run guest house situated in a quiet cul-de- sac close to a park, with easy access to shops, lake and all transport. B&B from £15.00. [🐾]

Key to Tourist Board Ratings

👑   **The Crown Scheme**
The **English Tourism Council** (formerly the English Tourist Board) has joined with the **AA** and **RAC** to create a new, easily understood quality rating for serviced accommodation.
Hotels will receive a grading ranging from **one to five STARS** (★). Other serviced accommodation such as **guest houses** and **B&B establishments** will be graded from **one to five DIAMONDS** (◆). These ratings represent Quality, Service and Hospitality not just facilities.
NB. Some properties had not been assessed at the time of going to press and in these cases the publishers have included the old CROWN gradings.

♀   **The Key Scheme**
The Key Scheme covering self-catering in cottages, bungalows, flats, houseboats, houses, chalets, etc remains unchanged. The classification from **One to Five KEYS** indicates the range of facilities and equipment. Higher quality standards are indicated by the terms APPROVED, COMMENDED, HIGHLY COMMENDED AND DE LUXE.

HILLTHWAITE HOUSE HOTEL, THORNBARROW ROAD, WINDERMERE LA23 2DF (015394 43636; Fax: 015394 88660). Set in 3 acres of secluded gardens. All bedrooms en suite with satellite TV; some with personal jacuzzi. Superb leisure facilities including indoor pool. Pets welcome. [🐾]

HOLBECK GYHLL HOTEL & SPA, HOLBECK LANE, WINDERMERE LA23 1LU (between Windermere and Ambleside). 19th century Hunting Lodge in 7 acres with breathtaking Lake views. Luxury accommodation and finest quality food combined with a warmth of hospitality for a relaxing stay. Rooms opening on to lawns and grounds. Tennis and Spa facilities. Direct access to mountains and fields for walking. Cumbria Tourist Board Hotel of the Year 1998, AA 3 Rosettes and 3 Red Stars, RAC ★★★ and Blue Ribbon. Tel: 015394 32375 for colour brochure. [Pets £3 per night]

KIRKWOOD, PRINCE'S ROAD, WINDERMERE LA23 2DD (015394 43907). A warm friendly atmosphere with individual personal service. En suite rooms with colour TV and tea/coffee making. Hosts pleased to help plan tours and walks. Two Crowns Highly Commended, RAC Highly Acclaimed, AA QQQQ. [🐾]
E-mail: neil.cox@kirkwood51.freeserve.co.uk
Website: www.kirkwood51.freeserve.co.uk

Many attractive self-catering holiday homes in a variety of good locations, all well equipped and managed by our caring staff. Pets welcome. For brochure, contact: LAKELOVERS, THE NEW TOFFEE LOFT, KENDAL ROAD, WINDER-MERE LA23 3RA (015394 88855; Fax: 015394 88857). [Pets £15.00 per week.]
E-mail: carol@lakelovers.co.uk
Website: www.lakelovers.co.uk

LOW SPRINGWOOD HOTEL, THORNBARROW ROAD, WINDERMERE LA23 2DF (015394 46383). Twiggy (Boxer) and Millie (Boxer) would like to welcome you to their peaceful Hotel in its own secluded gardens. Lovely views of the Lakes and Fells. All rooms en suite with colour TV etc. Some four-posters. Brochure available. 3 Crowns. [pw! 🐾]

THE MORTAL MAN HOTEL, TROUTBECK WINDERMERE LA23 1PL (015394 33193; Fax: 015394 31261). Set in beautiful Troutbeck Valley, good food and wine, real ales and a pefect location for walkers of all abilities. B&B from £40 pppn.. Dogs go free. ETC ★★, Silver Award for Quality. [🐾]
E-mail: the-mortalman@btinternet.com

WYN AND IAN CAPPER, UPPER OAKMERE, 3 UPPER OAK STREET, WINDER-MERE LA23 2LB (015394 45649). Built in traditional Lakeland stone and situated close to park. Warm, clean and very friendly. Single people welcome. Pets preferred to people. B&B from £10 winter to £18 in summer; children half price. Dinner optional. [🐾]

YORKSHIRE HOUSE, 1 UPPER OAK STREET, WINDERMERE LA23 2LB (015394 44689). A warm welcome, clean, comfortable rooms and a hearty breakfast awaits you in our family run guest house. Quiet yet convenient location. All rooms have colour TV and complimentary hot drinks. Non-smoking. B&B from £15 to £24 per person. Pets stay free. [🐾]

DERBYSHIRE

DERBYSHIRE *Ashbourne*

NOTE

All the information in this book is given in good faith in the belief that it is correct. However, the publishers cannot guarantee the facts given in these pages, neither are they responsible for changes in policy, ownership or terms that may take place after the date of going to press. Readers should always satisfy themselves that the facilities they require are available and that the terms, if quoted, still apply.

PEAK COTTAGES (0114 262 0777). Quality self catering accommodation in the Derbyshire Dales and Peaks. Whether you are a walker, climber, potholer, antiquarian, historian, naturalist, gardener or sportsman – Derbyshire has it all. Pets Welcome. Telephone for colour brochure.

WELCOME COTTAGE HOLIDAYS. Quality Cottages in wonderful locations at welcoming low prices. Pets, linen and fuel mostly included. PHONE FOR FREE 2000 FULL COLOUR BROCHURE 01756 702215.

Ashbourne

Market town on River Henmore, close to its junction with River Dove. Several interesting old buildings. Birmingham 42 miles, Nottingham 29, Derby 13.

BERESFORD ARMS HOTEL, STATION ROAD, ASHBOURNE DE6 1AA (01335 300035; Fax: 01335 300065). Situated in the centre of Ashbourne and offering a warm welcome, especially to pets and children. It makes a perfect starting point to explore the area or visit Alton Towers. 3 Crowns. [🐕]
Website: www.beresford-arms.demon.co.uk

TONY AND LINDA STODDART, CORNPARK COTTAGE, UPPER MAYFIELD, NEAR ASHBOURNE DE6 2HR. (Tel/Fax: 01335 345041). Self-catering open plan barn conversion. All modern conveniences. Large gardens, surrounded by fields. Sleeps up to four (plus pets!). Close to all Staffs/Derbys Beauty spots. Open all year, prices £105-£230. Brochure on request.

DERBYSHIRE COTTAGES. In the grounds of a 17th century Inn, close to Peak District, Alton Towers and Ashbourne. Each has own patio, fully fitted kitchen, colour TV. Children and pets welcome. Phone MARY (01335 300202) for further details. [🐕]

MRS M.M. STELFOX, DOG AND PARTRIDGE, SWINSCOE, ASHBOURNE DE6 2HS (01335 343183). 17th century Inn offering ideal holiday accommodation. Many leisure activities available. All bedrooms with washbasins, colour TV, telephone and private facilities. [🐕]
Website: www.dogandpartridge.co.uk

MRS M.A. RICHARDSON, THROWLEY HALL FARM, ILAM, ASHBOURNE DE6 2BB (01538 308202/308243). Self-catering accommodation in farmhouse for up to 12 and cottage for seven people. Also Bed and Breakfast in farmhouse. Central heating, washbasins, tea/coffee facilities in rooms. Children and pets welcome. Near Alton Towers and stately homes. Tourist Board 2 Crowns, ᵒᵒᵒᵒ Commended.

SYMBOLS

🐕   Indicates that pets are welcome free of charge.

£   Indicates that a charge is made for pets: nightly or weekly.

pw!   Shows some special provision for pets; exercise facility, feeding or accommodation arrangement.

⌂   Indicates separate pets accommodation.

Biggin

Situated 8 miles north of Ashbourne

THE KINGS AT IVY HOUSE, BIGGIN BY HARTINGTON, NEWHAVEN, BUXTON, SK17 0DT (01298 84709) Georgian Grade II Listed Guest House with many original features. Spectacular views. All rooms en suite with baths. B&B from £29, Dinner £15. Open all year. Dogs Welcome. ETC ◆◆◆◆. [🐾]
E–mail: kings.ivyhouse@lineone.net

Buxton

Well-known spa and centre for the Peak District. Beautiful scenery and good sporting amenities. Leeds 50 miles, Matlock 20, Macclesfield 12.

MRS JURY, BARN HOUSE, LITTON MILL, BUXTON SK17 8SW (Tel & Fax: 01298 872751). Located in Peak District National Park. Self-contained ground floor flat within an 18th century converted barn in the peaceful hamlet of Litton Mill. Ideal for walkers. Sleeps four.

BUXTON VIEW, 74 CORBAR ROAD, BUXTON SK17 6RJ (01298 79222). Attractive house very near moors and 10 minutes from town centre. En suite rooms. Bed and Breakfast from £20pppn; Evening Meals available. Pets very welcome. ETC /AA ◆◆◆◆.

THE CHARLES COTTON HOTEL, HARTINGTON, NEAR BUXTON SK17 0AL (01298 84229; Fax: 01298 84301). Small hotel, AA & RAC star rated. Good home cooking and hospitality. In heart of Derbyshire Dales. Special diets catered for. Ideal for relaxing, walking, cycling, hang-gliding. [🐾]
Website: www.charlescotton.co.uk

NICK & FIONA CLOUGH, THE DEVONSHIRE ARMS, PEAK FOREST, NEAR BUXTON SK17 8EJ (01298 23875) Situated in a village location in the heart of the Peak District. All rooms en suite with tea/coffee and colour TV. Meals served every day. Excellent walking area. Three Crowns Commended. [🐾]

MRS LYNNE P. FEARNS, HEATH FARM, SMALLDALE, BUXTON SK17 8EB (01298 24431). Farm in Peak District, 4½ miles from Buxton. Quiet location. Many activities locally. Cot and babysitting available. Car essential. Bed and Breakfast from £15, reductions children and weekly stays.

PRIORY LEA HOLIDAY FLATS. Close to Poole's Cavern Country Park. Fully equipped. Sleep 2/6. Cleanliness assured. Terms £80 - £210. Open all year. Short Breaks available. 2-3 Keys up to Commended. MRS GILL TAYLOR, 50 WHITE KNOWLE ROAD, BUXTON SK17 9NH (01298 23737). [pw! Pets £1 per night.]

WHEELDON TREES FARM, EARL STERNDALE, BUXTON SK17 0AA (Tel and Fax: 01298 83219). Eighteenth century barn conversion offers seven cosy self-catering holiday cottages. Sleep 2-6. Laundry, payphone and games room. ♔♔♔♔ Commended. [🐾]

Matlock

Inland resort and spa in the Derwent Valley. Chesterfield 9 miles.

MRS G. PARKINSON, DIMPLE HOUSE, DIMPLE ROAD, MATLOCK DE4 3JX (01629 583228). 19th Century house close to Matlock. Large garden. Ideal for visiting Chatsworth and Peak Park. TV and teamaking in all rooms. EMTB Listed Commended. B&B from £18. [🐕]

TUCKERS GUEST HOUSE, 48 DALE ROAD, MATLOCK DE4 3NB (01629 583018). A welcoming, pet loving home where you can feel totally relaxed. Wonderful scenery and walks in the Peak District and Derbyshire Dales. Dogs love it! No charge for them (or their breakfast)! Non-smokers preferred. Open all year. B&B £18.50 to £23 pp.

Peak District National Park

A green and unspoilt area at the southern end of the Pennines, covering 555 square miles.

BIGGIN HALL, PEAK PARK (01298 84451). Close Dove Dale. 17th century hall sympathetically restored. baths en suite, log fires, C/H comfort, warmth and quiet. Fresh home cooking. beautiful uncrowded footpaths. Brochure on request

SHEFFIELD/HATHERSAGE. Well equipped converted barn, fenced garden, in open countryside, ideal for Peak Park and Sheffield. Sleeps 4. ETC 🏠🏠🏠🏠 Highly Commended. For brochure phone 0114 2301949.

DEVON

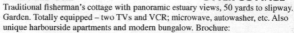

Readers are requested to mention this guidebook
when seeking accommodation
(and please enclose a stamped addressed envelope).

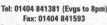

175

Watermill Cottages, Hansel, Dartmouth TQ6 0LN
Comfortable, well equipped, old stone cottages in peaceful riverside setting.
Wonderful walks in and around our idyllic valley near Slapton. 10 minutes
from sea. Sleep 3-8. Open all year. Children and Pets welcome.
Brochure: 01803 770219   Pam and Graham Spittle

PLEASE SEE OUR MAIN ADVERT IN THE COLOUR SECTION!

Welcome Family Holiday Park
DAWLISH WARREN SOUTH DEVON

First rate facilities and friendly personal service provide the perfect family holiday!

★ Stylish Dolphin Club, Entertainment Centre with Kaleidoscope Disco
★ Superb Indoor Heated Neptune Tropicana Water Leisure Complex - four feature packed Pools, Solarium and Spectator Viewing area.
★ Cruisers Adult Cocktail Bar with Big Screen TV

★ Childrens' Jolly Roger Club with Disco, Cinema and large Games Arcade
★ Short, level walk to safe sandy beach
★ Great value-for-money prices
★ Free electricity, linen, Colour TV
★ Welcome Movie Channel - great films for all the family

★ 3 Shops • Cafe • 2 Takeaways • Crazy Golf
★ Adventure Playground
★ Launderette
★ Hire service with Computer Games
★ Pets Welcome (at small charge)
★ Caravans, Villas, Apartments & Bungalows - Accommodation to suit all tastes and pockets.

 Enquiries / Reservations 01626 862070

See also Colour Advertisement on page 12

THE ROYAL OAK INN
Dunsford, Near Exeter EX6 7DA
Tel: 01647 252256
Tourist Board Approved. CAMRA, Good Pub Guide.
Please ring Mark or Judy Harrison for further details.

Enjoy a friendly welcome in our traditional Country Pub in the picturesque thatched village of Dunsford. Quiet en suite bedrooms are available in the tastefully converted cob barn. Ideal base for touring Dartmoor, Exeter and the coast, and the beautiful Teign Valley. Real Ale and home-made meals are served.
Well behaved children and dogs are welcome.
Bed & Breakfast from £20.

TEIGN VALLEY FOREST
HALDON LODGE FARM, KENNFORD
NEAR EXETER, DEVON EX6 7YG Tel: 01392 832312

Delightful modern 34ft Caravan only five miles from Exeter and short distance Dawlish, Teignmouth and Torbay, from £70 per week. Lounge (TV), two bedrooms, kitchen, bathroom (H&C) and toilet. *Attractive private grounds in peaceful surroundings. Famous village inns, two beautiful Coarse Fishing Lakes and farm shop.* Small private camping site. Pony trekking available. Special welcome to less experienced riders.

Pets Welcome ● Open all year ● Enquiries to D.L. Salter

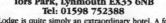

Readers are requested to mention this guidebook
when seeking accommodation
(and please enclose a stamped addressed envelope).

WEST AISH FARM
Morchard Bishop,

Contact:
Molly & Jeff Kingaby for brochure
Tel & Fax: 01363 877427
e-mail: su2195@eclipse.co.uk
Website: www. eclipse.co.uk/westaish

33% of our guests have stayed with us at least once before

Two self catering cottages.
(See classified ad under Morchard Bishop)

A warm welcome awaits you at Silver Birches, a comfortable riverside bungalow on the edge of Dartmoor. Good centre for bird-watching, forest walks, golf, riding; free salmon/trout fishing for residents. All rooms en suite. Guest lounge with TV, dining room, sun lounge. Two self-catering caravans in garden from £130 per week. *Bed and Full English Breakfast from £24 nightly.*

Silver Birches, Teign Valley, Trusham, Newton Abbot, Devon TQ13 0NJ Tel: 01626 852172

LYME BAY HOUSE HOTEL
Sea Front, Teignmouth, South Devon TQ14 8SZ (01626 772953)
On the level sea front within sight of station. Quiet atmosphere. Licensed. Comfortable rooms with refreshments and TV's, pleasing outlook across Lyme Bay. En suite rooms available. Lift – no steps.

PALFREYS BARTON
Cove, Tiverton EX16 7RZ Tel: 01398 331456

Four six-berth caravans on a 235 acre working dairy farm, beautifully sited in a paddock adjacent to the farmhouse with marvellous views. Ideally situated for both coasts and moors; 10 miles from M5 Junction 27, five miles from Tiverton. Enjoy a holiday in the quiet countryside. Lovely walks, golf, fishing and riding within easy reach. All caravans have shower, flush toilet, hot and cold water; gas cooker provided; electric fire, fridge and colour TV. Electricity metered. Fully equipped except linen. Available March to October.

AA QQQ RAC Listed   **CLEVEDON HOTEL**   Visa/Access welcome
Meadfoot Sea Road, Torquay, Devon TQ1 2LQ. Tel: 01803 294260

Bobby, the 6-year-old Golden Retriever, invites sociable, well-behaved fellow canines to his home set in its own peaceful grounds 300 yards from beach, woods and coastal paths. Facilities for owners include en suite rooms with TV, radio/alarm (for morning walkies) and tea/coffee making facilities; licensed bar; delicious breakfasts; traditional home-cooked evening meals. B&B from £21. Small charge for pets £1 per night.

Mr & Mrs K. Noton, Crossways and Sea View Holiday Apartments Maidencombe, Torquay TQ1 4TH
for free brochure
Tel/Fax: 01803 328369

Maidencombe ~ Torquay
★ Modern self-contained flats set in one-acre grounds
★ Sleep 2/5 persons
★ Some with magnificent sea views
★ Colour TV
★ Ample free parking
★ Pets welcome (large garden)
★ Safe beach nearby
★ Easy reach town centre
★ Bus stop close by
★ Beautiful coast and country walks
★ Children's play area
See also Colour Advertisement on page 17

Pets and their families most welcome at Fairlawns Hall

Delightful self-catering holiday apartments and mews cottages for 2–8 people. South facing gardens overlooking the bay and large woods nearby. Lawn badminton, children's splash pool and play area. Ample parking. laundry room.
Write or phone Mrs E. Hanbury for further details
Fairlawns Hall, 27 St Michaels Road, Torquay, Devon TQ1 4DD Telephone 01803 328904

FHG
FHG PUBLICATIONS
publish a large range of well-known accommodation guides. We will be happy to send you details or you can use the order form at the back of this book.

DEVON *Torquay, Totnes*

LORNA DOONE APARTMENTS
Torwood Gardens Road, Torquay, Devon
Situated 500 yards from Torquay Centre shops and seafront. Beautifully converted luxury apartments with colour TV, microwave, modern bathroom and fully fitted kitchen. Gardens. Families and dogs welcome. From £132 per week for 2 persons.
RESERVATIONS OFFICE: 01694 722244; www.longmynd.co.uk

PETITOR HOUSE, TORQUAY

Clifftop Victorian House. Panoramic sea views. South facing terrace and garden. Sleeps six.

Colour Brochure: Les & Ann Shaw, 52 Petitor Road, Torquay TQ1 4QF Tel: 01803 327943

Red House Hotel & Maxton Lodge Holiday Apartments
Red House Hotel, Rousdown Road, Chelston, Torquay TQ2 6PB
Telephone: 01803 607811; Fax: 01803 605357

• Serviced or self-catering accommodation available
• Indoor and Outdoor Swimming Pools
• Spa Pool, Sauna, Gym, Indoor Recreation Room
• Beauty Salon and Solarium • Licensed Bar and Restaurant
• Launderette, parking and garden • Close to shops, parks and seafront

See also Colour Advertisement on page 18

SOUTH SANDS APARTMENTS
Torbay Road, Livermead, Torquay TQ2 6RG
Tel: 01803 293521; Fax: 01803 293502; E-mail: southsands@easicom.com
Modern self-contained apartments on sea front. Beach 100 yards. Near Riviera Centre, Marina, etc. Good bus service. Open all year. Pets welcome. Central heating. Short-breaks except Summer Season.
Mastercard/Visa. Sleep 1/5. Commended Mr & Mrs P.W. Moorhouse

EDESWELL FARM
COUNTRY CARAVAN PARK
RATTERY, SOUTH BRENT, DEVON TQ10 9LN

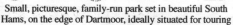

Small, picturesque, family-run park set in beautiful South Hams, on the edge of Dartmoor, ideally situated for touring Devon and Cornwall. 21 caravan holiday homes for hire, 46 terraced touring pitches. Indoor heated swimming pool, games room and TV lounge. Bar, shop, launderette, children's play area and covered floodlit badminton court.
Tel/Fax 01364 72177 • e-mail: welcome@edeswellfarm.co.uk • website: www.edeswellfarm.co.uk

Sea Trout Inn, Staverton, near Totnes, Devon TQ9 6PA
Tel: 01803 762274; Fax: 01803 762506
Hidden away in the tranquil Dart Valley but conveniently placed for Dartmoor, Torbay and the South Devon coast. Delightful cottage style bedrooms, two traditional English bars and elegant restaurant.
For a real taste of rural Devon, the Sea Trout has it all

194

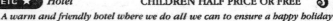

Key to Tourist Board Ratings

 The Crown Scheme

The **English Tourism Council** (formerly the English Tourist Board) has
joined with the **AA** and **RAC** to create a new, easily understood quality rating
for serviced accommodation.

Hotels will receive a grading ranging from **one to five STARS (★)**. Other
serviced accommodation such as **guest houses** and **B&B establishments**
will be graded from **one to five DIAMONDS (◆)**. These ratings represent
Quality, Service and Hospitality not just facilities.

*NB.Some properties had not been assessed at the time of going to press
and in these cases the publishers have included the old CROWN
gradings.*

The Key Scheme

The Key Scheme covering self-catering in cottages, bungalows, flats,
houseboats, houses, chalets, etc remains unchanged. The classification from
One to Five KEYS indicates the range of facilities and equipment. Higher
quality standards are indicated by the terms APPROVED, COMMENDED,
HIGHLY COMMENDED AND DE LUXE.

CLASSIC COTTAGES, HELSTON, CORNWALL TR13 8NA (01326 565555). Choose your cottage from 400 of the finest coastal and country cottages throughout the West Country. Many welcome pets.

A wonderful variety of over 450 cottages, houses and apartments all over the West Country, ideal for self catering holidays. Many accept pets. Free colour brochure from HELPFUL HOLIDAYS, COOMBE 49, CHAGFORD, DEVON TQ13 8DF (01647 433593 24hrs).

HOLIDAY HOMES & COTTAGES S.W, 365A TORQUAY ROAD, PAIGNTON TQ3 2BT (01803 663650; Fax: 01803 664037). Hundreds of Self-Catering Holiday Cottages, Houses, Bungalows, Apartments, Chalets and Caravans in Devon and Cornwall. Please write or phone for free colour brochure. [🐕]
E–mail: holcotts@aol.com

MARSDENS COTTAGE HOLIDAYS, DEPT 14, 2 THE SQUARE, BRAUNTON EX33 2JB (01271 813777; Fax: 01271 813664). Experience the charms of a North Devon holiday from the comfort and luxury of a Marsdens holiday cottage. Write or phone today for your free colour brochure.
E-mail: holidays@marsdens.co.uk
Website: www.marsdens.co.uk

POWELLS COTTAGE HOLIDAYS, HIGH STREET, SAUNDERSFOOT, PEM-BROKESHIRE SA69 9EJ. Many of our top quality holiday properties accept pets. Cottages in Devon, Cornwall, Cotswolds, Pembrokeshire and Heart of England. For colour brochure FREEPHONE 0800 378771 (24 hours).

SWEETCOMBE COTTAGE HOLIDAYS, ROSEMARY COTTAGE, WESTON, NEAR SIDMOUTH EX10 0PH (01395 512130; Fax: 01395 515680). Selection of Cottages, Farmhouses and Flats in Sidmouth and East Devon, all personally selected and very well-equipped. Gardens. Pets welcome. Please ask for our colour brochure. [🐕]
E–mail: enquiries@sweetcombe-ch.co.uk
Website: www.sweetcombe-ch.co.uk

TOAD HALL COTTAGES. 100 outstanding waterside and rural properties in truly beautiful locations in Devon. Call for our highly acclaimed brochure. Video also available. Tel: 01548 853089.
Website: www.toadhallcottages.com

WELCOME COTTAGE HOLIDAYS. Quality Cottages in wonderful locations at welcoming low prices. Pets, linen and fuel mostly included. PHONE FOR FREE 2000 FULL COLOUR BROCHURE 01756 702203.

SYMBOLS
🐕 Indicates that pets are welcome free of charge.
£ Indicates that a charge is made for pets: nightly or weekly.
pw! Shows some special provision for pets; exercise facility, feeding or accommodation arrangement.
⌂ Indicates separate pets accommodation.

WEST COUNTRY COTTAGES & WEST COUNTRY HOTELS, Guesthouses, Bed & Breakfasts, Caravan and Camping Sites. Lands End to the New Forest. Free Colour brochure 01626 333 679.
Website: www.westcountry-holidays.co.uk

WEST COUNTRY WALKS. Give your owner a Great Walkies Holiday in North Devon. Exhilarating walks with great smells along the spectacular South West Coast path. Call 01 271 33 60 30 for a brochure on all tailor-made walking holidays.

Appledore

Unspoilt resort and small port on estuaries of Taw and Torridge. Sandy beach, good bathing. Bideford 3 miles.

MARINERS COTTAGE, IRSHA STREET, APPLEDORE. Elizabethan fisherman's Cottage at sea edge. Extensive views of sea and boats. Enclosed garden. Sleeps 6: three bedrooms, lounge, dining room, own parking. Good fishing, coastal walks. SAE please to MRS P.A. BARNES, 140 BAY VIEW ROAD, NORTHAM, BIDEFORD EX39 1BJ or phone 01237 473801 for prices and vacancies only. [pw! Dog £5 per week.]

OTTER COTTAGE. Traditional fisherman's cottage. Totally equipped – 2 Tvs, VCR, microwave, autowasher etc. Also unique harbourside apartments and bungalow. Brochure from B.H. SMITH, 26 MARKET STREET, APPLEDORE EX39 1PR. Tel: 01237 47154/478206, (or our Agent: 01271 378907). [Pets £8 per week.]

SEA BIRDS, pretty Georgian cottage facing directly out to the open sea. Spacious cottage with large lounge, colour TV, dining room, modern fitted kitchen and 3 double bedrooms, own parking. Other cottages available. SAE to P.S. BARNES, 140 BAY VIEW ROAD, NORTHAM, BIDEFORD EX39 1BJ (01237 473801). [pw! Dog £5 per week.]

Ashburton

Delightful little town on southern fringe of Dartmoor. Centrally placed for touring and the Torbay resorts. Plymouth 24 miles, Exeter 20, Kingsbridge 20, Tavistock 20, Teignmouth 14, Torquay 14, Totnes 8, Newton Abbot 7.

MRS P.D. COULTER, 30 EAST STREET, ASHBURTON, NEWTON ABBOT, DEVON TQ13 7AZ (01364 652589). Completely self-contained furnished flat with colour TV; kitchen/diner. One double and one twin. Situated within the bounds of Dartmoor National Park. SAE please, for terms. [🐾]

THE CHURCH HOUSE INN, HOLNE, NEAR ASHBURTON TQ13 7SJ (01364 631208). 14th Century inn within Dartmoor National Park. En suite rooms available. Bars and restaurant; real ales. Great walks. [🐾]

PARKERS FARM HOLIDAY PARK, HIGHER MEAD FARM, ASHBURTON, NEWTON ABBOT TQ13 7LJ (01364 652598 Fax: 01364 654004). Farm Cottages and Caravans to let, also level touring site with two toilet/shower blocks and electric hook-ups. Central for touring; 12 miles Torquay. [pw! Pets welcome at a charge.]

MRS A. BELL, WOODER MANOR, WIDECOMBE-IN-THE-MOOR, NEAR ASH-BURTON TQ13 7TR (Tel & Fax: 01364 621391). Cottages on family farm. Surrounded by unspoilt woodland and moors. Clean and well equipped, colour TV, central heating, laundry room. Two properties suitable for disabled visitors. Colour brochure available. ⚘⚘⚘⚘ Commended. [pw! £15 per week for first dog; £10 per week for others. ▢]

Axminster

Small friendly market town, full of old world charm, set in the beautiful Axe Valley. Excellent centre for touring Devon, Somerset and Dorset. 5 miles from coast.

LILAC COTTAGE. A beautifully renovated cottage. Oil-fired central heating. All electric kitchen. Inglenook fireplace; beamed ceiling. Sleeps six plus cot. Colour TV. Garden. Garage. SAE please. APPLY – MRS J.M. STUART, MANOR FARM HOUSE, DEANE, BASINGSTOKE, HANTS RG25 3AS (Tel/Fax: 01256 782961) or Mrs Young (01769 573788). [Pets £5 per week.]
E–mail: bstuartb@compuserve.com

Bampton

Market town 6 miles north ot Tiverton.

COOMBE HOUSE, OAKFORD, TIVERTON EX16 9HF (01398 351281; Fax: 01398 351211). Self-contained annexe, fully equipped, two bedrooms. Access to large garden and paddock. [pw! 🐕]

MRS E. GOODWIN, LODFIN FARM, MOREBATH, BAMPTON EX16 9DD (Tel & Fax: 01398 331400). Three pretty bedrooms, one en suite, with tea making facil-ities and TV. Hearty Aga cooked breakfast served in the inglenook dining room. Sorry, no smoking. Children and pets welcome. Bed and Breakfast from £18.50 per person. ETC ◆◆. [Pets £1.50 per night]

Barnstaple

The largest town in Devon, once an important centre for the wool trade, now a lively shopping centre with thrice weekly market, modern leisure centre etc.

COASTAL EXMOOR HIDEAWAYS. House with indoor pool and jacuzzi; house on beach; riverside cottages in 80-acre valley with indoor pool and jacuzzi; plus many more properties. Dogs welcome. Breaks from £98. TELEPHONE 01598 763339. [Pets £10 per week]

NORTH DEVON HOLIDAY HOMES, 19 CROSS STREET, BARNSTAPLE EX31 1BD (01271 376322 (24 hours); Fax: 01271 346544). Send for guide to the 500 best value Cottages around Devon's National Trust coast. All regularly inspected and guaranteed to offer first class value. [Pets £10 per week.]
Website: www.northdevonholidays.co.uk

MRS V.M. CHUGG, VALLEY VIEW, MARWOOD, BARNSTAPLE EX31 4EA (01271 343458). Bungalow on 300 acre farm. Bed and Breakfast accommodation. Near Marwood Hill Gardens and Arlington Court. Children most welcome, free baby-sitting. Dogs by arrangement. Terms from £15. [pw!]

GILLIAN AND ROBERT SWANN, SPRINGFIELD GARDEN, ATHERINGTON, UMBERLEIGH, NORTH DEVON EX37 9JA (Tel & Fax: 01769 560034). A sub-stantial traditional English house on its own in a quiet countryside setting. Homely, clean, comfortable and friendly en suite B&B. Traditional English home cooking. B&B £18–£25 pppn.
E–mail: broadgdn@eurobell.co.uk
Website: broadgdn.eurobell.co.uk

Berrynarbor

This peaceful village overlooking the beautiful Sterridge valley, has a 17th cent. pub and even older church and is a half-mile from the coast road between Combe Martin (and Ilfracombe.

SANDY COVE HOTEL, BERRYNARBOR EX34 9SR (01271 882243 or 882888). Hotel set amidst acres of gardens and woods. Heated swimming pool. Children and pets welcome. A la carte restaurant. All rooms en suite with colour TV, tea-making. Free colour brochure on application. [🛖 One dog]
E–mail: rg14003483@aol.com

Bideford

Neat port and resort on River Torridge. Attractive, many-arched stone bridge, wooded hills. Boat trips from quay. The sea is 3 miles distant at Westward Ho! Exeter 43 miles, Launceston 32, Bude 26, Ilfracombe 21, Barnstaple 9, Torrington 7.

MRS V. PRICE, MEAD BARN COTTAGES, WELCOMBE, NEAR BIDEFORD EX39 6HQ (01288 331721). Enjoy our character barns all year. Close beautiful unre-stricted beaches, cliffs and country walks. Tranquil, unspoilt area. Weeks/breaks for 2-10 and pets.

JENNY AND BARRY JONES, THE PINES AT EASTLEIGH, NEAR BIDEFORD EX39 4PA (01271 860561; Fax: 01271 861248). A warm welcome and a peace-ful relaxing time. En suite rooms. Generous farmhouse style cooking. Open all year. Licensed. Children welcome. B&B from £29. No smoking. ETC ◆◆◆◆ Silver Award. [Pets £2 per night, £10 per week]
E–mail: barry@thepinesateastleigh.co.uk

SYMBOLS
🛖   Indicates that pets are welcome free of charge.
£   Indicates that a charge is made for pets: nightly or weekly.
pw!   Shows some special provision for pets; exercise facility, feeding or accommodation arrangement.
⌂   Indicates separate pets accommodation.

Bigbury on Sea

A scattered village overlooking superb coastal scenery and wide expanses of sand.

MR SCARTERFIELD, HENLEY HOTEL, FOLLY HILL, BIGBURY-ON-SEA TQ7 4AR (01548 810240). Edwardian cottage-style hotel, spectacular sea views. Near good beach, dog walking. en suite rooms with telephone, tea making, TV etc. Home cooking. No smoking establishment. Licensed. 3 Crowns Commended. AA ★★. [Pets £2.00 per night.]

PAT CHADWICK, "MARINERS", RINGMORE DRIVE, BIGBURY-ON-SEA, KINGS-BRIDGE TQ7 4AU (01548 810454). Two large flats with extensive sea views. Sandy beaches within yards. Golf nearby. Dogs welcome free.[🐕].
E–mail: chad.29upper@virgin.net

MRS J. TUCKER, MOUNT FOLLY FARM, BIGBURY-ON-SEA, KINGSBRIDGE TQ7 4AR (01548 810267). Cliff top position, with outstanding views of Bigbury Bay. Spacious, self catering wing of farmhouse, attractively furnished. Farm adjoins golf course and River Avon. Lovely coastal walks, ideal centre for South Hams and Dartmoor. No smoking. Always a warm welcome, pets too!

Bovey Tracey

Little town nestling on southern fringe of Dartmoor. Fine scenery including Haytor Rocks (4 miles) and Becky Falls (3 ½ miles). Exeter 14 miles, Torquay 13, Newton Abbot 6, Chudleigh 4.

BLENHEIM COUNTRY HOUSE HOTEL, BOVEY TRACEY TQ13 9DH (01626 832422). Family Hotel on edge of Dartmoor National Park. RSPCA member. Open all year. All pets free. 2 Crowns. [🐕]

Bradworthy

Village to the north of Holdsworthy. Well placed for North Devon and North Cornish coasts.

PETER & LESLEY LEWIN, LAKE HOUSE COTTAGES AND B&B (01409 241962). ETC ♛♛♛♛ Commended. Two well equipped cottages sleeping two to six. Quiet rural position; one acre gardens and tennis court. Half-a-mile from village shops and pubs. Spectacular coast eight miles. Also two lovely en suite B&B rooms, all facilities, from £18. [🐾]
E–mail: lakevilla@bradworthy.co.uk

Branscombe

Bright East Devon resort near Axe estuary. Shingle beach and chalk cliffs; good bathing, many lovely walks in vicinity. Exeter 23 miles, Sidmouth 11.

COOMBE VIEW FARM, BRANSCOMBE, SEATON EX12 3BT (01297 680218/ 680451). Beautiful East Devon. Small farm campsite. Two large, fully equipped caravans. Seaviews, walks, wildlife, beaches, fishing, from £75 per week.
E–mail: t.glasper@farmersweekly.net

Bratton Fleming

Village 6 miles north-east of Barnstaple..

MRS A. DOUGLAS, FRIENDSHIP FARM, BRATTON FLEMING, BARNSTAPLE, EX31 4SQ (01598 763291 evenings). Bungalow (sleeps six plus cot) quietly situated in its own garden, surrounded by fields. 12 miles from Barnstaple and Ilfracombe, within easy reach of the beaches of Woolacombe and Combe Martin, with Exmoor literally on the doorstep. Linen supplied, lounge with TV, well equipped kitchen/dining room. Weekly terms, low season from £100, high season £250.

Brixham

Lively resort and fishing port, with quaint houses and narrow winding streets. Ample opportunities for fishing and boat trips.

BRIXHAM HOLIDAY PARK, FISHCOMBE COVE, BRIXHAM (01803 853324). Situated on coastal path. Choice of one and two-bedroomed chalets. Indoor heated pool, free club membership, comfortable bar offering meals and takeaway service, launderette. 150 yards from beach with lovely walks through woods beyond. [Pets £20 per week]

DEVONCOURT HOLIDAY FLATS, BERRYHEAD ROAD, BRIXHAM TQ5 9AB (01803 853748 24 hours). 24 self-contained flats with private balcony, colour television, heating, private car park, all-electric kitchenette, separate bathroom and toilet. Open all year. [Pets £10 per week.]

HOLIDAYS TORBAY, 26 COTMORE CLOSE, BRIXHAM TQ5 0EF (01803 854708). Harbourside cottages, houses, flats. Sea views and close to beaches, town and coastal walks. Colour TV, clean and comfortable. [🐾]

THE SMUGGLERS HAUNT HOTEL, CHURCH HILL, BRIXHAM TQ5 8HH (01803 853050; Fax: 01803 858738). Friendly 300-year-old hotel in the centre of old Brixham. Quality bar and à la carte menus. En suite rooms. Children and pets welcome. From £21 pppn B&B. 3 Crowns, AA ★★. [🐕]
Website: smugglershaunt-hotel-devon.co.uk

ST. MARY'S BAY. A very special place! Award winning Holiday Park in an area of outstanding natural beauty. Close to Brixham on the English Riviera, over-looking its own superb, sandy beach. ◆◆◆◆. Telephone WESTSTAR HOLIDAY PARKS on 01392 447447 for further details.

Budleigh Salterton

South Devon resort of dignified charm. Attractive sea-front, shingle beach, pleasant walks in vicinity. Good fishing in sea and River Otter. Taunton 16 miles, Exeter 14, Exmouth 5.

TIDWELL HOUSE COUNTRY HOTEL, KNOWLE, BUDLEIGH SALTERTON EX9 7AG (01395 442444). Come and unwind at this listed Georgian house of great character set in three acres of gardens. Ideal centre for walking, touring, playing golf etc. Large en suite rooms. Pets and children welcome. [pw! Pets £1 per night.] E–mail: mcm@tidwellhouse.swinternet.co.uk
Website: www.SmoothHound.co.uk/hotels/tidwellh.html

Challacombe

Village west of Simonsbath on the edge of Exmoor.

MRS L. NASH, LITTLE SWINCOMBE FARM, CHALLACOMBE, NEAR BARN-STAPLE EX31 4TU (01598 763506). Exmoor – Pretty, airy stone cottage within working farm. Two bedrooms, sleeps four plus two. Kitchen/diner, large living room. CH fired by wood burner. Private garden. Children most welcome. Dog, horse by arrangement. Lovely situation on moor. Sea 15 minutes.
E–mail: nash@lineone.net

Chittlehamholt

Standing in beautiful countryside in the Taw Valley and just off the B3227. Barnstaple 9 miles, South Molton 6.

SNAPDOWN FARM CARAVANS, CHITTLEHAMHOLT, UMBERLEIGH, NORTH DEVON EX37 9PF (01769 540708). 12 only – 6 berth caravans with flush toilets, showers, colour TV, fridges, cookers and fires. Laundry room. Picnic tables. Unspoilt countryside – field and woodland walks. Terms £88 to £235 inc. gas and electricity in caravans. [Pets £8.75 per week.]

Chulmleigh

Mid-Devon village set in lovely countryside, just off A377 Exeter to Barnstaple road. Exeter 23 miles, Tiverton 19, Barnstaple 18.

SANDRA GAY, NORTHCOTT BARTON FARM COTTAGE, NORTHCOTT BARTON, ASHREIGNEY, CHULMLEIGH EX18 7PR (Tel/Fax: 01769 520259). ETC ♟♟♟ Commended. Three bedroom character cottage, large enclosed garden, log fire. Special rates low season, couples and short breaks. Near golf, riding, Tarka trail and R.H.S. Rosemoor. [🐕]

Combe Martin

Coastal village with harbour set in sandy bay. Good cliff and rock scenery. Of interest is the Church and "Pack of Cards" Inn. Barnstaple 14 miles, Lynton 12, Ilfracombe 6.

MR M. J. HUGHES, MANLEIGH HOLIDAY PARK, RECTORY ROAD, COMBE MARTIN EX34 0NS (01271 883353). Holiday Chalets, accommodate 4/6 persons. In 6 acres. Free use of swimming pool. Dogs welcome provided they are kept under control. Also 12 luxury Caravans to let. Graded ✓✓✓✓. [Pets £16 per week. pw!]

Crediton

Ancient small town. Chapter house with Cromwellian relics. Cidermaking. Cathedral-type church. 7 miles from Exeter.

COOMBE HOUSE COUNTRY HOTEL, COLEFORD, CREDITON EX17 5BY (01363 84487; Fax: 01363 84722). Peaceful and tranquil elegant Georgian manor house nestling in 5 acres of a hidden valley at the rural heart of Devon. RAC/AA ★★★, 4 Crowns Commended. [🐕]
E-mail: coombehs@eurobell.co.uk

Croyde

Village 7 miles south-west of Ilfracombe on the Golden Coast. Gem, rock and shell museum includes giant clams from the South Pacific.

MR A. BENNETT, 11 WEST CROYDE, CROYDE EX33 1QA (01271 890321). 2 bed-roomed bungalow (sleeps 4). Beautifully equipped with TV, video, washing machine etc. Large enclosed rear garden and patio within earshot of sea. Close to Devon Coastal Path and Tarka Trail. Village location near to local surfing, golf, cycling. [Pets £10 per week]

JOHN AND DIANA WOODINGTON, FIG TREE FARMHOUSE, ST MARY'S ROAD, CROYDE EX33 1PJ (Tel/Fax: 01271 890204). Bed and Breakfast and self catering (sleeping 5). Warm and friendly welcome in old thatched Devon longhouse. Edge of Croyde village. Acre garden. Dogs welcome in rooms or kennelling available. Canine Care Gold Award. [Pets £1 per night fl pw!] Website: www.jwoodington.freeserve.co.uk

MR AND MRS G. PADDISON, MANOR COTTAGE, 11 ST MARY'S ROAD, CROYDE EX33 1PE (Tel/Fax: 01271 890324). Comfortable bungalow, sleeps 5. Enclosed garden and car space. Easy walking distance to beach and village. Coastal footpath and golf course nearby. Available all year.

Croyde Bay

Charming village nestling in a sheltered combe behind Croyde Bay.

MRS JENNIFER PENNY, CROYDE BAY HOUSE HOTEL, CROYDE BAY, NORTH DEVON EX33 1PA (01271 890270). Small hotel beside beach at Croyde Bay. All rooms en suite with tea/coffee making facilities. Good food and friendly atmosphere. AA ◆◆◆◆◆. [🐾]

Cullompton

Small market town off the main A38 Taunton - Exeter road. Good touring centre. Noted for apple orchards which supply the local cider industry. Taunton 19 miles, Exeter 13, Honiton 11, Tiverton 9.

FOREST GLADE HOLIDAY PARK (PW), KENTISBEARE, CULLOMPTON EX15 2DT (01404 841381; Fax:01404 841593). Country estate with deluxe 2/4/6 berth caravans. All superbly equipped. Many amenities on site. Mother and Baby Room. Campers and tourers welcome. SAE for colour brochure. ✓✓✓✓ [pw! Pets 50p per night.]
E-mail: forestglade@cwcom.net;
Website: www.forestglade.mcmail.com

LYDENSIGN, MRS C. KING, DUNNS GREEN FARM, HEMYOCK, CULLOMPTON EX15 3PT (Tel: 01823 680447; Fax: 01823 681008). Three bedroom character cottage near village of Hemyock, good pub, very good food! Enjoy the peace and views of the Culm Valley on the Blackdown Hills. a designated area of Outstanding Natural Beauty. [🐾]
E-mail: 1daveking@lineone.net

MRS B. HILL, SUNNYSIDE FARM, BUTTERLEIGH, NEAR CULLOMPTON, TIVERTON EX15 1PP (01884 855322). 130-acre mixed farm, central for touring Dartmoor and Exmoor. En suite bedrooms with tea/coffee facilities. Bed and Breakfast; Evening Meal optional. Children welcome. [🐾]

Dartmoor

365 square miles of National Park with spectacular unspoiled scenery, fringed by picturesque villages.

CHERRYBROOK HOTEL, TWO BRIDGES, YELVERTON PL20 6SP (01822 880260). Set in the heart of Dartmoor National Park. Seven comfortably furnished en suite bedrooms. Good quality home-cooked food with menu choice. Ideal for touring. AA QQQQ SELECTED. WCTB ◆◆◆◆. [🐾]

MRS PIPER, DARTMOOR LADYMEDE, THROWLEIGH, NEAR OKEHAMPTON EX20 2HU (01647 231492). Delightful bungalow situated on edge of village of Throwleigh. All pets welcome. Local pub serves Evening Meals. Bed & Breakfast from £18.50 per person. Ample parking. Registered. [Pets £1 per night].

DEVONSHIRE INN, STICKLEPATH, OKEHAMPTON EX20 2NW (01837 840626). A real country pub! Out the back door past the water wheels, cross the river by ford or footbridge and up through the woods onto the north edge of Dartmoor proper. Dogs and horses always welcome, fed and watered. 1994 Winner National Beta Petfood Golden Bowl Competition for most dog-friendly pub!

MRS J. COLTON, PEEK HILL FARM, DOUSLAND, YELVERTON PL20 6PD (Tel/Fax: 01822 854808). The gateway to Dartmoor. Sunny, en suite rooms. The biggest breakfast. Packed lunches. Evening meal. Spectacular views. All pets welcomed. 2 Crowns Commended. [🐕]

P. WILKENS, POLTIMORE, RAMSLEY, SOUTH ZEAL EX20 2PD (01837 840209). Dartmoor National Park. Self catering accommodation consisting of summer chalet, granite barn conversion. Also pretty thatched guest house. All with direct access to the Moor. Write or phone for details. [1st dog free, others £7.50 per week]

PRINCE HALL HOTEL, TWO BRIDGES, DARTMOOR PL20 6SA (01822 890403; Fax: 01822 890676). Small, friendly, relaxed country house hotel with glorious views onto open moorland. Walks in all directions. Eight en suite bedrooms. Log fires. Gourmet cooking. Excellent wine list. Fishing, riding, golf nearby. 3 Day Break from £184 pp. 3 Crowns Highly Commended. [🐕]

SUE BOOTY, "ROGUES ROOST", POUNDSGATE, NEWTON ABBOT TQ13 7PS (01364 631223). Dartmoor National Park. Self-catering holiday accommodation, any number from 2 to 7. Excellent walking. Stunning Countryside. Off beaten track. [🐕]

THE ROSEMONT GUEST HOUSE, GREENBANK TERRACE, YELVERTON PL20 6DR (01822 852175). ◆◆◆. Large Victorian house overlooking the green at Yelverton, just yards from lovely open moorland. Most rooms en suite, all with TV and tea/coffee making. B&B from £20.00. [🐕]
E–mail: rosemont@members.swis.net

TWO BRIDGES HOTEL, TWO BRIDGES, DARTMOOR PL20 6SW (01822 890581; Fax: 01822 890575). Famous Olde World riverside Inn. Centre Dartmoor. Log fires, very comfortable, friendly, own brewed beer, excellent food. Ideal walking, touring, fishing, riding, golf. Warning – Addictive. [🐕]

Dartmouth

Historic port and resort on the estuary of the River Dart, with sandy coves and pleasure boat trips up the river. Car ferry to Kingswear.

DARTSIDE HOLIDAYS, RIVERSIDE COURT, SOUTH EMBANKMENT, DARTMOUTH TQ6 9BH (01803 832093; Fax: 01803 835135). Comfortable holiday apartments with private balconies and superb river and harbour views. Available all year with colour TV, linen and parking. From £79-£625 per week. Free Colour Brochure on request. [Pets £10 per week.]

MRS S.R. RIDALLS, THE OLD BAKEHOUSE, 7 BROADSTONE, DARTMOUTH TQ6 9NR (Tel & Fax: 01803 834585). Three Cottages (one with four-poster bed). Sleep 2–6. Near river, shops, restaurant. Blackpool Sands 15 minutes' drive. TV, linen free, baby-sitting. Open all year. ♔♔♔ up to Commended. [🐾]

TORCROSS APARTMENTS, SLAPTON SANDS, TORCROSS VILLAGE, NEAR KINGSBRIDGE, SOUTH DEVON TQ7 2TQ (Tel: 01548 580206). Fully equipped self-catering apartments with lovely lake and sea views. Resident owners and spotlessly clean. Brochure with pleasure or visit our website. WCTB, ETC ♔♔♔♔ Commended. [Pets £7 to £24 per week]
E–mail: torcross.apartments@eclipse.co.uk
Website: www.eclipse.co.uk/torcross.apartments

PAM & GRAHAM SPITTLE, WATERMILL COTTAGES, HANSEL, DARTMOUTH TQ6 0LN (01803 770219). Comfortable, well equipped, old stone cottages in peaceful riverside setting. Wonderful walks in and around our idyllic valley near Slapton. 10 minutes from sea. Sleep 3-8. Open all year. Children and pets welcome. Telephone for brochure. [Pets £15 per week]

Dawlish

Bright resort with sandy beach and sandstone cliffs. Lovely gardens with streams, waterfalls and famous black swans. Exeter 13 miles, Torquay 12.

MRS F. E. WINSTON, "STURWOOD", 1 OAK PARK VILLAS, DAWLISH EX7 0DE (01626 862660). Holiday flats. Comfortable, self-contained, accommodating 2-6. Own bathroom, 1/2 bedrooms. Colour television. Garden. Parking. Full Fire Certificate. Leisure centre and beach close by. Pets welcome. [🐾]

MRS P. KITSON, 3 CLEVELAND PLACE, DAWLISH EX7 9HZ (01626 865053). Town cottages – newly-built comfortable accommodation for two to five. two/three bedrooms. Parking. Patio garden. Three minutes' walk beaches. Special terms for couples. Also six bedroom family house accommodates ten. Parking. Garden. [🐾]

SYMBOLS

🐾   Indicates that pets are welcome free of charge.

£   Indicates that a charge is made for pets: nightly or weekly.

pw!   Shows some special provision for pets: exercise facility, feeding or accommodation arrangement.

⌂   Indicates separate pets accommodation.

Dawlish Warren

A 500 acre nature reserve with a sandy spit at the mouth of the River Exe.

WELCOME FAMILY HOLIDAY PARK, DAWLISH WARREN, SOUTH DEVON EX7 0PH (Reservations: 01626 862070, Dial-a-brochure: 01626 888323). Activities include the Dolphin Club Entertainment Centre, indoor heated four-pool complex, Children's Club with games arcade. Free electricity, linen. [Pets £25 per week.]

Dunsford

Attractive village in upper Teign valley with Dartmoor to the west. Plymouth 35 miles, Okehampton 16, Newton Abbot 13, Crediton 9, Exeter 8.

M.I. HARRISON, ROYAL OAK INN, DUNSFORD, NEAR EXETER EX6 7DA (01647 252256). Welcome to our Victorian country inn with real ales and home-made food. All en suite rooms are in a 300-year-old converted barn. Well behaved children and dogs welcome. [🛏]

Eggesford (Chulmleigh)

Picturesque village, central for north and south coasts, Exmoor and Dartmoor.

EGGESFORD COUNTRY HOTEL, EGGESFORD, CHULMLEIGH EX18 7JZ (01769 580345; Fax: 01769 580262). Family-run hotel in 10 acres of beautiful grounds with seven miles of fishing. Ideal centre for walking, touring and country pursuits. Open all year. Brochure. Pets welcome.

Exeter

Chief city of the South-West with a cathedral and university. Ample shopping, sports and leisure facilities.

MRS D.L. SALTER, HALDON LODGE FARM, KENNFORD, NEAR EXETER EX6 7YG (01392 832312). Modern Holiday Caravan. Two bedrooms, kitchen, lounge, bathroom/toilet. TV. Farm shop, famous village Inns. Sea short distance. Private grounds near Teign Valley Forest with two Coarse Fishing lakes. Pets welcome. [pw! 🛏]

MRS SALLY GLANVILL, RYDON FARM, WOODBURY, EXETER EX5 1LB (Tel and Fax: 01395 232341). 16th Century Devon Longhouse on working dairy farm. Bedrooms with private or en suite bathrooms, hairdryers, tea/coffee facilities. Romantic 4-poster. Open all year. 2 Crowns Highly Commended, AA QQQQ Selected. From £22 to £27. [🛏]

FHG PUBLICATIONS

publish a large range of well-known accommodation guides. We will be happy to send you details or you can use the order form at the back of this book.

Exmoor

265 square miles of unspoiled heather moorland with deep wooded valleys and rivers, ideal for a walking, pony trekking or fishing holiday.

MARTIN JONES, POLTIMORE INN, EAST STREET, NORTH MOLTON EX36 3HR (01598 740338). Edge of Exmoor. Twin and double rooms. Large garden restaurant. Real Ales. Five bedrooms. Pets and children welcome. B&B £17.50 per night. Good walks. Free car parking.

JAYE JONES AND HELEN ASHER, TWITCHEN FARM, CHALLACOMBE, BARNSTAPLE EX31 4TT (01598 763568). Comfort for country lovers in Exmoor National Park. All rooms en suite with TV. Meals prepared with local and some organic produce. Stabling £35 per week. Dogs no charge. B&B £19–£25, DB&B £34–£39. [🐕]
E–mail: holidays@twitchen.co.uk
Website: www.twitchen.co.uk

Harberton

Small picturesque village two miles from Totnes.

MIKE & JANET GRIFFITHS, "OLD HAZARD", HIGHER PLYMOUTH ROAD, HARBERTON, TOTNES TQ9 7LN (01803 862495). 3 miles Totnes. Attractive well-equipped cottage and spacious self-contained farmhouse flat. Convenient rural location. Open all year. Dogs welcome. Brochure on request. [Pets £7.00 p.w.]

Honiton

Busy South Devon town now happily by-passed. Noted for lace and pottery. Excellent touring centre. Newton Abbot 31 miles, Exmouth 18, Taunton 18, Exeter 17, Budleigh Salterton 16, Lyme Regis 15, Chard 13, Sidmouth 10.

THE BELFRY COUNTRY HOTEL, YARCOMBE, NEAR HONITON, DEVON EX14 9BD (Tel: 01404 861234; Fax: 01404 861579). Small luxury Hotel in converted Victorian village school. All rooms en suite with lovely views. Licensed restaurant, fine wines and superb food. Ideal base for touring, walking, gardens, antiques.

MRS S. KIDWELL, THE CREST, WILMINGTON, NR. HONITON EX14 9JU (01404 831 419). A modern chalet style house nestling in the picturesque Umborne Valley. The guest wing affords complete privacy with large modern en suite bedroom. Double glazed. Lying in two-and-a-half acres of garden. PETS WELCOME. [🐕]

MRS E. TUCKER, LOWER LUXTON FARM, UPOTTERY, HONITON EX14 9PB (01823 601269). Olde worlde Farmhouse in area of outstanding natural beauty. Ideal for touring. Carp and Tench fishing. Good home cooking. Children welcome. B&B nightly from £14. Weekly terms from £130, Six Dinners and Bed and Breakfast. [🐕]

Hope Cove

Attractive fishing village, flat sandy beach and safe bathing. Fine views towards Rame Head; cliffs. Kingsbridge 6 miles.

HOPE BARTON BARNS, HOPE COVE, NEAR SALCOMBE TQ7 3HT (01548 561393). 17 stone barns in two courtyards and three luxury apartments in farmhouse. Farmhouse meals. Free range children and well behaved dogs welcome. For full colour brochure please contact: Mike or Judy Tromans. [pw! 🐾]

MR AND MRS P.G. PEDRICK, HOPE BEACH HOUSE, HOPE COVE, NEAR KINGS-BRIDGE TQ7 3HH (01548 560151). Seven luxury 2 and 3 bedroom Apartments, all facilities, equipped to highest standards: ETC 🏵🏵🏵🏵 Commended. Linen supplied free. Open all year. Children/pets welcome. [Pets £12 weekly.]

Ilfracombe

This popular seaside resort clusters round a busy harbour. The surrounding area is ideal for coastal walks.

THE EXCELSIOR HOTEL TORRS PARK, ILFRACOMBE EX34 8AZ Tel & Fax: 01271 862919). Friendly licensed hotel in excellent location for pets and their owners. Direct access to famed Torr Walk. Tunnels, beaches, harbour and town five minutes walk. [🐾]

ST BRANNOCKS HOUSE HOTEL, ST BRANNOCKS ROAD, ILFRACOMBE EX34 8EQ (01271 863873). Good food and excellent accommodation guaranteed at this friendly Hotel. All rooms TV, tea making; most en suite. Licensed bar. Parking. Children and pets welcome. 3 Crowns Commended, RAC Acclaimed [🐾]

SUNNYMEADE COUNTRY HOTEL, WEST DOWN, ILFRACOMBE EX34 8NT (01271 863668). A few minutes away from the South West Coastal Path, Woolacombe, Ilfracombe and Exmoor. Award winning home cooked food, using local produce. Licenced Bar. Eight en suite rooms, two on the ground floor. Website: www.btinternet.com/~sunnymeade

VARLEY HOUSE, CHAMBERCOMBE PARK, ILFRACOMBE EX34 9QW (Tel: 01271 863927; Fax: 01271 869299). Relax with your dog, fabulous walks nearby. Fully en suite non-smoking rooms with lots of thoughtful extras. Superb food, beautiful surroundings. Bar. Car Park. Children welcome over five years. WE WANT YOU HERE WE WANT YOU TO RETURN. ETC ◆◆◆◆. AA QQQQ Selected Award. [🐾]
E–mail: info@varleyhouse.freeserve.co.uk

WESTWELL HALL HOTEL, TORRS PARK, ILFRACOMBE EX34 8AZ (Tel & Fax: 01271 862792). Elegant Victorian hotel in own grounds, adjacent to National Trust coastal walks. All spacious rooms en suite with colour TV and tea/coffee facilities. AA ★, RAC ★, ETC ★. [🐕]

Instow

On estuaries of Taw and Torridge, very popular with boating enthusiasts. Barnstaple 6 miles, Bideford 3.

BEACH HAVEN COTTAGE, INSTOW. Seafront cottage overlooking sandy beach. Extensive beach and sea views. Sleeps 5, own parking. Central heating, colour TV, coastal walks. Dog welcome. For colour brochure send SAE to 140 BAY VIEW ROAD, NORTHAM, BIDEFORD EX39 1BJ (01237 473801). [Dog £10 per week]

Kingsbridge

Pleasant town at head of picturesque Kingsbridge estuary. Centre for South Hams district with its lush scenery and quiet coves. Plymouth 21 miles, Dartmouth 15, Totnes 13.

BEACHDOWN, CHALLABOROUGH BAY, KINGSBRIDGE TQ7 4JB (Tel & Fax: 01548 810089). Self catering holidays for families in pleasant cedarwood bungalows 200 yards from quiet, sandy beach. Children's playground. Local shopping. Pets welcome. Fully furnished and equipped. ETC ♕♕♕♕ Approved Contact LIZ for details. [pw! £15 per week for first pet, £10 for second and subsequent.]

MRS B. KELLY, BLACKWELL PARK, LODDISWELL, KINGSBRIDGE TQ7 4EA (01548 821230). 17th century Farmhouse, 5 miles from Kingsbridge. Ideal centre for Dartmoor, Plymouth, Torbay, Dartmouth and many beaches. Some bedrooms en suite. Bed, Breakfast and Evening Meal or Bed and Breakfast. Pets welcome free of charge. ETC ♦♦. [pw!🐕]

MR AND MRS HUGHES, BUTSONS MAI, KILN LANE, STOKENHAM, KINGSBRIDGE TQ7 2SQ (01548 581106). B&B en suite double and family rooms. Pet friendly. Dogs £1.50 per night. Sea views. Near Slapton Ley. Walking and birdwatching. Colour TV. Tea/coffee making. [£1.50 per night]

RUTH & JON SAUNDERS, DITTISCOMBE FARMHOUSE & HOLIDAY COTTAGES, SLAPTON, KINGSBRIDGE TQ7 2QF (Tel: 01548 521272; Fax: 01548 521425). Individual and comfortable self-catering cottages with gardens. Set in private 20-acre conservation valley with ponds and wildlife. Two miles from historic Slapton village, Slapton Sands beach and South West Coast Path. Ideal area for dog-walking and bird watching. [Pets £15 per week for first pet, £10 for each subsequent pet]

FREE and REDUCED RATE Holiday Visits!
Don't miss our Readers' Offer Vouchers on pages 53 to 70

DEREK & JEAN IDE, FAIRFIELD, WALLINGFORD ROAD, KINGSBRIDGE TQ7 1NF (01548 852441). "Garden Flat" sleeps 2+2, £140 to £220 per week. Out of season breaks £20 per day (minimum £100). No smokers. Two off-road parking spaces. Direct access to well fenced garden, ideal for children (eight years and over). Dogs welcome free of charge. A friendly welcome and cream tea await you. [🐾]

GARA MILL. Self catering in comfortable detached lodges or flats in 16th century mill. TVs, laundry, play area, games room. Woodland walks. Ring or fax for brochure. ALLAN AND MARCIA GREEN, GARA MILL HOUSE, SLAPTON, KINGSBRIDGE TQ7 2RE (01803 770295). [Pets £12 per week.]

HALLSANDS HOTEL, NORTH HALLSANDS, KINGSBRIDGE (01548 511264). Fully licensed family Hotel offering Bed, Breakfast and Evening Meal. Good food. Fishing, bathing and compressed air available.

JOURNEYS END INN, RINGMORE, NEAR KINGSBRIDGE TQ7 4HL (01548 810205). Historic inn in unspoilt setting. Extensive food menu served in bar and dining room; wide range of real ales. Comfortable en suite bedrooms with colour TV. Golf, fishing nearby. [Pets £2.50 per night]

LIPTON FARM, EAST ALLINGTON, NEAR TOTNES TQ9 7RN (01548 521252) Luxury 30 ft six berth caravan in quiet valley. Bed linen, microwave, colour TV, swimming pool. Kingsbridge 5 miles. Ideal for beautiful beaches and Dartmoor. From £150.00 per week. [Pets £5 per week.]

THE SLOOP INN, BANTHAM, NEAR KINGSBRIDGE TQ7 3AJ. (01548 560489/560215; Fax: 01548 561940). Five en suite bedrooms, four luxury self-catering apartments. Pet friendly. Bed & Breakfast from £31 per person. Self-catering from £245 inclusive. Short breaks available. 2 Crowns Commended; ♔♔♔ Commended. AA QQQ Recommended.

King's Nympton

3 miles north of Chulmleigh. Winner of CPRE Award for Devon Village of the Year 1999.

Eight Country Cottages sleeping from 2 to 12 in rural area; lovely views, private patios and gardens. Well furnished and equipped. Heated pool, tennis court, BHS approved riding school. Laundry room. Open all year. APPLY: TERRY & JANE SHERAR, COLLACOTT FARM, KING'S NYMPTON, UMBERLEIGH, NORTH DEVON EX37 9TP. (01769 572491). [Pets £3 per night, £20 per week] Website: http://.members.aol.com/self.cater

Lynton/Lynmouth

Picturesque twin villages joined by a unique cliff railway (vertical height 500ft). Lynmouth has a quaint harbour and Lynton enjoys superb views over the rugged coastline.

MR AND MRS D. HILLIER, BRENDON HOUSE, BRENDON, LYNTON EX35 6PS (01598 741206). Charming country house in beautiful Lyn Valley. Licensed. Good Devon cooking. Fishing permits sold. Dogs welcome by arrangement. B&B from £19, DB &B from £34. 3 Crowns Commended. [🐕] Website: www.brendonvalley.co uk/Brendon_House.htm

COUNTISBURY LODGE HOTEL, TORS PARK, LYNMOUTH EX35 6NB (01598 752388). Former Victorian vicarage, peacefully secluded yet only 5 minutes to Lynmouth village. En suite rooms with tea/coffee facilities, central heating, and choice of menu. Log fires. Parking. Spring/Autumn Breaks. [🐕]

THE EXMOOR SANDPIPER INN, COUNTISBURY, NEAR LYNMOUTH EX35 6NE (01598 741263). This fine old coaching inn is in a beautiful setting with good food and hotel facilities for complete comfort. All 16 rooms en suite with colour TV, tea/coffee making. [🐕 one dog] E–mail: exmoorsandpiper.demon.co.uk

GABLE LODGE, LEE ROAD, LYNTON EX35 6BS (01598 752367). Grade II Listed building. Friendly and homely atmosphere. En suite rooms with TV and beverage trays. Licensed. Good home cooking. Car park and garden. Non-smoking. [🐕]

THE HEATHERVILLE HOTEL, TORS PARK, LYNMOUTH EX35 6NB (01598 752327). AA ◆◆◆◆. Country house hotel in peaceful setting with magnificent river and woodland views. Tea and coffee making in all rooms. Some en suite rooms with colour TV. Traditional English cooking. Licensed. Four minutes' walk to village. Parking. Bargain Breaks. Pets very welcome free of charge.[🐕]

R.S. BINGHAM, NEW MILL FARM, BARBROOK, LYNTON EX35 6JR (01598 753341). Exmoor Valley. Two delightful genuine modernised XVII century cottages by stream on 100-acre farm with A.B.R.S. Approved riding stables. Free fishing. ETC 🏠🏠🏠 commended. SAE for brochure. [pw! Pets £15 per week.]

ST VINCENT HOUSE HOTEL, CASTLE HILL, LYNTON EX35 6JA (Tel: 01598 752244; Fax: 01598 753971). Charming Grade II Listed building with many original features. Fully licensed bar. All double/twin rooms en suite with colour TV, tea/coffee making. Phone for brochure. Major credit cards accepted. AA/ETC ◆◆◆◆. NON-SMOKING. [🐾]
E–mail: keenstvins@lineone.net
Website: http://www.hotelsaccomodation.co.uk/DEVON/vincent.htn

MRS W. PRYOR, STATION HOUSE, LYNTON (01598 752275/752381 Fax: 01598 752475). Holiday Flat situated in the former narrow gauge railway station closed in 1935, overlooking the West Lyn Valley. Centrally placed for Doone Valley and Exmoor. Parking available. [🐾]

Modbury

Twin towns linked by a bridge over the River Looe. Capital of the shark fishing industry; nearby Monkey Sanctuary is well worth a visit.

THE LODGE, ERMINGTON. Pretty detached thatched cottage. Country near village. Overlooking fields. Area of outstanding natural beauty. Three miles coast. Comfortably furnished. Well equipped. Barbecue. Two bedrooms, sleeps four. ENQUIRIES: BARTERS OLD FARMHOUSE, NORTH WHILBOROUGH, NEWTON ABBOT TQ12 5LP (Tel: 01803 873213; Fax: 01803 875096)
E–mail: holcot@eclipse.co.uk

Morchard Bishop

An old traditional Devon village almost equal distance from both coasts and both moors.

MOLLY AND JEFF KINGABY, WEST AISH FARM, MORCHARD BISHOP, NEAR CREDITON EX17 6RX (Tel/Fax: 01363 877427). Two Self Catering Cottages set in a former cobbled farmyard on a southerly slope overlooking Dartmoor. One cottage sleeps 5. Bungalow sleeps 4. £148 – £295. Short Breaks (3 nights) £110. If you have forgotten what peace and quietness is like, come and stay with us! [🐾]
E–mail: su2195@eclipse.co.uk
Website: www. eclipse.co.uk/westaish

Mortehoe

Adjoining Woolacombe with cliffs and wide sands. Intresting rock scenery beyond Morte Point. Barnstaple 15 miles, Ilfracombe

LUNDY HOUSE HOTEL, MORTEHOE, WOOLACOMBE EX34 7DZ (01271 870372). Quality en suite accommodation in small, friendly hotel. Superb food, licensed bar lounge, restaurant. TV & tea-making facilities in all rooms. Write or phone for full details.[🐾]

SHAUN & JILL FERGUSON, THE SMUGGLERS, NORTH MORTE ROAD, MORTE-HOE EX34 7DR (Tel/Fax: 01271 870891). Luxury accommodation from twin rooms to family suites, in the pretty village of Mortehoe. En suite rooms, Satellite TV, Full English Breakfast, Licensed Bar, Beer Garden, Homecooked Meals . Well trained pets welcome. [🐾]

Newton Abbot

Known as the Gateway to Dartmoor and the coast, this lively market town has many fine buildings, parks and a racecourse.

ROSELANDS HOLIDAY CHALETS, TOTNES ROAD, IPPLEPEN, NEWTON ABBOT TQ12 5TD (01803 812701). Within easy reach of all South Devon attractions, detached, fully equipped chalets sleeping 2-6 persons; one suitable for wheelchairs. Sociable dogs have freedom of garden. Telephone for details. [pw! 1st pet free, extra pets £5 per week.]
E-mail: Roselands@FSBDial.co.uk

Okehampton

Market town on edge of Dartmoor

MR I. HOWARD, OLDITCH FARM CARAVAN & CAMPING PARK, STICKLE PATH, NEAR OKEHAMPTON EX20 2NT (01837 840734; Fax: 01837 840877). Small family-run site within Dartmoor National Park. Ideal base for touring Devon with easy access to both coasts. We welcome well-behaved dogs. Small restaurant on site. Open March to November. Terms from £4.50 to £8.50 per night. AA Three Pennant.

Ottery St Mary

Pleasant little town in East Devon, within easy reach of the sea. Many interesting buildings including 11th-century parish Church. Birthplace of the poet Coleridge.

MR AND MRS M. FORTH, FLUXTON FARM, OTTERY ST MARY EX11 1RJ (01404 812818). Charming 16th-century farmhouse with large garden. Good food, log fires. Peace and quiet. Cat lovers' paradise. Licensed. Three Crowns, AA Listed. [🐾 pw!]

SYMBOLS

🐾 Indicates that pets are welcome free of charge.

£ Indicates that a charge is made for pets: nightly or weekly.

pw! Shows some special provision for pets; exercise facility, feeding or accommodation arrangement.

⌂ Indicates separate pets accommodation.

Paignton

Popular family resort on Torbay with long, safe sandy beaches and small harbour. Exeter 25 miles, Newton Abbot 9, Torquay 3.

AMBER HOUSE HOTEL, 6 ROUNDHAM ROAD, PAIGNTON TQ4 6EZ (01803 558372). Family-run licensed hotel. En suite facilities and ground floor rooms. Good food. Highly recommended. A warm welcome assured to pets and their families. 3 Crowns. [🐾]

J. AND E. BALL, DEPARTMENT P.W., HIGHER WELL FARM HOLIDAY PARK, STOKE GABRIEL, TOTNES TQ9 6RN (01803 782289). Within 4 miles Torbay beaches and 1 mile of River Dart. Central for touring. Dogs on leads. Tourist Board Graded park ✓✓✓. [Pets £12 per week in statics, free in tents and tourers.]

Plymouth

Historic port and resort, impressively rebuilt after severe war damage. Large naval docks at Devonport. Beach of pebble and sand.

AVALON GUEST HOUSE, 167 CITADEL ROAD, THE HOE, PLYMOUTH PL1 2HU (01752 668127). Family run guest house, close to the sea front. All rooms have full central heating, colour TV and tea/coffee facilities. En suite available. Open all year round. [🐾]

CHURCHWOOD VALLEY, DEPT PW, WEMBURY BAY, NEAR PLYMOUTH PL9 0DZ (01752 862382). Relax in quality log cabins with own patio & BBQ. In wooded valley leading to beach. Licensed shop, launderette, riding stables. Two family pets welcome free of charge. ✓✓✓✓ [🐾]

CRANBOURNE HOTEL, 278/282 CITADEL ROAD, THE HOE, PLYMOUTH PL1 2PZ (01752 263858/661400/224646; Fax: 01752 263858). Convenient for Ferry Terminal and City Centre. All bedrooms with colour TV and tea/coffee. Licensed bar. Keys provided for access at all times. Under personal supervision. Pets by arrangement. Two Crowns Commended. [🐾]

Salcombe

Fishing and sailing centre in a sheltered position. Fine beaches and coastal walks nearby.

GRAFTON TOWERS HOTEL, MOULT ROAD, SALCOMBE TQ8 8LG (01548 842882; Fax: 01548 842857). Small luxury hotel, all en suite, overlooking magnificent coastline. Spectacular walks. [Pets £2.50 per night].

THE SALCOMBE BOAT COMPANY, WHITESTRAND, SALCOMBE TQ8 8ET (Tel: 01548 843420; Fax: 01548 844417). A holiday with a difference. Unwind with a houseboat holiday on Salcombe's tranquil estuary. Write or phone for brochure. [Pets £20 weekly.]

SAND PEBBLES HOTEL, HOPE COVE, NEAR KINGSBRIDGE TQ7 3HF (01548 561673). In own grounds overlooking sea and countryside. Tastefully furnished bedrooms with bathroom or shower, TV, beverage facilities. Excellent restaurant. Golf, tennis, riding, within easy reach.
Website: www.webmachine.co.uk/sandpebbles

SEAMARK, THURLESTONE SANDS, NEAR SALCOMBE TQ7 3JY (01548 561300). 5 lovely cottages adjoining coastal path. Beach 500 yards, golf one mile. Indoor heated pool, sauna and games room. Laundry room. Pay phone. Colour brochure. [🐾]

THE PORT LIGHT, BOLBERRY DOWN, MALBOROUGH, NEAR SALCOMBE TQ7 3DY (01548 561384 or 07970 859992). A totally unique location set amidst acres of National Trust coastline. Luxury en suite rooms. Superb home-cooked fare, specialising in local seafood. Licensed bar. Pets welcome throughout the hotel. Bargain Breaks throughout the year. [🐾]
E–mail: info@portlightsalcombe.co.uk
Website: www.portlightsalcombe.co.uk

MR & MRS JOHN WILTON, THORNLEA MEWS HOLIDAY COTTAGES, HOPE COVE, SALCOMBE TQ7 3HB (Tel & fax: 01548 561319). Attractive cottages 400 yards from safe sandy beaches. Lovely views, pretty garden with one acre play area. Ample parking. Pets welcome. Resident owners. Ten self-contained units sleeping two to seven. Open March to November. ♛♛♛ to ♛♛♛♛ and Commended. [Pets £20 per week]

Seaton

Bright East Devon resort near Axe estuary. Shingle beach and chalk cliffs; good bathing, many lovely walks in vicinity. Exeter 23 miles, Sidmouth 11.

MILKBERE HOLIDAYS, MILKBERE HOUSE, 14 FORE STREET, SEATON EX12 2LA (01297 22925 – brochure/01297 20729 – bookings). Attractive self-catering Cottages, Bungalows, Apartments. Coast and Country on Devon/Dorset border. Free colour brochure. Pets welcome. [£18 per week.]

Shaldon

Delightful little resort facing Teignmouth across the Teign estuary. Sheltered by the lofty prominence of Shaldon Ness, beach side activities are largely concerned with boats and sailing; beaches are mainly of sand. Mini-golf course. The attractions of Teignmouth are reached by a long road bridge or passenger ferry.

GLENSIDE HOTEL, RINGMOOR ROAD, SHALDON, TEIGNMOUTH TQ14 0EP (01626 872448). Charming, waterside, cottage hotel. Level river walks to beach. En suite available. Garden, car park. B&B from £20.00; DB&B from £33.00. Telephone for brochure. [Pets £2.50 daily, £10 weekly.]

MRS P. O'DONNELL, THE ROUND HOUSE, MARINE PARADE, SHALDON TEIGNMOUTHTQ14 0DP (01626 873328). Situated right on the beach with glorious views from all apartments in this pretty, olde worlde village. Full central heating. Parking. [£5 weekly per dog.]

Sidmouth

Sheltered resort, winner of many awards for its floral displays. Good sands at Jacob's Ladder beach.

ENID & BERT CARR, BARRINGTON VILLA GUEST HOUSE, SALCOMBE ROAD, SIDMOUTH EX10 8PU (01395 514252). A Regency Villa in beautiful gardens on the River Sid. Dog-walk riverside park nearby. Ample forecourt parking. Dogs with house trained owners most welcome. ETC ◆◆◆◆ Commended. [🐾]

MR & MRS B. P. DILLON, BOSWELL FARM COTTAGES, SIDMOUTH EX10 0PP (Tel & Fax: 01395 514162). Self-catering cottages with own gardens, TV, microwave, bedlinen, dishwasher, fridge freezer. Two miles from beaches. Inn and amenities within walking distance. Open all year. ♛♛♛ and ♛♛♛♛ Highly Commended. [Pets £15 per week, pw!]
E–mail: dillon@boswell-farm.co.uk
Website: www.boswell-farm.co.uk

LOWER KNAPP FARM, SIDBURY, SIDMOUTH EX10 0QN (Tel: 01404 871438; Fax: 01404 871597). Luxury self-catering cottages sleeping 2/9 set in 16 acres. Indoor heated pool, sauna, solarium. All cottages with fully fitted kitchens; colour TV etc. Linen supplied. Colour brochure on request. ♛♛♛. [Pets £15 per week.]

OAKDOWN TOURING AND HOLIDAY HOME PARK, WESTON, SIDMOUTH EX10 0PH (Tel: 01297 680387; Fax: 01297 680541). Privately owned park set in East Devon Heritage Coast. Level, well drained and close mown. Luxury holiday homes to hire, pitches for touring units. Colour brochure. Calor Gas Best Park, BGHP ★★★★★. [pw! from £1.00 per night.]

South Brent

Just off the busy A38 Plymouth to Exeter road, this is a good centre on the River Avon for Dartmoor and the South Devon resorts. Plymouth 15 miles, Ashburton 8.

Enchanting, select site for those seeking a quiet restful holiday amidst beautiful surroundings, overlooking the Dartmoor Hills. Fully serviced luxury caravans, with colour TV, fridge, heater and shower. Separate low density site for tents/tourers. Several acres for carefree exercising. ✓✓✓. APPLY – TREVOR AND JILL HORNE, WEBLAND FARM HOLIDAY PARK, AVONWICK, NEAR SOUTH BRENT TQ10 9EX (01364 73273). [pw! Pets £10 per week in caravans.]

SYMBOLS

🐾   Indicates that pets are welcome free of charge.

£   Indicates that a charge is made for pets: nightly or weekly.

pw!   Shows some special provision for pets; exercise facility, feeding or accommodation arrangement.

⌂   Indicates separate pets accommodation.

South Molton

On the southern edge of Exmoor, 12 miles east of Barnstaple, this busy market town is noted for its antiques and elegant Georgian buildings.

NORTH LEE HOLIDAY COTTAGES, NORTH LEE FARM, SOUTH MOLTON EX36 3EH (Tel: 01598 740248/740675; Fax: 01598 740248). Southern edge of Exmoor. Tastefully decorated barn conversions. Sleep 2-8. Working farm. Easy reach of Exmoor and Coast. Open all year. Weekend and short breaks available. ♛♛♛♛ Highly Commended [🐕pw!]

Tavistock

Birthplace of Sir Francis Drake and site of a fine ruined Benedictine Abbey. On edge of Dartmoor, 13 miles north of Plymouth.

MRS P.G.C. QUINTON, HIGHER QUITHER, MILTON ABBOT, TAVISTOCK PL19 0PZ (01822 860284). Modern self-contained barn conversion. Own private garden. Terms from £195 inc. linen, coal and logs. Electricity metered. [🐕]

Teign Valley

Picturesque area on edge of Dartmoor. The River Teign flows into the English Channel at Teignmouth.

S. & G. HARRISON-CRAWFORD, SILVER BIRCHES, TEIGN VALLEY, TRUSHAM, NEWTON ABBOT TQ13 0NJ (01626 852172). Comfortable riverside bungalow on the edge of Dartmoor. Good centre for bird-watching, forest walks, golf, riding; fishing. All rooms en suite. Two self-catering caravans inn garden from £130 per week. B&B from £24.00 nightly. [🐕]

Teignmouth

Resort at mouth of River Teign. Bridge connects with Shaldon on south side of estuary.

LYME BAY HOUSE HOTEL, DEN PROMENADE, TEIGNMOUTH TQ14 8SZ (01626 772953). Near rail and coach stations and shops. En suite facilities available. Licensed. Lift – no steps. Bed and Breakfast. [🐕]

Tiverton

Market town on River Exe 12 miles north of Exeter, centrally located for touring both North and South coasts.

MRS PRATT, MOOR BARTON, NOMANSLAND, TIVERTON EX16 8NN (01884 860325). 18th-century superior farmhouse on a 250-acre mixed farm, situated equidistant from North and South coasts. Double, family and twin-bedded rooms. Children welcome. B&B from £18.50 per night; DB&B £25 per night, £140 per week inclusive.

PALFREYS BARTON, COVE, TIVERTON EX16 7RZ (01398 331456). Four six-berth caravans on a 235 acre working dairy farm, beautifully sited adjacent to farmhouse with marvellous views. All caravans fully equipped. Available March to October.

Torquay

Popular resort on the English Riviera with a wide range of attractions and entertainments. Yachting and watersports centre with 10 superb beaches and coves.

CLEVEDON HOTEL, MEADFOOT SEA ROAD, TORQUAY TQ1 2LQ (01803 204260). Set in its own peaceful grounds 300 yards from beach and woods. En suite rooms with TV, radio/alarm and tea/coffee. Licensed bar and traditional home cooked meals. [Pets £1 per night]

MR AND MRS K. NOTON, CROSSWAYS AND SEA VIEW HOLIDAY APARTMENTS, MAIDENCOMBE, TORQUAY TQ1 4TH (Tel and Fax: 01803 328369). Modern self-contained flats set in one-acre grounds. Sleep 2/5. Colour TV. Pets welcome – exercise area. Children's play area. [pw! £10 per week.]

MR & MRS W.J. HANBURY AND FAMILY, FAIRLAWNS HALL, 27 ST MICHAELS ROAD, TORQUAY TQ1 4DD (01803 328904). Delightful self-catering holiday apartments and mews cottages. Pets welcome. Large woods nearby, gardens and parking. [Pets £15 per week]

FAIRMOUNT HOUSE HOTEL, HERBERT ROAD, CHELSTON, TORQUAY TQ2 6RW (01803 605446). Somewhere special – a small licensed hotel with comfortable en suite bedrooms, cosy bar, delicious home cooking. Peaceful setting. One mile town centre. B&B from £25 per person. Bargain Breaks available. [Pets £2 per night.]

MR & MRS EMERSON, FIRCROFT GUEST HOUSE, 69 AVENUE ROAD, TORQUAY TQ2 5LG (01803 211634; mobile: 0831 637798) Cosy en suite bedrooms with colour TV's and teamaking facilities. Car parking. Pets welcome free. AA QQ, 3 CROWNS. [🐕]
Website: www.english-riviera.co.uk/hotel/fircroft

HOTEL GLENEAGLES, TORQUAY (01803 293637). Top class live entertainment every night. Emphasis on relaxation. Renowned cuisine including six course silver service dinner. Panoramic sea views. Not suitable for children. Ring for Special Break Offers.
E–mail: hotelgleneagles@lineone.net
Website: http://website.lineone.net/~hotelgleneagles/

LORNA DOONE APARTMENTS, TORWOOD GARDENS ROAD, TORQUAY. (RESERVATIONS: 01694 722244) Situated 500 yards from town centre shops and seafront. Luxury apartments with colour TV, microwave, modern bathroom and kitchen. Families and dogs welcome. From £132 per week for 2 persons. [Pets £15 per week].
Website: www.longmynd.co.uk

PARKFIELD LUXURY HOLIDAY APARTMENTS. KITTY AND GORDON JONES, CLADDON LANE, MAIDENCOMBE, TORQUAY, DEVON TQ1 4TB (Tel & Fax: 01803 328952). We offer the warmest of welcomes to you, at the fairest of prices. Luxury 1, 2 and 3 bedroomed apartments with views overlooking Dartmoor in the distance. [🐾]

PETITOR HOUSE, TORQUAY. Beautiful Victorian House. Unique quiet idyllic clifftop position. House sleeps six in thre bedrooms and is well-furnished and equipped. Pets welcome. Colour brochure from: LES & ANN SHAW, 52 PETITOR ROAD, TQ1 4QF (01803 327943) [🐾]

RED HOUSE HOTEL AND MAXTON LODGE HOLIDAY APARTMENTS, ROUS-DOWN ROAD, CHELSTON, TORQUAY TQ2 6PB (01803 607811; Fax: 01803 605357). Choose either the friendly service and facilities of a hotel or the privacy and freedom of self-catering apartments. The best of both worlds! ♔♔♔♔, 3 Crowns Commended. See our colour display advert on page 18 [🐾 in flats; £3 per night in hotel]

SOUTH SANDS APARTMENTS, TORBAY ROAD, LIVERMEAD, TORQUAY TQ2 6RG (01803 293521; Fax: 01803 293502). 18 superior self-contained ground and first floor Apartments for 1–5 persons. Central heating. Open all year. Parking. Beach 100 yards. Convenient Riviera Centre, theatre, marina. Short Breaks except Summer season. [pw! from £1 per night.]
E–mail: southsands@easicom.com

Torrington

Pleasant market town on River Torridge. Good centre for moors and sea. Exeter 36 miles, Okehampton 20, Barnstaple 12, Bideford 7.

SALLY MILSOM, STOWFORD LODGE, LANGTREE, NEAR TORRINGTON EX38 8NU (01805 601540). Away from the crowds. Four luxury cottages with heated indoor pool, and two secluded period farm cottages. Sleep 4/6. Peaceful countryside, convenient North Devon coast and moors. Magnificent views and walks. ETC ♔♔♔♔ Highly Commended. Phone for brochure. [pw! Pets £10 per week.]

Totnes

Town at tidal estuary of River Dart, 7 miles west of Torquay.

EDESWELL FARM COUNTRY CARAVAN PARK, RATTERY, SOUTH BRENT TQ10 9LN (01364 72177). Picturesque Park in 21 acres wooded hillside. Ideally situated for Dartmoor, Torbay, South Devon. 21 caravan holiday homes for hire, 46 touring pitches. Indoor pool, games room; bar, shop, launderette. [pw! £8.00 weekly static, 50p per night touring.]
E–mail: welcome@edeswellfarm.co.uk
Website: www.edeswellfarm.co.uk

FLEAR FARM COTTAGES, EAST ALLINGTON, TOTNES, SOUTH DEVON TQ9 7RF (01548 521227; Fax 01548 521600). Superb cottages, indoor heated swimming pool, sauna, all weather tennis court, large indoor and outdoor play areas. Non-smokers only. Log fires and full central heating - perfect for off-season breaks.

SEA TROUT INN, STAVERTON, NEAR TOTNES, DEVON TQ9 6PA (Tel: 01803 762274; Fax: 01803 762506) Hidden away in the tranquil Dart Valley but conveniently placed for Dartmoor, Torbay and the South Devon coast. Delightful cottage style bedrooms, two traditional English bars and elegant restaurant.

Woolacombe

Favourite resort with long, wide stretches of sand. Barnstaple 15 miles, Ilfracombe 6.

MRS JOYCE BAGNALL, CHICHESTER HOUSE, THE ESPLANADE, WOOLACOMBE EX34 7DJ (01271 870761). Holiday apartments on sea front. Fully furnished, sea and coastal views. Watch the sun go down from your balcony. Open all year. SAE Resident Proprietor. [Pets £8 per week.]

PAT AND TONY WORTHINGTON, COMBE RIDGE HOTEL, THE ESPLANADE, WOOLACOMBE EX34 7DJ (01271 870321). 7 bedroomed detached hotel facing Combesgate Beach. Open April to end October. ETC ◆◆◆◆ Guest Accommodation Rating. Ample private parking. [Pets £1 per night, £7 per week]

CROSSWAYS HOTEL, SEAFRONT, WOOLACOMBE EX34 7DJ (Tel.& Fax: 01271 870395). Homely, family-run licensed Hotel surrounded by National Trust land. Children and pets welcome. ETC ★. [🐕]

EUROPA PARK, STATION ROAD, WOOLACOMBE (01271 870159). Luxury bungalows, superb views. Touring caravans and tents. Full facilities. Pets welcome, 6-acre dog park. Indoor heated swimming pool. [pw! £5 per week.]

PEBBLES HOTEL, COMBESGATE BEACH, WOOLACOMBE EX34 7EA (01271 870426). Family-run Hotel overlooking sea and beaches. All rooms en suite, with colour TV, tea/coffee making etc. Special Short Break packages. Write or phone for colour brochure. [🐕]

DORSET

DORSET *Abbotsbury, Blandford, Bournemouth*

Visit the **FHG** website

www.holidayguides.com

for details of the wide choice of accommodation featured in the full range of FHG titles

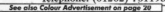

The Stables

ETC/AA/RAC ◆◆◆

Hyde Crook, Frampton, Dorchester DT2 9NW Tel: 01300 320075

The Stables is a large equestrian property which sits in a small area of woodland off the A37 which provides easy travelling to Dorchester from a location which enjoys uninterrupted views of open Dorset countryside. We are a registered small holding of approximately 20 acres, with sheep, ducks and horses, and specialise in providing accommodation and livery for cross country riding. Well behaved dogs welcome and should provide their own beds.

Situated in a secret spot, down a leafy lane, just a five minute walk from the sea. All 18 rooms en suite, with colour TV, tea and coffee making facilities and trouser press. Two of the rooms having four-poster beds. Restaurant with views over Lyme Bay. Smugglers Bar serving bar snacks lunchtimes and evenings with patio overlooking the sea. Enjoy the spectacular walks or just take in some of the many places of interest in the area. Don't just drive through Dorset, come and stay a while and experience the peace and tranquillity that still exists in this beautiful part of Dorset. Heidi our Dalmatian looks forward to meeting you and your Fido. Three day breaks available.

Eype's Mouth Country Hotel

Eype's Mouth Country Hotel, Eype, Bridport DT6 6AL
Tel: 01308 423300; Fax: 01308 420033
E-mail: eypehotel@aol.com

Proprietors: Elizabeth Tye and Steve Howley

Mrs J Tedbury, Little Paddocks, Yawl Hill Lane,
Lyme Regis DT7 3RW Tel: 01297 443085

A six-berth caravan on Devon/Dorset border in a well kept paddock overlooking Lyme Bay and surrounding countryside. Situated on a smallholding with animals, for perfect peace and quiet. Fully equipped except linen. Electric light, fridge, TV. Calor gas cooker and fire. Dogs welcome. Terms from £85. Also fully equipped chalet for two. (Terms from £70). SAE please.

WESTOVER FARM COTTAGES ℣℣℣ COMMENDED

In an area of outstanding beauty, Wootton Fitzpaine epitomizes picturesque West Dorset. Within walking distance of sea. 2 beautiful cottages sleep 6/7 with large secluded gardens. Car parking. Logs, Linen available, 3 bedrooms. £175-£495. Pets welcome.

Wootton Fitzpaine, Nr Lyme Regis, Dorset. DT6 6NE *Brochure: Debby Snook 01297 560451*

Country Inn set in the heart of lovely Piddle Valley. Within easy reach of all Dorset's attractions. All rooms en suite with colour TV, tea and coffee, telephone; swimming pool (May-September). Riverside garden, restaurant where Half Board guests choose from à la carte menu at no extra cost.
Bed and Breakfast: £27.50 per person per night.
Dinner, Bed and Breakfast: £41 per person per night.
10% discount for seven nights
Low Season Breaks: two nights Dinner, Bed and Breakfast £82 per person per night.
Third night Dinner, Bed and Breakfast – FREE.
ETC ◆◆◆◆ AA
Telephone: 01300 348358; Fax: 01300 348153
SEND FOR BROCHURE

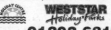

The Poachers Inn
Piddletrenthide, Dorset DT2 7QX

See also Colour Advertisement on page 20

SANDFORD
A Very Special Place!

Sandford Holiday Park is situated in an area of outstanding natural beauty near the New Forest, Bournemouth & Poole.

WESTSTAR Holiday Parks

01202 631600

THE
KNOLL HOUSE

A CIVILISED AND RELAXING HOLIDAY FOR ALL AGES.
AN INDEPENDENT COUNTRY-HOUSE HOTEL, IN AN UNRIVALLED POSITION ABOVE THREE
MILES OF GOLDEN BEACH. DOGS ARE ESPECIALLY WELCOME AND MAY SLEEP IN YOUR
ROOM. SPECIAL DIETS ARRANGED. OUR 100 ACRE GROUNDS OFFER NICE WALKS;
SQUIRRELS AND RABBITS!

~

GOOD FOOD AND A SENSIBLE WINE LIST. TENNIS COURTS; NINE ACRE GOLF COURSE AND
OUTDOOR HEATED POOL. HEALTH SPA WITH JACUZZI, SAUNA, TURKISH ROOM, PLUNGE
POOL AND GYM. MANY GROUND-FLOOR AND SINGLE ROOMS FOR OLDER GUESTS.

~

FAMILY SUITES, OF CONNECTING ROOMS WITH BATHROOM, SEPARATE YOUNG CHILDREN'S
DINING ROOM. PLAYROOMS AND FABULOUS **SAFE** ADVENTURE PLAYGROUND.

~

DAILY FULL BOARD TERMS: £65-£95. CHILDREN LESS, ACCORDING TO AGE.

~

OPEN EASTER - END OCTOBER

STUDLAND BAY DORSET
BH19 3AW
01929 450450 (FAX-450423)
e-mail: enquiries@knollhouse.co.uk
www.knollhouse.co.uk

See also Colour Advertisement on page 19

See also Colour Advertisement on page 21

DORSET *Swanage, Wareham, West bexington*

THE LITTLE MANOR SWANAGE

*Beautiful views. Informal friendly Guest
House with access at any time. Cheerful
personal service. Television, tea and coffee making
facilities in all rooms. Most en suite.
Dogs are welcome in bedrooms.*

s.a.e. Gillian MacDermott
389 HIGH STREET,
SWANAGE, DORSET BH19 2NP
Tel/Fax: 01929 422948

SWANAGE CARAVAN SITE
4/5/6 BERTH FULL MAINS CARAVANS
COMFORTABLE AND WELL EQUIPPED
Colour TV * Launderette * Sea Views * Parking space * Pets welcome
* Fully licensed club with entertainment. * Indoor swimming pool
EASTER – OCTOBER, REDUCED TERMS EARLY/LATE HOLIDAYS
S.A.E. M. Stockley, 17 Moor Road, Swanage, Dorset BH19 1RG Tel: 01929 424154

CROMWELL HOUSE HOTEL Lulworth Cove BH20 5RJ Tel: 01929 400253/400332; Fax: 01929 400566

Catriona and Alistair Miller welcome guests to their comfortable family-run hotel, set in secluded gardens with spectacular sea views. Situated 200 yards from Lulworth Cove, with direct access to the Dorset Coastal Footpath. A heated swimming pool is available for guests' use from May to October. Accommodation is in 14 en suite bedrooms, with TV, direct-dial telephone, and tea/coffee making facilities; most have spectacular sea views. Restaurant, bar wine list. AA**, RAC**. Two nights dinner, bed and breakfast (fully en suite) from £75. Off peak mid week breaks all year except Christmas. ❀❀❀ Commended.

Gorselands Caravan Park
"Peaceful and Pretty"

*Fully Serviced
  caravans
*Shop
*Launderette
*Games room

*Self contained flats
*Village Pub
  100 yards
*Beach car park
  3 mins by car

Attractive secluded park set in coastal valley overlooking Chesil Beach.
Tourist Board graded. Glorious sea views. Country and seaside walks. An
ideal base for discovering Dorset's charming villages and Heritage
coastline. The beach is a mile either by car or through the meadows, and
the fishing is excellent. Pets are most welcome

Colour brochure Dept. PW
Gorselands Caravan Park
West Bexington-on-Sea, Dorset DT2 9DJ
Tel: 01308 897232   Fax: 01308 897239

WELCOME COTTAGE HOLIDAYS. Quality Cottages in wonderful locations at welcoming low prices. Pets, linen and fuel mostly included. PHONE FOR FREE 2000 FULL COLOUR BROCHURE 01756 702204.

Abbotsbury

Village of thatched cottages; Benedictine monks created the famous Abbotsbury Swannery.

MRS JOSEPHINE PEARSE, TAMARISK FARM, WEST BEXINGTON, DORCHESTER DT2 9DF (01308 897784). Self Catering. Overlooking Chesil Beach: three large (one for disabled Cat 1) and two smaller Cottages (ETC ♕♕♕ Approved) and two secluded Chalets (not ETC graded) on mixed organic farm with arable, sheep, cattle, horses and market garden with vegetables on sale. Good centre for touring, sightseeing, walking. Pets and children welcome. Terms from £105 to £495. [🐾]

Blandford

Handsome Georgian town that rose from the ashes of 1731 fire; rebuilt with chequered brick and stone. Also known as Blandford Forum.

bold class

ANVIL HOTEL & RESTAURANT, PIMPERNE, BLANDFORD DT11 8UQ (01258 453431/480182). A typical Old English hostelry offering good old-fashioned English hospitality. Beamed restaurant and bar meals. All bedrooms with private facilities. Ample parking. 3 Crowns Commended, Les Routiers. [Pets £2.50 per night]

Bournemouth

One of Britain's premier holiday resorts with miles of golden sand, excellent shopping and leisure facilities. Lively entertainments include Festival of Lights at the beginning of September.

MRS W. HOLLAND, 12 AVONCLIFFE ROAD, SOUTHBOURNE, BOURNEMOUTH BH6 3NR (01202 426650). Self-catering flatlet on Southbourne cliff top. Fully equipped, close shops, buses; car parking available. Small dogs welcome. Open all year. Rates from £80. SAE Mrs W. Holland.[🐾]

MIKE AND LYN LAMBERT, AARON, 16 FLORENCE ROAD, BOURNEMOUTH BH5 1HF (01202 304925/01425 474007). Modern Holiday Apartments sleeping one to 10 persons, close to sea and shops. Recently extensively renovated with new kitchens and bathrooms. Clean well-equipped flats. Car park and garages. Write or phone for colour brochure and terms. [Pets £14 weekly]

ALUM DENE HOTEL, 2 BURNABY ROAD, ALUM CHINE, BOURNEMOUTH BH4 8JF (01202 764011) Renowned for good old fashioned hospitality and friendly service. Come and be spoilt at our licensed hotel. All rooms en suite, colour TV. Some have sea views. 200 metres sea. Parking. Christmas House party. No charge for pets. [🐾]

CAIRNSMORE PRIVATE HOTEL, 37 BEAULIEU ROAD, BOURNEMOUTH BH4 8HY (01202 763705). 4 minutes' walk through wooded glades to sea. Colour TV in all bedrooms, all en suite. Parking. BB&EM from £26 per person per day. Residential licence. Special diets catered for. No charge for pets. 3 Crowns Commended. [🐕 pw!]

THE CARISBROOKE HOTEL, 42 TREGONWELL ROAD, WEST CLIFF, BOURNEMOUTH BH2 5NT (01202 290432; Fax: 01202 310499). Within five minutes' walk you will find good exercise area for pets, golden beaches, town centre and shopping area. En suite rooms. Colour TV. Licensed bar. Reductions for children. [🐕].
Website: www.carisbrooke.co.uk

CRAVEN GRANGE HOLIDAY FLATS, 17 BODORGAN ROAD, BOURNEMOUTH BH2 6JY (01202 296234). Self-contained flats and cottage, 2–6 persons. Town centre, golf and parks nearby. Car parking. Free Welcome Pack. Pets welcome, not to be exercised in the garden area. Telephone or SAE for details.[🐕]

DENEWOOD HOTEL, 40 SEA ROAD, BOURNEMOUTH. BH5 1BQ (01202 309913; Fax: 391155). Most rooms en suite. Residential and Residents' licence. Two Crowns Commended. Special weekly rates available. TV, tea, coffee and Biscuits in rooms, Health and Beauty salon on site. Open all year. [🐕]

MRS LYNN WEETMAN, THE GOLDEN SOVEREIGN HOTEL, 97 ALUMHURST ROAD, ALUM CHINE, BOURNEMOUTH, DORSET BH4 8HR (Tel & Fax: 01202 762088) Charming Victorian Hotel close to award winning beaches and wooded chine walks. Cosy bar, freshly cooked optional evening meals. En suite rooms, all with tea/coffee making facilities, television, clock/radio alarm and direct dial telephones with extra point for internet access. [🐕]

SEAWAY HOLIDAY FLATS. Self-contained holiday flats with exercise area in garden. Three minutes' level walk between shops and cliffs, with lift to fine sandy "Pets Allowed" beach. Most reasonable terms early and late season. 41 GRAND AVENUE, SOUTHBOURNE, BOURNEMOUTH BH6 3SY (01202 300351). [🐕 pw!]

St George's Holiday Flats are near sea and shops; Questors overlooks quiet, wooded Pleasure Gardens; superb for you and your dog. Both properties have good car parks; pay-phones, laundry, TV, fridges in all units. Clean and fully equipped. We like dogs. Apply: SANDRA & BARRY GLENARD, 45 BRANKSOME WOOD ROAD, BOURNEMOUTH BH4 9JT (01202 763262) [Pets £14 per dog, per week]
E–mail: sun.sea@virgin.net

MRS JENNIE STARLING, STELLA MARIS GUEST HOUSE, 88 SOUTHBOURNE ROAD, BOURNEMOUTH BH6 3QQ (01202 426874). Friendly guest house near sea and shops. Clean and comfortable. Plenty of good home cooking; menu choice. All bedrooms with tea/coffee, colour TV, washbasins; some en suite. Guest lounge with Sky TV. Car park. Sensible prices; generous Senior Citizen and child discounts. [🐕]

Three self-contained apartments in quiet avenue, one minute from clean, sandy beaches and five minutes from shops. Sleep 3/6. Fully equipped including linen. All have fridge, toilet and shower room, microwave, colour TV, central heating, electric meter. Parking. Terms from £75. Contact: MRS HAMMOND, STOURCLIFFE COURT, 56 STOURCLIFFE AVENUE, SOUTHBOURNE, BOURNEMOUTH BH6 3PX (01202 420698). [Pets £5 weekly]

ALUM GRANGE HOTEL, 1 BURNABY ROAD, ALUM CHINE, BOURNEMOUTH BH4 8JF (01202 761195). Pets and owners are assured of a warm welcome at this superbly furnished hotel, 250 yards from the beach. All rooms with colour TV and tea/coffee making. [🐾]

ANNE & RICHARD REYNOLDS, THE VINE HOTEL, 22 SOUTHERN ROAD, SOUTHBOURNE, BOURNEMOUTH BH6 3SR (01202 428309). Small family Hotel only 3 minutes' walk from sea and shops. All rooms en suite. Residential licence. Pets welcome. Non smoking.[Dogs £1 per night]

BILL AND MARJORIE TITCHEN, WHITE TOPPS HOTEL, 45 CHURCH ROAD, SOUTHBOURNE, BOURNEMOUTH BH6 4BB (01202 428868). Situated in quiet position close to lovely walks and beach. Dogs welcome. Free parking. Residential licence. [🐾]

Bridport

Market town of Saxon origin noted for rope and net making. Harbour at West Bay has sheer cliffs rising from the beach.

BRIDPORT ARMS HOTEL, WEST BAY, BRIDPORT DT6 4EN (01308 422994). Thatched Hotel on edge of beach in picturesque West Bay. Two character bars, real ale, wide range of bar meals. A la oarte Restaurant featuring local fish. [🐾]

MRS S. NORMAN, FROGMORE FARM, CHIDEOCK, BRIDPORT DT6 6HT (01308 456159). The choice is yours - Bed and Breakfast, optional Evening meal, in charming farmhouse, OR self-catering Cottage equipped for six, pets welcome. Brochure and terms free on request. [1st dog free, 2nd dog £3.00 per night, £15 per week]

MRS CAROL MANSFIELD, LANCOMBES HOUSE, WEST MILTON, BRIDPORT DT6 3TN (01308 485375). 🏠🏠🏠 Commended. Pretty cottages in converted barns. Panoramic views to sea four miles away. Set in 10 acres, some have fenced gardens. Many walks from our land. [Pets £15.00 per week]

MR F. LOOSMORE, MANOR FARM HOLIDAY CENTRE, CHARMOUTH, BRIDPORT DT6 6QL (01297 560226). All units for four to six people, 10 minutes' level walk to beach, many fine local walks. Swimming pools, licensed bar with family room, shops, launderette. Sporting facilities nearby. Children and pets welcome. SAE. [Pets £15 per week]

Charmouth

Small resort on Lyme Bay, 3 miles Lyme Regis. Sandy beach backed by undulating cliffs where many fossils are found. Good walks.

DOLPHINS RIVER PARK, BERNE LANE, CHARMOUTH DT6 6RD (FREEPHONE 0800 0746375). Luxury 4 and 6 berth caravans on small, peaceful park. Coin-op laundry; children's play area. One mile from beach. Colour brochure available. [Pets £10 per week]

THE QUEEN'S ARMES HOTEL, THE STREET, CHARMOUTH, DORSET DT6 6QF (01297 560339). RAC ★★, Three Crowns Commended.Built around 1480 with oak beams, unique bedrooms and old world charm. Cosy bar and dining room, vegetarians welcome. En suite rooms. Abundance of National Trust land and cliff walks. Pets welcome. [🐾]

Christchurch

Residential town near coast. Yachting based on Christchurch harbour and Christchurch Bay.

Country Holiday Chalet on small, quiet, secluded woodland park. Fenced private garden. Dog welcome. Car parking. £100 to £295 per week. BH & HPA Member. Write enclosing SAE or telephone. APPLY – MRS L. M. BOWLING, OWLPEN, 148 BURLEY ROAD, BRANSGORE, DORSET BH23 8DB (01425 672875; mobile 0860 547391). [pw! 🐾]

Crewkerne

Market town on a sheltered slope of the Blackdown Hills 8 miles west of Yeovil.

MRS G. SWANN, BROADVIEW GARDENS, EAST CREWKERNE TA18 7AG (Tel & Fax: 01460 73424). Unusual Colonial bungalow built in an era of quality. En suite rooms with colour TV, C/H, Tea/Fac. Perfect touring base for country and garden lovers. Non-smoking. Bed and Breakfast £25-£30. [🐾 pw!]
E–mail: broadgdn@eurobell.co.uk
Website: www.eurobell.co.uk

Dorchester

Busy market town steeped in history. Roman remains include Amphitheatre and villa.

CHURCHVIEW GUEST HOUSE, WINTERBOURNE ABBAS, DORCHESTER DT2 9LS (01305 889296). Beautiful 17th Century Licensed Guest House set in the heart of West Dorset, character bedrooms, delightful period dining room, two lounges and bar. Non-smoking. B&B £21–£28pp. B&BEM £35–£42. ETC ◆◆◆, AA QQQ. [🐾]

SYMBOLS

🐾	Indicates that pets are welcome free of charge.
£	Indicates that a charge is made for pets: nightly or weekly.
pw!	Shows some special provision for pets; exercise facility, feeding or accommodation arrangement.
⌂	Indicates separate pets accommodation.

GRACE COTTAGE. Charming cottage with enclosed garden. Lounge/dining room, study/bedroom, two bedrooms, well equipped kitchen, two bathrooms. Pub nearby. Non smokers only Good touring centre. Apply: MRS WILLIS, LAMPERTS COTTAGE, SYDLING ST. NICHOLAS DT2 9NU (01300 341659; Fax: 01300 341699). [🐕]

MRS RITA BOWN, LAMPERTS FARMHOUSE AND COTTAGE, 11 DORCHESTER ROAD, SYDLING ST NICHOLAS, DORCHESTER DT2 9NU (01300 341790). 17th Century thatched listed farmhouse nestling in the Sydling valley. Choose self catering in our well-equipped farm cottage or B&B in our tastefully decorated en suite bedrooms. [🐕]

MRS JANE BOOTHAM, THE OLD POST OFFICE, MARTINSTOWN, DORCHESTER DT2 9LF (01305 889254). Situated in the Winterbourne Valley, The Old Post Office is a stone and slate Georgian cottage used as the village post office until 1950. Five miles from coast and beach, an ideal walking and touring base. Pets and children welcome. Bed and Breakfast from £15 to £20. [🐕]

MRS JACOBINA LANGLEY, THE STABLES, HYDE CROOK (OFF A37), FRAMPTON, DORCHESTER DT2 9NW (01300 320075). A comfortable equestrian property in some 20 acres grounds. Well situated for bridleways/footpaths. Guests' TV lounge, three bedrooms with en suite and private facilities. ETC/AA/RAC ◆◆◆. [pw! £1.50 per dog per night.]

Eype

Market town of Saxon origin noted for rope and net making. Harbour at West Bay has sheer cliffs rising from the beach.

EYPE'S MOUTH COUNTRY HOTEL EYPE, BRIDPORT DT6 6AL (TEL: 01308 423300; FAX: 01308 420033). Experience the tranquillity of Dorset. Situated in a secret spot, down a leafy lane, just a five minute walk from the sea. Restaurant with views over Lyme Bay.

Kington Magna

Village lying to the south west of Gillingham.

MRS G. GOSNEY, KINGTON MANOR FARM, CHURCH HILL, KINGTON MAGNA NEAR GILLINGHAM SP8 5EG (01747 838371). ◆◆◆◆. Attractive farmhouse situated in a quiet, pretty village, with splendid views over the pastoral Blackmore Vale. Near the historic towns of Shaftesbury and Sherborne; Stourhead National Trust house and gardens and stately home of Longleat and Safari Park nearby. Bath 45 minutes' drive. Breakfast £18.50 per person per night. Reductions for children. Excellent pub food nearby. Outdoor swimming pool.[🐕]

Lyme Regis

Picturesque little resort with harbour, once the haunt of smugglers. Shingle beach with sand at low tide. Fishing, sailing and water ski-ing in Lyme Bay. Taunton 28 miles, Dorchester 24, Seaton 8.

MRS J TEDBURY, LITTLE PADDOCKS, YAWL HILL LANE, LYME REGIS DT7 3RW (01297 443085). A six-berth caravan on Devon/Dorset border overlooking Lyme Bay and surrounding countryside. Situated on a smallholding with animals. Fully equipped. Also fully equipped chalet for two. [🛏]

WESTOVER FARM COTTAGES, WOOTTON FITZPAINE, NEAR LYME REGIS, DORSET DT6 6NE (01297 560451). Within walking distance of the sea. Two beautiful cottages, sleep 6/7, with large secluded gardens. Car parking. Logs, Linen available. 3 bedrooms. 🎖🎖🎖🎖 commended. Pets welcome. [Pets £1 per night.]

Piddletrenthide

Village 6 miles north of Dorchester.

THE POACHERS INN, PIDDLETRENTHIDE DT2 7QX (01300 348358; Fax: 01300 348153). On B3143 in lovely Piddle Valley, this delightful Inn offers en suite rooms with colour TV, tea/coffee making, phone. Swimming pool; residents' lounge. Restaurant or Bar meals available. Garden – good dog walks! B&B £27.50. ETC/AA ◆◆◆◆. [Pets £2 per night, £10 per week]

Poole

Popular resort, yachting and watersports centre with large harbour and many creeks. Sand and shingle beaches. Salisbury 30 miles, Dorchester 23, Blandford 14, Wareham 9, Bournemouth 5.

SANDFORD HOLIDAY PARK. A very special place! Situated in an area of outstanding natural beauty near the New Forest, Bournemouth and Poole. ★★★★. Phone WESTSTAR HOLIDAY PARKS on 01202 631600.

Sherbourne

Town with abbey and two castles, one of which was built by Sir Walter Raleigh with lakes and gardens by Capability Brown.

MRS S. STRETTON, BEECH FARM, SIGWELLS, CHARLTON HORETHORNE, NEAR SHERBORNE, DORSET DT9 4LN (01963 220524). Relaxed farmhouse accommodation on our 137 acre dairy farm. Centrally heated with double room en suite, a twin room and family room with guest bathroom. Pets and horses welcome. Evening meals available locally, or by prior arrangement. £16 per person. Open all year [🛏]

**Readers are requested to mention this guidebook
when seeking accommodation
(and please enclose a stamped addressed envelope).**

Studland

Unspoilt seaside village at south-western end of Poole Bay 3 miles north of Swanage.

THE MANOR HOUSE, STUDLAND BAY BH19 3AU (01929 450288). An 18th century Manor House, nestling in 20 acres of secluded grounds. All bedrooms en suite with central heating, colour TV, direct dial telephone, tea/coffee making facilities. 4 Crowns Commended. [Pets £3.00 per night.]

KNOLL HOUSE HOTEL, STUDLAND BN19 3AW (01929 450450; Fax: 01929 450423). Country House Hotel within National Trust reserve. Golden beach. 100 acre grounds. Family suites, six lounges. Tennis, golf, swimming, games rooms, health spa. Full board terms £65-£95 daily. See our Full Page Advertisement under Studland Bay. [pw! £4 nightly]
E-mail: enquiries@knollhouse.co.uk
Website: www.knollhouse.co.uk

Sturminster Newton

Small town on River Stour edged by Blackmoor Vale. Blandford Forum 8 miles.

MRS S. SOFIELD, THE OLD POST OFFICE GUEST HOUSE, HINTON ST. MARY, STURMINSTER NEWTON DT10 ING (Tel: 01258 472366; Fax: 01258 472173). Guests' lounge with games, TV, maps and books. Car Park. Large garden. Footpath and river nearby. Cottage sleeping three also available. Brochure on request. B&B en suite from £18pppn. [pw! Pets £1 per night, £5 per week].

Swanage

Traditional family holiday resort set in a sheltered bay ideal for water sports. Good base for a walking holiday.

FAIRFIELDS HOTEL, STUDLAND BAY, NEAR SWANAGE, DORSET BH19 3AE (Tel/Fax: 01929 450224). A private hotel, family-owned, at the rural heart of a National Trust Conservation area and Studland Nature Reserve. Short walk to three miles of sandy beach.

LIMES HOTEL, 48 PARK ROAD, SWANAGE BH19 2AE (Tel: 01929 422664; Fax: 0870 0548794). Small friendly Hotel. En suite rooms, tea/coffee facilities. Licensed bar. Central heating. Children and pets welcome. Telephone or SAE for brochure. [🐕]
E-mail: info@limeshotel.demon.co.uk
Website: www.limeshotel.demon.co.uk

MRS GILLIAN MACDERMOTT, THE LITTLE MANOR, 389 HIGH STREET, SWANAGE BH19 2NP (Tel & Fax: 01929 422948). A friendly small Guest House where pets are welcome. Television, tea and coffee making facilities in all rooms. Most en suite. [🐕]

MRS M. STOCKLEY, SWANAGE CARAVAN SITE, 17 MOOR ROAD, SWANAGE BH19 1RG (01929 424154). 4/5/6-berth Caravans. Pets welcome. Easter to October. Colour TV. Shop. Parking space. Rose Award Park ✓✓✓✓ [🐕]

Wareham

Picturesque riverside town almost surrounded by earthworks, considered pre-Roman. Nature reserves of great beauty nearby. Weymouth 19 miles, Bournemouth 14, Swanage 10, Poole 6.

CATRIONA AND ALISTAIR MILLER, CROMWELL HOUSE HOTEL LULWORTH COVE BH20 5RJ (01929 400253/400332; Fax: 01929 400566). Comfortable family-run hotel, set in secluded gardens with spectacular sea views. Heated swimming pool, 14 en suite bedrooms. Restaurant, bar wine list. AA★★, RAC ★★. 3 Crowns Commended.

MRS L. S. BARNES, LUCKFORD WOOD HOUSE, EAST STOKE, WAREHAM BH20 6AW (01929 463098; Fax: 01929 405715). Spacious, peaceful surroundings. B&B luxurious farmhouse. Full English breakfast. Camping facilities include showers, toilets. Near Lulworth Cove, Tank Museum and Studland Monkey World. Open all year. From £18. LISTED. AA QQ. [Pets £5 per night]

West Bexington

Seaside village with pebble beach. Chesil beach stretches eastwards. Nearby is Abbotsbury with its Benedictine Abbey and famous Swannery. Dorchester 13 miles, Weymouth 13, Bridport 6.

GORSELANDS CARAVAN PARK, DEPT PW, WEST BEXINGTON-ON-SEA DT2 9DJ (01308 897232; Fax: 01308 897239). Quality graded "very good" park. Fully serviced and equipped 4/6 berth caravans. Shop and launderette on site. Glorious sea views. Good country and seaside walks. One mile to beach. Personal attention. Holiday apartments with sea views and private garden. Pets most welcome. Colour brochure on request. [🐕]

Weymouth

Set in a beautiful bay with fine beaches and a picturesque 17th-century harbour, Weymouth has a wide range of entertainment and leisure amenities.

WEYMOUTH BAY HOLIDAY PARK, PRESTON. One 8-berth Caravan. Near sea. Dogs welcome. APPLY – MRS D. W. CANNON, 151 SANDSTONE ROAD, GROVE PARK, LONDON SE12 0UT (020 8857 7586) [🐕]

DURHAM

DURHAM *Barnard Castle, Cornforth*

Barnard Castle

Market town with Norman ruins. Bowes museum has forty rooms with paintings by El Greco, Goya and Canaletto.

JERSEY FARM HOTEL, DARLINGTON ROAD, BARNARD CASTLE, CO. DURHAM DL12 8TA (Tel: 01833 638223   Fax: 01833 631988). 20 En suite Rooms, five Luxury Suites. Renowned Carvery Restaurant open seven days. Alternative Menu available • Open all day for meals/drinks. Conservatory with Games. Licensed Bar. Mini Breaks available. [pw! Pets £3.50 per week, £15.00 per night] Website: jerseyfarmhotel.enta.net

Castleside

A suburb 2 miles south-west of Consett.

LIZ LAWSON, BEE COTTAGE FARM, CASTLESIDE, CONSETT DH8 9HW (01207 508224). Working farm in lovely surroundings. You will be made most welcome. Ideal for Metro Centre, Durham Cathedral, Beamish Museum etc. Bed and Breakfast; Evening Meal available. ETB 2 Crowns Highly Commended. [🐾]

Cornforth

Village 4 miles north-west of Sedgefield.

ASH HOUSE, 24 THE GREEN, CORNFORTH, DURHAM DL17 9JH (01740 654654). Ideally situated Victorian home, lovingly restored. The elegant rooms are spacious. Adjacent A1(M) Motorway. 10 minutes historic Durham. Excellent value from £18 (£22 single; £45 four-poster). [🐾]

Waterhouses

6 miles west of Durham

MRS P. A. BOOTH, IVESLEY EQUESTRIAN CENTRE, WATERHOUSES, DURHAM DH7 9HB (0191 373 4324; Fax: 0191 373 4757). Elegantly furnished comfortable country house set in 220 acres. Near Durham but quiet and rural. En suite bedrooms. Excellent food. Licensed. Equestrian facilities available.

GLOUCESTERSHIRE

GLOUCESTERSHIRE *Blakeney, Bourton-on-the-Water*

Many of our top quality holiday properties accept pets.

PETS WELCOME

Cottages in Devon, Cornwall, Cotswolds, Pembrokeshire & the Heart of England.

For 120 page 2000 Colour Brochure

FREEPHONE 0800 378771 (24 hrs)

Powells Cottage Holidays, High Street, Saundersfoot, Pembrokeshire SA69 9EJ

IN THE COTSWOLDS. QUALITY PROPERTIES IN WONDERFUL LOCATIONS AT WELCOMING LOW PRICES. MANY LESS THAN £150 PER WEEK FROM OCTOBER TO APRIL. LOTS AT LESS THAN £350 PER WEEK FROM MAY TO SEPTEMBER. PETS, LINEN AND FUEL MOSTLY INCLUDED.

01756 702212 **PHONE FOR FREE 2000 FULL COLOUR BROCHURE**

Oatfield Farm

ETB ♛♛♛ / ♛♛♛♛ *HIGHLY COMMENDED.*

Oatfield provides visitors to the delightful and unspoilt Forest of Dean and Wye Valley with a relaxing, quiet and luxurious holiday. The award-winning 17th century Listed farm buildings, in an old cider orchard 100ft above the Severn Estuary, offers accommodation for two to eight people in six cottages. Exposed beams, log fires, central heating, some four-poster beds, fully-equipped kitchens, laundry room, all weather tennis court and fully inclusive charges. Wide range of attractions and activities for people of all ages. Wonderful dog-walking country. Maximum two dogs. Short Breaks available. Prices per week low season from £228, high season £330.

Mrs Berrisford, Oatfield Farm, Etloe, Blakeney GL15 4AY Tel & Fax: 01594 510372

CHESTER HOUSE

—— Hotel ——

VICTORIA STREET, BOURTON-ON-THE-WATER, GLOUCESTERSHIRE. GL54 2BU

TELEPHONE 01451 820286 • FAX 01451 820471

FREEPHONE 0800 0199577

Bourton-on-the-Water The Venice of the Cotswolds

A haven of peace and comfort tucked away in a quiet backwater of this famous village

Julian & Sue Davies welcome you to Bourton-on-the-Water and the Cotswolds

See also Colour Advertisement on page 22

FHG

Visit the FHG website

www.holidayguides.com

for details of the wide choice of accommodation featured in the full range of FHG titles

The Laurels at Inchbrook

Mrs Lesley Williams-Allen, The Laurels at Inchbrook
Nailsworth GL5 5HA Tel & Fax: 01453 834021
A lovely rambling licensed house and cottage, where dogs and their owners are encouraged to relax and enjoy. All rooms are en suite and include family, twin and double rooms, each with colour TV and hospitality trays. There is wheelchair access and a ground floor room suitable for disabled guests. We have a ground floor panelled lounge full of interesting books and a piano, and on the top floor a games room. Smoking is not allowed (except in the courtyard and garden). The secluded garden with parking backs onto fields and offers a swimming pool and the opportunity to observe wildlife. We are ideally situated for touring all parts of the Cotswolds and West Country, surrounded by a wealth of beautiful countryside, first-class restaurants and pubs, and all kinds of activities. Children and pets welcome. Bed and Breakfast from £20 per person. Dinner by arrangement. Brochure on request. RAC Acclaimed.

The Golden Ball Inn

Delightful 17th Century Inn of warm Cotswold stone, offering good home cooked food, real ales and a welcoming friendly atmosphere. Situated on the beautiful "Donnington Way" (details on request). All rooms en suite. From £22.50 pppn. Honey, Jess and Scrumpy the cat look forward to welcoming you.

The Golden Ball Inn, Lower Swell, Near Stow-on-the-Wold, Cheltenham, Gloucestershire GL54 1LF Telephone 01451 830247

Established 22 years AA ◆◆◆ and RAC Listed
Large Country House with attractive garden, overlooking fields. Four minutes to town centre. One four-poster bedroom; double, twin or family rooms, all en suite. Tea/coffee making facilities, colour TV in all rooms. TV lounge. Central heating. Children and pets welcome. Car park. Bed and Full English Breakfast from £18.00 to £22.00. Open all year except Christmas.
THE LIMES
Evesham Road, Stow-on-the-Wold
GL54 1EN Tel: 01451 830034/831056

Court Farm Randwick, Stroud GL6 6HH. Tel: 01453 764210 Fax: 01453 766428
A 17th century beamed farmhouse, centre of hillside village of Randwick. Beautiful views over Stroud Valleys. Much of our food produced organically on seven acres of meadowland. A stream divides the sloping fields, haven for wildlife. Large garden for guests to enjoy, village pub food. Tourist attractions nearby include Wildfowl Trust, Gloucester Waterways, Prinknash Abbey, Berkeley Castle. Bed and Breakfast from £18 to £20; Evening Meal can be provided. Children and pets welcome.

Dear Rover,
Well, we've just got back from our holidays – absolute bliss and what a lovely place the Downfield is – we got a really warm welcome from the owners. Great walks in the Cotswolds, comfy rooms, a bar, delicious food and the Joneses I brought with me were really pleased as well. I made lots of new friends – there were even some cats to chase!
Why don't you come with me next year and bring your owners with you – Just call Nigel or Maura on the dog and bone on **01453 764496**
Lots of licks, *Toby*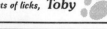

The Downfield Hotel
134 Cainscross Rd,
Stroud, Gloucestershire
GL5 4HN
AA QQQ
ETB 👑👑👑 Commended
RAC Acclaimed

FHG PUBLICATIONS
publish a large range of well-known accommodation guides. We will be happy to send you details or you can use the order form at the back of this book.

244

SYMONDS YAT ROCK

LODGE

SYMONDS YAT ROCK LODGE

Perfect location for walking and touring. Rural situation with forest tracks directly opposite hotel giving easy access to Wye Valley, Forest of Dean and stunning views from Symonds Yat Rock.

Canoeing, climbing, horse riding and cycle tracks all close by.

Accommodation is comfortable and smart and the welcome is friendly in this small family-run hotel. Rooms are all en suite and on the ground floor, directly accessed from the car park.

Six-berth static caravan with stunning views also on site and available for hire.

Licensed restaurant provides good choice of excellent food and wines.

Families catered for.

Dogs welcome. Most of our guests come with their dogs and come back time and again. Come and see for yourself!

HILLERSLAND NEAR COLEFORD GL16 7NY
TEL: 01594 836191 FAX: 01594 836626

Gundog DOGS UNLIMITED Agility

Four acres of Dog Secure grounds, Large Comfortable Farmhouse.
Come and relax in the Country with your Dogs.
Facilities include: Researched Walks, Agility and Gundog
Training by arrangement. See Classified for accommodation details
BAYS COURT, BOLLOW, WESTBURY-ON-SEVERN. 01452 750426

POWELLS COTTAGE HOLIDAYS, HIGH STREET, SAUNDERSFOOT, PEM-BROKESHIRE SA69 9EJ. Many of our top quality holiday properties accept pets. Cottages in Devon, Cornwall, Cotswolds, Pembrokeshire and Heart of England. For colour brochure FREEPHONE 0800 378771 (24 hours).

WELCOME COTTAGE HOLIDAYS. Quality Cottages in wonderful locations at welcoming low prices. Pets, linen and fuel mostly included. PHONE FOR FREE 2000 FULL COLOUR BROCHURE 01756 702208.

SYMBOLS

🐕 Indicates that pets are welcome free of charge.

£ Indicates that a charge is made for pets: nightly or weekly.

pw! Shows some special provision for pets; exercise facility, feeding or accommodation arrangement.

⌂ Indicates separate pets accommodation.

Blakeney

Village on the Severn Estuary, north east of Lydney

MRS BERRISFORD, OATFIELD FARM, ETLOE, BLAKENEY GL15 4AY (Telephone& Fax: 01594 510372). ETC 4/5 Keys HIGHLY COMMENDED. Six award-winning 17th century Listed farm buildings with exposed beams, log fires, central heating, some four-poster beds, fully-equipped kitchens, laundry room, all weather tennis court and fully inclusive charges. Short Breaks available. Prices per week: low season from £228, high season £330. [🐴]

Bourton-on-the-Water

Delightfully situated on the River Windrush which is crossed by miniature stone bridges. Stow-on-the-Wold 4 miles.

CHESTER HOUSE HOTEL, VICTORIA STREET, BOURTON-ON-THE-WATER GL54 2BU (01451 820286; FREEPHONE 0800 0199577). Personally supervised by proprietor Mr Julian Davies. All rooms en suite, all with central heating, colour TV, radio, phone, tea/coffee making facilities. Ideal for touring Cotswolds. [🐴]

Cheltenham

Anglo-Saxon market town transformed into elegant Regency resort with the discovery of medicinal springs. 8 miles east of Gloucester.

CHARLTON KINGS HOTEL, CHELTENHAM, GLOUCESTER GL52 6UU (01242 231061; Fax: 01242 241900). Ideal venue for Cheltenham and the Cotswolds. Most rooms have views of the Cotswold Hills. We offer a standard of service only a small hotel can provide. Four Crowns Highly Commended. [🐴]

Coleford

Small town in Forest of Dean 3 miles River Wye. Gloucester 19 miles, Chepstow 13, Monmouth 6.

TUDOR FARMHOUSE HOTEL & RESTAURANT, CLEARWELL, COLEFORD (01594 833046; Fax: 01594 837093). Extensive grounds (14 acres) ideal for dog walking. 14 bedrooms with bathrooms en suite, colour TV, tea/coffee facilities. Excellent traditional choice and a comprehensive wine list.
E–mail:reservations@tudorfarm.u-net.com

Forest of Dean

Formerly a royal hunting ground, this scenic area lies between the rivers Severn and Wye.

DRYSLADE FARM, ENGLISH BICKNOR, COLEFORD (Tel & Fax: 01594 860259). Daphne and Phil warmly welcome you and your dogs at their 17th century farmhouse on family working farm, in Royal Forest of Dean, with its woodland walking. B&B with excellent breakfast, also spacious self-contained ground floor flat, recommended for disabled. HTB ◆◆◆, ♔♔♔♔.

GLOUCESTERSHIRE

GUNN MILL HOUSE COUNTRY GUEST HOUSE, LOWER SPOUT LANE, MITCHELDEAN GL17 0EA (Tel & Fax: 01594 827577). Eight individually designed rooms including four-poster and suites with direct access to 5-acre garden and Forest of Dean. All en suite, TV. Fine dining. Licensed.[Pets £5 per stay]. SEE DISPLAY ADVERT.
E–mail: info@gunnmillhouse.co.uk
Website: www.gunnmillhouse.co.uk

THE SPEECH HOUSE, COLEFORD, FOREST OF DEAN GL16 7EL (01594 822607 Fax: 01594 823658). A friendly hotel set in the heart of the Forest of Dean, the perfect place to get away from it all. 14 en suite bedrooms. Lavish restaurant. Aqua spa and beauty suite. [Pets £10 per stay]

Lydney

Small town 8 miles north-east of Chepstow. Nearby Lydney Park has ruined 12th-century castle and remains of Roman temple set amongst woodland, lakes, fine shrubs and trees.

PARKEND HOUSE HOTEL, PARKEND, NEAR LYDNEY GL15 4HL (01594 563666). Small country hotel surrounded by parkland. All rooms en suite. Good food and friendly service. Pets and children welcome. Ideal for Cheltenham, Bath and Bristol. [Pets £1.50 per night.]

Nailsworth

Hilly town 4 miles south of Stroud.

LESLEY WILLIAMS-ALLEN, THE LAURELS, INCHBROOK, NAILSWORTH GL5 5HA (Tel/Fax: 01453 834021). A lovely rambling licensed house and cottage, where dogs and their owners are encouraged to relax and enjoy. Ideally situated for touring all parts of the Cotswolds and West Country. Brochure. B&B from £20. [🐕]

Painswick

Beautiful little Cotswold town with characteristic stone-built houses

MISS E. COLLETT, HAMBUTTS MYND, EDGE ROAD, PAINSWICK GL6 6UP (Tel/Fax:01452 812352). Bed and Breakfast in an old Converted Corn Mill. Very quiet with superb views. Three minutes to the centre of the village. Central heating. One double room, one twin, one single, all with TV. From £27 to £45 per night. ALL ROOMS EN SUITE. RAC Acclaimed, Commended. [🐕]

NOTE

All the information in this book is given in good faith in the belief that it is correct. However, the publishers cannot guarantee the facts given in these pages, neither are they responsible for changes in policy, ownership or terms that may take place after the date of going to press. Readers should always satisfy themselves that the facilities they require are available and that the terms, if quoted, still apply.

Stow-on-the-Wold

Charming Cotswold hill-top market town with several old inns and interesting buildings. Birmingham 45 miles, Gloucester 26, Stratford-upon-Avon 21, Cheltenham 18, Chipping Norton 9.

THE GOLDEN BALL INN, LOWER SWELL, NEAR STOW-ON-THE-WOLD, CHELTENHAM, GLOUCESTERSHIRE GL54 1LF (01451 830247). Delightful 17th Century Village Inn. Home cooked food, friendly atmosphere. Situated on the beautiful "Donnington Way" (details on request). All rooms en suite. From £22.50 pppn. [🐾]

THE LIMES, EVESHAM ROAD, STOW-ON-THE-WOLD GL54 1EN (01451 830034/831056). Large country house. Attractive garden, overlooking fields, 4 minutes town centre. Television lounge. Central heating. Car park. Bed and Breakfast from £18 to £22.00. Children and pets welcome. AA ◆◆◆, RAC Listed. Twin, double or family rooms, all en suite. [🐾]

Stroud

Cotswold town on River Frome below picturesque Stroudwater Hills, formerly renowned for cloth-making. Bristol 32 miles, Bath 29, Chippenham 25, Cheltenham 14, Gloucester 9.

COURT FARM, RANDWICK, STROUD GL6 6HH (01453 764210; Fax: 01453 766428). A 17th century beamed farmhouse on working farm. Much of our food produced organically. Large garden. Abundant wildlife. Children and pets welcome. [🐾]

DOWNFIELD HOTEL, CAINSCROSS ROAD, STROUD GL5 4HN (01453 764496). Dogs and children most welcome. Easy to find – just 5 miles from M5 – and easy to park. Ideal location for exploring Cotswolds. Comfortable lounges, home-cooked evening meal, cosy bar – all at sensible prices. 3 Crowns, AA QQQ, RAC Acclaimed. [🐾],

Symonds Yat

Popular beauty spot on River Wye, 4 miles north-east of Monmouth.

PAUL & CATHY KORN, SYMONDS YAT ROCK LODGE, HILLERSLAND, NEAR COLEFORD GL16 7NY (Tel: 01594 836191; Fax: 01594 836626). Family-run lodge in Royal Forest of Dean near Wye Valley. All rooms en suite, colour TV, central heating. Licensed restaurant. Dogs welcome. Brochure on request. [🐾]

Westbury-on-Severn

Village 4 miles east of Cinderford. Nearby Westbury Court (NT) has a lovely formal water garden.

BAYS COURT, BOLLOW, WESTBURY-ON-SEVERN GL14 1QX (01452 750426). Listed Country Farmhouse in four acres of dog-secure grounds. Large en suite rooms, TV, tea and coffee, guest lounge. Ideal for Forest of Dean and Cotswolds. B&B from £20 per night. See display for dog facilities. [pw! 🐾]

THE WOODLANDS LODGE HOTEL

Bartley Road, Woodlands, New Forest, Hampshire SO40 7GN

AA   AA   **Reservations: (023) 80 292257**   ETC
 ★★★   Fax: (023) 80 293090   ★★★

e-mail: woodlands@nortels.ltd.uk   Website: www.nortels.ltd.uk

RELAXATION, COMFORT AND TRANQUILLITY

The Woodlands Lodge Hotel is a luxuriously restored Georgian Country House, set within the beautiful New Forest, yet only 15 minutes from Southampton. This former hunting lodge has been totally refurbished and offers guests comfort, peace and tranquillity.

Our attractive gardens, set in three acres, have direct access to the forest, and are ideal for romantic walks. Golf and horse riding are both available nearby and can be arranged by the hotel. Come and unwind from the stress of everyday life and enjoy pure luxury without ostentation.

All bedrooms enjoy full en suite facilities of whirlpool bath and separate shower and have king size beds, 21" television, hairdryer, trouser press, tea and coffee making facilities and direct dial telephone. Some rooms have features including real flame fires, four-poster bed, balcony and forest views. The service is friendly, efficient and informal.

Our quality four course menu, served in the elegant dining room, is changed daily to make use of fresh local produce and has an AA rosette award for excellence. The menu is complemented by an interesting and reasonably priced wine list.

'Woodlands Lodge ~ where a
warm welcome awaits you'

FREE and REDUCED RATE Holiday Visits!
Don't miss our Readers' Offer Vouchers on pages 53 to 70

Ashurst

Three miles north-east of Lyndhurst.

WOODLANDS LODGE HOTEL, BARTLEY ROAD, ASHURST, WOODLANDS SO40 7GN (Tel: (023) 80 292257; Fax: (023) 80 293090). Luxury Hotel offering peace and tranquillity. 16 bedrooms, all en suite with whirlpool bath, with TV, hairdryer, telephone etc. AA Award Winning Restaurant. Excellent wine list. Stables available. ETC ★★★.
E–mail: woodlands@nortels.ltd.uk
Website: www.nortels.ltd.uk

Bramshaw

New Forest village surrounded by National Trust land. Southampton 10 miles, Lyndhurst 6.

BRAMBLE HILL HOTEL, BRAMSHAW, NEAR LYNDHURST SO43 7JG (023 8081 3165). Fully licensed country house hotel with own livery stables. Unique seclusion amidst glorious surroundings. Unlimited riding and walking territory. Dogs welcome. [Pets £4 per night.] DIY livery for horses.

Brockenhurst

Popular village attractively situated in New Forest. Golf course. Bournemouth 18 miles, Southampton 13, Lymington 5, Lyndhurst 4.

WHITLEY RIDGE COUNTRY HOUSE HOTEL, BEAULIEU ROAD, BROCKEN-HURST SO42 7QL (01590 622354; Fax: 01590 622856). Georgian Hotel set in 5 acres of secluded grounds. 14 bedrooms, all en suite, cosy bar and splendid dining room. Superb cuisine, friendly and efficient service. Ideally located for the New Forest. [Pets £3 per night]

Faccombe

Village south wesst of Newbury.

JACK RUSSELL INN, FACCOMBE, HAMPSHIRE SP11 0DS (01264 737315). In the tranquil heart of the verdant Hampshire countryside, this little pub represents the very essence of English rural life, real ale and first-rate wholesome food. Three miles off the A343. Three comfortable en suite bedrooms. Children welcome, beer garden and play equipment. [🐾]

Fareham

Old market town, six miles north-west of Portsmouth across the harbour

ELLERSLIE TOURING CARAVAN & CAMPING PARK, DOWNEND ROAD, FAREHAM PO16 8TS (Tel/Fax: 01329 822248; Mobile 0411 446701). Small partly wooded site. Close to stables, health club, golf course, boating facilities, sites of historic interest. Car and caravan plus two persons £7 per night. Chemical emptying. Food preparation and wash room. Raised barbecues allowed. Free showers. Southern Tourist Board Graded, AA & RAC Listed

Hayling Island

Resort with sandy beaches. Ferry to Portsmouth and Southsea. Linked by bridge to Havant (5 miles).

HAYLING HOLIDAYS LTD, 63 ELM GROVE, HAYLING ISLAND PO11 9EA (Tel/Fax: 023 9246 7271). ETC 𝔛𝔛𝔛 to 𝔛𝔛𝔛𝔛 up to Commended. Wide selection of holiday homes and caravans; superbly equipped and very clean. Self catering up to 7 persons. Telephone now for free colour brochure. [Pets £15 per week.]

Lymington

Residential town and yachting centre 15 miles east of Bournemouth.

MRS J. FINCH, "DOLPHINS", 6 EMSWORTH ROAD, LYMINGTON SO41 9BL (Tel: 01590 676108/679545 Fax: 01590 688275). Single, twin, double and family rooms all with colour TV and tea/coffee making facilities; king-size or twin en suite available. Doggy-bed provided if required. Park two minutes' walk. Please write or telephone for brochure. [🐕]

MRS P. J. ELLIS, EFFORD COTTAGE, EVERTON, LYMINGTON, HAMPSHIRE SO41 0JD (Tel & Fax: 01590 642315; Fax: 01590 641030). Friendly, award winning Georgian cottage in an acre of garden. Excellent centre for New Forest and South Coat. All rooms en suite with luxury facilities. B&B from £23pp. No children RAC/AA/STB ◆◆◆◆◆. [From £2 per night]
E–mail: effcottage@aol.com

Lyndhurst

Good base for enjoying the fascinating New Forest as well as the Hampshire coastal resorts. Bournemouth 20 miles, Southampton 9.

THE CROWN HOTEL, LYNDHURST, NEW FOREST S043 7NF (Tel: 023 8028 2922; Fax: 023 8028 2751). A mellow, listed building in the centre of the village, an ideal base for exploring the delights of the New Forest with your canine friend(s). Free parking, quiet garden, three star luxury and animal loving staff. [Pets £8.50 per night].
E–mail: crown@marsonhotels.co.uk

ORMONDE HOUSE HOTEL, SOUTHAMPTON ROAD, LYNDHURST SO43 7BT (023 8028 2806, Fax: 023 8028 2004). AA ◆◆◆◆. Opposite open forest, easy drive to Exbury Gardens and Bealieu. Pretty en suite rooms with Sky TV, phone and beverage making. Super lux rooms with whirlpool baths and kingsize beds. Bar, lounge and delicious dinners available. [Pets £2.50 per night — free from Nov-Feb]
Website: www.ormondehouse.co.uk

SYMBOLS

🐕   Indicates that pets are welcome free of charge.

£   Indicates that a charge is made for pets: nightly or weekly.

pw!   Shows some special provision for pets; exercise facility, feeding or accommodation arrangement.

⌂   Indicates separate pets accommodation.

New Forest

Area of heath and woodland of nearly 150 square miles, formerly Royal hunting grounds.

MRS J. PEARCE, ST. URSULA, 30 HOBART ROAD, NEW MILTON BH25 6EG (01425 613515). Excellent facilities and warm welcome for well behaved pets and owners! Ground floor suite suitable for disabled guests, plus single and twin rooms. Bed & Breakfast from £19. [🐎]

Luxury 2-bedroomed residential-type caravan, (sleeps 4/6). Maintained to high standard, full kItchen, bathroom, sitting/dining room, own garden. Idyllic setting in heart of New Forest. Non-smoking, ample parking. Children over 5 years. Well behaved dogs welcome. £185-£255 (May-Sept). MRS E. MATTHEWS, THE ACORNS, OGDENS, NEAR FORDINGBRIDGE SP6 2PY (01425 655552) [Pets £10 per week]

THE WATERSPLASH HOTEL, THE RISE, BROCKENHURST SO42 7ZP. Prestigious New Forest family-run country house hotel set in large garden. Noted for fine personal service, accommodation and traditional English cuisine at its best. All rooms en suite. Luxury 4 poster with double spa bath. Swimming pool. RAC, AA ★★, 4 Crowns Commended, Les Routiers, Ashley Courtenay. Colour brochure available (01590 622344).[🐎]

Portsmouth

Historic port and naval base, with Nelson's flagship HMS Victory in harbour.

The best of 2 star accommodation with a superb location on Southsea seafront. All rooms en suite, Satellite TV etc. Passenger lift, Licensed bar and Restaurant, Car Park. Brochure with pleasure. ANTOINETTE STRETTON, THE SEACREST HOTEL, 12 SOUTH PARADE, SOUTHSEA, PORTSMOUTH PO5 2JB (Tel: 02392 733192; Fax: 02392 832523)

Ringwood

Busy market town, centre for trout fishing, trekking and rambling. Bournemouth 13 miles

MR AND MRS D. C. HAYLES, BURBUSH FARM, POUND LANE, BURLEY, NEAR RINGWOOD BE24 4EF (01425 403238). Character cottages delightfully situated in the heart of the New Forest close to Burley village. Equipped to highest standard with central heating. Each sleeps five. From £200 per week. [Pets £15 per week]

JENNY MONGER, LITTLE HORSESHOES, SOUTH GORLEY, RINGWOOD BH24 3NL (01425 479340). ETC 🏠🏠🏠 Commended. Cosy, superior modern bungalow set in 3½ acres, with wild ponies grazing outside our gate. Wonderful walking and riding in the ancient hunting forests/heaths. Horses and dogs welcome. E-mail: jenny@littlehorseshoes.freeserve.co.uk

Sway

Village in southern part of New Forest and within easy reach of sea. Lymington 4 miles south east

MRS THELMA ROWE, 9 CRUSE CLOSE, SWAY SO41 6AY (01590 683092). Ground floor suite of rooms (bedroom, bathroom, sitting room) plus 1st floor bedroom. Tea-making, fridge, TV. Quiet, very comfortable and friendly accommodation.

Winchester

Site of an old Roman town. Ancient capital of Wessex and of England. Notable Cathedral, famous boys' public school, a wealth of old and historic buildings.

ROYAL HOTEL, ST PETER STREET, WINCHESTER SO23 8BS (01962 840840; Fax: 01962 841582). Quality hotel of character quietly located in the heart of England's ancient capital. All rooms en suite with satellite TV, tea and coffee and telephone. 5 Crowns Highly Commended. [🐾]

Woodfalls

Village on the hampshire/Wiltshire border south of Salisbury.

THE WOODFALLS INN, THE RIDGE, WOODFALLS, HAMPSHIRE SP5 2LN (Tel: 01725 513222; Fax: 01725 513220). AA QQQQQ Premier selected, ETC ◆◆◆◆◆ Silver Award. Nestling on the northern edge of the New Forest, this award-winning inn has a restaurant and a bar serving food and real ales. [Pets £4.95 per night, £25.00 per week]
E–mail: woodfalls@aol.com
Website: www.trad-inns.co.uk

Key to Tourist Board Ratings

 The Crown Scheme

The English Tourism Council (formerly the English Tourist Board) has joined with the **AA** and **RAC** to create a new, easily understood quality rating for serviced accommodation.

Hotels will receive a grading ranging from **one to five STARS (★)**. Other serviced accommodation such as **guest houses** and **B&B establishments** will be graded from **one to five DIAMONDS (◆)**. These ratings represent Quality, Service and Hospitality not just facilities.

NB.Some properties had not been assessed at the time of going to press and in these cases the publishers have included the old CROWN gradings.

The Key Scheme

The Key Scheme covering self-catering in cottages, bungalows, flats, houseboats, houses, chalets, etc remains unchanged. The classification from **One to Five KEYS** indicates the range of facilities and equipment. Higher quality standards are indicated by the terms APPROVED, COMMENDED, HIGHLY COMMENDED AND DE LUXE.

HEREFORDSHIRE

HEREFORDSHIRE *Felton, Hereford, Kington, Ledbury*

257

Ye Hostelrie Hotel

AA ★★   ETC ★★ Hotel

GOODRICH, ROSS ON WYE, HEREFORDSHIRE HR9 6HX

Tel: 01600 890241 Fax: 01600 890838

Enjoy comfort and good food at this fully centrally heated 17th Century Inn. Situated near to Goodrich Castle in a beautiful part of the Wye Valley, it affords easy access to the Forest of Dean, rural Herefordshire and Wales; although in a quiet village it is only a mile from the A40. Dine in the elegant surroundings of the restaurant, choosing from either the table d'hôte or à la carte Menus. In addition on offer is a very extensive Bar Menu. All of the dishes are home-made on the premises, using locally grown produce. A choice of real ales and fine wines, Morning Coffee and Afternoon Cream Tea is also available.

Prices: Bed and Breakfast in a double, twin bedded room or family room with en suite facilities, colour television, courtesy tray, clock radio, from: Double £48, Single £31.50; a cot can be provided.

Pets are welcome in the bedrooms and garden.

RAC ACCLAIMED **W O O D L E A   H O T E L** ❦❦❦ COMMENDED

Symonds Yat West, Ross-on-Wye, Herefordshire HR9 6BL Tel and Fax: 01600 890206

Residential and restaurant licence; 7 bedrooms, all with private facilities; Pets most welcome.

Family-run hotel overlooking the famous Wye Rapids in peaceful and picturesque surroundings. Highest quality food and attentive service. Recommended for a quiet country holiday at any time of year, the hotel has splendidly equipped double, twin, single and family-size guest rooms, all with colour television; special 'bargain breaks' represent excellent value.

Felton

Village on the A4103 north east of Hereford.

MARJORIE AND BRIAN ROBY, FELTON HOUSE, FELTON, NEAR HEREFORD HR1 3PH (Tel & Fax: 01432 820366). AA ◆◆◆◆. Period-furnished Country House in tranquil setting. Double, single, twin-bedded rooms. Bed and Breakfast £23.00. Vegetarian choice. Good local Inns for evening meals. Ideal locality for touring. Non-smoking. [🐕]
Website: www.smoothhound.co.uk/hotels/felton.html

Hereford

Well-known touring centre on River Wye. Good sport and entertainment facilities including steeple-chasing. Cheltenham 37 miles, Gloucester 28, Ross-on-Wye 15.

DIANA SINCLAIR, HOLLY HOUSE FARM, ALLENSMORE, HEREFORD HR2 9BH (01432 277294; Fax: 01432 261285; Mobile: 0589 830 223). Escape with your horse or dog to our spacious luxury farmhouse. Bed and Breakfast from £20.

NEW PRIORY HOTEL, STRETTON SUGWAS, HEREFORD HR4 7AR (01432 760264; Fax: 01432 761809). The New Priory Hotel is situated just a short distance from the Hereford city limits in 3½ acre grounds. 10 bedrooms all with private bath or shower except for single rooms which have an adjacent shower. Two Four-poster beds. 3 Crowns. [🐕]

THE STEPPES, ULLINGSWICK, NEAR HEREFORD HR1 3JG (01432 820424; Fax: 01432 820042). Award-winning hotel with intimate atmosphere. Large luxury en suite bedrooms. Set in Wye Valley within easy reach of Malverns and Black Mountains. Non-smoking. WHICH? Hotel Guide, AA ★★, 2 Food Rosettes, Good Hotel Guide, Johansens, Four Crowns Highly Commended. [Pets £3 per week]

Kington

Town on River Arrow, close to Welsh border, 12 miles north of Leominster.

MRS C. D. WILLIAMS, RADNOR'S END, HUNTINGTON, KINGTON HR5 3NZ (01544 370289). Detached cottage (sleeps 5) in lovely unspoiled Welsh border countryside, where rolling hills are home to Buzzard, Kestrel, Red Kite and a rich variety of other birds and wild flowers. Offa's Dyke footpath and Kilvert's Country nearby. Ample parking, lawn. [🐕]

RIDGE VIEW COTTAGE, BRADNOR GREEN, KINGTON. Detached 17th century cottage in beautiful location. Sleeps 5/7 plus cot. All electric. Terms from £130-£230 per week. Apply: MR AND MRS THOMAS, 228 MARY VALE ROAD, BOURNVILLE, BIRMINGHAM B30 1PJ (0121 628 0164). [🐕]

Ledbury

Pleasant town ideally situated for Cotswolds and Wye Valley. Good centre for bowls, fishing, riding and tennis. Monmouth 23 miles, Leominster 22, Gloucester 17, Tewkesbury 14, Malvern 8.

CHURCH FARM, CODDINGTON, LEDBURY HR8 1JJ (01531 640271). Black and white 16th-century Farmhouse on a working farm close to the Malvern Hills — ideal for touring and walking. Two double and one twin bedrooms. Excellent home cooking. Warm welcome assured. Open all year. [🐕]

Much Birch

Village six miles south of Hereford.

POOLSPRINGE FARM COTTAGES. Barn conversion on 17th century, 50 acre farm. Ideal for touring. Indoor heated swimming pool, games room and sauna. 🏠🏠🏠🏠. APPLY: DAVID AND VAL BEAUMONT, POOLSPRINGE FARM, MUCH BIRCH, HEREFORD HR2 8JJ (Tel & Fax: 01981 540355). Pets welcome.

SYMBOLS

🐕   Indicates that pets are welcome free of charge.

£   Indicates that a charge is made for pets: nightly or weekly.

pw!   Shows some special provision for pets; exercise facility, feeding or accommodation arrangement.

⌂   Indicates separate pets accommodation.

Much Cowarne

Village 5 miles south west of Bromyard.

MR & MRS R.M. BRADBURY, COWARNE HALL COTTAGES, MUCH COWARNE
HR7 4JQ (Tel: 01432 820317; Fax: 01432 820093). Luxurious holiday cottage
accommodation, centrally heated, with patio, garden and parking. Within easy
reach of Malvern, Bromyard, Hereford and Worcester. Ideal for dog walks. [pw!
£12 per week per pet].
E–mail: rm@cowarnehall.freeserve.co.uk

Pembridge

Tiny mediaeval village surrounded by meadows and orchards.

MRS N. OWENS, THE GROVE, PEMBRIDGE, LEOMINSTER. HR6 9HP (01544
388268). The farm is mixed arable and stock and there are lovely little woodland and riverside walks on the farm itself. Pets welcome under strict control.
Friendly farm atmosphere. Sleeps 4. Terms from £140 per week. ♔♔♔♔
Commended. [Pets £5 per week]

Ross-on-Wye

*An attractive town standing on a hill rising from the left bank on the Wye. Cardiff 47 miles,
Gloucester 17.*

THE KING'S HEAD HOTEL, 8 HIGH STREET, ROSS-ON-WYE HR9 5HL (FREEP-
HONE: 0800 801098). Small coaching inn dating back to the 14th century with
all bedrooms offering en suite bathrooms and a full range of modern amenities.
A la carte menu offers home-cooked food which is served in a warm and
friendly atmosphere. [🐾]
Website: www.kingshead.co.uk

THE ARCHES HOTEL, WALFORD ROAD, ROSS-ON-WYE HR9 5PT (01989
563348). Georgian-style House. Lovely rooms with all facilities; en suite available. Centrally heated. Pets welcome. Bed and Breakfast or Half Board, weekly
reductions available. AA QQQQ Selected, RAC Acclaimed, Les Routiers, Three
Crowns. [Pets £1 per night]

THE INN ON THE WYE, KERNE BRIDGE, GOODRICH, NR. ROSS-ON-WYE HR9
5QT (Tel: 01600 890872 Fax: 01600 890594). Beautifully restored 18th century
coaching inn, near Goodrich Castle on the banks of the River Wye. All bedrooms
en suite. Peaceful country walks, ideal base for touring.
E–mail: theinnonthewye@kernebridge.freeserve.co.uk

WOODLEA HOTEL SYMONDS YAT WEST, ROSS-ON-WYE, HEREFORDSHIRE
HR9 6BL (Tel and Fax: 01600 890206). Family-run hotel in peaceful and picturesque surroundings. Highest quality food and attentive service. Double,
twin, single and family-size guest rooms. Special 'bargain breaks' represent
excellent value. 3 Crowns Commended, RAC Acclaimed.

YE HOSTELRIE, GOODRICH, ROSS-ON-WYE HR9 6HX (01600 890241). Enjoy comfort and good food at this fully centrally heated 17th Century Inn. We have a reputation for quality food at a reasonable price. [🛏]

ISLES OF SCILLY

St Mary's

Largest of group of granite islands and islets off Cornish Coast. Terminus for air and sea services from mainland. Main income from flower-growing. Seabirds, dolphins and seals abound.

MRS PAMELA MUMFORD, SALLAKEE FARM, ST. MARY'S TR21 0NZ (01720 422391). Self catering farm cottage, available all year round. Sleeps 5. Woodburner. Near beach and coastal paths. Pets welcome. Write or phone for details. ♔♔♔.

FOR THE MUTUAL GUIDANCE OF GUEST AND HOST

Every year literally thousands of holidays, short breaks and overnight stops are arranged through our guides, the vast majority without any problems at all. In a handful of cases, however, difficulties do arise about bookings, which often could have been prevented from the outset.

It is important to remember that when accommodation has been booked, both parties – guests and hosts – have entered into a form of contract. We hope that the following points will provide helpful guidance.

GUESTS: When enquiring about accommodation, be as precise as possible. Give exact dates, numbers in your party and the ages of any children. State the number and type of rooms wanted and also what catering you require – bed and breakfast, full board etc. Make sure that the position about evening meals is clear – and about pets, reductions for children or any other special points.

Read our reviews carefully to ensure that the proprietors you are going to contact can supply what you want. Ask for a letter confirming all arrangements, if possible.

If you have to cancel, do so as soon as possible. Proprietors do have the right to retain deposits and under certain circumstances to charge for cancelled holidays if adequate notice is not given and they cannot re-let the accommodation.

HOSTS: Give details about your facilities and about any special conditions. Explain your deposit system clearly and arrangements for cancellations, charges etc. and whether or not your terms include VAT.

If for any reason you are unable to fulfil an agreed booking without adequate notice, you may be under an obligation to arrange suitable alternative accommodation or to make some form of compensation.

While every effort is made to ensure accuracy, we regret that FHG Publications cannot accept responsibility for errors, omissions or misrepresentations in our entries or any consequences thereof.

Prices in particular should be checked because we go to press early. We will follow up complaints but cannot act as arbiters or agents for either party.

ISLE OF WIGHT

ISLE OF WIGHT *Alum Bay, Bonchurch, Cowes, Freshwater*

 **Holiday Apartments** 🏆🏆🏆 Commended
In acres of National Trust land with breathtaking
views over the Needles. Lovely two-bedroom
apartments – fully equipped for four including
colour television. Licensed restaurant on site –
10% discount to residents. Own two acre pitch and putt course (good greens),
free to residents. Open all year. Dogs welcome
Colour brochure: **Marion Smith, Headon Hall, Alum Bay,
Isle of Wight PO39 0JD. Tel: 01983 752123**

ASHCLIFF HOLIDAY APARTMENTS
Bonchurch, Isle of Wight PO38 1NT
Idyllic and secluded position in the picturesque seaside village of Bonchurch.
Four self-contained apartments within Victorian house, set in large south-
facing gardens with sea views and sheltered by a thickly wooded cliff. Large,
private car park. ETC 🏆🏆🏆 Commended. Dogs very welcome. *For free brochure Tel: (01983) 853919*

RAC ★★★ **BONCHURCH MANOR** AA ★★★
Bonchurch, Isle of Wight PO38 1NU Tel: 01983 852868
Bonchurch Manor is situated on the sheltered south coast of the Isle of
Wight with spacious grounds overlooking the sea. All bedrooms with private
facilities, colour TV, telephone and hair dryer. Five course table d'hôte and à la carte menu.
Hospitality and Restaurant Merit, Ashley Courtenay. Dogs not to be left in rooms unattended.

20 Deluxe and Luxury 4 and 6 berth Caravans on quiet country Park in rural surroundings close to
Cowes. All caravans are fully self-contained and are connected to all mains services. There is a
Laundry Room on the Park and a Shop which can cater for all your daily needs.
Bring your pets for a holiday too!
Fax or Phone: 01983 292859 for brochure. Member of BH & HPA & STB.

 MOUNTFIELD Holiday Park BHHPA STB

Freshwater, Isle of Wight. Telephone: Freshwater (01983) 752993
Set in four acres of beautiful countryside, 2/6 berth Bungalows, 2/6
berth Chalets, 2/6 berth Caravans all with own toilet, bath or shower,
TV. Table tennis room. Heated swimming pool. Play area for children
with swings etc. SAE, please.
Proprietors: **The Roberts Family, Mountfield Holiday Park,
Norton Green, Freshwater, Isle of Wight.**

Readers are requested to mention this guidebook
when seeking accommodation
(and please enclose a stamped addressed envelope).

Alum Bay

On west of island, one mile from the Needles and lighthouse. Newport 13 miles, Yarmouth 5.

MARION SMITH, HEADON HALL, ALUM BAY PO39 0JD (01983 752123). Lovely two bedroom apartments, fully equipped for 4/6, including colour television. Breathtaking views. Dogs welcome. [Pets £10 per week.]

Bonchurch

One mile north-east of Ventnor

MR & MRS T.J. FOLEY, ASHCLIFF HOLIDAY APARTMENTS, BONCHURCH PO38 1NT(01983 853919). Four self-contained apartments within Victorian house. Large south facing gardens. Sea views. Large private car park. ♀♀♀♀ Commended. [🐾],

BONCHURCH MANOR, BONCHURCH PO38 1NU (01983 852868). Bonchurch Manor combines elegance and comfort to provide a perfect setting for a holiday at any time of the year. Tastefully furnished bedrooms all with private facilities. Restaurant is regarded as one of the finest on the island. [🐾]

Cowes

Yachting centre with yearly regatta since 1814. Newport 4 miles.

SUNNYCOTT CARAVAN PARK, COWES PO31 8NN (Tel & Fax: 01983 292859). 20 Deluxe and Luxury 4 and 6 berth caravans on quiet country park in rural surroundings. Laundry room and shop on site. Bring your pets for a holiday too! [🐾]

Freshwater

Pleasant and quiet resort on Freshwater Bay, near the start of the Tennyson Trail. Sandown 20 miles, Cowes 15, Newport 11, Yarmouth 4.

THE ROBERTS FAMILY, MOUNTFIELD HOLIDAY PARK, NORTON GREEN, FRESHWATER (01983 752993). 2/6-berth Bungalows, Chalets and Caravans, all set in beautiful countryside. Television. ✓✓✓✓. [Pets £15 per week].

Niton Undercliffe

Delightful village near sea at the southernmost part of the island. Several secluded chines nearby, cliff walks. Ventnor 5 miles.

MR AND MRS D. A. HERON, WINDCLIFFE MANOR, SANDROCK ROAD, NITON UNDERCLIFFE PO38 2NG (Tel & Fax: 01983 730215). Bed, Breakfast and Evening Meal in a historic Manor House set in wooded gardens. Heated pool. Colour television. Games room. Children and dogs welcome. Three Crowns Highly Commended. [pw!]

Ryde

Popular resort and yachting centre, fine sands, pier. Shanklin 9 miles, Newport 7, Sandown 6.

HILLGROVE PARK, FIELD LANE, ST HELENS, NEAR RYDE PO33 1UT (01983 872802). Select site 10 minutes sea, 3 minutes bus stop. Self-service shop, heated swimming pool. Pets welcome. Phone for brochure. [Pets £14.00 per week]

Shanklin

Safe sandy beaches and traditional entertainments make this a family favourite. Cliff lift connects the beach to the cliff top.

FARRINGFORD HOTEL, 19 HOPE ROAD, SHANKLIN PO37 6EA (01983 862176). 3 Crowns Commended. Licensed hotel, close to beach and old village. TV, tea/coffee, hairdryer all rooms. En suite available. Parking. B&B from £18. [🐕]
E–mail: farr-shanklin@netguides.co.uk

ISLAND COTTAGE HOLIDAYS. Charming cottages in lovely rural surroundings and close to the sea. Some cottages on farms - some with swimming pools - some in walking distance of sandy beaches. All cottages equipped to a high standard and graded for quality by the Tourist Board. Brochure: HONOR VASS, THE OLD VICARAGE, KINGSTON, CORFE CASTLE, DORSET BH20 5LH. (Tel: 01929 480080; Fax: 01929 481070)

ALAN AND LYN AYLOTT, HARROW LODGE HOTEL, EASTCLIFF PROMENADE, SHANKLIN (01983 862800; Fax: 01983 868889). Family-run hotel, all rooms en suite with colour TV. Licensed bar, varied menu. Open March to October. Three Crowns Commended. [Pets £10 per week]

Totland

Little resort with good sands, safe bathing and high cliffs. Newport 13 miles, Yarmouth 3, Freshwater 2.

COUNTRY GARDEN HOTEL, CHURCH HILL, TOTLAND BAY PO39 OET (01983 754521: Fax: 01983 754421). Overlooking the sea, superb hotel; all rooms with bath and shower, TV, telephone, fridge, hairdryer etc. Telephone for brochure, tariff. Special spring and autumn rates. [pw!] pets £2 per day]

MRS J. SIMMONDS, NORTON LODGE, GRANVILLE ROAD, TOTLAND PO39 0AZ (01983 752772). Two purpose built holiday bungalows and one large caravan, all situated on a pleasant grassy site with beaches and breathtaking walks. Well behaved dogs most welcome. Prices from £95. [🐕]

SENTRY MEAD HOTEL, MADEIRA ROAD, TOTLAND BAY PO39 OBJ (01983 753212). Get away from it all at this friendly and comfortable haven, just two minutes from a sandy beach and cliff walks. Bedrooms have en suite bath or shower, colour TV and radio. Delicious table d'hôte dinners; lunchtime bar menu. [Pets £3 per night]

THE NODES COUNTRY HOTEL, ALUM BAY ROAD, TOTLAND BAY PO39 0HZ (01983 752859). Glorious walks, safe sandy beaches and facilities for horse riding, fishing, sailing and golf nearby. Full C/H, en suite rooms with tea/coffee making facilities. AA, RAC Approved. "Pets Choice Gold Award" 96/97. UK top ten establishments for pets. [🐕]

Ventnor

Well-known resort with good sands, downs, popular as a winter holiday resort. Nearby is St Boniface Down, the highest point on the island. Ryde 13 miles, Newport 12, Sandown 7, Shanklin 4.

RAVENSCOURT HOLIDAY BUNGALOWS 2 OCEAN VIEW ROAD, VENTNOR, ISLE OF WIGHT PO38 1AA (01983 852555). Self catering holiday chalets In woodland. Small, quiet site, wonderful walks. Two bedrooms plus sofa bed, bathroom, kitchenette and TV. £99 per bungalow (including your pet!). Website: http://isleofwight.webjump.com/

A. EVANS, "THE WATERFALL", SHORE ROAD, BONCHURCH, VENTNOR PO38 1RN (01983 852246). Spacious, self-contained Flat. Sleep up to 4. Colour TV. Sun verandah and garden. The beach, the sea and the downs. [🐕]

WOODLYNCH HOLIDAY APARTMENTS, SHORE ROAD, BONCHURCH, VENTNOR PO38 1RF (01983 852513). Comfortable self-contained holiday apartments in picturesque seaside village. Pleasant seaside and country walks, gardens and private parking. Dogs welcome. Tourist Board Member. Please write or phone for brochure and tariff. ♔♔♔ Commended. [🐕]

Yarmouth

Coastal resort situated 9 miles west of Newport. Castle built by Henry VIII for coastal defence.

THE ORCHARDS HOLIDAY CARAVAN & CAMPING PARK, NEWBRIDGE, YARMOUTH PO41 0TS (Dial-a-brochure 01983 531331; Fax: 01983 531666). Luxury holiday caravans, some with central heating. Excellent facilities including indoor pool with licensed cafe. Dog exercise areas. Coarse fishing; ideal walking, cycling and golf Open late February to New Year. [Pets from £0.50 to £2.50 per night]
E–mail: info@orchards-holiday-park.co.uk
Website: www.orchards-holiday-park.co.uk

TUCKAWAY" – Holiday Chalet in private, secluded position. Sleeps six. swimming pool. Dogs welcome. Large grassed area. Tourist Board Approved. APPLY – G. BAYLDON, FURZEBREAK, CRANMORE AVENUE, YARMOUTH PO41 OXR (01983 760082). [🐕]

SYMBOLS

🐕   Indicates that pets are welcome free of charge.

£   Indicates that a charge is made for pets: nightly or weekly.

pw!   Shows some special provision for pets; exercise facility, feeding or accommodation arrangement.

⌂   Indicates separate pets accommodation.

KENT

KENT Broadstairs, Canterbury, Hythe

HANSON HOTEL (Lic.) 41 Belvedere Road, Broadstairs CT10 1PF Tel: (01843) 868936
A small friendly Georgian hotel with relaxed atmosphere, centrally situated for beach, shops
and transport. B/B only or renowned for excellent food, we offer a 5-course Evening Dinner
with choice of menu prepared by Chef/Proprietor ★ Attractive Bar ★ Most en suite.
Children and pets welcome.

OPEN ALL YEAR   *S.A.E. or telephone for brochure to Trevor and Jean Webb*   SPRING AND WINTER BREAKS

The Tanner of Wingham

Tel/Fax: 01227 720532
Website: www.ttow.freeserve.co.uk

Family-run restaurant with bed and breakfast accommodation, situated in a building dating from 1440. Convenient
for docks and Chunnel. Rooms are individually decorated with antique beds and furniture – some rooms heavily
beamed. Families welcome, cot available. The many local attractions include historic houses and gardens, wildlife
and bird parks. Bed and Breakfast from £39 double; Evening Meal £14.

Mrs D.J. Martin, The Tanner of Wingham, 44 High Street, Wingham, Canterbury CT3 1AB

STADE COURT

♛♛♛ Highly Commended. AA ★★★ RAC
DOGS WELCOME
★ Delightful location on seafront of historic
Cinque Port of Hythe
★ Award Winning Restaurant ★ Terrace Bar
★ Single/Twin/Double/Split Level Rooms
★ Free access to Leisure Facilities 600 metres
away at sister hotel

West Parade, Hythe, Kent CT21 6DT
Tel: 01303 268263, Fax: 01303 261803
Web Site http://www.marstonhotels.co.uk

*"Give your dog a break
(and we'll provide the 'steak'!)"*

Broadstairs

Quiet resort, once a favourite of Charles Dickens. Good sands and promenades.

TREVOR AND JEAN WEBB, HANSON HOTEL, 41 BELVEDERE ROAD, BROAD-
STAIRS (01843 868936). Small, friendly licensed Georgian Hotel. Home
comforts; children and pets welcome. Attractive bar. SAE. [pw! Pets 50p p.n.]

Canterbury

*Cathedral and university city on River Great Stour, 54 miles from London. Roman and medieval
remains including city walls.*

THE TANNER OF WINGHAM, 44 HIGH STREET, WINGHAM, CANTERBURY CT3
1AB (Tel & Fax: 01227 720532) Family-run restaurant with bed and breakfast
accommodation. Convenient for docks and Chunnel. Rooms are individually
decorated with antique beds and furniture. [🐕]
Website: www.ttow.freeserve.co.uk

FREE and REDUCED RATE Holiday Visits!
Don't miss our Readers' Offer Vouchers
on pages 53 to 70

Folkestone

Cross-Channel port with good sandy beach and narrow old streets winding down to the harbour.

THE HORSESHOE HOTEL, 29 WESTBOURNE GARDENS, FOLKESTONE CT20 2HY (01303 258643). Spacious hotel, close to promenade and town centre. All rooms colour TV, washbasins, tea/coffee making facilities. Some en suite; family rooms. Licensed bar, friendly hospitality. Details on request. Hotel and Catering Reg. B&B from £20. [🐕]

Herne Bay

Homely family resort on North Kent coast. Shingle beach with sand at low tide. Maidstone 32 miles, Faversham 13, Canterbury 9, Whitstable 5.

MR AND MRS N. EVANS, 156 BELTINGE ROAD, HERNE BAY CT6 6JE (01227 375750). A fully furnished detached bungalow for three people (double and single bedrooms). Car parking space and enclosed rear garden. Brochure on request. [🐕]

Hythe

Village on west bank of Southampton Water. Ferry connection for pedestrians.

STADE COURT, HYTHE CT21 6DT. (01303 268263; Fax: 01303 261803). Situated on seafront close to beach and parks, the hotel has comfortable, well-equipped en suite bedrooms including colour TV and tea/coffee facilities. Free access to superb leisure and golf at sister hotel close by. Telephone for brochure and tariff. 'Doggie Dinner' [pw! £8.00 per night]
Website: www.marstonhotels.co.uk

St Margaret's Bay

4 miles north-east of Dover.

DEREK AND JACQUI MITCHELL, REACH COURT FARM COTTAGES, REACH COURT FARM, ST MARGARET'S BAY, DOVER CT15 6AQ (01304 852159; TEL/FAX: 01304 853902). Situated in the heart of the Mitchell family farm, surrounded by open countryside, these five luxury self-contained cottages are very special. The cottages are set around the old farmyard, which has been attractively set to lawns and shrubs, with open views of the rural valley both front and back. ♕♕♕♕ HIGHLY COMMENDED.

NOTE

All the information in this book is given in good faith in the belief that it is correct. However, the publishers cannot guarantee the facts given in these pages, neither are they responsible for changes in policy, ownership or terms that may take place after the date of going to press. Readers should always satisfy themselves that the facilities they require are available and that the terms, if quoted, still apply.

LANCASHIRE

Hillcrest ~ Morecambe

*Hillcrest is a self-catering bungalow in a quiet cul-de-sac in Heysham. Five minutes
sea-front. Fitted kitchen, washer, fridge-freezer, microwave, hot water, central
heating, no meters, colour TV, payphone. All linen supplied (except towels). Lovely
gardens and patio. Children and pets welcome. Weekly terms £275.*

Brochure: Mrs Bruce 01539 444436

Bell Farm Beryl and Peter welcome you to their 18th century farmhouse in the quiet village of Pilling.
The area has many footpaths and is ideal for cycling. Easy access to Blackpool, Lancaster, the Forest of Bowland
and the Lake District. One family room with en suite facilities, one double and one twin with private bathroom. Tea
and coffee making facilities. Lounge and dining room. Children and pets welcome. Open all year except Christmas
and New Year. Bed and Breakfast from £20.00.
Beryl and Peter Richardson, Bell Farm, Bradshaw Lane, Scronkey, Pilling, Preston PR3 6SN. Tel: 01253 790324.

SIX ARCHES CARAVAN PARK **SCORTON, GARSTANG** **NEAR PRESTON,** **LANCS PR3 1AL** **TEL: 01524 791683** **FAX: 01524 792926**	Situated on the banks of the River Wyre. Modern 6-berth caravans, fully equipped; touring pitches, some with electric hook-ups; large two-bedroom flats to sleep 6. Ideal for touring: Blackpool 14 miles, Lake District 30 miles. Facilities include licensed club with entertainment, heated pool, children's playground, fishing. Controlled dogs welcome. Write or phone for brochure. ✓✓✓

Blackpool

*Famous resort with fine sands and many attractions and vast variety of entertainments. Blackpool
Tower (500ft). Three piers. Manchester 47 miles, Lancaster 26, Preston 17, Fleetwood 9.*

**THE BRAYTON HOTEL, 7-8 FINCHLEY ROAD, GYNN SQUARE, BLACKPOOL
FY1 2LP. The small hotel with the BIG reputation. A family-run hotel overlooking Gynn gardens and the promenade offering quality food from a varied
menu. Comfortable rooms and a licensed bar, easy parking. Open all year. For
tariff and brochure ring 01253 351645. [🐾]
E–mail: brayton@globalnet.co.uk**

MRS C. MOORE, COTSWOLD HOLIDAY FLATLETS, 2A HADDON ROAD, NOR-
BRECK, BLACKPOOL FY2 9AH (01253 352227). Holiday Flatlets fully equipped.
Cross road to beach and trams. Select area. Open all year. Short Breaks early
season and Illuminations. Phone or SAE for brochure. [🐾]

Clitheroe

Pleasant market town, with ruined Norman keep standing on limestone cliff above grey roofs. Pendle Hill 4 miles to the east, from where there are spectacular views of the Forest of Bowland.

MRS FRANCES OLIVER, WYTHA FARM, RIMINGTON, CLITHEROE BB7 4EQ (01200 445295). Farmhouse accommodation in heart of countryside. Panoramic views. Warm welcome. Double and family rooms. Ideal touring centre. Bed and Breakfast from £15. Evening Meal £7. [pw! Pets £1 per day]

Mellor

Vilalge 3 miles north-west of Blackburn

ROSE COTTAGE, LONGSIGHT ROAD, CLAYTON-LE-DALE BB1 9EX (01254 813223; Fax: 01254 813831). Picturesque 200-year-old cottage on A59 close to M6 and M65. Established by present owners 1984. Charming well-appointed rooms with private facilities and many extras. Stabling opposite. Kennels/cattery nearby. Excellent one night stop travelling to and from Scotland. Credit Cards accepted. [🐾]

Morecambe

Popular family holiday resort 3 miles north-west of Lancaster

MRS BRUCE, HILLCREST, MORECAMBE (01539 444436). Self-catering bungalow in a quiet cul-de-sac in Heysham with lovely gardens and patio and only five minutes from the sea-front. Children and pets welcome. Weekly terms £275. Brochure available. [🐾]

VENTURE CARAVAN PARK, LANGRIDGE WAY, WESTGATE, MORECAMBE LA4 4TQ (01524 412986; Fax: 01524 422029). Relaxing family park. Tourers and Tents welcome. Hire caravans including vans for disabled. Promenade ¾ mile. Bar. Entertainment. Food. Shop. Off licence. Launderette. Indoor heated pool. Pets on lead. AA/RAC.

Pilling

Small village 3 miles from Preesall, 12 miles from Blackpool

18th century farmhouse with one family room with en suite facilities, one double and one twin with private bathroom. All centrally heated. Full English breakfast is served. Open all year except Christmas and New Year. B&B from £20. BERYL AND PETER RICHARDSON, BELL FARM, BRADSHAW LANE, SCRONKEY, PILLING, PRESTON PR3 6SN (01253 790324).

Preston

Large town on River Ribble, 27 miles from Manchester.

SIX ARCHES CARAVAN PARK, SCORTON, GARSTANG, NEAR PRESTON PR3 1AL (01524 791683; Fax: 01524 792926). Modern 6-berth caravans, touring pitches; large two-bedroom flats to sleep 6. Blackpool 14 miles, Lake District 30 miles. Licensed club with entertainment. Controlled dogs welcome. [🐾]

Southport

Elegant seaside resort with Victorian feel. Amusement park, zoo and Royal Birkdale championship golf course.

THE GARDEN COURT HOTEL, 22 BANK SQUARE, SOUTHPORT PR9 0DG (Tel/Fax: 01704 530219). Recently renovated Victorian town house overlooking Floral Hall, Marine Lake and sea. All amenities and attractions within easy walking distance. Standard, en suite and four poster bedrooms with central heating, colour television etc. Licensed bar. Friendly, comfortable accommodation from £14.50 B&B pppn. [🐕]
E-mail: gardencourt@merseymail.co.uk

St Annes

Very poular family resort with good sands. Good shopping centre. Preston 15 miles, Blackpool 5 miles.

MRS M. MACKOON, ORCHARD COURT, 50/52 ORCHARD ROAD, ST ANNES FY8 1PJ (01253 712653). Self-catering flats with en suite facilities and large gardens. 2 minutes to shops, cafes, beach. Linen provided. Car park. Open all year, Short Breaks. Brochure. [🐕 pw!]

LEICESTERSHIRE

LEICESTERSHIRE *Market Harborough, Melton Mowbray*

Market Harborough

Town on River Welland 14 miles south-east of Leicester

BROOK MEADOW HOLIDAYS. 3-4 Keys Up to Highly Commended. Three self-catering chalets, farmhouse Bed and Breakfast, Carp fishing, camping and caravan site with electric hookups. Phone for brochure. MRS MARY HART, WELFORD ROAD, SIBBERTOFT, MARKET HARBOROUGH LE16 9UJ (01858 880886). [🐕 camping, £5 per week B&B, £10 Self-catering]

Melton Mowbray

Old market town, centre of hunting country. Large cattle market. Church and Anne of Cleves' House are of interest. Kettering 29 miles, Market Harborough 22, Notttingham 18, Leicester 15.

SYSONBY KNOLL HOTEL, ASFORDBY ROAD, MELTON MOWBRAY LE13 OHP (01664 563563; Fax: 01664 410364.). Traditional family-run hotel; all bedrooms (some ground floor) en suite with TV and hospitality tray. Outdoor swimming pool; bar and restaurant. Four Crowns Commended, AA and RAC ★★★. [🐕] Website: www.btinternet.com/~sysonby.knoll

LINCOLNSHIRE (including Rutland)

Mablethorpe

Coastal resort 11 miles from Louth.

MRS GRAVES, GRANGE FARM, MALTBY-LE-MARSH, ALFORD LN13 0JP (01507 450267; Fax: 01507 450180). Farmhouse B & B set in six idyllic acres of Lincolnshire countryside. Peaceful base for leisure and sightseeing. Private fishing lake, many farm animals. Pets welcome.

Market Rasen

Market town and agricultural centre 14 miles north-east of Lincoln

MRS M. F. DAWSON-MARGRAVE, THE WAVENEY GUEST HOUSE, WILLINGHAM ROAD, MARKET RASEN LN8 3DN (01673 843236). Very comfortable, smoke-free accommodation in small market town surrounded by woodland and close to Lincolnshire Wolds; golf and race courses. All rooms with private facilities, colour TV, tea-making equipment. Guests' own lounge and dining room. Excellent food. Private parking. Brochure available. 2 Crowns Commended. [🐕]

ST ATHANS HOTEL
20 Tavistock Place, Russell Square, LONDON WC1H 9RE
Tel: 0207-837 9140; Fax: 0207-833 8352
Bed and Breakfast, comfortable, ideal for families. Hotel situated near British Museum,
convenient for shops, parks and theatres. Only 10 minutes from Euston and King's Cross.
Pets welcome FREE.

London

*Legislative capital of UK and major port. Theatres, shops, museums, places of historic interest.
Airports at Heathrow and Gatwick.*

THE DRAGON HOUSE, 39 MARMORA ROAD, LONDON SE22 0RX (0208 693
4355; or 0956 645 894). London Tourist Board ◆◆◆◆. Nearest thing to a farmhouse in London. Large freshly decorated rooms in peaceful cosseted
atmosphere. Flowers, toiletries, television, magazines, tea/coffee, en suite.
Evening meal available. Single £30, Double £50. Dog's beds, walks, sitting services provided. Central London 10 minutes. Local pick up. Parking. [pw! 🐾]

ST ATHANS HOTEL, 20 TAVISTOCK PLACE, RUSSELL SQUARE, LONDON
WC1H 9RE (Tel: 0207-837 9140; Fax: 0207-833 8352). Family Bed and Breakfast
near British Museum, shops, parks and theatres. Russell Square two blocks
away, Euston and King's Cross stations ten minutes. LTB LISTED. [🐾]

Key to Tourist Board Ratings
👑   ## The Crown Scheme

The English Tourism Council (formerly the English Tourist Board) has
joined with the **AA** and **RAC** to create a new, easily understood quality rating
for serviced accommodation.
Hotels will receive a grading ranging from **one to five STARS (★)**. Other
serviced accommodation such as **guest houses** and **B&B establishments**
will be graded from **one to five DIAMONDS (◆)**. These ratings represent
Quality, Service and Hospitality not just facilities.
*NB. Some properties had not been assessed at the time of going to press
and in these cases the publishers have included the old CROWN
gradings.*

🔑   ## The Key Scheme

The Key Scheme covering self-catering in cottages, bungalows, flats,
houseboats, houses, chalets, etc remains unchanged. The classification from
One to Five KEYS indicates the range of facilities and equipment. Higher
quality standards are indicated by the terms APPROVED, COMMENDED,
HIGHLY COMMENDED AND DE LUXE.

NORFOLK

NORFOLK *Acle, Bacton-on-Sea*

Readers are requested to mention this guidebook
when seeking accommodation
(and please enclose a stamped addressed envelope).

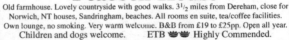

Visit the FHG website
www.holidayguides.com
for details of the wide choice of accommodation
featured in the full range of FHG titles

FREE and REDUCED RATE Holiday Visits!
Don't miss our Readers' Offer Vouchers
on pages 53 to 70

Country Bed and Breakfast
STRENNETH

Airfield Road
Fersfield, Diss
Norfolk IP22 2BP
Telephone: 01379 688182
Fax: 01379 688260
E-mail ken@mainline.co.uk
Website: www.abreakwithtradition.co.uk/

STRENNETH is a well-established, family-run business, situated in unspoiled country-side just a short drive from Bressingham Gardens and the picturesque market town of Diss. Offering first-class accommodation, the original 17th Century building has been carefully renovated to a high standard with a wealth of exposed oak beams and a newer single storey courtyard wing. There is ample off road parking and plenty of nice walks nearby. All seven bedrooms, including a Four Poster and an Executive, are tastefully arranged with period furniture and distinctive beds. Each having remote colour television, hospitality trays, central heating and full en suite facilities. The establishment is smoke free and the guest lounge has a log fire on cold winter evenings. There is an extensive breakfast menu using local produce. Ideal touring base. Pets most welcome at no extra charge. Outside kennels with runs if required. Hair and Beauty Salons now open. ETC 4 Diamonds. Bed and Breakfast from £23.00

CROSSKEYS RIVERSIDE HOTEL Tel: 01366 387777
BRIDGE STREET, HILGAY, NEAR DOWNHAM MARKET, NORFOLK PE38 0LD.
Country hotel beside River Wissey in converted 17th century buildings, renovations have retained the original character with oak beams and inglenook fireplace complemented by a rustic bar. All bedrooms have en suite bathrooms, colour TV, coffee/tea making facilities; 3 four-poster beds. Ideally suited for touring Norfolk and Cambridgeshire Fens. Two ground floor rooms. Free fishing from the hotel frontage. Pets most welcome.

See also Colour Advertisement on page 25

Fakenham Racecourse Caravan & Camping Site
Set in beautiful countryside and sheltered by tall conifers, the grounds and modern facilities are excellently maintained. 120 pitches accommodating touring caravans, motorcaravans and tents. Centrally heated lavatories and shower blocks. Disabled facilities, Laundry rooms and mothercare unit. Site shop. Cable TV. Sports Centre on site (golf, tennis, squash, meals and licensed bar). Ideally located for visiting Norfolk's coastal resorts, stately homes, wildlife and bird sanctuaries and many other attractions.
From £8.50 to £11.00 for 2 adults per night. *Open all year round* ✓✓✓ **Tourist Board rating**
The Racecourse, Fakenham, Norfolk NR21 7NY Tel: (01328) 862388 Fax: (01328) 855908

See also Colour Advertisement on page 25

NOTE

All the information in this book is given in good faith in the belief that it is correct. However, the publishers cannot guarantee the facts given in these pages, neither are they responsible for changes in policy, ownership or terms that may take place after the date of going to press. Readers should always satisfy themselves that the facilities they require are available and that the terms, if quoted, still apply.

COME TO BEAUTIFUL NORFOLK with Blue Riband Holidays
Super Quality Bungalows, Chalets & Seafront Caravans
in GREAT YARMOUTH's Coastal Villages
One Dog Free; Extra Pets £6 per Holiday

✳ **Detached Bungalows** in village of Hemsby, Satellite TV, Children's Playground, Miniature Railway.
✳ **Seafront Bungalows** at Caister-on-Sea with enclosed rear gardens leading to beach.
✳ **Seafront Caravans** at Caister-on-Sea, 4-8 berth. Clubhouse and swimming pool.
✳ **Detached Chalets on Sea-Dell Park** a lovely, quiet location on Beach Road, Hemsby.
✳ **Belle Aire Park, Beach Road, Hemsby,** Super Chalets with Free Electricity and Clubhouse.
✳ **Cottages,** in central Great Yarmouth.
✳ **Scratby & California,** Chalets and Caravans with family entertainment and swimming pools.

Free Colour Brochure:- DON WITHERIDGE, BLUE RIBAND HOUSE,
PARKLANDS, HEMSBY, GREAT YARMOUTH NR29 4HA Website: www.blue-riband.com
Direct Line for Bookings & Brochures: 01493 730445; all calls personally answered.

See also Colour Advertisement on page 1

 **Chapel Briers, Yarmouth Road,**
Hemsby, Great Yarmouth. NR29 4NJ
www.uktourism.com/nr-carefreeholidays

Inexpensive, live-as-you-please Self Catering
Holidays near Great Yarmouth and Norfolk Broads

The Laurels – Superb Bungalows close to beach. Private car park.

The Jasmines – Lovely cottages. 100 yards to golden sandy beach.

Belle-Aire – Family chalets, clubhouse. Free Electric and Linen.

Seadell – Fully detached. Parking in front of chalet.

Winterton Valley – Chalets in pretty fishing village.

Fennside – Detached 3 bedroom bungalow. In residential Hemsby.

DIAL -A -BROCHURE 7 DAYS 01493 732176
ALL CALLS PERSONALLY ANSWERED

• Colour TV and fitted carpets in all properties • Free club membership • Short Breaks available from £55 • Discounts April to September for small families and Senior Citizens
• Pets welcome on all parks (2nd pet free) • Children welcome – cots and high chairs for hire.

See also Colour Advertisement on page 26

WINTERTON-ON-SEA
(Near Great Yarmouth)

For a quiet, relaxing holiday – modern, personally maintained holiday
chalets. Each sleeps 6 and is fully equipped for self-catering, on a
beautiful grassed site, close to sandy beach with marvellous sea views.
Lovely valley area – this is a pets' paradise.

For further details contact:

Mrs J.S. Cooper, Silverlea, Mile Road, Carleton Rode,
Norwich NR16 1NE Tel: 01953 789407

Pott Row

Detached 2 bedroom bungalow sleeps 4. In quiet rural Norfolk village close to Sandringham and beaches. Facilities include colour TV, video, microwave, fridge/freezer, washing machine, off road parking, dog run. All dogs welcome FREE. Open all year. Please telephone for brochure.

Mrs. J.E. Ford, 129 Leziate Drove, Pott Row, King's Lynn PE32 1DE Tel: 01553 630356

KILN CLIFFS CARAVAN PARK

Peaceful family-run site with NO clubhouse situated around an historic brick kiln. Luxury 1997 six-berth caravans for hire, standing on ten acres of grassy cliff top. Magnificent view out over the sea; private path leads down to extensive stretches of unspoilt sandy beach. All caravans fully equipped (except linen) and price includes all gas and electricity. Caravans always available for sale or for hire. Within easy reach are the Broads, Norwich, the Shire Horse Centre, local markets, nature reserves, bird sanctuaries; nearby golf, riding and fishing. Facilities on site include general store and launderette. Responsible pet owners welcome.

Substantial discounts for off-peak bookings – phone for details.
Call for brochure. Mr G. Malone, Kiln Cliffs Caravan Park,
Cromer Road, Mundesley, Norfolk NR11 8DF.   Tel: 01263 720449

Roseacre Country House   **West Runton, Cromer, Norfolk NR27 9QS,**
Telephone: West Runton (01263) 837221 Resident Proprietors: Greg & Sue Lunken
Roseacre stands in grounds of one acre in a secluded position just off the coast road between Cromer and Sheringham and is ideal for a friendly relaxing holiday. The sandy beach with safe bathing is a mere five minutes walk away. The village boasts two high class restaurants and a village pub. Golf, fishing and riding facilities are all close by. Your pets are welcome too as long as they are kept on a lead while in the grounds.

Winterton Valley Holidays

offer a selection of modern, superior, fully appointed holiday chalets, sleeping 2 to 6 people. Duvets and colour TV in all chalets. Panoramic views of sand-duned valley and sea from the front of this quiet 35 acre estate. Five minutes from beach and eight miles North of Great Yarmouth.

PETS VERY WELCOME

For colour brochure please ring 01493 377175 or write to
15 Kingston Avenue, Caister-on-Sea, Norfolk, NR30 5ET

THE BROADS HOTEL Station Road, Wroxham, Norwich NR12 8UR

Highly Commended RAC ★★ AA ★★   Tel: 01603 782869 Fax: 01603 784066

Comfortable hotel renowned for its high standard cuisine. Owned and run by dog-loving family. Ideally situated for boating, fishing and exploring the beautiful Norfolk countryside and coastline. All rooms fully en suite with tea/coffee making, colour TV etc. For brochure please telephone.

SYMBOLS

🐕 Indicates that pets are welcome free of charge.

£ Indicates that a charge is made for pets: nightly or weekly.

pw! Shows some special provision for pets; exercise facility, feeding or accommodation arrangement.

⌂ Indicates separate pets accommodation.

286

NORFOLK COUNTRY COTTAGES, MARKET PLACE, REEPHAM NR10 7JJ. Widest ever selection of cottages throughout Norfolk. Phone for brochure 01603 871872. [Pets £12 per week]

WELCOME COTTAGE HOLIDAYS. Quality Cottages in wonderful locations at welcoming low prices. Pets, linen and fuel mostly included. PHONE FOR FREE 2000 FULL COLOUR BROCHURE 01756 702205.

Acle

Small town 8 miles west of Great Yarmouth.

EAST NORWICH INN, OLD ROAD, ACLE, NORWICH NR13 3QN (01493 751112; Fax: 01493 751109). Midway between Norwich and Great Yarmouth, ideal for holiday attractions. All rooms en suite with colour TV and tea/coffee making. Pets welcome by arrangement. [🐕]

Bacton-on-Sea

Village on coast, 5 miles from North Walsham.

CASTAWAYS HOLIDAY PARK, PASTON ROAD, BACTON-ON-SEA, NORFOLK NR12 0JB (01692 650436 and 650418). In peaceful village with direct access to sandy beach. Modern caravans with all amenities. Licensed club, entertainment, children's play area. Ideal for touring Norfolk. [Pets £15 per week/£2.50 p.n.]

RED HOUSE CHALET AND CARAVAN PARK, PASTON ROAD, BACTON-ON-SEA NR12 0JB (01692 650815). Small family-run site, ideal for touring Broads. Chalets, caravans and flats all with showers, fridges and colour TV. Some with sea views. Licensed. Open March–January. [Pets £10 weekly.]

Beetley

Village 4 miles/6 km north of East Dereham, which is notable for old buildings, inc. parish church

MRS JENNY BELL, PEACOCK HOUSE, PEACOCK LANE, OLD BEETLEY, DEREHAM NR20 4DG (01362 860371). Old farmhouse in lovely countryside. All rooms en suite, tea / coffee facilities. Own lounge, B&B from £19 to £25 pp. Open all year. Two Crowns Highly Commended. Non-smoking. Children and dogs welcome. [pw! 🐕]

Blakeney

Popular sailing village with brightly coloured cottages.

SNUGGLER'S DEN, HIGH STREET, BLAKENEY Tourist Board Rating: 🛏🛏🛏 Highly Commended. Secluded romantic hideaway to access peaceful walks, sailing, bird watching and all the amenities the North Norfolk coast has to offer. Sleeps two. Full facilities, television, CD and radio, telephone. For further details and bookings please call: 07041-564005 or 01582-460961. [Pets £10 per week]

Breckland

Area of sandy heaths on borders of Norfolk and Suffolk.

THE THATCHED COTTAGE AND PEARTREE COTTAGE. Two idyllic detached cottages; open fires, beams and cottage-style furniture. Modern kitchens and bathrooms. Sleep 4/5. Beaches, Broads, Cambridge all within the hour. Children and pets welcome. JCR PROPERTIES, THE OLD HALL, HARDINGHAM, NORWICH NR9 4EW (01953 851641).

Brooke

Attractive small village 8 miles south of Norwich; Lowestoft 20 miles, Great Yarmouth 25.

DAPHNE VIVIAN-NEAL, WELBECK HOUSE, BROOKE, NEAR NORWICH NR15 1AT (Telephone & Fax: 01508 550292). 300-year-old Farmhouse; double, twin and single bedrooms, central heating, tea/coffee. Near Norwich, sea, nature reserves, the Broads, local walks, theatre, pub food nearby. B&B from £18-£20. Long stay and child reductions on request. [Pets £1 per night].

Burnham Market

Village five miles west of Wells-next-the-Sea.

THE HOSTE ARMS, THE GREEN, BURNHAM MARKET PE31 8HD (Tel: 01328 738257/738777; Fax: 01328 730103). 17th century Hotel overlooking village green. 28 bedrooms, elegantly furnished, all en suite with colour TV and telephone. Bar and restaurant menus, AA 2 Rosettes. [🐾]
E-mail: TheHosteArms@compuserve.com
Website: www.hostearms.co.uk

Caister-on-Sea

Historic site with Roman ruins and 15th century Caister Castle with 100 foot tower.

Go BLUE RIBAND for quality inexpensive self-catering holidays where your dog is welcome – choice of locations all in the borough of Great Yarmouth. Detached 3 bedroom bungalows, seafront bungalows, detached Sea-Dell chalets and modern sea front caravans. Free colour brochure: DON WITHERIDGE, BLUE RIBAND HOUSE, PARKLANDS, HEMSBY, GREAT YARMOUTH NR29 4HA (01493 730445). [pw! 🐾].

Coltishall

Village to the north east of Norwich

THE NORFOLK MEAD HOTEL, COLTISHALL, NORWICH, NORFOLK. NR12 7DN (01603 737531 or 737521). Three Crowns HIGHLY COMMENDED. Renowned restaurant offering superb cuisine and a comprehensive wine list. Well mannered dogs welcome. Johansen recommended. Best loved hotel. [Pets £5 per week]

Cromer

Attractive resort built round old fishing village. Norwich 21 miles.

CHALET 49 ~ KINGS CHALET PARK, MRS M. WALKER, WHITE BARN, SANDY LANE, WEST RUNTON, NORFOLK NR27 9NB (01263 837494) Luxury, well equipped chalet , adjacent to beaches, woods, cliff-top walks and golf courses. Local shops. Two bedrooms, bathroom, fitted kitchen, microwave, color TV, etc. Sleeps four to five. Cleaned and maintained by owner. Pets welcome.Open March to October. [Pets £10]

CLIFTONVILLE HOTEL, SEAFRONT, CROMER NR27 9AS (01263 512543; Fax: 01263 515700). Ideally situated on the Norfolk coast. Beautifully restored Edwardian Hotel. 30 en suite bedrooms all with sea view. Executive suites. Seafood Bistro. A la carte Restaurant. Dogs welcome. [pw! pets £4 per night]

KINGS CHALET PARK, CROMER NR27 0AL (01263 511308). Well-equipped chalets sleeping 2 to 6; shower/bathroom, microwave, TV, videos in some chalets. Tourist Board and NNH/GHA Approved. Quiet site adjacent to woods, golf club and beaches. Local shops nearby. Pleasant walks. 10 minutes' walk to town. Children and pets welcome. ♈. [🐕]

KINGS CHALET PARK, CROMER. Comfortable well-equipped chalets on quiet site; ideally placed for woodland and beach walks. 10 minutes' walk to town, shops nearby. Details from MRS I. SCOLTOCK, SHANGRI-LA, LITTLE CAMBRIDGE, DUTON HILL, DUNMOW, ESSEX (01371 870482). [🐕]

MERIBEL B&B, 126 CROMER ROAD, WEST RUNTON, CROMER NR27 9QA (01263 837456). Comfortable bungalow with lovely views. Situated between Cromer and Sheringham. No smoking. Colour TV's etc. Parking, private garden. Close to beaches, golf, riding, shops. £18-£22 pppn. [🐕]

All-electric two and three bedroom Holiday Cottages accommodating four to sixpersons in beautiful surroundings. Sandy beaches, sports facilities, Cinema and Pier (live shows). Parking. Children and pets welcome. Brochure: NORTHREPPS HOLIDAY PROPERTIES, CROMER, NORFOLK NR27 0JW (01263 512236 (am) /513969 (pm) / Fax: 01263 515588). [Pets £12 weekly].

Dereham

Situated 16 miles west of Norwich. St Nicholas Church has16th century bell tower.

BARTLES LODGE, CHURCH STREET, ELSING, DEREHAM NR20 3EA (01362 637177). Stay in the peaceful, tranquil heart of Norfolk's most beautiful countryside. All rooms en suite, TVs, tea/coffee making facilities, etc. Recommended by "Which?" Good Bed & Breakfast Guide. [pw! Pets £1 per night, £5 per week]

SCARNING DALE, SCARNING, EAST DEREHAM NR19 2QN (01362 687269). Self catering cottages (not commercialised) in grounds of owner's house. On-site indoor heated swimming pool and full-size snooker table. B&B for six also available in house (sorry no pets).

Diss

Twisting streets with Tudor, Georgian and Victorian architecture. 12th century St. Mary's Church and 6 acre mere, haven for wildfowl.

BRENDA WEBB, STRENNETH, AIRFIELD ROAD, FERSFIELD, DISS IP22 2BP (01379 688182 Fax 01379 688260). Family run, fully renovated period property. All rooms en suite, colour TVs, hospitality trays. Ground floor rooms. Non smoking. Extensive breakfast menu. Licensed. ETC ◆◆◆◆. Bed and Breakfast from £23.00. [🛏] E-mail ken@mainline.co.uk, Website: www.abreakwithtradition.co.uk/

Downham Market

Market town and agricultural centre on River Ouse, 10 miles south of King's Lynn.

CROSSKEYS RIVERSIDE HOTEL, BRIDGE STREET, HILGAY, NEAR DOWNHAM MARKET, NORFOLK PE38 0LD (01366 387777). A small country hotel beside the River Wissey. With free fishing from hotel frontage. All bedrooms (three four posters) have en suite bathrooms, colour TV, tea/coffee making facilities. Ground floor bedrooms available. Pets most welcome. Reductions of 10% for long stays. [Pets £3.50 per visit]

Fakenham

Agricultural centre on River Wensum 23 miles north-west of Norwich.

FAKENHAM RACECOURSE CARAVAN & CAMPING SITE, THE RACECOURSE, FAKENHAM, NORFOLK NR21 7NY (Tel: 01328 862388 Fax: 01328 855908). ✓✓✓ Tourist Board rating. A beautiful site, with excellently maintained grounds and facilities. 140 pitches accommodating touring caravans, motorvans and tents. Sports Centre on site (golf, tennis, squash, meals, licensed bar).

VERE LODGE, NEAR FAKENHAM (01328 838261). 14 superbly equipped cottages with leisure centre and heated indoor pool. 8 acres of lawns, paddock and woodland, with Norfolk's vast beaches nearby. [pw! Pets £20 per week]

Foxley

Village 6 miles east of East Dereham.

Self Catering Chalets (2/3 bedrooms) on working farm. All fully equipped, with central heating. 20 miles from coast, 15 from Broads. Mature woodland nearby. Ideal for walking. ♔♔♔ Approved. MOOR FARM HOLIDAYS (PW), FOXLEY NR20 4QN (01362 688523). [Pets £10 per week]

Visit the FHG website
www.holidayguides.com
for details of the wide choice of accommodation
featured in the full range of FHG titles

Great Yarmouth

Traditional lively seaside resort with a wide range of amusements, including the Marina Centre and Sealife Centre.

MR & MRS COLLIS, "ANCHOR", 21 NORTH DENES ROAD, GREAT YARMOUTH NR30 4LW (01493 844339/300050). Completely self-contained Flats with own shower and toilet. Fully equipped at no extra cost. Reduced terms early and late season. Close by public amenities. Children and pets welcome. [🐾]

Go BLUE RIBAND for quality inexpensive self-catering holidays where your dog is welcome – choice of locations all in the borough of Great Yarmouth. Detached 3 bedroom bungalows, seafront bungalows, detached Sea-Dell chalets and modern sea front caravans. Free colour brochure: DON WITHERIDGE, BLUE RIBAND HOUSE, PARKLANDS, HEMSBY, GREAT YARMOUTH NR29 4HA (01493 730445). [pw! 🐾].

CAREFREE HOLIDAYS, CHAPEL BRIERS, YARMOUTH ROAD, HEMSBY, GREAT YARMOUTH NR29 4NJ (01493 732176). A wide selection of superior chalets for live-as-you-please holidays near Great Yarmouth and Norfolk Broads. All amenities on site. Parking. Children and pets welcome. [Pets £10 per week, £5 on short breaks, 2nd pet free.]

Superior brick built tiled roof cottages. Adjacent golf course. Lovely walks on dunes and coast. 2-4 night breaks early/late season, Christmas and New Year. SAND DUNE COTTAGES, TAN LANE, CAISTER-ON-SEA, GREAT YARMOUTH NR30 5DT (01493 667786 / 03855 61363).

SUNDOWNER AND BELLE AIRE HOLIDAY PARKS, HEMSBY ON SEA. Self contained holiday chalets suitable for 2-8 persons. Fully equipped. Licensed clubhouses, indoor heated pools. Convenient Great Yarmouth and Broads. For details tel 01493 377932 or SAE to MRS R. LAWRENCE, 1 CAISTERSANDS AVENUE, CAISTER ON SEA, GREAT YARMOUTH NR30 5PF.

MRS J. S. COOPER, SILVERLEA, MILE ROAD, CARLETON RODE, NORWICH NR16 1NE (01953 789407). Modern holiday chalets at Winterton-on-Sea. Sleep six. Grassed site close to beach with marvellous sea views. A pets' paradise! [Pets £8 per week.]

Horning

Lovely riverside village ideally placed for exploring the Broads. Great Yarmouth 17 miles.

BROADLAND HOLIDAYS, 17 LOWER STREET, HORNING NR12 8AA (01692 630177). Riverside and waterside individual, comfortable thatched bungalows, cottages, townhouses with own private lawns and moorings in delightful riverside village. Day-launch available. Open all year. [Pets welcome £15 per week].

SILVER BIRCHES HOLIDAYS, GREBE ISLAND, LOWER STREET, HORNING NR12 8PF (01692 630858). Five individual houseboats and seven all-weather motor day launches. All the comforts of a caravan afloat! Surrounded by lawns, adjacent parking. Ideal for families, fishermen and their pets. [Pets £15 per stay]

Hunstanton

Neat little resort which faces west across The Wash. Norwich 47 miles, Cromer 38.

COBBLERS COTTAGE, 3 WODEHOUSE ROAD, OLD HUNSTANTON PE36 6JD (01485 534036). Two Crowns Commended, ♕♕♕ Commended. Near Royal Sandringham/Norfolk Lavender. All en suite twin/double rooms. Colour TV and tea-making. Near the beach, golf, bird watching, pubs and restaurants. Sauna and jacuzzi. Also self catering annexe. [🐕]
E–mail: cobblerscottage@dial.pipex.com

MRS BROWN, MARINE HOTEL, HUNSTANTON PE36 5EH (01485 533310). Overlooking sea and green. Pets welcome, free of charge. Colour TV in all bedrooms. Open all year except Christmas period. SAE for terms and brochure. [🐕]

King's Lynn

Ancient market town and port on the Wash with many beautiful medieval and Georgian buildings.

MRS G. DAVIDSON, HOLMDENE FARM, BEESTON, KING'S LYNN PE32 2NJ (01328 701284). 17th century farmhouse situated in central Norfolk within easy reach of the coast and Broads. Sporting activities available locally, village pub nearby. One double room, one twin and two singles. Pets welcome. Bed and Breakfast from £18 per person; Evening Meal from £10. Weekly terms available and child reductions. Two self-catering cottages. Sleeping 4/8. Terms on request.

MRS J. E. FORD, LEZIATE DROVE, POTT ROW, KING'S LYNN PE32 1DE (01553 630356). Detached bungalow sleeps 4. In quiet village close to Sandringham and beaches. Facilities include colour TV, video, microwave, fridge/freezer, washing machine, off road parking, dog run. [🐕]

MRS JOAN BASTONE, MARANATHA GUEST HOUSE, 115 GAYWOOD ROAD, KING'S LYNN PE30 2PU (01553 774596). Charming Victorian guest house within easy walking distance of town centre. Close to Sandringham and coast. Pets welcome free of charge, children special rates. Terms from £14 pp. RAC, AA QQ 2 Crowns Approved.

Mundesley-on-Sea

Small resort backed by low cliffs. Good sands and bathing. Norwich 20 miles, Cromer 7.

47 SEAWARD CREST, MUNDESLEY. West-facing brick built chalet on private site with lawns, flowers and parking. Large lounge/dining room, kitchenette, two bedrooms, bathroom. Beach and shops nearby. Pets most welcome. Weekly terms from £90. SAE please: MRS DOAR, 4 DENBURY ROAD, RAVENSHEAD, NOTTS, NG15 9FQ (01623 798032).

---

*When making enquiries or bookings,
a stamped addressed envelope is always appreciated.*

KILN CLIFFS CARAVAN PARK, CROMER ROAD, MUNDESLEY NR11 8DF (01263 720449). Peaceful family-run site situated around an historic brick kiln. Six-berth caravans for hire, standing on ten acres of grassy cliff top. All caravans fully equipped (except linen) and price includes all gas and electricity. [Pets £5 per week].

"WHINCLIFF", CROMER ROAD, MUNDESLEY NR11 8DU (01263 720961). Clifftop house, sea views and sandy beaches. Rooms with colour TV and tea-making. En suite family/twin room. Evening Meal optional, not Sundays. An abundance of coastal and woodland walks; many places of interest and local crafts. Well-behaved dogs welcome. Contact Mrs G. Faulkner. [🐾]

Neatishead

Ideal for touring East Anglia. Close to Norwich. Aylsham 14 miles, Norwich 10, Wroxham 3.

ALAN AND SUE WRIGLEY, REGENCY GUEST HOUSE, THE STREET, NEATISHEAD, NORFOLK BROADS NR12 8AD (Tel & Fax: 01692 630233). 18th century five-bedroom guest house renowned for generous English breakfasts. Ideal East Anglian touring base. Accent on personal service. ETC/AA ◆◆◆◆. Dogs welcome. [Pets £3 per night.]

North Walsham

Market town 14 miles north of Norwich, traditional centre of the Norfolk reed thatching industry.

MRS V. O'HARA, GEOFFREY THE DYER'S HOUSE, CHURCH PLAIN, WORSTEAD, NORTH WALSHAM NR28 9AL (01692 536562). 17th century Listed weaver's house in centre of conservation village. Close to Broads, Coast, Norwich. Good walking and touring. All rooms en suite. Wholesome, well-cooked food. Dogs welcome. Two Crowns. [🐾]
E-mail: oharafamily@freeserve.co.uk

Sheringham

Small, traditional resort built around a flint-built fishing village. Sandy beaches and amusements.

ACHIMOTA, 31 NORTH STREET, SHERINGHAM NR26 8LW (01263 822379). Award-winning small guest house in quiet part of Sheringham in "Area of Outstanding Natural Beauty", with Blue Flag beach and walks galore. All rooms have private facilities, easy chairs, T.V, beverage tray and central heating. ETC ◆◆◆. NO SMOKING. Brochure on request. [🐾]
Website: www.broadland.com/achimota.

Thurne

Idyllic Broadland village. Great Yarmouth 10 miles.

HEDERA HOUSE AND PLANTATION BUNGALOWS, THURNE NR29 3BU (01692 670242). Adjacent river, 7 bedroomed farmhouse, 10 competitively priced bungalows in lovely peaceful gardens. Outdoor heated pool. Enjoy boating, fishing, walking, touring, nearby golf, horseriding, sandy beaches and popular resorts.

Wells-next-the-Sea

Lovely little resort with interesting harbour, famous for its cockles, whelks and shrimps. A winding creek leads to a beach of fine sands with dunes. Norwich 31 miles, King's Lynn 27, Cromer 19.

MRS J. M. COURT, EASTDENE, NORTHFIELD LANE, WELLS-NEXT-THE-SEA NR23 1LH (01328 710381). Homely Guest House offers warm welcome. Bed and Breakfast from £18. Two double, one twin bedded rooms, all en suite; tea /coffee facilities and colour TV. Private parking. [Pets £1 per night].

West Runton

Resort with sandy beach east of Sheringham

GREG & SUE LUNKEN, ROSEACRE COUNTRY HOUSE, WEST RUNTON, CROMER, NORFOLK NR27 9QS (01263 837221). In a secluded position just off the coast road between Cromer and Sheringham. Ideal for a friendly relaxing holiday. Safe sandy beach five minutes walk. The village boasts two high class restaurants and a village pub. Golf, fishing and riding facilities are all close by. Your pets are welcome too as long as they are kept on a lead while in the grounds. [Pets £1 per night, £6 per week]

Winterton-On-Sea

Good sands and bathing. Great Yarmouth 8 miles.

TIMBERS, WINTERTON-ON-SEA. Self-contained ground floor of cottage in quiet seaside village. Broad sandy beach and pleasant walks. Close to Norfolk Broads. Secluded garden. Double, twin and single bedrooms, sleep 5 plus cot. Bed linen provided. Fully equipped for self-catering family holiday. £200-£320 per week. Full details from MR M. J. ISHERWOOD, 79 OAKLEIGH AVENUE, LONDON N20 9JG (0208 445 2192). [Pets £5 per week]

WINTERTON VALLEY HOLIDAYS. A selection of modern superior fully appointed holiday chalets sleeping 2-6 persons. Duvets and colour TV in all chalets. Panoramic views of the sea from this quiet 35 acre estate. 5 minutes beach, 8 miles Great Yarmouth. Pets very welcome. For colour brochure; 15 KINGSTON AVENUE, CAISTER-ON-SEA NR30 5ET (01493 377175). [Pets £15 per week].,

Wroxham

Village 7 miles north east of Norwich.

THE BROADS HOTEL, STATION ROAD, WROXHAM, NORWICH NR12 8UR (01603 782869; Fax: 01603 784066). Comfortable hotel owned and run by dog-loving family. Ideally situated for boating, fishing and exploring the beautiful Norfolk countryside and coastline. All rooms fully en suite. [🐾]

**Readers are requested to mention this guidebook
when seeking accommodation
(and please enclose a stamped addressed envelope).**

The Globe Hotel

High Street, Weedon, Northampton NN7 4QD

👑👑👑👑 Commended   RAC★★

While retaining its historic character, The Globe has been completely refurbished to a most comfortable standard. 18 en suite bedrooms. Within easy touring distance of Warwick, Leamington Spa, Stratford, Naseby Battlefield and Silverstone. Close to Grand Union Canal. Comprehensive food operation OPEN ALL DAY features home fayre bar meals and à la carte menu. Special weekend Giveaway Breaks. Country walks abound.

A Countryside Inn

Tel: 01327 340336 Fax: 01327 349058

WEEDON

Village to the south east of Daventry, near the M1

THE GLOBE HOTEL, HIGH STREET, WEEDON, NORTHAMPTON NN7 4QD (01327 340336; Fax: 01327 349058). Set in countryside close to Grand Union Canal. 18 en suite bedrooms. Comprehensive food operation. Convenient for Warwick, Stratford, Silverstone. Special Weekend Giveaway Breaks. Four Crowns Commended. [pw! 🐕]

NORTHUMBERLAND
NORTHUMBERLAND *Alnmouth, Alnwick*

The Hope & Anchor Hotel ♕♕♕ *Commended*

44 Northumberland St, Alnmouth, Alnwick, Northumberland NE66 2RA

01665 830363

The Hope & Anchor....friendly, clean and comfortable with good food. Set in this historic coastal village yet only minutes' drive from open countryside. Ideal base from which to explore unspoilt Northumberland. Call/write for details. Proprietors Carol & Alan Sweet. ' *Sam', our chihuahua says "great for pets, sorry ......people as well"*

John & Christina Tanney   Marine Road, Alnmouth NE66 2RW Tel: 01665 830349

MARINE HOUSE PRIVATE HOTEL

Charming hotel in fine sea front location. 10 individually appointed en suite bedrooms, four course gourmet candlelit dinner, cocktail bar, games room. Children over seven years and pets very welcome.

ETC ♦♦♦♦ Highly Commended   AA Selected ♦♦♦♦
RAC Highly Acclaimed   Hospitality Awards.

Dinner, Bed and Breakfast   Low season from £38
Daily per person: High season from £44

Northumbrian Log Fire Breaks: Oct/Apr

Mount Pleasant Farm
Alnmouth, Alnwick NE66 3BY

Situated on the outskirts of Alnmouth, Mount Pleasant Farm is an ideal base for touring castles, the Farnes and the Holy Island. Self-contained annexe sleeps 2 adults and one child; open plan kitchen. Also chalet comprising double/twin bedded rooms. Plus 6 berth caravan

Telephone 01665 830 215
for more details.

Prices on application.

NORTHUMBRIA COAST AND COUNTRY COTTAGES LTD
Self-Catering Holiday Cottage Agency. ETC Registered.
A superb selection of cottages in beautiful Northumberland
Website: www.alnmarin.co.uk/nccc
FREE COLOUR BROCHURE: 01665 830783 (24HRS)

Titlington Hall Farm   4 KEYS COMMENDED

Two lovely country cottages available for let all year round. They are situated in a quiet and beautiful area with many interesting places just a short drive away. Facilities include central heating, TV, fridge, microwave, washing machine, tumble dryer and linen. Children welcome, pets by arrangement. From £195 to £315 per week.

MRS V. PURVIS, TITLINGTON HALL FARM, ALNWICK NE66 2EB (01665 578253)

VILLAGE FARM   Town Foot Farm, Shilbottle, Alnwick, Northumberland NE66 2HG
SELF CATERING   Tel/Fax: 01665 575591; e-mail: crissy@villagefarm.demon.co.uk

Top-quality accommodation with a choice of 17th Century farmhouse or Scandinavian lodges and cottages. Indoor pool, sauna, gymnasium, solarium, games room, riding, tennis court, fishing pond and award-winning beaches within 3 miles. Castles and Hills close by. Open all year. Short Breaks Autumn/Winter.

Comprehensive brochure.   **3-5 Keys up to Highly Commended**.

NORTHUMBERLAND *Bamburgh, Belsay, Corbridge, Haltwhistle, Hexham, Warkworth*

Waren House Hotel AA★★ RAC ★★★

Waren House Hotel, Waren Mill, Bamburgh, Northumberland. NE70 7EE
Why not let your best friend join you and your partner at our luxurious Country
House Hotel. Excellent accommodation, superb food and extensive moderately
priced wine list. Rural setting in six acres of grounds on edge of Budle Bay 2
miles from Bamburgh Castle. No children under 14 please.   ★★★

Tel: 01668 214581

Bounder House Stone built farmhouse situated in beautiful Northumbrian countryside. Ideally situated for touring
the Borders or convenient overnight stop en route for Scotland. Two double rooms and a twin all
with en suite facilities and a family room with private bathroom. All rooms have TV and tea/coffee
facilities. Microwave and fridge available. £38 twin or double room en suite £25 single, family room
with private bathroom on application. All including full English breakfast. **Mrs Kath Fearns,
Bounder House, Belsay, Newcastle-upon-Tyne NE20 0JR Tel: 01661 881267**
Fax: 01661 881266 Web: http://freespace.virgin.net/k.fearns// e-mail: k.fearns@bigfoot.com

---

The Hayes

Large, spacious stone-built country house set in seven acres of gardens and woodland, on
the edge of this historic village and with easy nearby access to the A69 and A1M. All rooms
with tea/coffee facilities and TV, and most en suite. Stair lift available. Well furnished
throughout. Plenty of car parking. Bed and Breakfast from £18.50 with reductions for
children. Further details/brochure on request. ™ Commended **ETC** ◆◆

Self-catering cottages also available. **Mrs M. J. Matthews, The Hayes, Newcastle Road, Corbridge NE45 5LP**
Tel: 01434 632010   E-mail: mmatthews.fsbusiness.co.uk

SAUGHY RIGG FARM • TEL: 01434 344120 • 🏵🏵 APPROVED

Kathryn McNulty, Twice Brewed, Haltwhistle. NE49 9PT

Close to the best parts of Hadrian's Wall. A warm welcome, real fires and
good food. Parking. TV. Central heating. Children and pets welcome.
Open January to February. Prices from £15.00.

Taylor Burn, Ninebanks, Hexham, Northumberland NE47 8DE

Warm welcome and good food on quiet working hill farm with spectacular views. Large comfortable
farmhouse with spacious bedrooms; guests' lounge and bathroom; You will be our only visitors.
No Smoking. Guests can join in farm activities; excellent for walkers and country lovers.

10% reduction for weekly stays - B&B £18 pppn

Mrs Mavis Ostler   **Tel: 01434 345343**

BIRLING VALE, WARKWORTH.

Attractive stone built detached house in secluded garden. Fully equipped, two double bedrooms,
one twin, cot. Free central heating. Close to sandy beaches, trout and salmon rivers and many
places of interest. Well-trained dogs welcome. Weekly rates from £120 – £425.

SAE to Mrs J. Brewis, Woodhouse Farm, Shilbottle, Near Alnwick NE66 2HR Tel: 01665 575222

NOTE

All the information in this book is given in good faith in the
belief that it is correct. However, the publishers cannot
guarantee the facts given in these pages, neither are they
responsible for changes in policy, ownership or terms that may
take place after the date of going to press. Readers should
always satisfy themselves that the facilities they require are
available and that the terms, if quoted, still apply.

Alnmouth

Quiet little resort with wide sands. Alnwick with its impressive Norman Castle is 5 miles north west.

CAROL AND ALAN SWEET, THE HOPE & ANCHOR HOTEL, 44 NORTHUMBERLAND STREET, ALNMOUTH, ALNWICK NE66 2RA (01665 830363). Three Crowns Commended. "Sam" our cheeky chihuahua says "Great for pets..., sorry people as well!". Close to the beach yet on the edge of Northumberland's magnificent countryside. [🐕]

JOHN AND CHRISTINA TANNEY, MARINE HOUSE PRIVATE HOTEL, 1 MARINE ROAD, ALNMOUTH NE66 2RW (01665 830349). Charming hotel in fine seafront location. Home cooking, cocktail bar, games room. Children over seven and pets very welcome. ETC ◆◆◆◆ AA ◆◆◆◆. [🐕]

MRS A. STANTON, MOUNT PLEASANT FARM, ALNMOUTH, ALNWICK NE66 3BY (01665 830215). Situated at top of hill on outskirts of village; convenient for castles and Holy Island. Self-contained annexe sleeps 2 adults and one child; open-plan kitchen, shower room. Chalet and 6-berth caravan also available. [🐕]

NORTHUMBRIA COAST AND COUNTRY COTTAGES LTD. Selected self-catering holiday cottages. ETC Registered Agency. Discover beautiful unspoilt Northumberland in one of our personally selected properties – over 130 to choose from – pets welcome in many. Colour brochure: 01665 830783 / 830902 (24hrs) [Pets £4.00 per week.]
Website: www.alnmarin.co.uk/nccc

Alnwick

Local attractions include the Norman castle, Dunstanburgh Castle and Warkworth Castle. Nine-hole golf course, fishing, riding, tennis. Newcastle-upon-Tyne 34 miles, Berwick-upon-Tweed 30.

MRS V. PURVIS, TITLINGTON HALL FARM, ALNWICK NE66 2EB (01665 578253) ♛♛♛♛ COMMENDED. Two lovely country cottages in a quiet and beautiful area, available for let all year round. Central heating, TV, fridge, microwave, washing machine, tumble dryer and linen. Children welcome, pets by arrangement. From £195 to £315 per week. [🐾]

VILLAGE FARM SELF CATERING, TOWN FOOT FARM, SHILBOTTLE, ALNWICK NE66 2HG (Tel/Fax: 01665 575591). Top quality accommodation with a choice of 17th century farmhouse or Scandinavian lodges and cottages. Indoor pool, gymnasium, games room, tennis court and award-winning beaches within 3 miles. Open all year. Short Breaks Autumn/Winter. Comprehensive brochure. [Pets £10 pw].
E–mail: crissy@villagefarm.demon.co.uk

Bamburgh

Village on North Sea coast with magnificent castle. Grace Darling buried in churchyard.

THE MIZEN HEAD HOTEL, BAMBURGH NE69 7BS (Tel: 01668 214254; Fax: 01668 214104) AA ★★ Three Crowns Commended. A warm welcome awaits owners and pets alike at the Mizen Head. Close to the beautiful Northumbrian coastline and just a short drive from many lovely walks in the Ingram Valley. The hotel boasts log fires, good food and real ales.

MR P. LAVERACK, WAREN HOUSE HOTEL, WAREN MILL, BAMBURGH, NORTHUMBERLAND. NE70 7EE (01668 214581). Luxurious Country House Hotel. Excellent accommodation, superb food, moderately priced wine list. Rural setting. No children under 14 please. ★★★.

Beadnell

Fishing village and resort on North Sea coast.

MARILYN DAVIDSON, 7 BENTHALL, BEADNELL NE67 5BQ (Tel & Fax: 01665 720900). Small non-smoking pet-friendly B&B, luxury en suite bedrooms, sitting room with TV and tea tray. Near picturesque harbour, glorious beaches and surrounded by super opportunities foe walkers and riders, golfers and divers, artists and birdwatchers. [🐾]

Belsay

Village five miles north west of Ponteland. Belsay Hall is a Neo-Classical building resembling a Greek temple, has extensive gardens. 14th century castle.

MRS. KATH FEARNS, BOUNDER HOUSE, BELSAY, NEWCASTLE-UPON-TYNE NE20 0JR (01661 881267). Stone-built farmhouse situated in beautiful Northumbrian countryside. Two double rooms and a twin all with en suite facilities and a family room with private bathroom. All with colour TV and tea/coffee facilities. Pets welcome. Open all year.

Berwick-on-Tweed

The most northerly town in England with elegant streets and 18th century town hall.

MRS M. J. MARTIN, FELKINGTON FARM, BERWICK-UPON-TWEED TD15 2NR (01289 387220). Comfortable cottages – ideal base to explore the coast and Border country. Playground, games room, woodland walk. Children and pets welcome. ♥♥♥♥ Commended. Colour Brochure available.

Corbridge

Small town on north bank of River Tyne, 3 miles east of Hexham. Nearby are remains of Roman military town of Corstopitum.

MRS M. J. MATTHEWS, THE HAYES, NEWCASTLE ROAD, CORBRIDGE NE45 5LP (01434 632010). ETC ◆◆. Large, spacious stone-built country house set in seven acres of gardens and woodland. Stair lift available. B&B from £18.50. Reductions for children. Further details/brochure on request (ref. FHG). ♥♥♥ Commended self-catering cottages also available [🐾]
E–mail: mmatthews.fsbusiness.co.uk

Haltwhistle

Small market town about one mile south of Hadrian's Wall.

MRS CAROLINE CLAYTON, HOLE HOUSE, BLENKINSOPP, NEAR HALTWHISTLE NE49 0LQ (016977 47383). Labrador Nell thoroughly recommends Stable Cottage – luxurious stone byre with log burning stove. Excellent walking – Hadrian's Wall/North Pennines. ETC ♥♥♥♥ Highly Commended (and 4 Paws!).

SAUGHY RIGG FARM, KATHRYN McNULTY, TWICE BREWED, HALTWHISTLE. NE49 9PT (01434 344120). Close to the best parts of Hadrian's Wall. A warm welcome, real fires and good food. Parking. TV. Central heating. Children and pets welcome. Open January to Febuary. Prices from £15.00. Two Crowns.

SYMBOLS

🐾	Indicates that pets are welcome free of charge.
£	Indicates that a charge is made for pets: nightly or weekly.
pw!	Shows some special provision for pets; exercise facility, feeding or accommodation arrangement.
⌂	Indicates separate pets accommodation.

Hexham

Market town on bank of River Tyne, with medieval priory church. Racecourse 2 miles, Newcastle upon Tyne 20 miles.

RYE HILL FARM, SLALEY, NEAR HEXHAM NE47 OAH (01434 673259). Pleasant family atmosphere in cosy farmhouse. Bed and Breakfast and optional Evening Meal. Bedrooms with TV and tea/coffee facilities. All en suite. Laundry facilities. Table licence. 3 Crowns Highly Commended. [pw! Pets £1 per night.]

MRS MAVIS OSTLER, TAYLOR BURN, NINEBANKS, HEXHAM NE47 8DE (01434 345343). Warm welcome and good food on quiet working hill farm. Large comfortable farmhouse with spacious bedrooms; guests' lounge and bathroom. No smoking. Join in farm activities. [pw! Pets £1 per night, £5 per week]

Warkworth

Village on River Coquet near North Sea Coast north-west of Amble with several interesting historic remains.

WARKWORTH HOUSE HOTEL, BRIDGE STREET, WARKWORTH NE65 OXB (01665 711276; Fax: 01665 713323). Set in heart of small village, ideal for dog walking. Miles of open uncrowded beaches. Delicious evening meals. Phone for brochure. [🐕]

Birling Vale is an attractive stone built detached house in secluded garden. Fully equipped, two double bedrooms, one twin, cot. Free central heating. Close to sandy beaches, trout and salmon rivers and many places of interest. Well-trained dogs welcome. Weekly rates from £120 – £425. SAE to MRS J. BREWIS, WOODHOUSE FARM, SHILBOTTLE, NEAR ALNWICK NE66 2HR (01665 575222). [🐕]

Priory Farm Guest House ◆◆◆

Hodsock Priory Estate, Blyth, Notts S81 0TY   Tel: 01909 591515
e-mail: vera@guesthse.force9.co.uk   http://www.guesthse.force9.co.uk

Located within five minutes of A1 and 10 miles of M1, giving easy access to North Yorkshire and Nottingham Borders. Country Walks. All four bedrooms have tea/coffee making facilities; two are en suite. Lounge with log fire and TV. B&B from £18. For details please contact Mrs Vera Hambleton.

BEECHLEA GUEST HOUSE

Our Victorian Guest House is conveniently situated a short walk from Newark's historic town centre (map supplied free of charge). Two en suite and one family rooms, one further double and three singles, all centrally heated with washbasins, colour TV, tea and coffee making facilities. Guests' lounge. All our visitors are assured of a warm, friendly welcome. Children and pets gladly accepted. Non-smoking accommodation. Bed and Breakfast from £18.

Mrs Elaine Sanders, Beechlea Guest House, 2 London Road, Balderton, Newark NG24 3AJ
Tel: 01636 672480; Fax: 01636 707716

Blyth

Village 6 miles from Retford.

MRS V. HAMBLETON, PRIORY FARM GUEST HOUSE, HODSOCK PRIORY ESTATE, BLYTH S81 0TY (01909 591515). Convenient for A1 and M1. All rooms with tea/coffee making; two en suite. Lounge with log fire and TV. B&B from £18. Children and dogs welcome. [🐾]
E–mail: vera@guesthse.force9.co.uk
Website: www.guesthse.force9.co.uk

Burton Joyce

Residential area 4 miles north-east of Nottingham.

MRS V. BAKER, WILLOW HOUSE, 12 WILLOW WONG, BURTON JOYCE, NOTTINGHAM NG14 5FD (0115 931 2070). Large Victorian house in quiet village location, two minutes walk River Trent, four miles city. Attractive accommodation in bright, clean rooms with tea/coffee facilities, TV. Good local eating. Private parking. From £17 pppn. Reduced rates for children. Please phone first for directions.

Newark

Famous as the place where King John died in 1216 at Newark Castle which was reduced to ruins in the civil war. Also Newark Air Museum.

MRS ELAINE SANDERS, BEECHLEA GUEST HOUSE, 2 LONDON ROAD, BALDERTON, NEWARK NG24 3AJ (Tel: 01636 672480; Fax: 01636 707716). Victorian Guest House. Two en suite and one family rooms, one further double and three singles, all centrally heated. Children and pets welcome. Non-smoking accommodation. Bed and Breakfast from £18.

Southwell

Beautiful Southwell Minster has splendid towers and spires dating from 1108.

THE OLD FORGE, BURGAGE LANE, SOUTHWELL NG25 0ER. Charming village house within a short walk of historic Minster, pubs and restaurants, shops and country walks. All rooms en suite, one ground floor. Private parking. B&B from £28 sharing. Reductions for longer stays. (01636 812809; Fax: 01636 816302).

OXFORDSHIRE

NOTTINGHAMSHIRE *Chipping Norton, Thame*

Crown and Cushion Hotel and Leisure Centre
High Street, Chipping Norton, Near Oxford OX7 5AD

500-year-old Coaching Inn, tastefully modernised to provide 40 excellent en suite bedrooms; some four-poster suites. "Old World" bar, log fires, real ale, good food, 👑👑👑👑 Egon Ronay Recommended. Indoor pool, multi-gym, solarium etc. Modern Commended conference centre. Located in picturesque Cotswolds town midway between Oxford and Stratford-upon-Avon. Convenient London, Heathrow, M40. Blenheim Palace, Bourton-on-the-Water, Stow-on-the-Wold, Shakespeare Country all nearby. Pets welcome.

Price Busters start at £19.50; D,B&B at just £34.50

Tel: 01608 642533 Fax: 01608 642926. Colour brochure Freephone 0800 585251.

LITTLE ACRE

Charming country retreat with pretty landscaped gardens and waterfall. Quiet location but only two miles from J6 M40. Near Chilterns, Oxford, Cotswolds, Heathrow Airport. Comfy beds, hearty breakfasts, 'olde worlde' style dining room. Open all year with friendly, relaxed atmosphere. En suite rooms; ground floor bedrooms. Tea/coffee making and TV in rooms. Pets welcome. Highly recommended by previous guests. Bed and Breakfast from £18. **Tel: 01844 281423**

Chipping Norton

Cotswold town 18 miles north-west of Oxford.

CROWN & CUSHION HOTEL AND LEISURE CENTRE, HIGH STREET, CHIPPING NORTON, NEAR OXFORD OX7 5AD (01608 642533; Fax: 01608 642926; Colour Brochure Freephone 0800 585251). 500-year-old coaching inn tastefully modernised. En suite bedrooms; some four-posters. Old World bar; indoor pool, solarium etc. Convenient Stratford, Oxford, London, Shakespeare Country. Price Busters from £19.50.

Faringdon

Town on the A417 north east of Swindon

FARINGDON HOTEL, 1 MARKET PLACE, FARINGDON SN7 7HL (01367 240536; Fax: 01367 243250) 3 Crowns, AA/RAC ★★. Delightful 17th century coaching inn and authentic Thai restaurant. Located just south of the famous city of Oxford and close to the Cotswolds. For that quiet country break we provide traditional hospitality that allows you to relax in the beauty of the English countryside. [Pets £10 per night]

Oxford

Ancient university city on the Thames, here known as the Isis. Apart from the colleges there are many fine buildings, particularly churches and inns. London 56 miles, Stratford-upon-Avon 39, Windsor 39, Henley-on-Thames 24, Banbury 23, Chipping Norton 20, Burford 19.

MRS B.A. DOWNES, BRAVALLA GUEST HOUSE, 242 IFFLEY ROAD, OXFORD OX4 1SE (01865 241326; Fax: 01865 250511). Bravalla is a late Victorian house convenient for city, Ring Road and River. Rooms have bathrooms, colour TV, tea/coffee facilities. We use environmentally friendly products and vegetarians are catered for. Pets are most welcome. Double from £20 per person.

Thame

Town on River Thame 9 miles south west of Aylesbury. Airport at Haddenham.

MS. JULIA TANNER, LITTLE ACRE, TETSWORTH, NEAR THAME OX9 7AT (01844 281423). A country house retreat offering every comfort, set in several private acres. Most rooms en suite. A perfect place to relax . . . your dog will love it. Three minutes Junction 6 M40. [🐾– Bring dog basket with you.]

Woodstock

Old town 8 miles north-west of Oxford. Home to Oxford City and County Museum.

MRS B. JONES, GORSELANDS FARMHOUSE AUBERGE, NEAR LONG HANBOROUGH, WOODSTOCK OX8 6PU (01993 881895; Fax: 01993 882799). Old Cotswold Stone House with flagstone floors and oak beams situated in peaceful countryside. Convenient for many attractions. B&B from £19.25. En suite rooms. Evening Meals £11.95. ★★, RAC Listed. [🐾].

SHROPSHIRE

SHROPSHIRE *Church Stretton*

BED & BREAKFAST   **SELF CATERING**
Central for Shrewsbury, Ironbridge, Ludlow
BED & BREAKFAST: from £18 per person. Enjoy a large country breakfast and a warm welcome. Four-poster en suite rooms, tea trays. Short Breaks available.

SELF-CATERING: three beautifully converted barn cottages, equipped and furnished to a high standard, Ground floor bedroom sleeps 2 to 8 people.
Touring caravans and tents welcome.
**Virginia Evans, Church Farm, Rowton, Near Wellington,
Telford, Shropshire TF6 6QY
Telephone and Fax: 01952 770381**
Commended
E-mail: church.farm@pipemedia.co.uk
Commended

Church Stretton

Delightful little town in lee of Shropshire Hills. Walking and riding country. Facilities for tennis, bowls, gliding and golf. Knighton 22 miles, Bridgnorth 19, Ludlow 15, Shrewsbury 12.

DON AND RITA ROGERS, BELVEDERE GUEST HOUSE, BURWAY ROAD, CHURCH STRETTON SY6 6DP (01694 722232). Pleasant, centrally heated family Guest House – attractive gardens. Parking. Hairdryers, shaver points, Teasmaids all rooms. Two lounges – TV. Packed lunches available. Bed and Breakfast from £24. Evening Meal £11. 10% reduction for weekly/party bookings. AA QQQQ, RAC Acclaimed. 3 Crowns Commended. [⚲]

THE LONGMYND HOTEL, CHURCH STRETTON SY6 6AG (01694 722244; Fax: 01694 722718). Situated overlooking the beautiful Welsh border this hotel has a subtle mixture of superb modern and period rooms equipped with every refinement demanded by the discerning guest of today. 4 Crowns. [pw! Pets £2 per night.]

MYND HOUSE HOTEL, LITTLE STRETTON, CHURCH STRETTON SY6 6RB (01694 722212). Distinguished 7 bedroomed hotel and restaurant in rural hamlet. At base of Long Mynd. Iron Bridge, Shrewsbury and Ludlow 15 miles. Award winning food. Dogs free. 4 Crowns HIGHLY COMMENDED. [⚲]

MRS C.F. BRANDON-LODGE, NORTH HILL FARM, CARDINGTON, CHURCH STRETTON SY6 7LL (01694 771532). Rooms with a view! B&B in beautiful Shropshire hills. TV in rooms, tea etc. Ideal walking country.[⚲ ◻]

F. & M. ALLISON, TRAVELLERS REST INN, UPPER AFFCOT, NEAR CHURCH STRETTON SY6 6RL (01694 781275; Fax: 01694 781555). RAC Inn. Fully licensed inn on the main A49. Good base for touring. Ample parking space. Children and dogs welcome. 2 Crowns Approved. SAE or phone for further details. [pw! ⚲]

Cleobury Mortimer

Charming little town of timbered and Georgian house. There is fishing on the River Rea, and walking in the Wyre Forest or on Clee Hill, which rises to over 1,600 ft. Ludlow 10 miles.

THE REDFERN HOTEL, CLEOBURY MORTIMER DY14 8AA (01299 270395). Eleven well-equipped bedrooms, all with private facilities and some on the ground floor. Award-winning restaurant noted for fine food. No charge for pets to PETS WELCOME! readers. AA ★★★. [🐾]

Craven Arms

Attractive little town with some interesting old half-timbered houses. Weekly cattle and sheep sales. Nearby is imposing Stokesay Castle (13th cent.). Bridgnorth 21 miles, Shrewsbury 20, Ludlow 8.

MRS J. WILLIAMS, HURST HILL FARM, CLUN, CRAVEN ARMS SY7 OJA (01588 640224). Comfortable riverside farmhouse. Woodlands, riding ponies. Convenient for Offa's Dyke, Stiperstones. Bed and Breakfast from £19, Dinner, Bed and Breakfast from £27. 2 Crowns Commended. AA Recommended. Winner "Great Farm Breakfast".

Ludlow

Lovely and historic town on Rivers Teme and Corve with numerous old half-timbered houses and inns. Impressive Norman castle; river and woodland walks. Golf, tennis, bowls, steeplechase course. Worcester 29 miles, Shrewsbury 27, Hereford 24, Bridgnorth 19, Church Stretton 16.

HENWICK HOUSE, GRAVEL HILL, LUDLOW SY8 1QU (01584 873338). Warm, comfortable Georgian coach house, good traditional English Breakfast. Easy walking distance from town centre and local inns. lots of nice local walks. One double/ one twin en suite, one twin private bathroom. £20pp

CLIVE AND CYNTHIA PRIOR, MOCKTREE BARNS, LEINTWARDINE, LUDLOW SY7 0LY (01547 540441). Self-catering character cottages around sunny courtyard. ETC ♔♔♔. Sleep two to six. Comfortable, well-equipped. Friendly owners nearby. Dogs and children welcome. Lovely country walks from door. Ludlow seven miles. Brochure. [Pets £10 per week]

Mrs S.E. JONES, SPARCHFORD FARM, CULMONGTON, LUDLOW SY8 2DE (01584 861 222; MOBILE: 07974 744 203). Six berth caravan on hard standing, also camping and touring caravan site. Children and pets welcome. Toilets, showers, washing up and food preparation area. Situated on a working farm four miles from the medieval town of Ludlow. Ideally placed for walkers. Open March to November.

SYMBOLS

🐾   Indicates that pets are welcome free of charge.

£   Indicates that a charge is made for pets: nightly or weekly.

pw!   Shows some special provision for pets; exercise facility, feeding or accommodation arrangement.

⌂   Indicates separate pets accommodation.

Oswestry

Borderland Market town. Many old castles and fortifications including 13th century Chirk Castle, Whittington Castle, Oswestry's huge Iron Age hill fort, Offa's Dyke. Shrewsbury 16, Vyrnwy 18.

PEN-Y-DYFFRYN COUNTRY HOUSE HOTEL, NEAR RHYDYCROESAU, OSWESTRY SY10 7JD (01691 653700). Picturesque Georgian Rectory quietly set in Shropshire/ Welsh Hills. Ten en suite bedrooms, two with private patios. 5-acre grounds. No passing traffic. Johansens recommended. Dinner, Bed and Breakfast from £53.00 per person per day. ETC ★★★. [🐕 pw!]

Shrewsbury

Fine Tudor Town with many beautiful black and white timber buildings, Abbey and Castle. Riverside walks, Quarry Park and Dingle flower garden. 39 miles north-west of Birmingham.

RYTON FARM HOLIDAY COTTAGES, RYTON, DORRINGTON, SHREWSBURY SY5 7LY (01743 718449). Traditional country cottage sleeping 6 or converted barn for 2 or 4 persons. Well-equipped kitchens, colour TV, fitted carpets. Pets especially welcome. 🔑🔑🔑 Commended. [Pets £22 per week].

MR DAVID COLLINGWOOD, "WEAVER HOUSE", 26 GRANVILLE STREET, SHREWSBURY SY3 8NE (01743 344 266). Everything you could wish for: comfort, relaxation, freedom, extra facilities, with friendly, helpful host. Situated in a very quiet area, easy reach of riverside park and town centre. Only guests with dogs accommodated – only one booking taken at any one time and minimum stay is two nights. SEE DISPLAY ADVERT. [🐕]

Telford

New town (1963). Ten miles east of Shrewsbury. Includes the south bank of the River Severn above and below Ironbridge, site of the world's first iron bridge (1777).

BOURTON MANOR, BOURTON, MUCH WENLOCK TF13 6QE(01746 785531). Set in small hamlet nestling close to Wenlock Edge. Single, twin and double luxury bedrooms each with radio, colour TV etc. Ideal for walking and riding; Telford, Shrewsbury nearby. Dogs welcome. [pw! Pets £2 per night]

B&B and self-catering in a quiet village yet equidistant from Shrewsbury and Ironbridge. Listed Grade II farmhouse; en suite rooms from £18pp. Self-catering barn conversion cottages sleeping 2-8 people. Ground floor bedroom from £160 per week. VIRGINIA AND ROBERT EVANS, CHURCH FARM, ROWTON, WELLINGTON, TELFORD TF6 6QY (01952 770381). [Pets £5 per week]
E–mail: church.farm@pipemedia.co.uk

MRS RICHARDS, THORPE HOUSE, COALPORT, TELFORD TF8 7HP (01952 586789). Victorian House in Ironbridge Gorge World Heritage Site, beautiful views, peaceful. Breakfasts with free range meat and eggs. Teletext televisions, tea making facilities, magazines all rooms. Riverside/woodland walks, fishing, close Victorian Town and China Museum. Dogs Allowed.

Highercombe Farm

Dulverton, Exmoor, Somerset TA22 9PT. Tel: 01398 323616

A 450 acre farm on Exmoor and 100 acres of woodland in peaceful setting.
Spectacular views. All rooms en suite. Bring your dog or horse and enjoy
walking/riding directly onto moorland. Log fires, farmhouse cooking and much
more. ETC ◆◆◆◆ Silver Award.

Also private self-catering wing of farmhouse. ꝑꝑꝑꝑ **Commended.**

Brochure available. **Contact: Abigail Humphrey**

THE YARN MARKET HOTEL
High Street, Dunster TA24 6SF
Tel: **01643 821425**
Fax: **01643 821475**
E-mail:
yarnmarket.hotel@virgin.net

In the centre of quaint English village, an ideal location for walking and
exploring Exmoor, the surrounding coastline and the many local attractions.
Comfortable, family-run hotel which provides a friendly, relaxed atmosphere,
home cooking, en suite rooms with colour TV, tea making facilities and a
residents' lounge. Packed lunches and drying facilities available. Non-smoking.
Well behaved dogs welcome. 🦌🦌🦌 Commended. B&B From £30.

HUNTERS MOON
Exford, Near Minehead, Somerset TA24 7PP
Cosy bungalow smallholding in the heart of Exmoor
★★ Glorious views ★★ Good food ★★ Friendly atmosphere ★★ Open all year ★★
Pets welcome free   Stabling available   Optional Evening Meal
Bryan and Jane Jackson   Tel: 01643 831695

THE
𝔇unkery 𝔅eacon
HOTEL

WOOTTON COURTENAY,
WEST SOMERSET TA24 8RH
TELEPHONE 01643 841241
For full information and brochure write
or telephone Kenneth or Daphne Midwood

PETS WELCOME FREE

IN THE BEAUTIFUL EXMOOR NATIONAL PARK
Country house hotel in fabulous unrivalled setting.

The superb views can be absorbed at leisure
from the terrace or lawns and gardens.

Fully en-suite rooms • Colour TV • Radio Alarm
Coffee and tea making facilities • **No single supplement**
Car park • Lots of lovely "walkies"

Special Spring and Autumn Bargains Breaks
Meet our two Old English sheepdogs Bronte and Bonnie

YOU WILL BE WARMLY WELCOMED ON ARRIVAL, BUT IT IS QUITE
POSSIBLE THAT YOUR PET WILL GET EVEN MORE FUSS

See also Colour Advertisement on page 31

Riscombe Farm Holiday Cottages – Exmoor National Park

Brochure from the resident owners:
Leone & Brian Martin,
Riscombe Farm, Exford,
Somerset TA24 7NH
Tel & Fax: 01643 831480

Four charming self-catering stone cottages converted from
barns surrounding an attractive courtyard with stables.
Very comfortable, with log fires and equipped to a high
standard, sleeping 2-7.
Peaceful, relaxing location beside the River Exe in the centre
of Exmoor National Park.
Excellent walking and riding country in the valleys, across
the moors or along the spectacular coast.
One and a half miles from Exford Village.
Dogs and horses welcome. Open all year.
ETC Rating: Four Keys Highly Commended.

BRAESIDE
Tel/Fax: (01934) 626642 HOTEL
2 VICTORIA PARK, WESTON-SUPER-MARE BS23 2HZ

Delightful, family-run hotel, ideally situated near sandy beach (dogs allowed all year) and park. All rooms en suite. Unrestricted on street parking. Open all year. Although fairly small, we have been awarded ◆◆◆◆ from the RAC, the AA and The English Tourism Council... expect quality and service.

Special B&B Offer: November to April inclusive ... THIRD NIGHT FREE. **E-mail: braeside@tesco.net**

MARION COFFMAN, BARKA PARKA BEAN BEDS, HEATHBURY, BAKER'S LANE, CHILCOMPTON, BATH BA3 4EW (FREEPHONE/Fax: 0800 096 2443; Tel & Fax 01205 270505). Stop wasting money on beds that don't last. Barka Parka Means Quality – Our Two-Year Warranty Guarantees It!

CLASSIC COTTAGES, HELSTON, CORNWALL TR13 8NA (01326 565555). Choose your cottage from 400 of the finest coastal and country cottages throughout the West Country. Many welcome pets.

POWELLS COTTAGE HOLIDAYS, HIGH STREET, SAUNDERSFOOT, PEMBROKESHIRE SA69 9EJ. Many of our top quality holiday properties accept pets. Cottages in Devon, Cornwall, Cotswolds, Pembrokeshire and Heart of England. For colour brochure FREEPHONE 0800 378771 (24 hours).

Bath

The best-preserved Georgian city in Britain, Bath has been famous since Roman times for its mineral springs. It is a noted centre for music and the arts, with a wide range of leisure facilities.

MR AND MRS S.G. MORRIS, "MIDSTFIELDS", FROME ROAD, RADSTOCK, NEAR BATH BA3 5UD (01761 434440). Large house in two-acre gardens. Tennis, Indoor heated pool, sauna. Rooms with washbasins, TV; one en suite. Ample parking. Terms £18 – £25pp. Pets and children welcome.

THE OLD MALT HOUSE HOTEL, RADFORD, TIMSBURY, NEAR BATH BA3 1QF (Tel: 01761 470106; Fax: 01761 472726). A relaxing, comfortable hotel, in beautiful surroundings between Bath and Wells. Gardens, lawns. All bedrooms en suite. Restaurant and bar meals. ETC/AA ★★. [Pets £3 per night.] E–mail: hotel@oldmalthouse.co.uk
Website: www.oldmalthouse.co.uk

DAVID & JACKIE BISHOP, TOGHILL HOUSE FARM, FREEZING HILL, WICK, NEAR BATH BS30 5RT (01225 891261; Fax: 01225 892128). Luxury barn conversions on working farm 3 miles north of Bath. Each equipped to very high standard, bed linen provided. Also en suite B&B accommodation in 17th century farmhouse. [pw! Pets £8 per week]

Brean

Coastal village with extensive sands. To the north is the promontory of Brean Down. Weston super-Mare 9 miles, Burnham-on-Sea 5.

EMBELLE HOLIDAY PARK, COAST ROAD, BREAN SANDS TA8 2QZ (Freephone 0800 190 322). Chalets and holiday homes on quiet park. Direct access to beach. Full facilities. Colour television. Pets welcome. Near entertainments. Club and restaurant. Free brochure. [Pets £15.00 per week].

WESTWARD RISE HOLIDAY PARK, SOUTH ROAD, BREAN, NEAR BURNHAM ON-SEA TA8 2RD (01278 751310). Highly Recommended Luxury 2/6 berth Chalet bungalows. 2 double bedrooms, shower, toilet, TV, fridge, cooker, duvets and linen. Open all year. Call for free brochure. [Pets £10 per week.]

Bristol

Busy university city on River Avon, which is spanned by Brunel's famous suspension bridge. SS Great Britain, Brunel's iron ship, is moored in the old docks. Bath 13 miles.

MRS C. B. PERRY, CLEVE HILL FARM, UBLEY, NEAR BRISTOL BS18 6PG (01761 462410). Family-run dairy farm in beautiful countryside. Self-catering accommodation in "The Cider House". Fully equipped except towels and linen. £1 electricity meter. One double, one twin room, one double bed settee. Terms from £95 to £220 per week. Obedient pets welcome. [🐕]

Cheddar

Picturesque little town in the Mendips, famous for its Gorge and unique caves. Cheese making is a speciality. Good touring centre. Bath 24 miles, Burnham-on-sea 13, Weston-super-Mare 11.

BROADWAY HOUSE HOLIDAY TOURING CARAVAN & CAMPING PARK, CHEDDAR BS27 3DB (01934 742610; Fax: 01934 744950). ★★★★. Holiday caravans for hire; premier touring and camping pitches. Heated pool, adventure playground, pub, shop. launderette. Superb range of activities.

Mrs Jennifer Buckland, Spring Cottages, Venns Gate, Cheddar BS27 3LW (Tel/Fax: 01934 742493).Three single bedroom cottages sleeping 2/4 persons. The Gorge/Caves are within walking distance. An acre of paddock to exercise your pet. Non-smoking. Short breaks. ♔♔♔♔ Commended. [Pets £3 per night, £20 per week].

Churchill

Village below the north slopes of the Mendip Hills.

WINSTON MANOR HOTEL, CHURCHILL BS25 5NL (01934 852348). Pets and well-trained owners most welcome! Secluded walled garden. Close to Wells, Glastonbury, Bath and Cheddar. Excellent walking country. Our guests tell us the food is excellent too! [🐕]

Dulverton

Attractively set between Exmoor and Brendon Hills. Good fishing. In vicinity, prehistoric Tarr Steps (A.M and N.T.). Exeter 27 miles, Taunton 26, Lynton 23, Minehead 19, Tiverton 13.

ABIGAIL HUMPHREY, HIGHERCOMBE FARM, DULVERTON, EXMOOR TA22 9PT (01398 323616). A 450 acre farm on Exmoor in peaceful setting. All rooms en suite. Log fires, farmhouse cooking and much more. ETC ◆◆◆ Silver Award. Also private self-catering wing of farmhouse. ⚑⚑⚑⚑ Commended. [🐾]

TARR STEPS HOTEL, HAWKRIDGE, NEAR DULVERTON TA22 9PY (01643 851293). Delightful Country House Hotel nestling against the wooded slopes of the River Barle. A paradise for walking, riding, fishing. Dogs, horses and children welcome! Superb cuisine, very comfortable en suite rooms. [Pets £3.50 nightly, ⌂]

Dunster

Pretty village with interesting features, including Yarn Market, imposing 14th century Castle. Priory Church and old houses and cottages. Minehead 3 miles.

THE YARN MARKET HOTEL, HIGH STREET, DUNSTER TA24 6SF (01643 821425; Fax: 01643 821475). An ideal location for walking and exploring Exmoor. Family-run hotel with a friendly, relaxed atmosphere, home cooking, en suite rooms with colour TV and tea making facilities. Non-smoking. [pw! 🐾, Please notify when booking.]
E–mail: yarnmarket.hotel@virgin.net

Exford

Fine touring centre for Exmoor and North Devon, on River Exe. Dulverton 10 miles.

EXMOOR HOUSE HOTEL, CHAPEL STREET, EXFORD TA24 7PY (01643 831304). Situated in picturesque village (central Exmoor). Comfortable accommodation, en suite rooms with colour TV and beverage facilities. B&B from £25.00pp. [🐾]

BRYAN & JANE JACKSON, HUNTERS MOON, EXFORD, NEAR MINEHEAD TA24 7PP (01643 831695). Cosy bungalow smallholding in the heart of Exmoor. Good food (optional Evening Meal), glorious views, friendly atmosphere. Pets welcome free, stabling available. Open all year. [pw! 🐾]

SYMBOLS

🐾 Indicates that pets are welcome free of charge.
£ Indicates that a charge is made for pets: nightly or weekly.
pw! Shows some special provision for pets; exercise facility, feeding or accommodation arrangement.
⌂ Indicates separate pets accommodation.

Exmoor

265 square miles of unspoiled heather moorland with deep wooded valleys and rivers, ideal for a walking, pony trekking or fishing holiday.

CUTTHORNE, LUCKWELL BRIDGE, WHEDDON CROSS TA24 7EW (01643 831255). Enjoy a touch of sheer luxury at our 14th century country house in glorious Exmoor. En suite facilities, log fires, candlelit dinners. Three Crowns Highly Commended. [🐴 in B&B; Pets £11.75 per week S/C]
E–mail: durbin@cutthorne.co.uk
Website: www.cutthorne.co.uk

DRAYDON COTTAGES, EXMOOR. 7 attractive s/c barn conversion cottages situated 2 miles north-west of Dulverton. Well equipped and maintained with heating throughout. Excellent base for exploring Exmoor. KATHARINE HARRIS, 6 CRABB LANE, ALPHINGTON, EXETER, DEVON EX2 9JD (01392 433524). [Dogs £10.50 weekly.]
E–mail: Kate@draydon-cottages-exmoor.freeserve.co.uk

DUNKERY BEACON HOTEL, WOOTTON COURTENAY TA24 8RH (01643 841241). Country House Hotel with superb views. Fully en suite rooms, colour TV. Lots of lovely "walkies". Special autumn and spring breaks. Write or phone Kenneth or Daphne Midwood for details.[🐴] .

THE EXMOOR WHITE HORSE INN, EXFORD TA24 7PY (01643 831229; Fax: 01643 831246). Family-run 16th century inn situated in charming Exmoor village. 26 bedrooms all en suite, with colour TV and tea making. Fully licensed. Restaurant with varied menu. [🐴](one dog),
E–mail:exmoorwhitehorse.demon.co.uk

MRS JONES, HIGHER TOWN, DULVERTON, EXMOOR TA22 9RX (01398 341272). Bungalow set on its own, where visitors are welcome to walk over our beef and sheep farm. 80 acres set in National Parkland. Walkers paradise; half-a-mile walk from open moorland. Sleeps six, centrally heated, double glazed. Bed linen and electricity provided.

EXMOOR – LOWER CHILCOTT FARM, DULVERTON TA22 9OQ (01398 323439). Self catering character cottages. Walks, adjacent riding school. Children, pets and mothers-in-law welcome. Sleep 2–9. [🐴]

LEONE & BRIAN MARTIN, RISCOMBE FARM HOLIDAY COTTAGES, EXFORD, MINEHEAD TA24 7NH (Tel & Fax: 01643 831480). Four self-catering stone cottages in the centre of Exmoor National Park. Excellent walking and riding country. Dogs and horses welcome. Open all year. 🏠🏠🏠 Highly Commended. [Pets £1 per night, £7 per week.]

THE CROWN HOTEL, EXFORD TA24 7PP (01643 831554/5; Fax: 01643 831665). Situated in rural England. All bedrooms with bath, colour television, hairdryer. Excellent cuisine and fine wines. Bargain Breaks. Superb dog holiday country. [pw! 🏠]

THE ROYAL OAK INN, WITHYPOOL, EXMOOR NATIONAL PARK TA24 7QP (01643 831506/7; Fax: 01643 831659). The Royal Oak Inn has been renowned for its comfort and food for approximately three centuries and has many awards for the latter. It is an ideal base for riding, fishing or simply to walk and enjoy the calm and beauty of the moors. [🐴 🏠]

MRS J. ROBINSON, THE SHIP INN, HIGH STREET, PORLOCK TA24 8QT (01643 862507). Thatched 13th cent. Inn within walking distance of sea and moor. 11 en suite bedrooms. Local produce supplements traditional English cooking in candlelit restaurant. [🛏🗋]

Two cottages and two bungalows on 10 acre estate overlooking Barle Valley. Dogs and horses welcome. Shop and pub 300 metres. JULIA AND JERRY BEGGS, WESTERCLOSE HOUSE, WITHYPOOL TA24 7QR (01643 831302). [pw! Dogs £7 per week]
Website: www.westerclose.f9.co.uk

MRS P. EDWARDS, WESTERMILL FARM, EXFORD TA24 7NJ (01643 831238; Fax: 01643 831660). Delightful Scandinavian pine log Cottages and a Cottage attached to farmhouse. Campsite for Tents/Dormobiles. Information centre and small shop. One/Four Keys Commended. 500 acre farm, varied way-marked walks. [Pets £8+ per week]

JANE STYLES, WINTERSHEAD FARM, SIMONSBATH TA24 7LF (01643 831222; Fax: 01643 831628). Five tastefully furnished and well equipped cottages situated in the midst of beautiful Exmoor. Pets welcome, stables and grazing available. Colour brochure on request. [Dogs and horses £12 per week.]

WOODCOMBE LODGES, BRATTON, NEAR MINEHEAD TA24 8SQ (Tel/Fax: 01643 702789). Four self-catering lodges in a tranquil rural setting on the edge of Exmoor National Park, standing in a beautiful three acre garden with wonderful views.
E–mail: woodcombe@classicfm.net
Website: exmoortourism.org/woodcombe.htm

Hillfarrance

4 miles west of Taunton with its 12th century castle. Situated in valley of Taunton Deane, famed for its apples and cider.

ANCHOR COTTAGES, THE ANCHOR INN, HILLFARRANCE, TAUNTON TA4 1AW (01823 461334). Three self-catering cottages, each sleeps up to five. Full central heating, colour TV; tastefully furnished to high standard. Private gardens and ample parking. Anchor Inn renowned for good food. [🛏]

Ilminster

Market town founded in Saxon times, with charming Georgian houses and a 15th century minster.

MRS GRACE BOND, GRADEN, PEASMARSH, NEAR DONYATT, ILMINSTER TA19 0SG (01460 52371). Comfortable home with pretty garden in peaceful location, close Devon, Dorset borders, ideal for touring Quantock Hills, Lyme Regis, Taunton, Wells and Glastonbury. Many local pubs serving good food. One family, two double rooms with all usual facilities. B&B £15 per night. [Pets £1 per night, £7 per week]

FHG PUBLICATIONS LIMITED publish a large range of well-known accommodation guides. We will be happy to send you details or you can use the order form at the back of this book.

Minehead

Neat and stylish resort on Bristol Channel. Sandy bathing beach, attractive gardens, golf course and good facilities for tennis, bowls and horse riding. Within easy reach of the beauties of Exmoor.

MINEHEAD – SEA – EXMOOR –HOLIDAY FLATS. 30 yards to seafront, Level walk to town centre, Self contained, Fully furnished, Bath/shower, Colour TV, Large garden, Car park, Dogs welcomed SAE: MR T. STONE, TROYTES FARMSTEAD, TIVINGTON, MINEHEAD TA24 8SU (Tel: 01643 704531). [🐾]

Porlock

Most attractive village beneath the tree-clad slopes of Exmoor. Picturesque cottages, old Ship Inn and interesting church). Good bathing from pebble beach at delightful Porlock Weir (2 miles).

CASTLE HOTEL, PORLOCK TA24 8PY (01643 862504). Fully licensed, family-run hotel in centre of lovely Exmoor village. 13 en suite bedrooms, all with colour TV. Bar snacks and meals. Well-behaved children and pets welcome. [🐾]

MR & MRS A. D. HARDICK, PORLOCK CARAVAN PARK, HIGHBANKS, PORLOCK, NEAR MINEHEAD TA24 8NS (Tel/Fax:01643 862269). Well-equipped Caravans for hire, with main drains and water, electric light, TV, launderette. Dogs welcome. Touring caravans, Dormobiles and tents welcome. Write or phone for a brochure. [Pets 50p per night]

MRS CHRISTINE FITZGERALD, "SEAPOINT", UPWAY, PORLOCK TA24 8QE (Tel/Fax:01643 862289). Spacious Edwardian house overlooking Porlock Bay. Open log fires. Coastal/moorland walks. Excellent traditional or vegetarian food. All bedrooms en suite with tea/coffee facilities. ETC ◆◆◆◆. [🐾]

Taunton

County town, rich in historical associations. Good touring centre. Many sporting attractions. Bristol 43 miles, Exeter 32, Weston-super-Mare 29.

MR & MRS D.A. SMALL, ASHE FARM CARAVAN AND CAMPING SITE, THORN-FALCON, TAUNTON TA3 5NW (01823 442567; Fax: 01823 443372). Quiet farm site with 30 touring pitches and two holiday caravans. Showers, toilet, electric hook-ups, shop, games room, tennis court. Ideal for touring coast, Exmoor and Somerset Levels. Fully equipped caravans sleep 6. Open April to October. Pets welcome. WCTB ✓✓✓✓. AA 3 Pennants. [🐾]

MRS PAM GROOME, EXMOOR GATE HOLIDAY LODGES, WATERROW, TAUNTON TA4 2AU (01984 623322). Six pine lodges in secluded woodland setting. Sleep up to six. Colour TV, fitted kitchens and bathrooms. Laundry, fitness suite etc. Bed, Breakfast and Evening Meal also available.

Templecombe

Attractive village 4 miles south of Wincanton.

JUDITH HARTSILVER, PERHAMS FARM, SALLY LOVELLS LANE, YENSTON, TEMPLECOMBE BA8 0NE (01963 371123). Newly renovated period farmhouse. En suite shower room or own bathroom. Peaceful location on public footpath. Large safe gardens. B&B £16 per night. [Pets £1 per night]

Watchet

Small port and resort with rocks and sands. Good centre for Exmoor and the Quantocks. Bathing, boating, fishing, rambling. Tiverton 24 miles, Bridgwater 19, Taunton 17, Dunster 6.

MR D. ALBUTT, CROFT HOLIDAY COTTAGES, THE CROFT, ANCHOR STREET, WATCHET. TA23 0AZ. (Tel & Fax: 01984 631121). Cottages and Bungalow. Private parking, central heating, TV, washing machine, fridge, microwave. Use of lawned area and heated indoor swimming pool. Each unit has barbecue. Five self-contained units; sleeping 2-8. £100 to £470 per unit per week. [🐾]

LORNA DOONE CARAVAN PARK, WATCHET TA23 0BJ (01984 631206). Small quiet park with beautiful views of the coastline and Quantock Hills. Fully equipped luxury caravans. Rose Award Park. [Pets £2 per night, £12 weekly]

SUNNY BANK HOLIDAY CARAVANS, DONIFORD, WATCHET TA23 0UD (01984 632237). Small picturesque family park overlooking sea. All caravans with mains services. Colour TV. Showers. Heated swimming pool. Shop. Launderette. Tourist Board ✓✓✓✓. Also caravans for sale. Brochure. [Pets £2 per night.]

WEST BAY CARAVAN PARK, WATCHET TA23 OBJ (Tel: 01984 631261). Small, quiet park with panoramic sea views. Ideal for relaxing and touring Exmoor and Quantock Hills. Open March-October. ETC ★★★★ Rose Award. Pets welcome. [Pets £2 per night, £12 weekly.]

Weston-Super-Mare

Popular resort on the Bristol Channel with a wide range of entertainments and leisure facilities. An ideal base for touring the West Country.

MR AND MRS C. G. THOMAS, ARDNAVE CARAVAN PARK, KEWSTOKE, WESTON-SUPER-MARE BS22 9XJ (01934 622319). Caravans — de luxe. 2-3 bedrooms, shower, toilet, colour TV's, duvets and covers included. Parking. Dogs welcome. Graded ✓✓✓✓. [🐾 pw!]

BRAESIDE HOTEL, 2 VICTORIA PARK, WESTON-SUPER-MARE BS23 2HZ (Tel/Fax: 01934 626642). ETC/AA/RAC ◆◆◆◆. Delightful, family-run hotel, close to shops and sea front. All rooms en suite, colour TV, tea/coffee making. November to April THIRD NIGHT FREE. See display advertisement. [🐾] E-mail: braeside@tesco.net

---

When making enquiries or bookings, a stamped addressed envelope is always appreciated.

STAFFORDSHIRE

Leek

Village 10 miles north-east of Stoke-on-Trent

ROSEWOOD HOLIDAY FLATS, LOWER BERKHAMSYTCH FARM, BOTTOM HOUSE, NEAR LEEK ST13 7QP (Tel & Fax: 01538 308213). 2 cosy flats each with private entrance. Ground floor flat sleeps 6. First floor flat sleeps 7. Colour TV, microwave, and shower rooms in both flats. Play area and patio sitting area. Terms from £120 to £235 per week, includes electricity and linen. Well behaved pets welcome. ꙮꙮꙮ Commended.

Tutbury

To the north of Burton-on-Trent and overlooked by ruins of twelfth century castle where Mary Queen of Scots was imprisoned.

LITTLE PARK HOLIDAY HOMES, PARK LANE, TUTBURY, NR BURTON-ON-TRENT, DE13 9JQ (Tel & Fax: 01283 812654; Mobile: 0771 4004638). Barn Conversion Units. Full self-catering. Facilities situated next to medieval castle and tourist village. Spectacular views. Near Alton Towers and other theme parks. Ample parking. Please phone for brochure.

SUFFOLK

Aldeburgh

Coastal town 6 miles south-east of Saxmundham. Annual music festival at Snape Maltings.

WENTWORTH HOTEL, ALDEBURGH IP15 5BD (01728 452312). Country House
Hotel overlooking the sea. Immediate access to the beach and walks. Two
comfortable lounges with log fires and antique furniture. Refurbished bedrooms with all facilities and many with sea views. Restaurant specialises in fresh
produce and sea food. [Pets £2 per week]

Bury St Edmunds

This prosperous market town on the River Lark lies 28 miles east of Cambridge.

RAVENWOOD HALL COUNTRY HOUSE HOTEL AND RESTAURANT,
ROUGHAM, BURY ST EDMUNDS IP30 9JA (01359 270345; Fax: 01359 270788).
16th century heavily beamed Tudor Hall set in seven acres of perfect dog
walks. Beautifully furnished en suite bedrooms; renowned restaurant; relaxing
inglenook fires. AA ★★★. [pw!🐾]

Dunwich

Small village on coast, 4 miles south west of Southwold.

MRS ELIZABETH COLE, MIDDLEGATE COTTAGES, MIDDLEGATE BARN,
DUNWICH IP17 3DW (01728 648741). Three cottages situated in quiet, private
road 200 yards from the sea. All furnished and equipped to a high standard.
Centrally heated; available all year. Bookings taken from 1st January 2000. [🐾]

Hadleigh

*Historic town on River Brett with several old buildings of interest including unusual 14th century
church. Bury St Edmunds 20 miles, Harwich 20, Colchester 14, Sudbury 11, Ipswich 10.*

EDGEHILL HOTEL, 2 HIGH STREET, HADLEIGH IP7 5AP (01473 822458; Fax:
01473 823848). 16th-century property offering a warm welcome. Comfortable
accommodation and good home-cooked food. Licensed. Pets welcome. SAE
or telephone for details. 3 Crowns Commended. [🐾]

Kessingland

Little seaside place with expansive sandy beach, safe bathing, wildlife park, lake fishing. To the south is Benacre Broad, a beauty spot. Norwich 26 miles, Aldeburgh 23, Lowestoft 5.

Quality seaside Bungalows, open all year, central heating. Colour TV, parking, bed-linen, heat and light included. 2/8 people. Direct access to award winning beach. Pets very welcome. APPLY– KNIGHTS HOLIDAY HOMES, 198 CHURCH ROAD, KESSINGLAND, SUFFOLK NR33 7SF (FREEPHONE 0800 269067).

Comfortable well-equipped bungalow on lawned site overlooking beach, next to Heritage Coast. Panoramic sea views. Easy beach access. Unspoiled walking area. ETC ♙♙ Commended. MR AND MRS J. SAUNDERS, 22 WANSTEAD PARK AVENUE, LONDON E12 5EN (020 8989 5636). [Pets £10 per week].

Lowestoft

Holiday resort and fishing port. Britains most easterly point. Maritime museum traces seafaring history.

IVY HOUSE FARM HOTEL, IVY LANE, OULTON BROAD, LOWESTOFT, NORFOLK NR33 8HY (01502 501353/588144; Fax: 01502 501539). A relaxing, tranquil location with walks from your bedroom door. 'Oulton Broad's hidden oasis'. See our full colour advert under Norfolk.

Sudbury

Birthplace of Thomas Gainsborough, with a museum illustrating his career. Colchester 13 miles.

Situated in small, picturesque village within 15 miles of Sudbury, Newmarket Racecourse and historic Bury St Edmunds. Bungalow well equipped to accommodate 4 people. All facilities. Car essential, parking. Children and pets welcome. Terms from £55 to £112 per week. For further details send SAE to MRS M. WINCH, PLOUGH HOUSE, STANSFIELD, SUDBURY CO10 8LT (01284 789253).

Wenhaston

Village 3 miles south-east of Halesworth.

THE COMPASSES INN, WENHASTON IP19 9EF (01502 478319). B&B in cosy country inn run by dog lovers. Real ale, log fires and evening bistro. Many walks, commons and river. Garden. Car park. Stairlift. No children. [pw! ♙]

SYMBOLS

♙	Indicates that pets are welcome free of charge.
£	Indicates that a charge is made for pets: nightly or weekly.
pw!	Shows some special provision for pets; exercise facility, feeding or accommodation arrangement.
⌂	Indicates separate pets accommodation.

SURREY

Kingston-upon-Thames

Market town, Royal borough, and administrative centre of Surrey, Kingston is ideally placed for London and environs.

CHASE LODGE HOTEL, 10 PARK ROAD, HAMPTON WICK, KINGSTON-UPON-THAMES KT1 4AS (020 8943 1862; Fax: 020 8943 9363). Award-winning hotel offering quality en suite bedrooms. Easy access to town centre and major transport links. A la carte menu, licensed bar. AA QQQQ, RAC Highly Acclaimed. [🐾]

EAST SUSSEX

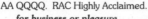

JEAKE'S HOUSE
Mermaid Street, Rye, East Sussex TN31 7ET
Telephone: 01797 222828 Fax: 01797 222623

Dating from 1689, this beautiful Listed Building stands in one of England's most famous streets. Oak-beamed and panelled bedrooms overlook the marsh to the sea. Brass, mahogany or four-poster beds with linen sheets and lace; honeymoon suite. En suite facilities, TV, radio, telephone. Residential licence. Traditional and vegetarian breakfast served. £25.50-£45.50pp. Private car park. Access, Visa and Mastercard accepted.

AA QQQQQ PREMIER SELECTED   RAC Highly Acclaimed   César Award

Good Hotel Guide   ETB ♕♕ Highly Commended

---

4 BEACH COTTAGES, CLAREMONT ROAD, SEAFORD BN25 2QQ

Well-equipped, three-bedroomed terraced cottage on seafront. CH, open fire and woodburner. South-facing patio overlooking sea. Downland walks (wonderful for dogs), fishing, golf, wind-surfing, etc. *Details from*
Julia Lewis, 47 Wandle Bank, London SW19 1DW Tel: 0208 542 5073

♕♕♕ — ♕♕♕♕♕ *Up to Highly Commended*
DUCK BARN HOLIDAYS, TELSCOMBE VILLAGE

DUCK BARN Beautifully converted BARN for 8/10 in large garden; attractive COACH HOUSE for 4/5 and cosy COTTAGE for 2/3. CH and woodburners. Exposed beams, pine furniture. Children, horses and dogs welcome. Brochure from: **Duck Barn Holidays, 51 The Street, Firle, Near Lewes BN8 6LF (01273 858221) e-mail: duck.barn@which.net**

Arlington

Village in valley of River Cuckmere below the South Downs. Hailsham 3 miles.

MRS P. BONIFACE, LAKESIDE FARM, ARLINGTON, POLEGATE BN26 6SB (01323 870111). Situated on the edge of Arlington Reservoir. Eastbourne within 15 miles. Accommodation sleeps 4–6 with two double rooms, lounge, dining area, kitchen, bathroom. Open April to October. Weekly from £175. [🐾]

Battle

Site of the famous victory of William the Conqueror; remains of an abbey mark the spot where Harold fell.

BURNT WOOD HOUSE HOTEL & RESTAURANT, POWDERMILL LANE, BATTLE TN33 0SU (01424 775151). Set in 18 acres of beautiful gardens and ancient woodlands, Burnt Wood House Hotel, with its superb facilities and gentle country atmosphere, is an ideal retreat to relax, unwind and really enjoy your stay. Four Crowns Commended, AA ★★★.

LITTLE HEMINGFOLD HOTEL, TELHAM, BATTLE TN33 0TT (01424 774338). In the heart of 1066 Country, 40 acres of bliss for you and your pets. Farmhouse hotel, all facilities. Fishing, boating, swimming, tennis. Special Breaks all year. Discounts for children. FREE accommodation for pets. [🐾]

Brighton

Famous resort with shingle beach and sand at low tide. Varied entertainment and nightlife; excellent shops and restaurants. Portsmouth 48 miles, Hastings 37, Newhaven 9.

BEST OF BRIGHTON & SUSSEX COTTAGES has available a very good selection of houses, flats, apartments and cottages in Brighton and Hove as well as East and West Sussex from Eastbourne to Chichester. Town centre/seaside and countryside locations – many taking pets. (01273 308779; Fax: 01273 300266). [Pets £15/£20 per week.]

KEMPTON HOUSE HOTEL, 33/34 MARINE PARADE, BRIGHTON BN2 1TR (01273 570248). Private seafront hotel, relaxed and friendly atmosphere, overlooking beach and pier. En suite rooms available, all modern facilities. Satellite TV. Choice of breakfasts. B&B from £25 to £35. Pets and children always welcome. [🐕]

ST BENEDICT'S, 1 MANOR ROAD, BRIGHTON BN2 5EA (01273 674140). Convent Guest House. Comfortable rooms, mostly en suite. TV. also self-catering flat (sleeps 6). Hermitage (1). Near sea, on bus route. Daily mass available. Pets welcome. Apply to Sister Superior. [🐕]

Chiddingly

Charming village, 4 miles north-west of Hailsham. Off the A22 London-Eastbourne road.

Adorable, small, well-equipped cottage in grounds of Tudor Manor. Two bedrooms. Full central heating. Colour TV. Fridge/freezer, laundry facilities. Large safe garden. Use indoor heated swimming pool, sauna/jacuzzi and tennis. From £350 to £625 per week inclusive. ♛♛♛♛♛ Commended. Contact: EVA MORRIS, "PEKES", 124 ELM PARK MANSIONS, PARK WALK, LONDON SW10 0AR (020 7352 8088; Fax: 020 7362 8125). [2 dogs free, extra dog £5 (max. 4) pw!] E–mail: pekes.afa@virgin.net

Fairlight

Village 3 miles east of Hastings.

JANET & RAY ADAMS, FAIRLIGHT COTTAGE, WARREN ROAD, FAIRLIGHT TN35 4AG (01424 812545). A warm welcome awaits you at our comfortable country house. Tasteful en suite bedrooms with central heating, tea/coffee. TV lounge and good home cooking. No smoking. Ample parking. [🐕]

Hastings

Seaside resort with a famous past — the ruins of William the Conqueror's castle lie above the Old Town. Many places of historic interest in the area, plus entertainments for all the family.

BEAUPORT PARK HOTEL, BATTLE ROAD, HASTINGS TN38 8EA (01424 851222). Georgian country mansion in 33 acres. All rooms private bath, colour television, trouser press, hairdryer, telephone. Country house breaks available all year. [pw!]

Herstmonceaux

Small village four miles north-east of Hailsham. Royal Observatory at Herstmonceux Castle.

CLEAVERS LYNG 16th-CENTURY COUNTRY HOTEL, CHURCH ROAD, HERST-MONCEUX BN27 1QJ (01323 833131; Fax: 01323 833617). Privately owned country hotel in heart of rural East Sussex. Bedrooms en suite with tea making, direct dial telephones. Oak-beamed non-smoking restaurant, bar, lounge bar, residents' lounge. Pets welcome. [🐴]

Polegate

Quiet position, 5 miles from the popular seaside resort of Eastbourne. London 58 miles, Lewes 12

MRS P. FIELD, 20 ST JOHN'S ROAD, POLEGATE BN26 5BP (01323 482691). Homely private house. Quiet location; large enclosed garden. Parking space. Ideally situated for walking on South Downs and Forestry Commission land. All rooms washbasins and tea coffee facilities. Bed and Breakfast. Pets very welcome. [pw!]

Rye

Picturesque hill town with steep cobbled streets. Many fine buildings of historic interest. Hastings 12 miles, Tunbridge Wells 28.

FLACKLEY ASH HOTEL, PEASMARSH, RYE TN31 6YH (01797 230651; Fax: 01797 230510). Georgian Country House Hotel in beautiful grounds. Indoor swimming pool and Leisure Centre. AA Rosette for our food. Visit Rye and the castles and gardens of East Sussex and Kent. 4 Crowns Highly Commended. [Pets £7.50 per night.]

JEAKE'S HOUSE, MERMAID STREET, RYE TN31 7ET (01797 222828; Fax: 01797 222623). Dating from 1689, this Listed Building has oak-beamed and panelled bedrooms overlooking the marsh. En suite facilities, TV, radio, telephone. £25.50-£45.50 per person. AA QQQQQ. [🐴]

RYE LODGE HOTEL, HILDER'S CLIFF, RYE TN31 7LD (01797 223838; Fax: 01797 223585). Elegant deluxe rooms named after French wine regions, tastefully furnished. Delicious food, candlelit dinners, fine wines, room service and private car park. The stylish place to stay at this ancient Cinque Ports town. [Pets £3 per night] Website: www.ryelodge.co.uk

Seaford

On the coast midway between Newhaven and Beachy head.

4 BEACH COTTAGES, CLAREMONT ROAD, SEAFORD. BN25 2QQ. Well-equipped, three-bedroomed terraced cottage on seafront. CH, open fire and woodburner. South-facing patio overlooking sea. Downland walks (wonderful for dogs), fishing, golf, wind-surfing, etc. Details from JULIA LEWIS, 47 WANDLE BANK, LONDON SW19 1DW (0208 542 5073). [🐴]

Telscombe

Tranquil Downland hamlet close to South Downs Way. 4 miles from Lewes and 2 miles from coast.

DUCK BARN HOLIDAYS, 51 THE STREET, FIRLE, NEAR LEWES BN8 6LF (01273 858221). Beautiful converted Barn, sleeps 8/10; Coach House for 4/5; Cosy Cottage for 2/3. Central heating, woodburners. Exposed beams– pine furniture. Children, dogs and horses welcome. Brochure. [pw! £10 weekly.]
e-mail: duck.barn@which.net

WEST SUSSEX

WEST SUSSEX *Chichester, Eastergate*

THE MILLSTREAM
HOTEL AND RESTAURANT
BOSHAM

*Ideal setting in a tranquil quayside village
with beautiful shoreline walks – 4 miles west
of Chichester. Dogs very welcome – £2 per day
(inc blanket and dinner of fresh meat and vegetables).*

• *RAC/AA ★★★ and Rosette Award for Food Excellence*
• *'Johansens', 'Which? Hotel' and 'Good Hotel' guides recommended*
• *English Tourist Council Silver Award*

Bosham, Chichester PO18 8HL **01243 573234**

See also Colour Advertisement on page 34

Wandleys Caravan Park
Eastergate, West Sussex PO20 6SE
(01243 543235) or
01243 543384 (evenings/weekends)

You will find peace, tranquillity and relaxation in one of our comfortable holiday caravans. All have internal WC and shower. Dogs welcome. The Sussex Downs, Chichester, Bognor Regis, Arundel, Littlehampton – all these historic and interesting places are only 15 minutes from our beautiful, small and quiet country park. SAE please for brochure.

FHG
Visit the website
www.holidayguides.com
for details of the wide choice of
accommodation featured in the full
range of FHG titles

Chichester

County town dating from Roman times. Festival Theatre holds annual summer season.

THE MILLSTREAM HOTEL AND RESTAURANT, BOSHAM, CHICHESTER PO18 8HL (01243 573234). Ideal setting in a tranquil quayside village with beautiful shoreline walks. Dogs very welcome – £2 per day (inc blanket and dinner of fresh meat and vegetables). [pw!]

Eastergate

Village between the sea and South Downs. Fontwell Park nearby. Bognor Regis 5 miles south.

WANDLEYS CARAVAN PARK, EASTERGATE PO20 6SE (01243 543235 or 01243 543384 evenings/weekends). You will find peace, tranquillity and relaxation in one of our comfortable holiday caravans. All have internal WC and shower. Dogs welcome. Many historic and interesting places nearby. SAE for brochure. [🐕]

Pulborough

Popular fishing centre on the River Arun. South Downs Way nearb; Arundel 8 miles.

BEACON LODGE, LONDON ROAD, WATERSFIELD, PULBOROUGH RH20 1NH (Tel/Fax: 01798 831026). Charming self-contained annexe. B&B accommodation, en suite, TV, coffee/tea making facilities. Wonderful countryside views. B&B from £24pppn. No charge for your pets!. Telephone for more details. [🐕]

CHEQUERS HOTEL, PULBOROUGH RH20 IAD (01798 872486). Lovely Queen Anne house in village overlooking Arun Valley. Excellent food. Children and dogs welcome. AA/RAC ★★. 4 Crowns Highly Commended. No charge for dogs belonging to readers of Pets Welcome! [pw! 🐕]

Selsey

Seaside resort 8 miles south of Chichester. Selsey Bill is headland extending into English Channel.

SELSEY BILL, NEAR CHICHESTER. Delightful detached self-catering cottages and one railway carriage, sleep 2/6, 6/12 plus cot. One suitable for disabled. Superb walks; ideal for touring. Chidren and pets welcome. Colour brochure: MRS SUE GRAVES, 28 WISE LANE, MILL HILL, LONDON NW7 2RE (Tel & Fax: 0208 959 2848).
E–mail: sue@suegraves.demon.co.uk
Website: www.shortlet.dircon.co.uk

ST ANDREWS LODGE HOTEL, CHICHESTER ROAD, SELSEY PO20 0LX (01243 606899; Fax: 01243 607826). 10 bedrooms, all en suite, with direct dial telephones and modem point, some on ground floor. Spacious lounges with log fire; friendly bar for residents only. Excellent Grade 1 wheelchair access. Evening meals by prior arrangement. 3 Crowns Commended. AA QQQQ Selected.

Worthing

Residential town and seaside resort with 5-mile seafront. Situated 10 miles west of Brighton.

CAVENDISH HOTEL, 115 MARINE PARADE, WORTHING BN11 3QG (01903 236767; Fax: 01903 823840). Ideal base for touring Sussex villages and the rolling South Downs. All rooms are en suite, have TV, direct-dial telephone and tea/coffee facilities. No charge for dogs belonging to readers of Pets Welcome!. [🐾]
E–mail: thecavendish@mistral.co.uk
Website: www3.mistral.co.uk/thecavendish/

WARWICKSHIRE

WARWICKSHIRE   *Stratford-upon-Avon*

Mrs Hazel Mellor
ARRANDALE
208 Evesham Road,
Stratford-upon-Avon CV37 9AS

Tel: (01789) 267112

Comfortable family Guest House situated at the town end of Evesham Road on the B439 (Bidford). 10 minutes' walk to River Avon, Shakespearean properties, theatre. One hour's drive to Cotswolds. Washbasins, tea-making facilities and TV in bedrooms; centrally heated. Pets in room. Parking, though car not essential. Lift from bus or train station by arrangement. Bed and Breakfast: room with shower £15.50 per person, en suite at £18 per person. Weekly terms £105-£120. Evening Meals £6.50 extra.

RAYFORD CARAVAN PARK

RIVERSIDE, TIDDINGTON ROAD,
STRATFORD-UPON-AVON CV37 7BE
Tel: (01789) 293964

PETS WELCOME. A HAPPY AND INTERESTING HOLIDAY FOR ALL

Avon Estates Ltd

Holiday & Home Parks

**River
Launch
Service
to
Stratford**

Situated within the town of Stratford-upon-Avon, on the banks of the river, Rayford Park is ideally placed for visiting all Shakespearean attractions and the beautiful Cotswolds. In Stratford itself there is everything you could wish for: shops, pubs, restaurants, swimming pool, sports centre, the Royal Shakespeare Theatre, and a generous helping of history and the Bard! The luxury 12ft wide Caravan Holiday Homes accommodate up to 6 persons in comfort. All have kitchen with full-size cooker, fridge; bathroom with shower/washbasin/WC; two bedrooms, one double-bedded and one with two single beds (cot available);double dinette/two single settees in lounge; gas fires, colour TV, carpeted throughout.Also available: TWO COTTAGES, "Sleepy Hollow" and "Kingfisher Cottage", all modern facilities, set on riverside. Private fishing. BROCHURE ON REQUEST.

THE CROFT Haseley Knob, Warwick CV35 7NL
Tel and Fax: 01926 484447
This four-acre smallholding has a friendly, family atmosphere and is situated in picturesque rural surroundings. Very comfortable accommodation. Bedrooms, most en suite, with colour TV, tea/coffee facilities. Ground floor en suite bedrooms available. Bed and Full English Breakfast from £23. Pets welcome.

Woodside Guest House
Langley Road, Claverdon, Warwick CV35 8PJ
Tel: 01926 842446; Fax: 01926 843697
A peaceful family guest house in 22 acres of own gardens and woodland. Lovely views, walks, log fires. Happy to welcome four-legged guests. ETB One Crown. Brochure available. Special Autumn Breaks.

Stratford-Upon-Avon

Historic town famous as Shakespeare's birthplace and home. Birmingham 24, Warwick 8.

MRS H. J. MELLOR, ARRANDALE, 208 EVESHAM ROAD, STRATFORD-UPON-AVON CV37 9AS (01789 267112). Guest House situated near River Avon, theatre, Shakespeare properties. Washbasins, tea making, TV, central heating, en suite available. Children, pets welcome. Parking. Bed and Breakfast £15.50-£18.00. Weekly terms £105-£120. Evening Meal £6.50. [🐕]

RAYFORD CARAVAN PARK, TIDDINGTON ROAD, STRATFORD-UPON-AVON CV37 7BE (01789 293964). Luxury Caravans, sleep 6. Fully equipped kitchens, bathroom/ shower/WC. Also two riverside Cottages, all modern facilities to first-class standards. Private fishing. On banks of River Avon. [Pets £12 weekly.]

Warwick

Town on the River Avon, 9 miles south-west of Coventry, with medieval castle and many fine old buildings.

MR & MRS D. CLAPP, THE CROFT, HASELEY KNOB, WARWICK CV35 7NL (Tel & Fax: 01926 484447). Smallholding with a friendly, family atmosphere and situated in picturesque rural surroundings. Very comfortable accommodation. Bedrooms, most en suite, with colour TV, tea/coffee facilities. Ground floor en suite bedrooms available. Bed and Full English Breakfast from £23. Pets welcome. [Pets £2 per night]

THE OLD RECTORY, VICARAGE LANE, STRATFORD ROAD, SHERBOURNE, WARWICK CV35 8AB (Tel: 01926 624562; Fax: 01926 624995). Grade II Listed Georgian country house with 14 elegantly appointed en suite bedrooms, some antique brass beds. Four-posters and spa baths available. À la carte restaurant. Beautiful surroundings. Ideal for Stratford, Cotswolds and many National Trust properties. Half-mile M40 Junction 15. AA/ETC ◆◆◆◆. [🐕]

WOODSIDE GUEST HOUSE, CLAVERDON, NEAR WARWICK CV35 8PJ (Tel: 01926 842446; Fax: 01926 843697). A peaceful family guest house in 22 acres of own gardens and woodland. Lovely views, walks, log fires. Happy to welcome four-legged guests. One Crown. Brochure available. Special Autumn Breaks.

WEST MIDLANDS

Birmingham

The second-largest city in Britain, with Art Galleries to rival London. The Bull Ring has been modernised and includes an impressive shopping centre, but there is still plenty of the old town to see; the town hall, the concert hall and the Cathedral Church of St Philip.

ANGELA AND IAN KERR, THE AWENTSBURY HOTEL, 21 SERPENTINE ROAD, SELLY PARK, BIRMINGHAM B29 7HU (0121-472 1258). Victorian Country House. Large gardens. All rooms have colour TV, telephones and tea/coffee making facilities. Some rooms en suite, some with showers. All rooms central heating, wash-basins. Near BBC Pebble Mill, transport, University, city centre. Bed and Breakfast from £32 Single Room, from £46 Twin Room, inclusive of VAT.

WILTSHIRE
WILTSHIRE *Malmesbury, Salisbury*

 Dairy Farm on the Wiltshire/Gloucestershire borders. Malmesbury 3 miles, 15 minutes M4 (junction 16 or 17). **SELF CATERING:** The Bull Pen and Cow Byre each sleep 2/3 plus cot. Double bedded room, bathroom, kitchen, lounge. 3 KEYS COMMENDED . **B&B** in 15C farmhouse – three comfortable rooms, one en suite. Listed COMMENDED.

John & Edna Edwards, Stonehill Farm, Charlton, Malmesbury SN16 9DY Tel: 01666 823310

Swaynes Firs Farm
Grimsdyke, Coombe Bissett, Salisbury, Wiltshire SP5 5RF
Small working farm with horses, cattle, poultry, geese and duck ponds. Spacious rooms, all en suite with colour TV and country views. Ideal for visiting the many historic sites in the area. Rates: Adults £22 per night B/B. Children £11 sharing adults' room. Dogs– Free.

Mr A. Shering   AA QQ   ☸ Approved   **Tel: 01725 519240**

Chippenham

Town on River Avon 12 miles north-east of Bath.

ROWARD FARM, DRAYCOT CERNE, CHIPPENHAM SN15 4SG (01249 758147). Three self-catering cottages (🏠🏠🏠🏠 Highly Commended) in peaceful Wiltshire countryside, overlooking open fields. Convenient for Cotswolds and Bath. Sleep two to four people in fully-equipped accommodation. Non-smoking. Well behaved pets welcome. Call or write for brochure.

Malmesbury

Country town on River Avon with a late medieval market cross. Remains of medieval abbey.

MRS A. HILLIER, LOWER FARM, SHERSTON, MALMESBURY SN16 0PS (01666 840391). Self-contained wing of farmhouse. Sleeps 3/5. Working farm. Large lawn and fields. Ideal for pets and children. Fishing. Half-mile from shops and pubs. Wiltshire/Gloucestershire Borders, ideal for Bath, Cotswolds, etc. £95-£180 per week. Electricity £1 meter. [Pets £5 each per week.]

JOHN AND EDNA EDWARDS, STONEHILL FARM, CHARLTON, MALMESBURY SN16 9DY (01666 823310). Family-run dairy farm, ideal for touring. 3 comfortable rooms, one en suite. Also 2 fully equipped bungalow-style barns, each sleeps 2/3 plus cot, self catering. [Pets £10 per week]

Salisbury

13th century cathedral city, with England's highest spire at 404ft. Many fine buildings.

MR A. SHERING, SWAYNES FIRS FARM, GRIMSDYKE, COOMBE BISSETT, SALISBURY SP5 5RF (01725 519240). Small working farm with horses, poultry, geese and duck ponds. Spacious rooms, all en suite with colour TV. Ideal for visiting the many historic sites in the area. [🐾]

WORCESTERSHIRE

WORCESTERSHIRE   *Great Malvern*

Croft Guest House, Bransford, Worcester WR6 5JD

16th-18th Century country house, 10 minutes from Worcester, Malvern and M5. En suite rooms, tea/coffee trays, central heating. Dinners available; residential licence. TV's in bedrooms, sauna and family jacuzzi. Dogs and children welcome; cot and baby listening service; family room. Bed & Breakfast from £19.50 to £28 single, £38 to £48 double. Festive Christmas and New Year breaks available.

Ann & Brian Porter: Tel: 01886 832227   Fax: 01886 830037   AA / ETC ◆◆

Russeldene Hotel

40 Priory Road, Great Malvern, Worcestershire WR14 3DN
Elegantly restored Victorian house, close to Malvern hills, convenient for town.
comfortable rooms, good food (including vegetarian). Licensed bar. Parking. Dogs
welcome. Non-smoking. Colour brochure. ***Call Janet or Peter on: (01684 562121).***

WHITEWELLS FARM COTTAGES

Ridgeway Cross, Malvern, Worcestershire WR13 5JS   Highly Commended - 🏵🏵🏵🏵
Tel: 01886 880607; Fax: 01886 880360   E-mail: Whitewells.Farm@btinternet.com

Seven cottages including one for disabled, full of charm and character, converted from historic farm buildings. Fully furnished and equipped to the highest standards. Exceptionally clean and comfortable. Set in 9 acres of unspoilt Herefordshire countryside, this is an ideal base for touring Herefordshire, Worcestershire, Gloucestershire, Cotswolds, Welsh mountains, Shakespeare country. All electricity, linen, towels, cleaning materials, central heating in winter months included in price. Laundry room. Open all year. Short breaks in low season. Dogs welcome.
Mr and Mrs Kavanagh

SYMBOLS

🐾   Indicates that pets are welcome free of charge.
£   Indicates that a charge is made for pets: nightly or weekly.
pw! Shows some special provision for pets; exercise facility, feeding or accommodation arrangement.
⌂   Indicates separate pets accommodation.

Great Malvern

Fashionable spa town in last century with echoes of that period.

ANN AND BRIAN PORTER, CROFT GUEST HOUSE, BRANSFORD, WORCESTER
WR6 5JD (Tel: 01886 832227; Fax: 01886 830037). 16th-18th century country
house, 10 minutes from Worcester, Malvern and M5. En suite rooms, tea coffee
trays, central heating. Dinners available; residential licence. Sauna and family
jacuzzi. Dogs and children welcome; cot and baby listening service; family
room. ETC/AA two diamonds. []

**MALVERN HILLS HOTEL, WYNDS POINT, MALVERN WR13 6DW (01684
540690). Enchanting family owned and run hotel nestling high in the hills.
Direct access to superb walking with magnificent views.Oak-panelled lounge,
log fire, real ales, fine food and friendly staff. Great animal lovers. AA ★★
RAC ★★, 4 Crowns Commended []**

RUSSELDENE HOTEL 40 PRIORY ROAD, GREAT MALVERN WR14 3DN Elegantly
restored Victorian house. close to Malvern hills, convenient for town.
comfortable rooms, good food (including vegetarian). Licensed bar. Parking.
Dogs welcome. Non-smoking. Colour brochure. Call Janet or Peter on: (01684
562121).

MR AND MRS D. KAVANAGH, WHITEWELLS FARM COTTAGES, RIDGEWAY
CROSS, NEAR MALVERN WR13 5JS (Tel: 01886 880607; Fax: 01886 880360).
Charming converted Cottages, sleep 2–6. Fully equipped with colour TV,
microwave, barbecue, fridge, iron, etc. Linen, towels also supplied. One cottage
suitable for disabled guests. Short Breaks available. ETC ♔♔♔♔ Highly
Commended. [Pets £12 per week.]
E–mail: Whitewells.Farm@btinternet.com

Key to Tourist Board Ratings

The Crown Scheme

The English Tourism Council (formerly the English Tourist Board) has joined with the
AA and **RAC** to create a new, easily understood quality rating for serviced
accommodation.

Hotels will receive a grading ranging from **one to five STARS (★)**. Other serviced
accommodation such as **guest houses** and **B&B establishments** will be graded from
one to five DIAMONDS (◆). These ratings represent Quality, Service and Hospitality
not just facilities.

*NB.Some properties had not been assessed at the time of going to press and in
these cases the publishers have included the old CROWN gradings.*

The Key Scheme

The Key Scheme covering self-catering in cottages, bungalows, flats, houseboats, houses,
chalets, etc remains unchanged. The classification from **One to Five KEYS** indicates the
range of facilities and equipment. Higher quality standards are indicated by the terms
APPROVED, COMMENDED, HIGHLY COMMENDED AND DE LUXE.

WELCOME COTTAGE HOLIDAYS. Quality Cottages in wonderful locations at welcoming low prices. Pets, linen and fuel mostly included. PHONE FOR FREE 2000 FULL COLOUR BROCHURE 01756 702209.

Bridlington

Traditional family holiday resort with picturesque harbour and a wide range of entertainments and leisure facilities. Ideal for exploring the Heritage coastline and the Wolds.

THE TENNYSON HOTEL, 19 TENNYSON AVENUE, BRIDLINGTON YO15 2EU (Tel & Fax: 01262 604382). 1994 Golden Bowl Award Winner for the Most Pet-Friendly Hotel in Yorkshire. Offering fine cuisine in attractive surroundings. Close to beach and cliff walks. ETC ◆◆◆. [🐾 pw!]

North Dalton

On the Yorkshire Wolds between Great Driffield and Pocklington.

THE STAR INN, WARTER ROAD, NORTH DALTON, EAST RIDING OF YORKSHIRE YO25 9UX (01377 217688; Fax: 01377 217791). Delightful 18th Century Coaching Inn. Excellent à la carte Restaurant, Bar meals and pulled beers. Seven en-suite bedrooms. Ideal for walking, rambling and touring. Four Crowns Commended. For more details contact Keith or Jo.

NORTH YORKSHIRE *Harrogate, Harwood Dale, Hawes*

AA★★ **ABBATT & YOUNG'S HOTEL, HARROGATE** ETC ◆◆◆
Telephone: 01423 567336 Fax: 01423 500042
Private hotel in exclusive conservation area of Harrogate close to town centre
and Valley Gardens. Nine individually decorated en suite bedrooms.
ATTRACTIVE GARDENS   AMPLE CAR PARKING   E-mail: abbat@aol.com
15 YORK ROAD (off Swan Road), HARROGATE HG1 2QL

OLD SPRING WOOD LODGES AND COTTAGES
FREEDOM HOLIDAYS
Ideal for Discriminating Dogs
Rosemary Helme, Old Spring Wood Lodges & Cottages, Helme Pasture, Hartwith Bank, Summerbridge, Harrogate, N. Yorks HG3 4DR

* Great sniffing trails, highest paw category walks in the heart of unspoilt Nidderdale.
* Renowned snooze spots while owners explore.
* Central for Harrogate, York, Herriot and Brontë Country. National Trust area; outstanding natural beauty.
* After your hard day, stretch out and watch woodland wildlife from the luxurious comfort of your Scandinavian lodge or converted Yorkshire Dales barn.
* David Bellamy Gold Conservation Award
* ETB Welcome Host Award.   UP TO HIGHLY COMMENDED
* Accessible Category 3.

Tel: 01423 780279   Fax: 01423 780994
E-mail: info@oldspringwoodlodges.co.uk
Website: www.oldspringwoodlodges.co.uk

Superior Holiday Cottages and Lodges in picturesque surroundings near Harrogate

RUDDING holiday **PARK**
Your gateway to the Yorkshire Dales
Please send for free illustrated brochure:
ETC 🏠🏠🏠/🏠🏠🏠🏠🏠
UP TO HIGHLY COMMENDED

Rudding Holiday Park, Follifoot, Harrogate, HG3 1JH Telephone: 01423 870439 Fax: 01423 870859
See also Colour Advertisement on page 35

SCOTIA HOUSE HOTEL
66 KINGS ROAD, HARROGATE HG1 5JR
Tel: 01423 504361 Fax: 01423 526578
Award winning licensed Hotel five minutes' walk from the town centre.
En suite bedrooms, some on ground floor. CTV, hospitality tray and telephone. Central
heating throughout. On site parking. Pets and owners welcome.
👑👑👑 Commended   AA★ RAC★

Two very well equipped self-contained cottages sleeping 2-6. Reduction for 2 people in either cottage. En suite Bed and Breakfast also available. All set in 30 acres of gardens and open countryside including wood and stream. Many excellent walks from your back door for you and your pet. (Maybe not for the tortoise we had staying last week!) PETS FREE.
Rosalie's
Rosalie & Howard Richardson, Chapel Farm, Harwood Dale, Scarborough YO13 0LB Tel/Fax: 01723 870288

COUNTRY COTTAGE HOLIDAYS
DRYDEN HOUSE ◆ MARKET PLACE ◆ HAWES ◆ N.YORKS DL8 3RA
100 Cottages in the lovely Yorkshire Dales. Our Cottages feature
colour TV, central heating, open fires, superb views, gardens, private
parking and many allow pets. Sleep 1-10. Short breaks throughout
the year. Rents £135 – £495 per week. Brochure / Booking Line
open 9.00am - 7.00pm daily (Answer machine out of these hours)
Telephone **WENSLEYDALE (01 969) 667 654**

346

STONE HOUSE HOTEL

👑👑👑 Commended

Licensed Country House Hotel & Restaurant overlooking Magnificent Wensleydale

~ *21 Quality En Suite Bedrooms* ~
(some with private conservatories opening onto Gardens)
~ *Delicious food & Fine Wines* ~
The Perfect Venue for a relaxing break deep in the heart of the Yorkshire Dales.
Dogs genuinely welcome – Short Breaks available now
Sedbusk, Hawes, North Yorkshire DL8 3PT
Tel: 01969 667571 Fax: 01969 667720

See also Colour Advertisement on page 31

Crief
L O D G E S

NORTH YORKSHIRE MOORS NATIONAL PARK

9 Scandinavian Pine Lodges near Helmsley. Set within 60 acres of owner's land with magnificent views, surrounded by pine forests. There are endless perfect dog walks and seclusion. Crief Lodges are a convenient centre for visits to Brontë and Herriot countryside, Castle Howard, North York Moors, steam railway, York and East Coast resorts.

Each lodge sleeps up to five persons, is fully centrally heated and double glazed to give maximum comfort with all modern facilities.

We are open all year round including Christmas and New Year.
Please phone or fax for booking forms and full colour brochure.
Tel: 01347 868207   Fax: 01347 868202
24 hour answering service

1637   **OVER 350**   **2000**
YEARS OF GOOD SERVICE

Formerly a Posting House in coaching days, and full of character, a convenient centre for the North Yorkshire Moors and east coast, with Castle Howard and Rievaulx and Byland Abbeys within easy distance. 12 en suite rooms, all with colour TV, tea and coffee facilities, radio, and direct-dial telephone. One private lounge. Jacobean dining room offering traditional country-style cooking, with many choices. Special Breaks all year. Dogs welcome (no charge). Under the same ownership for 40 years. Brochure sent on request.

Dinner, Bed and Breakfast from £42.00.

AA/RAC ★★
Ashley Courtenay   **THE CROWN HOTEL**   👑👑👑 Commended

Helmsley, North Yorkshire YO62 5BJ Tel: Helmsley (01439) 770297

THE PREMIER HOTEL
66 Esplanade, South Cliff, Scarborough YO11 2UZ

AA *QQQ*
Recommended

A Premier Location

The Premier occupies a superb position on Scarborough's famous Esplanade, with breathtaking views of sea and coastline in this beautiful, quiet, elegant, unspoilt area.

This lovely Victorian hotel is privately owned and run, with the advantages of both a **lift** to all the very comfortable en suite bedrooms and a **private car park**. Relax in our sea-view lounge or enjoy a quiet drink in our residents' bar. We specialise in traditional English cuisine of the highest standard, using the very best fresh local produce.

Just cross the road, linger awhile in the beautiful Italian and Rose Gardens, or let the magnificence of the sea enthral you.

DOGS VERY WELCOME in all areas of the Hotel
except the dining room.

❖ All rooms en suite with colour TV, tea/coffee facilities,
clock radio and hairdryers
❖ Full central heating
❖ Residential licence

or details TEL: 01723 501062 FAX: 01723 501112
or E-MAIL: ThePremierScarborough@btinternet.com

FREE and REDUCED RATE Holiday Visits!
Don't miss our Readers' Offer Vouchers on pages 53 to 70

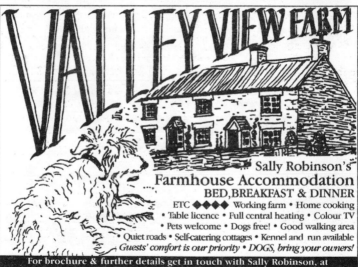

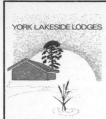

YORK LAKESIDE LODGES
Moor Lane, York YO24 2QU
Tel: 01904 702346
Fax: 01904 701631

Unique in a city! Luxurious Scandinavian lodges, and cottages in mature parkland overlooking large private fishing lake. Nearby superstore with coach to centre every 10 minutes. Easy access to ring road for touring. Open year round.

YORKSHIRE & HUMBERSIDE
TOURIST BOARD
WHITE ROSE AWARDS
FOR TOURISM
WINNER

Award – British
Holiday Home
Parks Association

Ⓨ Ⓨ Ⓨ Ⓨ UP TO DELUXE   *Website: www.yorkll.u-net.com* ♿

DALES HOLIDAY COTTAGES offer a choice of over 400 superb, self catering, holiday properties in beautiful rural and coastal locations from Bronte, Herriot and Heartbeat country to Yorkshire's Coastline. Cosy cottages to country houses, many open all year. For FREE Brochure contact Dales Holiday Cottages, Carleton Business Park, Skipton BD23 2DG (01756 799821/790919). E–mail: enq@dalesholcot.com

WELCOME COTTAGE HOLIDAYS. Quality Cottages in wonderful locations at welcoming low prices. Pets, linen and fuel mostly included. PHONE FOR FREE 2000 FULL COLOUR BROCHURE 01756 702209.

Askrigg

TV series based on popular "Vet" stories by James Herriot filmed here. St. Oswald 's Church, "Cathedral of Wensleydale", dates from late 15th and early 16th centuries.

WINVILLE HOTEL & RESTAURANT, MAIN STREET, ASKRIGG, LEYBURN DL8 3HG (01969 650515; Fax: 01969 650594). 19th Century Georgian residence in centre of "Herriot" village. Excellent touring centre for Lakes and Dales. Bar, residents' lounge, gardens and car park. B&B from £22.

Bentham

Quiet village amidst the fells. Good centre for rambling and fishing. Ingleton 5 miles N.E.

MRS L. J. STORY, HOLMES FARM, LOW BENTHAM, LANCASTER LA2 7DE (015242 61198). Cottage conversion in easy reach of Dales, Lake District and coast. Central heating, fridge, TV, washer, games room. ⓎⓎⓎ Commended. [🐕]

SYMBOLS

🐕   Indicates that pets are welcome free of charge.

£   Indicates that a charge is made for pets: nightly or weekly.

pw!   Shows some special provision for pets; exercise facility, feeding or accommodation arrangement.

⌂   Indicates separate pets accommodation.

Clapham

Attractive village with caves and pot-holes in vicinity, including Gaping Ghyll. Nearby lofty peaks include Ingleborough (2,373ft.) to the north. Kendal 24 miles, Settle 6.

DAVID & JACKIE KINGSLEY, ARBUTUS GUEST HOUSE, RIVERSIDE, CLAPHAM, NEAR SETTLE LA2 8DS (015242 51240). ETC/AA ◆◆◆◆. Restored Georgian vicarage in a delightful setting. All rooms en suite, or private facilities. TV, tea/coffee. Central heating. Delicious home cooking. Open all year round. Pets welcome. [🐾]
E–mail: info@arbutus.co.uk
Website: www.arbutus.co.uk

NEW INN HOTEL, CLAPHAM, NEAR SETTLE LA2 8HH (015242 51203, Fax: 015242 51496). Friendly 18th century coaching inn. Ideal centre for walking. All rooms en suite, with colour TV and tea/coffee facilities. Restaurant and bar meals. Dogs welcome.

Coverdale

Small village set in Yorkshire Dales, in heart of Herriot Country.

MRS JULIE CLARKE, MIDDLE FARM, WOODALE, COVERDALE, LEYBURN DL8 4TY (01969 640271). Peacefully situated farmhouse. B&B with optional Evening Meal. Home cooking. Pets sleep where you prefer. Ideally positioned for exploring the Dales. [🐾 fl]

Danby

Village on River Esk 12 miles west of Whitby.

THE FOX & HOUNDS INN, AINTHORPE, DANBY YO21 2LD (01287 660218; Fax: 01287 660030). Residential 16th Century Coaching Inn. Comfortable en suite bedrooms available. Enjoy our real ales or quality wines. Special mid-week breaks available Oct - May. Open all year. [🐾]

Dunnington

Village four miles east of York.

KAREN & ALAN JACKSON FIFTH MILESTONE COTTAGE, HULL ROAD, DUNNINGTON, YORKS YO19 5LR (01904 489361). We stand in a rural setting close to York, views over open fields with car parking to rear of house. Central heating, colour television, hospitality tray, ground floor rooms, two en suite with conservatory to relax in overlooking large gardens. B&B from £16.50. [🐾pw!]

Visit the FHG website
www.holidayguides.com
for details of the wide choice of accommodation
featured in the full range of FHG titles

Easingwold

Small market town with cobbled streets where weathered red brick dwellings are grouped around a large green. 12 miles north-west of York.

GARBUTTS GHYLL, THORNTON HILL, NEAR EASINGWOLD YO6 3PZ (01347 868644). Georgian working farm set in its own secluded valley. Homely, friendly, family atmosphere with home cooking and open log fires. Pets and children welcome, babysitting available. Open March-November

MRS R RITCHIE, THE OLD RECTORY, THORMANBY, EASINGWOLD, YORK YO61 4NN (01845 501417). Ideal for touring Herriot Country, Moors, Dales. TWO SELF-CONTAINED COTTAGES sleeping four to six. Also Bed and Breakfast. Three spacious bedrooms, two en suite. SAE or phone for brochure. [🐾]

Filey

Well-known resort with sandy beach. Off-shore is Filey Brig. Hull 40 miles, Bridlington 11, Scarborough 7.

SEA BRINK HOTEL, 3 THE BEACH, FILEY (01723 513257 Fax: 01723 514139). Seafront accommodation with restaurant/coffee shop and licensed bar Room amenities: Colour TV, Clock/radio, Central heating, Direct dial phones, Coffee/tea making facilities, Sea views. [Pets £2 per night]

MAYFIELD GUEST HOUSE, 2 BROOKLANDS, FILEY YO14 9BA (01723 514557). Close to all amenities. En suite rooms – one ground floor. Open all year. Ideal centre for touring. Bed and Breakfast £19, dinner £9. Out of season breaks. [🐾]

Goathland

Centre for moorland and woodland walks and waterfalls. Village of 19th century houses scattered over several heaths.

MRS MARION COCKREM, DALE END FARM, GREEN END, GOATHLAND, NEAR WHITBY YO22 5LJ (01947 895371). 500-year-old stone-built farmhouse on 140-acre working farm in North York Moors National Park. Rare breeds kept; emus, miniature ponies. Excellent children's playground. Generous portions home-cooked food. Guest lounge with colour TV and log fire. Homely olde-worlde interior. Many repeat bookings. SAE for brochure. [🐾]

WHITFIELD HOUSE HOTEL, DARNHOLM, GOATHLAND, NORTH YORKSHIRE YO22 5LA (01947 896215/896214) AA and Tourist Board Two Star. GuestAccom Good Room Award. A former 17th Century farmhouse in the beautiful North York Moors National Park, Whitfield House Hotel offers a relaxed and friendly atmosphere with superb cuisine, fully equipped bedrooms and a lounge and lounge bar. [Pets £1.50 per night]

Grassington

Wharfedale village in attractive moorland setting. Ripon 22 miles, Skipton 9.

GRASSINGTON HOUSE HOTEL, THE SQUARE, GRASSINGTON BD23 5AQ (01756 752406; Fax: 01756 752135). A small hotel with a big reputation. All rooms en suite, colour TV, tea making. Parking. Ideal for walking or touring. AA Rosette for Food. ETC ★★. [🐾]

JERRY & BEN'S HOLIDAY COTTAGES. Seven comfortable properties on private estate near Grassington in Yorkshire Dales National Park. Wooded mountain becks, waterfalls, rocky crags and accessible hill and footpath walking. Brochure from: MRS J.M.JOY, HOLEBOTTOM FARM, HEBDEN, SKIPTON BD23 5DL (01756 752369; Fax: 01756 753370). [pw! 🐾 one pet free, subsequent pets £5 per week]

FORESTERS ARMS, MAIN STREET, GRASSINGTON, SKIPTON BD23 5AA (Tel: 01756 752349; Fax: 01756 753633). The Foresters Arms is situated in the heart of the Yorkshire Dales and provides an ideal centre for walking or touring. Within easy reach of York and Harrogate. [🐾]

Harrogate

Charming and elegant spa town set amid some of Britain's most scenic countryside. Ideal for exploring Herriot Country and the moors and dales. York 22 miles, Bradford 19, Leeds 16.

ABBATT & YOUNG'S HOTEL, 15 YORK ROAD (OFF SWAN ROAD), HARROGATE HG1 2QL (Tel: 01423 567336; Fax: 01423 500042). Licensed Hotel with attractive gardens. Colour television, tea/coffee making facilities in all rooms, all with en suite bathrooms. ETC ◆◆◆. AA ★★. [🐾]
E–mail: abbat@aol.com

ROSEMARY HELME, OLD SPRING WOOD LODGES & COTTAGES, HELME PASTURE, HARTWITH BANK, SUMMERBRIDGE, HARROGATE HG3 4DR (Tel: 01423 780279, Fax: 01423 780994). Country accommodation for dogs and numerous walks in unspoilt Nidderdale. Central for Harrogate, York, Herriot and Bronte country. National Trust area. 3/4 keys up to Highly Commended. [pw! Pets £3 per night, £15 per week.]
E–mail: info@oldspringwoodlodges.co.uk
Website: oldspringwoodlodges.co.uk

RUDDING HOLIDAY PARK, FOLLIFOOT, HARROGATE HG3 1JH (01423 870439; Fax: 01423 870859). Luxury cottages and lodges sleeping two to ten people. All equipped to a high standard. Pool, licensed bar, golf and children's playground on estate. Illustrated brochure available. ♥♥♥/♥♥♥♥♥. [🐾]

SCOTIA HOUSE HOTEL, 66 KINGS ROAD, HARROGATE HG1 5JR (01423 504361; Fax: 01423 526578). Award winning licensed Hotel five minutes' walk town centre. En suite bedrooms with colour TV, hospitality tray, telephone. Central heating throughout. On site parking. Pets and owners welcome. ETB 3 Crowns Commended, AA, RAC One Star. [🐾]

Harwood Dale

Very popular family resort with good sands. York 41 miles, Whitby 20, Bridlington 17, Filey 7.

ROSALIE'S, ROSALIE & HOWARD RICHARDSON, CHAPEL FARM, HARWOOD DALE, SCARBOROUGH YO13 0LB (Tel & Fax: 01723 870288) Two very well equipped self-contained cottages sleeping 2-6. Reduction for 2 people in either cottage. En suite Bed and Breakfast also available. All set in 30 acres of gardens and open countryside including wood and stream. Many excellent walks from your back door for you and your pet. [🐾]

Hawes

Small town in Wensleydale. Situated 14 miles south-east of Kirkby Stephen.

COUNTRY COTTAGE HOLIDAYS, DRYDEN HOUSE, MARKET PLACE, HAWES DL8 3RA (01969 667654). 100 cottages in the lovely Yorkshire Dales. Colour TV, central heating, open fires. Gardens, private parking. Many allow pets. Rents £135 – £495 per week. Sleeep 1-10.

STONE HOUSE HOTEL, SEDBUSK, HAWES DL8 3PT (01969 667571; Fax: 01969 667720). This fine Edwardian country house has spectacular views and serves delicious Yorkshire cooking with fine wines. Comfortable en suite bedrooms, some ground floor. Phone for details. [🐾]

Hawes near (Mallerstang)

12 miles north west on the Hawes to Kirkby Stephen road.

COCKLAKE HOUSE, MALLERSTANG CA17 4JT (017683 72080). Charming, High Pennine Country House B&B in unique position above Pendragon Castle in Upper Mallerstang Dale offering good food and exceptional comfort to a small number of guests. Two double rooms with large private bathrooms. Three acres riverside grounds. Dogs welcome.

Helmsley

A delightful stone-built town on River Rye with a large cobbled square. Thirsk 12 miles.

Scandinavian Pine Lodges, each sleeping up to five persons. Fully centrally heated and double glazed. Set in 60 acres, surrounded by pine forests. Open all year. CRIEF LODGE HOLIDAY HOMES, WASS, YORK YO61 4AY (01347 868207 or Fax: 01347 868202) [🐾]

CROWN HOTEL, MARKET SQUARE, HELMSLEY YO62 5BJ (01439 770297). Fully residential old coaching inn. Bedrooms are very well appointed, all have tea and coffee-making facilities, colour TV, radio and telephones. Traditional country cooking. AA and RAC ★★. [🐾]

MRS ELIZABETH EASTON, LOCKTON HOUSE FARM, BILSDALE, HELMSLEY YO6 5NE (01439 798303). 16th century Farmhouse; oak beams, central heating. All rooms washbasins, tea/coffee facilities. Good home cooking. Panoramic views. Bed and Breakfast from £17; BB & EM from £26.

Huby

Small village 9 miles north of York. Ideal as base for exploring Dales, Moors and coast

THE NEW INN MOTEL, MAIN STREET, HUBY, YORK YO61 1HQ (01347 810219). Ideal base for Yorkshire attractions. Ground floor rooms, en suite, colour TVs etc. Bed and Breakfast from £25 pppn (EM available). Pets welcome. Special 3 & 4 day breaks. Telephone for brochure. AA ◆◆◆. [🐾],

Kilburn

Village to south of Hambleton Hills. Near White Horse carved into hillside. Helmsley 9 miles, Thirsk 6.

CHAPEL BARN. Converted barn, one bedroom, in excellent area for touring Moors, Dales and coast. Range of sports facilities and restaurants in area. No children please. CLAIRE STRAFFORD, CHAPEL COTTAGE, KILBURN, YORK YO61 4AH (01347 868383). ALL PETS VERY WELCOME. [pw! 🐾]

Kirkbymoorside

Small town below North Yorkshire Moors, 7 miles west of Pickering. Traces of a medieval castle.

MRS F. WILES, SINNINGTON COMMON FARM, KIRKBYMOORSIDE, YORK YO62 6NX (01751 431719). Newly converted cottages, tastefully furnished and well equipped, on working family farm. Sleep 2/8 from £115 per week including linen and heating. Also spacious ground floor accommodation (teamakers, colour TV, fridge, radio). Disabled facilities, separate outside entrances. B&B from £18.00. [🐾]

Knaresborough

Market town with narrow streets dominated by ruins of Norman castle partly demolished by Roundheads.

GENERAL TARLETON INN, FERRENSBY, NEAR KNARESBOROUGH, NORTH YORKSHIRE, HG5 OQB (Tel: 01423 340284; Fax: 01423 340288) Traditional 18th century coaching inn surrounded by the glorious countryside of the Yorkshire Moors and Dales National Park. Exciting pub dining is enhanced by an imaginative wine list and hand pulled ales. Restful en suite bedrooms are well appointed and pleasingly decorated. 4 Crowns Highly Commended, ★★★ AA 2 Rosettes, Good Food Guide 5 points, Michelin Red 'M' - Bib Gourmande for Food. [🐾]

NOTE

All the information in this book is given in good faith in the belief that it is correct. However, the publishers cannot guarantee the facts given in these pages, neither are they responsible for changes in policy, ownership or terms that may take place after the date of going to press. Readers should always satisfy themselves that the facilities they require are available and that the terms, if quoted, still apply.

Leeming Bar

Small, pretty village two miles north-east of Bedale.

THE WHITE ROSE HOTEL, LEEMING BAR, NORTHALLERTON DL7 9AY (01677 422707/424941, Fax: 01677 425123). Ideally situated for touring the spectacular scenery of two National Parks,Yorkshire Dales, coastal resorts, Herriot & Heartbeat Country. 18 rooms, all private bathroom, Colour TV/Radio, Tea & Coffee, hair dryer, trouser press and telephone. B&B from £24 per person. AA/RAC ★★★ [🐾]

Leyburn

Small market town, 8 miles south-west of Richmond, standing above the River Ure in Wensleydale.

PARK GRANGE HOLIDAY FARM. Working farm. Spend leisurely days walking, riding and exploring the Yorkshire Dales. Children, dogs and horses welcome. Yorkshire Welcome Pack for every booking etc. Contact: PAM SHEPPARD, LOW GILL FARM, AGGLETHORPE, LEYBURN DL8 4TN (01969 640258) [◻ 🐾 first pet, others £4 per night. Horses & ponies £22.50 per week. Dogs in kennels £1.50 per night.]

BARBARA & BARRIE MARTIN, THE OLD STAR, WEST WITTON, LEYBURN DL8 4LU (01969 622949). Former 17th century Coaching Inn now run as a guest house. Oak beams, log fire, home cooking. En suite from £17. Two Crowns Approved. [🐾]

Malham

In picturesque Craven District with spectacular Malham Cove (300ft.) and Gordale Scar with waterfalls. Malham Tarn (N T.) is 4 miles north, Skipton 12 miles.

MRS V. SHARP, MIRESFIELD FARM, MALHAM, SKIPTON BD23 4DA (01729 830414). In beautiful gardens bordering village green and stream. Excellent food. 14 bedrooms, 12 with private facilities. Full central heating. Two well-furnished lounges and conservatory. 3 Crowns Commended. B&B from £20pppn. [🐾]

Oldstead

Hamlet 7 miles east of Thirsk in beautiful North Yorkshire Moors.

THE BLACK SWAN INN, OLDSTEAD, COXWOLD, YORK YO61 4BL (01347 868387). 18th-century Country Freehouse offers Chalet-style accommodation, en suite, colour TV, central heating, tea/coffee facilities. Real ale. A la Carte Restaurant. Fine wines. Brochure available. [Pets £1 per night]

SYMBOLS

🐾   Indicates that pets are welcome free of charge.

£   Indicates that a charge is made for pets: nightly or weekly.

pw!   Shows some special provision for pets; exercise facility, feeding or accommodation arrangement.

◻   Indicates separate pets accommodation.

Pately Bridge

Small town in the heart of beautiful Nidderdale, bordering the Dales National Park. Excellent walking country and a good centre for touring the Dales, Moors, Herriot Country etc.

RIVULET COURT, PATELEY BRIDGE. ♕♕♕♕♕ Highly Commended (ETC). Spacious 18th century cottage, comfortable for six, plus children. Owner managed. Private gated garden. Convenient village amenities. Cenral heating, dishwasher, fridge freezer, laundry. Rates £230-£420. No extras. For colour brochure contact: ANNE RACK, BLAZEFIELD, BEWERLEY, HARROGATE HG 23 5BS (01423 711001

Pickering

Pleasant market town on southern fringe of North Yorkshire Moors National Park with moated Castle (Norm.). Bridlington 31 miles, Whitby 20, Scarborough 16, Helmsley 13, Malton 3.

MRS ELLA BOWES, BANAVIE, ROXBY ROAD, THORNTON-LE-DALE, PICKERING YO18 7SX (01751 474616). ETC ◆◆◆◆. Large stone-built semi-detached house set in Thornton-le-Dale. Ideal for touring. One family bedroom and two double bedrooms, all en suite. All with TV, shaver points, central heating and tea-making facilities. Open all year. Car park, cycle shed. B&B from £18. Welcome Host and Hygiene Certificate held. [🐕]

MRS S. M. PICKERING 'NABGATE', WILTON ROAD, THORNTON-LE-DALE, PICKERING, YO18 7QP (01751 474279; mobile: 077 03 804859). Good food and a very warm welcome for pets and owners. Car park. Hygiene and Welcome Host Certificates. Open all year. Bed and Breakfast from £18.00. [🐕]

VIVERS MILL, MILL LANE, PICKERING YO18 8DJ (01751 473640). Bed and Breakfast in ancient Watermill in peaceful surroundings. Comfortable TV lounge and en suite rooms with beamed ceilings. Tea making facilities. Ideal for Moors, coastline, and York. Bed and Breakfast from £24 per day, £160 weekly. [🐕]

Robin Hood's Bay

Fishing village where legend says Robin Hood repelled Danish invaders. Smuggling museum recalls the area's history.

MR T.R. NOBLE, SUMMERFIELD FARM, HAWSKER, WHITBY YO22 4LA (01947 602677). Six-berth caravan with all modern conveniences, on secluded private farm site. Safe for children and pets. It is two miles from Whitby and 17 miles from Scarborough, near Robin Hood's Bay. Beautiful coast, sandy beach one mile. Many local attractions. Dogs welcome. SAE for details.

Rosedale Abbey

Village 6 miles north of Kirkbymoorside, with remains of 12th century priory.

THE WHITE HORSE FARM HOTEL, ROSEDALE ABBEY, NORTH YORKSHIRE YO18 8SE (Tel: 01751 417239; Fax: 01751 417781). A charming Georgian Country Inn with panoramic views over the Moors. Ideal for walkers. All rooms en suite. BB / DBB. Mid-week breaks available. [🐕]

Scalby Nabs

Hamlet close to Scarborough, yet still in the beautiful North York Moors National Park.

EAST FARM COUNTRY COTTAGES, SCALBY NABS, SCALBY, SCARBOROUGH (Tel: 01723 506406; Fax; 01723 507356). Delightful single-storey two-bedroom stone cottages (no steps/stairs) set in the area's prettiest location. Ideal base for walking or touring. ♖♖♖♖ Commended. [🐾]

Scarborough

Very popular family resort with good sands. York 41 miles, Whitby 20, Bridlington 17, Filey 7.

FORGE VALLEY COTTAGES. Three superb stone-built cottages (sleeping 1-5) in delightful village on River Derwent, Gateway to the North Yorks Moors and coast, yet only 10 minutes from Scarborough. Highly equipped, cosy and comfortable — the perfect holiday base. ♖♖♖♖♖ Highly Commended. For colour brochure: DAVID BEELEY, BARN HOUSE, WESTGATE, OLD MALTON YO17 7HE (01653 698251). [🐾]

SUE AND TONY HEWITT, HARMONY COUNTRY LODGE, LIMESTONE ROAD, BURNISTON, SCARBOROUGH YO13 0DG (0800 2985840). A peaceful and relaxing retreat set in two acres of private grounds overlooking the National Park and sea. An ideal centre for walking or touring. En suite centrally heated rooms with superb views. Fragrant massage available. B&B from £20 to £28. Non smoking, licensed, private parking facilities. ◆◆◆◆. [Pets £2 per night, £10 per week]
Website: www.spiderweb.co.uk/Harmony

HARMONY GUEST HOUSE, PRINCESS ROYAL TERRACE, SCARBOROUGH YO11 2RP (01723 373562). Friendly licensed guest house, near South Bay attractions. We offer quality en suite and four-poster rooms. Excellent food. Bar and parking. Brochure on request. Five bedrooms B&B from £18, DB&B from £24.

KERRY LEE (100% NON SMOKING) HOTEL, 60 TRAFALGAR SQUARE, SCARBOROUGH YO12 7PY (01723 363845). Small North Bay hotel. Open all year. B&B from £12. Also cottage near castle. Log fire, sea view, microwave etc. Sleeps 4 – 6. Non smokers only. [🐾]

PARADE HOTEL, 29 ESPLANADE, SCARBOROUGH YO11 2AQ (01723 361285). Victorian Licensed Hotel with enviable sea views! Comfortable en suite rooms. Bed & Breakfast from £25. Dinner, Bed & Breakfast £34. YTB Member. RAC Acclaimed. [🐾]

THE PREMIER HOTEL, ESPLANADE, SOUTH CLIFF, SCARBOROUGH YO11 2UZ (01723 501062). The Premier Hotel is situated on the Esplanade. All rooms have private bath/shower and toilet en suite, colour TV, radio, tea/coffee facilities and full central heating. [Pets £3 per night]
E–mail: ThePremierScarborough@btinternet.com

Skipton

Airedale market town, centre for picturesque Craven district. Fine Castle (14th cent). York 43 miles, Manchester 42, Leeds 26, Harrogate 22, Settle 16.

Over 200 super self-catering Cottages, Houses and Flats throughout Yorkshire Dales, York, Moors, Coast, Peak and Lake District. Telephone for free illustrated brochure. APPLY– HOLIDAY COTTAGES (YORKSHIRE) LTD, WATER STREET, SKIPTON (18) BD23 1PB (01756 700872). [🐕]

Staithes

Coastal village with harbour sheltered by sandstone cliffs.

SUNNYSIDE COTTAGE, STAITHES, YORKSHIRE COAST. Two well-appointed cottages opening early spring. Sleeping two to six. Pets welcome. Also cottages available in Dundee. Telephone and details to DEBORAH TAYLOR, THE CHERRIES, PRIORY CLOSE, RIVERSIDE, LIVERPOOL L17 7EL (Tel: 0151 727 4208; Mobile: 07889 437 207)

Stokesley

Small town 8 miles south of Middlesbrough.

RED HALL, GREAT BROUGHTON, STOKESLEY, NEAR MIDDLESBROUGH TS9 7ET (Tel: 01642 712300; Fax: 01642 714023). Elegant 17th Century Grade II Listed country home. Family-run business provides personal service in warm friendly atmosphere. Centrally heated en suite bedrooms. Set in meadows and woodland at foot of North York Moors National Park. AA ◆◆◆◆. [pw! 🐕] E–mail: nathan@mythral.demon.co.uk

Thirsk

Market town with attractive square. Excellent touring area. Northallerton 3 miles.

FOXHILLS HIDEAWAYS, FELIXKIRK, THIRSK YO7 2DS (01845 537575). Scandinavian, heated throughout, linen provided. A supremely relaxed atmosphere on the edge of the North Yorkshire Moors National Park. Open all year. Village pub round the corner. [🐕]

GOLDEN FLEECE HOTEL, MARKET SQUARE, THIRSK YO7 1LL (01845 523108; Fax: 01845 523996). Characterful Coaching Inn offering good food and up to date facilities. All rooms have new bathrooms, satellite TV, phone, trouser press, hairdryer. AA ★★. 3 Crowns Commended. [🐕]

Wensleydale

Possibly the most picturesque of all the Dales, ideal for touring some of the most beautiful parts of Yorkshire and nearby Herriot Country. Kendal 25 miles, Kirkby Stephen 15.

MRS PAT COOPER, MOORCOTE FARM, ELLINGSTRING, MASHAM HG4 4PL (01677 460315). Three delightful cottages around a sunny courtyard, sleeping 4-6. All equipped to very high standard. Children and pets welcome. Open all year round. [Pets £10 per week.]

MRS SUE COOPER, ST. EDMUNDS, CRAKEHALL, BEDALE DL8 1HP (01677 423584). Set in Swaledale and Wensleydale, these recently renovated cottages are fully equipped and are an ideal base for exploring the Dales and Moors. Sleep 2–7 plus cot. Up to ♛♛♛♛ Commended. Brochure available. [🐾]

THE WENSLEYDALE HEIFER INN, WEST WITTON, WENSLEYDALE DL8 4LS (01969 622322; Fax: 01969 624183). A 17th Century Inn of character and style offering eleven en suite bedrooms and 3 Four Posters. Real Ales with Bistro and Bar Food. Home cooking specialising in Fish and Seafood. ETC ★★. [Pets £3 per night, £20 per week]
E–mail: heifer@daelnet.co.uk

West Scrafton

Village 3 miles south of Wensley

ADRIAN CAVE, WESTCLOSE HOUSE, WEST SCRAFTON, NEAR MIDDLEHAM DL8 4RM (020 8567 4862 for bookings). Traditional stone farmhouse. Three bedrooms sleeping six/seven. Storage heating. Microwave, fridge, electric cooker, colour TV. Large barn/playroom and garden. Pets welcome. Ideal for families/walkers. Self-catering from £300 per week. [pw 🐾],

Whitby

Charming resort with harbour and sands. Of note is the 13th-century ruined Abbey. Stockton-on-Tees 34 miles, Scarborough 20, Saltburn-by-the-Sea 19.

PAT & RUTH DONEGAN, ARGYLE HOUSE, 18 HUDSON STREET, WEST CLIFF, WHITBY YO21 3EP (01947 602733). Comfortable friendly guest house, en suites, four-posters, CTVs, hairdryers, courtesy trays, central heating. Hearty Breakfasts! Close sea and town centre. Non-smoking. Open all year. Pets welcome.
Website: www.argylehouse.co.uk

JOHN & JO HALTON, KIRKLANDS PRIVATE HOTEL, 17 ABBEY TERRACE, WEST CLIFF, WHITBY YO21 3HQ (01947 603868). Bed, Breakfast and Evening Meal. Family-run hotel, good home cooking. Licensed. Some rooms en suite; all have tea/coffee making facilities and colour TV. Pets welcome. [Pets £2 per day]

PARTRIDGE NEST FARM, ESKDALESIDE, SLEIGHTS, WHITBY YO22 5ES (01947 810450). Six caravans on secluded site, five miles from Whitby and sea. Ideal touring centre. All have mains electricity, colour TV, fridge, gas cooker. [Dogs £1 per day per dog]

JULIE A. WILSON, THE SEACLIFFE HOTEL, WEST CLIFF, WHITBY YO21 3JX (Tel & Fax:01947 603139). Friendly family run hotel overlooking the sea. Licensed à la carte restaurant specialising in fresh local seafoods, steaks and vegetarian dishes. 3 Crowns Commended. Freephone 0800 191747. [🐾]

SNEATON HALL HOTEL, SNEATON, WHITBY YO22 5HP (01947 605929; Fax: 01947 820177). Small, friendly ★★ country hotel, three miles south of Whitby. All rooms en suite; tea making facilities, TV. Good food, pleasant gardens. Panoramic sea views. Fully licensed; open to non-residents. Pets most welcome. [Pets £2 to £6 per night]

BOB & KAY HARTLEY, THE SHIP INN, PORT MULGRAVE, HINDERWELL, NEAR WHITBY TS13 5JZ (01947 840303). A traditional family-run pub set in a small seaside hamlet, with a choice of cask conditioned ales and good home cooked meals. B&B from £16.50pppn.

WHITE ROSE HOLIDAY COTTAGES, NEAR WHITBY. Superior C/H village cottages and bungalows. Available all year. Ideal for coast and country. Up to 3 Keys Highly Commended. APPLY: MRS J. ROBERTS (PW), 5 BROOK PARK, SLEIGHTS, NEAR WHITBY YO21 1RT (01947 810763) [pw! £5 per week.]

York

Historic cathedral city and former Roman Station on River Ouse. Magnificent Minster and 3 miles of ancient walls. Facilities for a wide range of sports and entertainments. Horse-racing on Knavesmire. Bridlington 41 miles, Filey 41, Leeds 24, Harrogate 22.

ASHCROFT HOTEL, 294 BISHOPTHORPE ROAD, YORK YO23 1LH (01904 659286; Fax: 01904 640107) Set in 2 acres of wooded grounds. All rooms en suite. Pets and owners accommodated in Coach House, giving easy access. 4 Crowns Commended.[Pets £2 per night]

THE BLOSSOMS, YORK CITY CENTRE (01904 652391). Family-run hotel just five minutes' walk from all attractions. Rooms en suite with TV, phone, tea/coffee. Licensed bar, restaurant, car park. B&B from £20pppn.

MRS LYNN MANNERS, CHURCH VIEW, STOCKTON ON THE FOREST, YORK YO32 9UP (01904 400403). 200-year-old cottage three miles from York in pretty village. Lounge, games room, full size snooker table. Children and pets welcome. Ideal for visiting York, East Coast, North York Moors. Lovely walks. [Pets £2 per night, £10 per week]

CLIFTON VIEW GUEST HOUSE, 118/120 CLIFTON, YORK YO3 6BQ (01904 625047). Victorian family-run guest house 12 minutes' walk from City Centre. All rooms have colour TV, tea coffee facilities; most have shower. Private car park. B&B from £13 to £18 p.p.p.n. One Crown [🐾]

HIGH BELTHORPE, BISHOP WILTON, YORK YO4 1SB (01759 368238; Mobile: 0802 270970). Set on an ancient moated site at the foot of the Yorkshire Wolds, this spacious Victorian farmhouse offers huge breakfasts, open fires, private fishing and fabulous walks. Dogs and owners will love it! One Crown Commended. Open all year. Prices from £15.00 +VAT. [pw! 🐾]

3 attractive self-catering choices. 12 miles from York. WOODLEA detached house sleeping 5–6, with kitchen, dining area, large lounge and colour TV, bathroom, cloakroom, 3 bedrooms. BUNGALOW adjacent to farmhouse sleeps 2–4. Kitchen, bathroom, lounge/dining room with colour TV and double bed settee. Twin room with cot. STUDIO adjacent to farmhouse, sleeping 2. Kitchen, lounge/dining room with colour TV, twin bedroom, bathroom/toilet. SAE for details: MRS M. S. A. WOODLIFFE, MILL FARM, YAPHAM, POCKLINGTON, YORK YO4 2PH (01759 302172).

ST. GEORGE'S HOUSE HOTEL, 6 ST. GEORGE'S PLACE, YORK YO24 1DR (01904 625056). Family-run licensed Hotel in quiet cul-de-sac near racecourse. All rooms en suite with colour TV, tea/coffee facilities. Private parking. Pets welcome. 3 Crowns Commended. RAC, AA. [🐕]
E–mail: sixstgeorg@aol.com
Website: membersaol.com/6stgeorg/

MRS SALLY ROBINSON, VALLEY VIEW FARM, OLD BYLAND, HELMSLEY, YORK YO6 5LG (01439 798221). ETC ◆◆◆◆. B&B £30. BB&D £43.50 Working farm, home cooking, table licence, private parking, full central heating, colour TV. Self catering cottages. Kennel and run available. Pets Welcome. [🐕]
E–mail: valleyview@tesconet
Website: www.valleyviewfarm.com

MRS S. JACKSON, VICTORIA VILLA GUEST HOUSE, 72 HESLINGTON ROAD, YORK YO10 5AU (01904 631647). Ten minutes' walk from city centre. Comfortable double, twin, single and family bedrooms, all with TV. Children and pets welcome. Open all year. B&B from £13 to £20 per person. [pw! 🐕]

YORK LAKESIDE LODGES, MOOR LANE, YORK YO24 2QU (01904 702346; Fax: 01904 701631). Self-catering pine lodges. Mature parkland setting. Large fishing lake. Nearby superstore with coach to centre every 10 mins. ETC ⚬⚬⚬⚬ up to De Luxe. [pw! Pets £15 per week]
Website: www.yorkll.u-net.com

WEST YORKSHIRE
WEST YORKSHIRE *Haworth*

HAWORTH 7 UPPER MARSH, OXENHOPE.

A small stone cottage and patio on the edge of moorland, one mile from Haworth. Sleeps six in two bedrooms and the lounge. The cottage has sunny rooms, lovely views, colour TV, gas central heating, well equipped kitchen including washing machine. Waymarked walks to miles of moorland start near the cottage. Spectacular countryside close by and you are within easy driving distance of the beautiful Yorkshire Dales with Skipton, Bolton Abbey, Burnsall and Malham not forgetting the historic and popular village of Haworth. We are pleased to have children and dogs to stay and personal supervision assures you of a very warm welcome. Prices £210 to £320 including linen and heating.

Details from **Mrs P. M. Seabrook, 30 Newcombe Street, Market Harborough, Leicestershire LE16 9PB Tel: 01858 463723 E-mail: LarkForge@courtyard9.freeserve.co.uk**

Bingley

Town on River Aire five miles north-west of Bradford.

MRS P. OXLEY, FIVE RISE LOCKS HOTEL, BECK LANE, BINGLEY BD16 4DD (01274 565296; Fax: 01274 568828). ETC , RAC, AA ◆◆◆◆. Charming Victorian Mill owner's house in mature terraced gardens, minutes walk from the famous Five Rise Locks. Individually designed and furnished en suite bedrooms with panoramic views of the Aire Valley. Relaxed atmosphere complemented by interesting menus and wine list. [🐴].

Haworth

Above the River Worth Valley. The one-time home of the Brontë Family, now a museum.

7 UPPER MARSH, OXENHOPE. Sleeps six in two bedrooms and the lounge. The cottage has sunny rooms, lovely views, colour TV, gas central heating, well equipped kitchen including washing machine. We are pleased to have children and dogs to stay and personal supervision assures you of a very warm welcome. Prices £210 to £320 including linen and heating. Details from MRS P. M. SEABROOK, 30 NEWCOMBE STREET, MARKET HARBOROUGH, LEICESTERSHIRE LE16 9PB (01858 463723).
E–mail: LarkForge@courtyard9.freeserve.co.uk

CHANNEL ISLANDS

CHANNEL ISLANDS *Jersey*

HOLIDAY **• JERSEY •** *BUNGALOWS*

Three bungalows a few metres direct access to beach. Reasonable rates.
Electric cooking and heating. Near golf course, shops and bus.
Family accommodation with cot. Open most of the year with reduced rates out of season. Well equipped. Jersey is a beautiful place to visit all year round.
Plenty to see and do on the island. Excellent restaurants, shops (no VAT) and entertainment. Easy access to the other Channel Islands and France for day trips.
Access by air and boat from Poole and Weymouth (both take cars).
Please phone **(01534) 853333** early evening, or write to:
**Mrs. P. Johnson, 'Mon Repos', Coast Road, Grouville, Jersey C.I. JE3 9FG
PETS MOST WELCOME (FREE)**

Jersey

The Island of flowers and friendliness. Marvellous coastline and enchanting, unspoilt countryside. Island's capital, St helier, includes Jersey museum among its many attractions.

MRS. P. JOHNSON, 'MON REPOS', COAST ROAD, GROUVILLE, JERSEY C.I. JE3 9FG (01534 853333). Three well equipped bungalows. Direct access to beach, Near golf course, shops and bus. Reasonable rates. Electric cooking and heating. Family accommodation with cot. [🐴]

Pictures of pets required!

For our next edition of the unique guide *Pets Welcome!*, we would like to feature a series of pictures of readers', or advertisers', pets.

If you have a photo of your pet you would be willing to have included we would be grateful if you could forward it along with a brief note of the pet's name and any interesting anecdotes about them. Please remember to include your own name and address and let us know if you would like the pictures returned.

Everyone sending a photo can select a *FREE* copy of any of FHG's year 2000 guides from the list shown at the back of this book. If your picture is featured in the next issue we will also pay £10 – and if the photo proves suitable for use on the front cover of the guide we will pay £100.

We will be happy to receive prints, transparencies or pictures on disk or by e-mail to **fhg@ipc.co.uk**. Please let us know which of our guides you would prefer as your free gift.

All pictures should be forwarded by September 1st 2000 to be considered for inclusion in the 2001 edition of *Pets Welcome!.*

Send to: FHG Publications, Abbey Mill Business Centre, Seedhill, Paisley PA1 1TJ.

SCOTLAND

SCOTLAND'S HOTELS OF DISTINCTION – FOR THE REAL TASTE OF SCOT-
LAND. A unique group of unique hotels. Please call us on 0800 975 5975 for
assistance with your reservation or visit our
Website: www.scotlands-hotels.com

WELCOME COTTAGE HOLIDAYS. Quality Cottages in wonderful locations at
welcoming low prices. Pets, linen and fuel mostly included. PHONE FOR FREE
2000 FULL COLOUR BROCHURE 01756 702213.

HOSEASONS COUNTRY COTTAGES. You can bring your pet to hundreds of our
cottages. Our brochure presents a delightful choice throughout Britain. For
your copy call 01502 502601 Quote H0004.

Key to Tourist Board Ratings ~ Scotland

The Scottish Tourist Board Star Grading System. This easy-to-understand system tells you at a glance the
quality standard you can expect. The gradings range from ★ (Fair and acceptable) to ★★★★★ (Exceptional,
world-class) and will also include the type of accommodation eg ★★★ Self-catering or ★★ Hotel.

Ballindalloch

Baronial Castle with modern additions and alterations is the most noteworthy building in this area; set on right bank of River Avon near its confluence with River Spey, 7 miles south-west of Charleston of Aberlour.

MRS J. WHITE, BEECHGROVE COTTAGES, TOMNAVOULIN, BALLINDALLOCH AB37 9JA (01807 590220). Traditional Highland Cottages in scenic area. Each sleeps 6 maximum – two double bedrooms, fully equipped dining/kitchen, living room, colour TV. All electric. Linen supplied. Central for coast and ski slopes. Open all year. Car essential. Children and pets welcome. [🐾]

MINMORE HOUSE HOTEL, GLENLIVET, BALLINDALLOCH, BANFFSHIRE AB37 9DB (Tel: 01807 590378; Fax: 01807 590472). Quality Scottish cooking and well appointed en suite bedrooms awaits you at Minmore, which overlooks the secluded Glenlivet Crown Estate. Many golf courses nearby and private salmon and trout fishing available. Families and pets very welcome. [🐾]

Banchory

Small town on River Dee 11 miles north-west of Stonehaven.

RAEMOIR HOUSE HOTEL, RAEMOIR, BANCHORY, KINCARDINSHIRE, AB31 4ED (01330 824884; Fax: 01330 822171). Original coach house and stable buildings have been converted into four de luxe self-catering cottages with one, two or three bedrooms, sleeping up to 8 people. Full details available on request. STB ★★★★.

WOODEND CHALET HOLIDAYS, ROSE COTTAGE, GLASSEL, BANCHORY AB31 4DD (013398 82562). Seven timber chalets, set in beautiful woodland surroundings, on a quiet spacious site 20 miles west of Aberdeen. Private parking on site. Write or phone for brochure. Prices £99 — £272 per week per chalet. [Pets £5 per week]

Ellon

Small town 15 miles north of Aberdeen.

MRS CHRISTINE STAFF, SUNNYBRAE FARM, GIGHT, METHLICK, ELLON AB41 7JA (01651 806456). Comfortable accommodation on a working farm situated in a quiet, peaceful location with superb views. Centrally situated for many places of interest. Double and twin rooms, all en suite. Open all year. Bed and Breakfast from £17. STB ★★. [🐾]

Grantown-On-Spey

Market town 19 miles south of Forres.

MR AND MRS J. R. TAYLOR, MILTON OF CROMDALE, GRANTOWN-ON-SPEY PH26 3PH (01479 872415). Fully modernised Cottage with large garden and views of River Spey and Cromdale Hills. Golf, tennis and trekking within easy reach. Fully equipped except linen. Two double bedrooms. Shower, refrigerator, electric cooker, colour television. Car desirable. Children and pets welcome. Open all year. £100 per week. [🐾]

Keith

Small town on banks of River Isla 15 miles south-east of Elgin.

MRS SMART, ERROLBANK, 134 FIFE STREET, DUFFTOWN, KEITH AB55 4DP (01340 820229). Small friendly guest house on Whisky Trail. Children and pets welcome. Full Scottish breakfast our speciality. From £13.50 per person.

Turriff

Small town in agricultural area, 9 miles south of Banff.

MRS P E. BATES, HOLIDAY COTTAGES, FORGLEN ESTATE, TURRIFF AB53 4JP (01888 562918/562518). Estate on the beautiful Deveron River. Sea only nine miles away, Turriff two miles. 10 cottages sleeping 6–9. From £145 weekly. Special Winter lets. Children and reasonable dogs welcome. [🐕]

ARGYLL & BUTE

ARGYLL & BUTE *Acharacle, Ballachulish, Dalmally*

West Loch Hotel **By Tarbert, Loch Fyne, Argyll PA29 6YF**
Very attractive traditional coaching inn situated on the
shore of West Loch. Bright, comfortable accommodation, cosy atmosphere, superb food and
wines. Open all year. Single, twin, double and family rooms; all with private facilities.
Tel: 01880 820283   **Fax: 01880 820930**

Acharacle

On the Ardnamurchan Peninsula, the most westerly point on the British mainland.

STEADING HOLIDAYS, KILCHOAN, BY ACHARACLE, ARGYLL PH36 4LH (01972
510262; Fax: 01972 510337). Escape to Ardnamurchan, the most westerly
point of the British mainland. Enjoy sea views, beaches and peace from a well
managed and comfortable home. Regular crossings to Tobermory, fishing and
walking are a few of the attractions. Open All Year. [£15 per week for first dog,
£10 for second. Maximum 2.]

Ardbeg

*Popular resort reached by ferry from Wemyss Bay. Overlooked by ruined castle; nearby Ardencraig
Gardens are noted for magnificent floral displays; another attraction is Mount Stuart.*

**ARDMORY HOUSE HOTEL AND RESTAURANT, ARDMORY ROAD, ARDBEG,
ISLE OF BUTE PA20 0PG (Tel: 01700 502346; Fax: 01700 505596). STB ★★★★
HOTEL. Great doggy smells in our country retreat with three-quarters-of-an-
acre mature grounds. The hotel has five well appointed en suite bedrooms,
restaurant, bar. Open all year. Bed and Breakfast from £37.50. Bedrooms and
restaurant are non-smoking. Ample parking. RAC ★★, AA 1 Rosette.
E-mail: ardmory.house.hotel@dial.pipex.com**

Ballachulish

*Impressively placed village at entrance to Glencoe and on Loch Leven. Magnificent mountain
scenery including Sgorr Dhearg (3362 ft). Good centre for boating, climbing and sailing. Glasgow
89 miles, Oban 38, Fort William 14, Kinlochleven 9.*

Cottages and Chalets in natural woodland sleeping two to six people. The
Glencoe area is lovely for walking and perfect for nature lovers too. Pets
welcome. Regret no smokers. No VAT. Brochure available. APPLY – HOUSE IN
THE WOOD HOLIDAYS, GLENACHULISH, BALLACHULISH PA39 4JZ (01855
811379). [🐕]

ISLES OF GLENCOE HOTEL AND LEISURE CENTRE, BALLACHULISH, NEAR
FORT WILLIAM PA39 4HL (01855 811602; Fax: 01855 821463). Almost afloat,
this stylish, modern Hotel nestles on the lochside. Spacious bedrooms offer a
commanding panorama of sky, mountain and loch. Delicious cuisine in
Conservatory Restaurant. Heated pool & Leisure Centre. [pw! £3.50 per night]
E-mail: reservations@freedomglen.co.uk
Website: www.freedomglen.co.uk

Dalmally

Small town in Glen Orchy. To the south-west is Loch Awe with romantic Kilchurn Castle (14th century) Edinburgh 98 miles, Glasgow 69, Ardrishaig 42, Oban 25, Inveraray 16.

ARDBRECKNISH HOUSE, SOUTH LOCHAWESIDE, BY DALMALLY, ARGYLL PA33 1BH (01866 833223/833242). Self-catering apartments and holiday cottages set in 20 acres of garden woodland on the south shore of Loch Awe. Breathtaking panoramic views over loch, mountain and glen.
E–mail: ardbreck01@aol.com
Website: www.ardbrecknish.com

ROCKHILL WATERSIDE COUNTRY HOUSE, ARDBRECKNISH, BY DALMALLY PA33 1BH (01866 833218). 17th Century guest house on waterside with spectacular views over Loch Awe. Five delightful rooms with all modern facilities. First class home cooking with much home grown produce.

Dunoon

Lively resort reached by car ferry from Gourock. Cowal Highland Gathering held at end of August.

ABBOT'S BRAE HOTEL, WEST BAY, DUNOON PA23 7QJ (Tel: 01369 705021; Fax: 01369 701191). Small welcoming hotel at the gateway to the Western Highlands with breathtaking views. Comfortable, spacious, en suite bedrooms, quality home cooking and select wines. [🐴],
E–mail: enquiry@abbotsbrae.co.uk
Website: www.abbotsbrae.co.uk

ENMORE HOTEL, MARINE PARADE, DUNOON PA23 8HH (01369 702230; Fax: 01369 702148). Small luxury Hotel with well-tended garden, situated overlooking the beautiful Firth of Clyde. Own shingle beach. Promenade and superb walking in the hills and forests within five minutes' drive. Owners have retriever and standard poodle. STB 4 Star HOTEL. AA **. AA Rosette. [pw! Pets £3.75 per night.]

Inveraray

Hereditary seat of the Dukes of Argyll situated on Loch Fyne. Tapestries, paintings and arms on display in the castle.

KILBLAAN FARMHOUSE, INVERARAY. A Victorian farmhouse situated in a beautiful glen close to Loch Fyne with lovely views. Wonderful hill walks and bird watching. Sleeps eight. A well kept garden, safe for animals. Car parking. Open March to October. Pets welcome free of charge. SAE to MRS MACLEAN, BRICKMAKERS COTTAGE, LAMBOURN WOODLANDS, HUNGERFORD, BERKSHIRE RG17 7TS (01488 71474).[🐴]

SYMBOLS

🐴 Indicates that pets are welcome free of charge.

£   Indicates that a charge is made for pets: nightly or weekly.

pw! Shows some special provision for pets; exercise facility, feeding or accommodation arrangement.

◻   Indicates separate pets accommodation.

Kintyre

Narrow peninsula of great beauty connected to mainland by Tarbert Isthmus.

PUTECHAN LODGE HOTEL, BELLOCHANTUY, BY CAMPBELTOWN, MULL OF KINTYRE PA28 6QF (01583 421323). Spectacular views over Islay and Jura. All rooms en suite. Most with sea view. Walking, bird watching, wildlife and golf nearby. Dogs welcome. Self-catering also available. B&B from £19.50 pppn. [🐾]

Loch Goil

Peaceful loch running from Lochgoilhead to Loch Long.

Five self catering Chalets on the shores of Loch Goil in the heart of Argyll Forest Park. Fully equipped except linen. Colour TV, fitted kitchen, carpeted. Pets very welcome. Open all year. DARROCH MHOR, CARRICK CASTLE, LOCH GOIL PA24 8AF (01301 703249/703432). [🐾]

Lochgoilhead

Village at head of Loch Goil in Argyll

MRS ROSEMARY DOLAN, THE SHOREHOUSE INN, LOCHGOILHEAD PA24 8AJ (01301 703340). Small friendly informal Inn with panoramic views down Loch Goil. Seven letting rooms, Bar and Restaurant. Local amenities include swimming pool, golf course, tennis, bowls, water sports, fishing. Good area for walking. Rates from £16 pp B&B. Well-trained dogs welcome. [🐾]

Luing(Oban)

Island to the south of Oban. Linked to mainland by "Bridge over the Atlantic" designed by Thomas Telford.

SUNNYBRAE CARAVAN PARK SOUTH CUAN, ISLE OF LUING, BY OBAN PA34 4TU (01852 314274). Escape from city life on the west coast of Scotland. This beautiful island is a tranquil haven amid spectacular scenery. Call for Colour Brochure. [pw! 🐾]

Oban

Popular Highland resort and port, yachting centre, ferry services to Inner and Outer Hebrides. Sandy bathing beach at Ganavan Bay. McCaig's Tower above town is Colosseum replica built in 1890s.

ELSPETH CAMPBELL, ASKNISH COTTAGE, ARDUAINE, BY OBAN PA34 4XQ (01852 200247). Superb views overlooking islands. Ideal base for touring, activities or relaxation; walking, boat-trips, diving, horseriding. Wild garden, tame owner. Double/twin, prices from £16.50. Owners welcome too. [Pets £1 per night, £3 per week.]

MRS LINDA BATTISON, COLOGIN FARM HOLIDAY CHALETS, LERAGS GLEN, BY OBAN PA34 4SE (Tel: 01631 564501; Fax: 01631 566925). Cosy timber chalets, sleep two to six, all conveniences. Situated on farm, wildlife abundant. Games room, Launderette, licensed bar serving home-cooked food. Free fishing. Playpark. Live entertainment. [pw! Pets £1.50 per night, £10.50 per week.]

Well equipped Scandinavian chalets in breathtaking scenery near Oban. Chalets sleep 4–7, are widely spaced and close to Loch Tralaig. Car parking. From £205 per week per chalet. Available March to October. STB ★★ Self Catering. APPLY – ANN & ROBIN GREY, ELERAIG HIGHLAND CHALETS, KIL-NINVER, BY OBAN PA34 4UX (01852 200225) [🐾]
Website: www.scotland2000.com/eleraig

LAGNAKEIL HIGHLAND LODGES, LERAGS, OBAN, ARGYLL PA34 4SE (01631 562746; Fax: 01631 570225). Our timber lodges are nestled in 7 acres of scenic wooded glen overlooking Loch Feochan, only 3.5 miles from the picturesque harbour town of Oban: "Gateway to the Isles". Fully equipped lodges to a high standard, including linen and towels, country pub a short walk. O.A.P. discount. Free loch fishing. Special Breaks from £29 per lodge per night, weekly from £135. Our colour brochure will tell lots more. [Pets £10 per week].
E–mail: lagnakeil@aol.com

MELFORT PIER AND HARBOUR, KILMELFORD, BY OBAN PA34 4XD (Tel: 01852 200333; Fax: 01852 200329). Superb lochside houses each with sauna, spa, satellite TV, telephone, on the shores of Loch Melfort. Excellent base for touring Argyll and the Isles. From £80 to £185 per house/night. Minimum stay of two consecutive nights. Boats and pets very welcome. STB ★★★★★ Self Catering. [pw! Pets £10 per stay]
E–mail: melharbour@aol.com.
Website: www.scotland2000.com/melfort

WILLOWBURN HOTEL, CLACHAN SEIL, BY OBAN PA34 4TJ (01852 300276). Peaceful, relaxing, informal and addictive. Superb setting overlooking the Sound of Seil. Walk, fish, birdwatch or simply just laze. Tempted? Bring your owners too! [🐾]

Onich

On shores of Loch Linnhe. Good boating, fishing. Fort William 10 miles.

CREAG MHOR HOTEL, ONICH, BY GLENCOE, FORT WILLIAM PH33 6RY (01855 821379; Fax: 01855 821579). Enjoy our famed Highland hospitality in hotel with en suite rooms (phones), cheery bar, fine home cooking; Bed and Breakfast from £27.50 per person. Ideal for a host of outdoors activities. AA/STB ★★ Hotel. [🐾]

Strontian

Beautifully situated at head of Loch Sunart which stretches 20 miles to the sea..

SEAVIEW GRAZINGS HOLIDAYS, STRONTIAN PH36 4HZ (01967 402191). Quality self catering in Scandinavian log houses overlooking Loch Sunart. Sleep up to eight. TV, washer/dryer etc. Pubs/hotels five minutes. Pets welcome. Ideal touring centre. Send for colour brochure. [🐾]

Tarbert

Fishing port on Isthmus connecting Kintyre to the mainland.

MRS MEG MACKINNON, DUNMORE, NEAR TARBERT PA29 6XZ (01880 820654). Luxury villa and four cottages on 1000 acre estate with three miles of shore on Loch Tarbert. Bird watching, sailing, sea fishing, unrestricted walking. Pets welcome. Terms from £165 – £750. STB ★★ to ★★★ SC. [🐾]

Peaceful, unspoilt West Highland estate. Traditional Cottages, well equipped including TV, dinghy in summer and open fires. Sleep 4–10. Pets welcome. Walks, pony trekking, golf nearby. APPLY SOPHIE JAMES, SKIPNESS CASTLE, BY TARBERT PA29 6XU (01880 760207; Fax: 01880 760208). [🐾]

WEST LOCH HOTEL, BY TARBERT, LOCH FYNE PA29 6YF (01880 820283). Attractive traditional coaching inn on the shore of West Loch. Bright, comfortable accommodation, cosy atmosphere, superb food and wines. Open all year. [🐾]

FHG PUBLICATIONS

publish a large range of well-known accommodation guides. We will be happy to send you details or you can use the order form at the back of this book.

NOTE

All the information in this book is given in good faith in the belief that it is correct. However, the publishers cannot guarantee the facts given in these pages, neither are they responsible for changes in policy, ownership or terms that may take place after the date of going to press. Readers should always satisfy themselves that the facilities they require are available and that the terms, if quoted, still apply.

Ayr

Popular family holiday resort with sandy beaches. Excellent shopping; theatre; racecourse.

HORIZON HOTEL, ESPLANADE, AYR KA7 1DT (01292 264383; Fax: 01292 264011). Highly recommended for golf breaks; special midweek rates. Coach parties welcome. Lunches, high teas, dinners and bar suppers served. Phone for colour brochure. [🐕]
E–mail: mail@horizonhotel.com; Web-site: www.horizonhotel.com

Lamlash (Isle of Arran)

Small port on the east coast of Arran.

THE LILYBANK, LAMLASH, ISLE OF ARRAN KA27 8LS. Situated on the shores of Lamlash Bay, overlooking Holy Isle. Comfortable en suite bedrooms. Delicious breakfasts using local produce. Restricted smoking areas. Private parking and gardens. Well-behaved dogs welcome. STB ★★★★ Guest House. Tel & Fax: 01770 600230 for your brochure. [🐕]

Lochranza (Isle of Arran)

Village at north end of Arran.

CATACOL BAY HOTEL, CATACOL, LOCHRANZA KA27 8HN (01770 830231; Fax: 01770 830350). Comfortable, friendly, small country house hotel where good cooking is our speciality. Extensive bar menu, meals are served from noon until 10pm. Centrally heated. Open all year. Details of Special Breaks and brochure on request. Les Routiers. Children and pets welcome.
E-mail: davecatbay@lineone.net
Website: www.catacol.co.uk

Monkton

Small village near Prestwick Airport, 4 miles north of Ayr.

MUIRHOUSE GUEST HOUSE, MUIRHOUSE, KILMARNOCK ROAD, MONKTON, BY PRESTWICK KA9 2RJ (01292 475726). Small, family owned guest house in quiet location, within easy reach of airport and station. All rooms with central heating, colour TV and tea-making. En suite available.

BORDERS

BORDERS *Duns, Jedburgh, Melrose, Peebles*

Give yourself and your dogs a quality holiday break
in beautiful Duns, Berwickshire, South East Scotland

The Barniken House Hotel

• Dogs most welcome • Your dogs sleep with you in your bedroom
• Satellite TV, tea/coffee making in all bedrooms • Central heating • Sun lounge
• Luxurious Lounge Bar (with 100 Malt Whiskies) and Dining Room, both furnished to a very
high standard • Large garden with 9-hole putting green and patio • Large car park • 18 hole
course • Near spectacular scenery and ideal walks for dogs • Within easy reach of sandy beaches

For free colour brochure write to:
**The Barniken House Hotel,
Duns, Berwickshire,
S.E. Scotland TD11 3DE
Tel: 01361 882466**

Bed, Breakfast and Evening Dinner from ONLY £175 per week.
Special 6-day Spring and Autumn Breaks: ONLY £30 per day Dinner, Bed and Breakfast.
Special 6-day Christmas Break: ONLY £195 Dinner, Bed and Breakfast.
Special 6-day Millenium New Year Hogmanay Break: ONLY £300 Dinner, Bed and Breakfast.
All prices include VAT.

See also Colour Advertisement on page 38

FERNIEHIRST MILL LODGE & RIDING CENTRE

A chalet style guest house set in grounds of 25 acres beside the River Jed. Large lounge with TV
and log fire. All rooms en suite with tea/coffee making facilities. Home cooking. Licensed for
residents. Riding for experienced, adult riders from own stables. Well behaved pets (including
horses) welcome by arrangement. STB, AA, RAC, ABRS, TRSS Approved. For brochure contact;
Alan and Christine Swanston, Ferniehirst Mill Lodge, Jedburgh TD8 6PQ Tel & Fax: 01835 863279

UNIQUE SCOTLAND

Your pets are welcomed as part of the family at an especially attractive selection of
holiday cottages ALL OVER SCOTLAND. Please write or phone for our 96-page colour
brochure by return of post.
ECOSSE UNIQUE LTD, LILLIESLEAF, MELROSE, ROXBURGHSHIRE TD6 9JD
TEL: 01835 870779   FAX: 01835 870417   WWW.UNIQUESCOTLAND.COM

Beautiful Farmhouse and five modern
country cottages in peaceful location, all
within 12 minutes from Peebles. 25 - 30
minutes by car from Edinburgh city or
Airport. Excellent walking to suit all tastes
ranging from mountains rising to 2,600 feet to
lovely valley walks along the Manor Water or River Tweed which runs through
our farms. CHILDRENS PARADISE. DOGS ESPECIALLY WELCOME. Mountain
biking, bird watching, fishing, pony trekking and golf. All properties have central
heating, washer/dryer, microwave, TV/video. Most have dishwasher. Bed linen
supplied. Weekly prices from £190 - £705. Telephone for brochure.

**Glenrath Farm, Kirkton
Manor, Peebles, EH45 9JW**
Tel: (01721) 740??? /740???
Fax: (01721) 740314
★★★ to ★★★★ SELF-CATERING

NOTE

All the information in this book is given in good faith in the
belief that it is correct. However, the publishers cannot
guarantee the facts given in these pages, neither are they
responsible for changes in policy, ownership or terms that may
take place after the date of going to press. Readers should
always satisfy themselves that the facilities they require are
available and that the terms, if quoted, still apply.

Mrs C.M. KILPATRICK
Slipperfield House
West Linton EH46 7AA
Tel and Fax: 01968 660401

Two Cottages a mile from West Linton at the foot of the Pentland Hills, set in 100 acres of lochs and woodlands. Only 19 miles from Edinburgh City Centre.

AMERICA COTTAGE, which sleeps six people in three bedrooms, is secluded and has been completely modernised Off-peak electric heating.

LOCH COTTAGE, which sleeps four people in two bedrooms, is attached to the owners' house and has magnificent loch views and oil-fired heating.

STB ★★★ SC.

Both Cottages have sitting rooms with dining areas and colour TV; modern bathrooms and excellently equipped kitchens with washing and drying machines, microwave oven, central heating, telephone and open fires.

** Controlled pets welcomed ** Ample parking ** Car essential
** Edinburgh 19 miles ** Golf and private fishing ** Available all year.
E-mail: hols@kilpat.demon.co.uk   Website: www.kilpat.demon.co.uk

Duns

Picturesque Borders town with nearby ancient fort, castle, and Covenanters' stone to commemorate the army's encampment here in 1639. Excellent touring centre. Berwick-upon-Tweed 13 miles.

BARNIKEN HOUSE HOTEL, MURRAY STREET, DUNS TD11 3DE (01361 882466). Dogs most welcome, colour TV and tea coffee facilities in all rooms. Luxurious bar, sun lounge, large garden and car park. Central heating. Near spectacular scenery and ideal for walks for dogs. [🐎]

Innerleithen

An old woollen-manufacturing town set in beautiful Borders countryside. Peebles 6 miles.

MRS JENNIFER CAIRD, TRAQUAIR BANK, INNERLEITHEN EH44 6PR (01896 830425). Stone house with rambling garden, overlooks Tweed. Walking, fishing, riding. Help on farm. Edinburgh 3/4 hour. Animals welcome. Bed and Breakfast, Evening Meals by arrangement. STB Listed Commended. [🐎]

SYMBOLS

🐎　Indicates that pets are welcome free of charge.

£　Indicates that a charge is made for pets: nightly or weekly.

pw!　Shows some special provision for pets; exercise facility, feeding or accommodation arrangement.

⌂　Indicates separate pets accommodation.

Jedburgh

Small town on Jed Water, 10 miles north east of Hawick. Ruins of abbey founded in 1138.

ALAN & CHRISTINE SWANSTON, FERNIEHIRST MILL LODGE & RIDING CENTRE, JEDBURGH TD8 6PQ (Tel & Fax: 01835 863279). A chalet style guest house set in grounds of 25 acres. All rooms en suite with tea/coffee making facilities. Licensed for residents. Well behaved pets (including horses) welcome by arrangement. STB, AA, RAC, ABRS, TRSS Approved. [🐾]

Melrose

Picturesque village ideal for touring scenic Borders country. Famous for its medieval abbey. Edinburgh 37 miles, Galashiels 5.

Your pets are welcomed as part of the family at an especially attractive selection of holiday cottages ALL OVER SCOTLAND. Please write or phone for our 96-page colour brochure. ECOSSE UNIQUE LTD, LILLIESLEAF, , MELROSE, ROXBURGHSHIRE TD6 9JD (01835 870779; Fax: 01835 870417; www.Uniquescotland.com). [pw! £10 per week],

Peebles

On the River Tweed, famous for tweeds and knitwear.

GLENRATH FARM, KIRKTON MANOR, PEEBLES. EH45 9JW (01721 740221/740226; Fax: 01721 740314). Beautiful Farmhouse and five modern country cottages in peaceful location, all within 12 minutes from Peebles. Dogs especially welcome. Mountain biking, bird watching, fishing, pony trekking and golf. All properties have central heating, washer/dryer, microwave, TV/video. Most have dishwasher. Bed linen supplied. Weekly prices from £190 - £705. ★★★ to ★★★★ self-catering. Telephone for brochure.

West Linton

Village on east side of Pentland Hills, 7 miles south-west of Penicuik. Edinburgh 18 miles.

MRS C. M. KILPATRICK, SLIPPERFIELD HOUSE, WEST LINTON EH46 7AA (Tel & Fax: 01968 660401). Two excellently equipped converted cottages set in 100 acres of lochs and woodlands. America Cottage sleeps 6, Loch Cottage sleeps 4. Car essential. STB ★★★ Self Catering. [🐾]
E–mail: hols@kilpat.demon.co.uk
Website: www.kilpat.demon.co.uk

AA ◆◆◆,
Restricted Licence

BARNHILL SPRINGS

STB ★★ *Guest House*

Country Guest House, Moffat, Dumfriesshire DG10 9QS Tel: 01683 220580

Early Victorian country house overlooking some of the finest views of Upper Annandale. Comfortable accommodation, residents' lounge with open fire. Ideal centre for touring South-West Scotland and the Borders, or for an overnight stop. Situated on the Southern Upland Way half-a-mile from A74/M74 Moffat Junction. Pets free of charge. Bed & Breakfast from £20; Evening Meal (optional) from £14.

BUCCLEUCH ARMS HOTEL

Dating from the 18th century, the Buccleuch Arms is a Listed building, ideally situated for exploring the unspoilt South West of Scotland. Single, double/twin and family rooms, all with private bathroom. Open all year. B&B from £40 single, £32.50 double/twin.

High Street, Moffat, Dumfriesshire DG10 9ET   Tel: 01683 220003; Fax: 01683 221291

MORLICH HOUSE Ballplay Road, Moffat DG10 9JU

In beautiful 'Burns Country', this superb Victorian country house is set in quiet elevated grounds overlooking the town and surrounding hills. Just 5 minutes' walk from town centre. Rooms are en suite with colour TV, radio alarm, tea/coffee private bar and direct-dial telephone, four poster available. Evening meals (menu choice), licensed, private car park. B&B from £19pp, 3 course evening meal from £9.50 Weekly terms. Well behaved dogs welcome. Open Feb/Nov. STB ★★ GUESTHOUSE.

e-mail: morlich.house@ndirect.co.uk.   www.morlich-house.ndirect.co.uk

Tel: 01683 220589
Fax: 01683 221032

Creebridge House Hotel, Minnigaff, Newton Stewart, DG8 6NP

The Creebridge House Hotel sits in 3 acres of idyllic gardens and woodlands a mere 2 minutes walk from the bustling market town of Newton Stewart. Built in 1760 and originally home to the Earl of Galloway it has been tastefully converted into a 20 bedroom country house hotel renowned throughout the country for fine food and warm hospitality.

Tel: 01671 402121; Fax: 01671 403258 E-mail: creebridge.hotel@daelnet.co.uk Website: www.creebridge.co.uk

---

All rooms en suite with colour TV and tea and coffee making facilities and private car parking. Evening meals usually available with prior arrangement. STB ★★★. Single from £30. Double/twin from £20 – £25 depending on room and season. March to October. Self-catering studio apartment also available by day or week.

Rockcliffe, Dalbeattie, Kirkcudbrightshire DG5 4QG
Tel: 01556 630217; Fax: 01556 630489

TIGH-NA-MARA HOTEL Main Street, Sandhead DG9 9JF
Tel: 01776 830210   Fax: 01776 830432

Norman and Ellis McIntyre are very pleased to welcome you to Tigh-na-Mara, described in the Hidden Places Hotel Guide as "the place you hear about but can never find. Food – just simply at its best". All our cosy rooms are en suite, with colour TV and tea/coffee making facilities. Situated just 6 miles from Stranraer and overlooking the beach, the hotel serves a variety of menus and has an attractive beer garden, with pets and families made most welcome. Les Routiers Recommended

---

SYMBOLS

🐕 Indicates that pets are welcome free of charge.

£ Indicates that a charge is made for pets: nightly or weekly.

pw! Shows some special provision for pets; exercise facility, feeding or accommodation arrangement.

⌂ Indicates separate pets accommodation.

Annan

Victorian red brick town overlooking River Annan, famous for trout and salmon.

POWFOOT GOLF HOTEL, LINK AVENUE, POWFOOT, NR. ANNAN (01461 700254; Fax: 01461 700288). On the shores of the Solway Firth. Well located for wildfowler, salmon and trout fishing. Bird watching. Les Routiers. AA ★★ 68%. Minotels. Pets Welcome.

WARMANBIE COUNTRY HOUSE HOTEL & RESTAURANT, ANNAN, DUM-FRIESSHIRE, DG12 5LL (01461 204015). Dogs very welcome (we have three ourselves), allowed in bedrooms and ground floor. Beautiful walks. Creative cooking. Two four posters. Selection of malts. Free fishing, golf nearby. [Pets £3.25 per night]

Auchencairn

Spectacular cliffs, and sandy beaches lie near this whitewashed village.

MR AND MRS BARDSLEY, THE ROSSAN, AUCHENCAIRN, CASTLE DOUGLAS DG7 1QR (01556 640269; Fax: 01556 640278). STB One Star B&B. Small, homely, early Victorian guest house. B&B. Optional evening meal. Organic produce when possible. Ideal centre for bird watching, golf, hill walking. [🐕],

Beattock

Picturesque Dumfriesshire village, ideally placed for touring Borders region and Upper Clyde Valley.

BEATTOCK HOUSE HOTEL AND CARAVAN PARK, BEATTOCK DG10 9QB (01683 300403). Ideally situated Hotel and Caravan Park for travellers wishing to rest awhile from the busy A74 or to tour the lovely Borders country, Burns Country and the Lake District. Fishing, stalking and rough shooting available. Restaurant; all-day bar licence. AA, RAC. [🐕]

Borgue

Village south west of Kircudbright, setting for Robert Louis Stevenson's "Master of Ballantrae".

FOUR QUALITY CARAVAN PARKS IN BEAUTIFUL S.W. SCOTLAND. Touring caravans, lodges and holiday caravans to rent or buy. Family camping. For details: MR D. GILLESPIE, BRIGHOUSE BAY, BORGUE, KIRKCUDBRIGHTSHIRE, DUMFRIES & GALLOWAY DG6 4TS (01557 870267). E-mail: fhg@gillespie.leisure.co.uk

Castle Douglas

Old market town at the northern end of Carlingwalk Loch, good touring centre for Galloway.

MR P. W. BALL, BARNCROSH FARM, CASTLE DOUGLAS DG7 1TX (01556 680216). Comfortable Cottages and flats for 2/4/6/9. Fully equipped, including linen. Colour TV. Children and dogs welcome. Beautiful rural surroundings. Brochure on request. [Pets £20 weekly]

MRS CELIA PICKUP, "CRAIGADAM", CASTLE DOUGLAS DG7 3HU (Tel & Fax: 01556 650233). Family-run 18th century famhouse. All bedrooms en suite. Billiard room. Lovely oak-panelled dining room offering Cordon Bleu cooking using local produce such as venison, pheasant and salmon. Trout fishing, walking and golfing available. 3 Crowns Commended. [🐾]

RUSKO HOLIDAYS, RUSKO, GATEHOUSE OF FLEET, CASTLE DOUGLAS. DG7 2BS (01557 814215; Fax: 01557 814679). Spacious farmhouse and cosy, comfortable cottages near beaches, hills and golf course. Walking, fishing, tennis, pets, including horses, welcome. Rates £150-£600. ★★ to ★★★ Self Catering.

Dalbeattie

Small granite town on Kirkgunzeon Lane (or Burn), 13 miles south-west of Dumfries.

BAREND HOLIDAY VILLAGE, DALBEATTIE (Tel: 01387 780663; Fax: 01387 780283). Enjoy the quiet and comfort of our centrally heated, well equipped Scandinavian style log chalets overlooking loch and golf course. Bar, restaurant, indoor heated pool and sauna on site, beach nearby. Brochure on request. [Pets £21 per week]
Website: www.barendholidayvillage.co.uk

Drummore

Peaceful village 4 miles north of Mull of Galloway.

MRS SALLY COLMAN, HARBOUR ROW, DRUMMORE, STRANRAER DG9 9QX (01776 840631). Five cottages and two houses benefiting from southerly exposure. Open fires for evening relaxation. Highest quality furnishings and equipment. Garden with children's playground. Pets welcome. Prices £195 – £455. STB ★★★★ SC. [🐾]

Dumfries

County town of Dumfriesshire and a former seaport, Dumfries contains many interesting buildings including an 18th century windmill containing a camera obscura. Robert Burns lived in the town before his death in 1796

BARNSOUL FARM, IRONGRAY, SHAWHEAD, DUMFRIES DG2 9SQ (Tel/Fax 01387 730249). Barnsoul, one of Galloway's scenic working farms. Birdwatching, walking, fishing on your doorstep. Spot the dog awaits your arrival. Open Easter-October. [🐾]
Website: BarnsoulDG@aol.com

DAVID & GILL STEWART, GUBHILL FARM, AE, NEAR DUMFRIES DG1 1RL (01387 860648). Listed farm steading flats in peaceful pastoral valley surrounded by wooded hills and forest lanes. Nature-friendly management. Lower flat wheelchair compatible. Riding, fishing, mountain biking and hillwalking all nearby.
E–mail: stewart@creaturefeature.freeserve.co.uk

Glenluce

Village 9 miles east of Stranraer.

KELVIN HOUSE HOTEL, 53 MAIN STREET, GLENLUCE DG8 0PP (Tel/Fax: 01581 300303). Built c.1700, an unpretentious, recently renovated hotel situated on the village main street. Excellent reputation for food. Family-run, with emphasis on relaxation. Sporting parties catered for. [🐕],
E–mail: kelvinhouse@lineone.net.

Gretna Green

Village close to border famous for runaway weddings.

JANE LAWSON, CHERRY BANK, SPRINGFIELD, GRETNA GREEN, DUM-FRIESSHIRE DG16 5EH (01461 337569). An ideal stopoff on the journey north and only half-a-mile from Gretna Green. Cherry bank is an unusual house, fea-turing en suite rooms, a four poster, and a welcome that will speed your return. [🐕]

Kirkcudbright

Small town on River Dee estuary 10 miles south of Castle Douglas.

GORDON HOUSE HOTEL, 116 HIGH STREET, KIRKCUDBRIGHT DG6 4JQ (Tel & Fax: 01557 330670). 12 comfortable bedrooms with TVs, tea/coffee, radio alarms, washbasins and central heating. Private residents' lounge. Restaurant – Scottish/Italian cuisine. Lounge bar. Garden. Dogs welcome! STB ★★ Inn.

Langholm

Small mill town at the junction of three rivers. Common Riding held in July.

THE ESKDALE HOTEL, LANGHOLM DG13 0JH (Tel & Fax: 013873 80357). Former Coaching Inn. All rooms with central heating, colour TV, radio. En suite available. Licensed. Two bars. Restaurant. Games room. Golf, shooting, fishing. AA ★★. STB ★★ Hotel. [🐕]

Lockerbie

Market town 11 miles east of Dumfries.

DINWOODIE LODGE, COUNTRY HOUSE HOTEL, NEAR LOCKERBIE, DUM-FRIESSHIRE DG11 2SL (01576 470289). Fishing, golf, shooting available in area. Ideal centre for touring Borders, Galloway. Full central heating. Breakfast, Lunches, Bar Meals, Licensed Bar, Separate Pool Room and Darts Board.

LOCKERBIE MANOR COUNTRY HOTEL, LOCKERBIE DG11 2RG (01576 202610/ 203939). Splendid Georgian mansion house set in 78 acres of beautiful grounds. Ideal base for exploring countryside. Single, twin, double and family rooms, all en suite, and equipped with colour TV, tea-making etc. [pw! 🐕]

Moffat

At head of lovely Annandale, grand mountain scenery. Good centre for rambling, climbing, angling and golf. The 'Devil's Beef Tub' is 5 miles, Edinburgh 52 miles, Peebles 33, Dumfries 21.

ANNANDALE ARMS HOTEL, HIGH STREET, MOFFAT DG1O 9HF (Tel: 01683 220013 Fax: 01683 221395). A warm welcome is offered at the Annandale Arms to dogs with well-mannered and house-trained owners. Excellent restaurant and a relaxing panelled bar. Large private parking area. £64.00 per room for two; £45.00 per room for one. [🐕]

BARNHILL SPRINGS COUNTRY GUEST HOUSE, MOFFAT DG10 9QS (01683 220580). Early Victorian country house overlooking some of the finest views of Upper Annandale. Comfortable accommodation, residents' lounge with open fire. Situated on the Southern Upland Way half-a-mile from A74/M74 Moffat Junction. Pets free of charge. Bed & Breakfast from £20; Evening Meal (optional) from £14. STB ★★ Guest House. AA ◆◆◆. [🐕]

BUCCLEUCH ARMS HOTEL, HIGH STREET, MOFFAT DG10 9ET (01683 220003; Fax: 01683 221291). Ideally situated for exploring the unspoilt South West of Scotland. Single, double/twin and family rooms, all with private bathroom. Open all year. B&B from £40 single, £32.50 double/twin. [🐕]

MORLICH LICENSED GUEST HOUSE, BALLPLAY ROAD, MOFFAT DG10 9JU (Tel: 01683 220589; Fax: 01683 221032). Set in beautiful 'Burns Country' Morlich House is a superb Victorian country house. Rooms are en suite with TV, radio alarm, tea/coffee and telephone, four-poster available. Private car park. B&B from £19pp, 3 course evening meal from £9.50. Weekly terms. Open Feb/Nov. STB ★★. [🐕]

Newton Stewart

Town on the edge of the Galloway Forest Park. Central for touring south west Scotland.

CREEBRIDGE HOUSE HOTEL, MINNIGAFF, NEWTON STEWART DG8 6NP (Tel: 01671 402121; Fax: 01671 403258). The Creebridge House Hotel sits in 3 acres of idyllic gardens and woodlands a mere 2 minutes walk from Newton Stewart. It has been tastefully converted into a 20 bedroom country house hotel renowned throughout the country for fine food and warm hospitality. [🐕]
E–mail: creebridge.hotel@daelnet.co.uk
Website: www.creebridge.co.uk

Rockcliffe

Enchanting coastal village in a "National Scenic Area" five miles south of Dalbeattie.

MILLBRAE HOUSE, ROCKCLIFFE, DALBEATTIE, KIRKCUDBRIGHTSHIRE DG5 4QG (01556 630217; Fax: 01556 630489). STB ★★★. All rooms en suite, TV and tea /coffee facilities, private car parking. Evening meals usually available with prior arrangement. From £20. March to October. Also, self-catering studio apartment. [🐕]

Sandhead

Coastal village on west side of Luce Bay, 7 miles south of Stranraer.

TIGH-NA-MARA HOTEL, MAIN STREET, SANDHEAD DG9 9JF (01776 830210; Fax: 01776 830432). All rooms en suite, with colour TV and tea/coffee facilities. The hotel serves a variety of menus and has an attractive beer garden, with pets and families welcome. Les Routiers Recommended. [🐾]

DUNBARTONSHIRE

Loch Lomond

Largest loch in Scotland –23 miles long, up to 5 miles wide, and 630 ft at deepest point – with 30 islands. Pleasure boats and paddle steamer offer rides. Surrounded by beautiful woodland areas.

MRS SALLY MACDONELL, MARDELLA FARMHOUSE, OLD SCHOOL ROAD, GARTOCHARN, LOCH LOMOND G83 8SD (01389 830428). Set on a quiet country lane, surrounded by fields. Friendly and comfortable, where the kettle's always boiling. AA QQQQ, RAC Listed, AA "Landlady of the Year" 1995 Finalist; Winner AA Scotland B&B of the Year 1995. [🐾]

DUNDEE & ANGUS

DUNDEE & ANGUS *Broughty Ferry*

KINGENNIE LODGES STB ★★★★ *SELF-CATERING* TEL: 01382 350777 FAX: 01382 350400
Kingennie, Broughty Ferry, By Dundee. DD5 3RD
All lodges furnished to the highest standards and are open plan and centrally heated. Each has a double and twin bedrrom as well as folding futon bed in the lounge; bathroom with shower over bath; fully-equipped kitchen with dishwasher, microwave and washer/dryer. Our "Clova" Lodge has full disabled facilities. Bed linen and towels provided, cot and highchair available upon request. Pets welcome. Lodge terms weekly from £200. Further details contact: **Neil Anderson.**

Broughty Ferry

On the outskirts of Dundee with restored 15th century castle housing a museum of Tayside's natural history and whaling industry.

KINGENNIE FISHING & WOODLAND LODGES, KINGENNIE, BROUGHTY FERRY, BY DUNDEE. DD5 3RD (01382 350777; Fax: 01382 350400). Each has a double and twin bedroom as well as folding futon bed in the lounge; bathroom with shower over bath; fully-equipped kitchen with dishwasher, microwave and washer/dryer. Our "Clova" Lodge has full disabled facilities. Pets welcome. Further details contact: NEIL ANDERSON. [Pets £15 per week]

EDINBURGH & LOTHIANS

THE MONKS' MUIR

Haddington EH41 3SB
Tel: 01620 860340; Fax: 01620 861770

A secluded, friendly, green, sheltered place, but with direct access to the main A1 road. One of the oldest and best-loved caravan and camping parks in Scotland, only 15 minutes from the fringes of famous Edinburgh, in an area of great beauty, with glorious beaches, rich farmland, a plethora of golf courses and fascinating villages. Excellent facilities include the best park shop and cafe/bistro in the business! Appointed by every motoring and caravanning organisation, with the Scottish Tourist Board "Thistle" Award for Excellence,'Green Apple' Environmental Award, David Bellamy Gold Environmental Award, 1999 Finalist Calor 'Best Park in Scotland'. Tourers, campervans and tents all welcome. Luxury four/six berth caravans to rent. Open all year.

Hunter Holiday Cottages Rosewell, Edinburgh. Contact Duncan Hunter Tel: 0131 448 0888 Fax: 0131 440 2082
E-mail: hunter@holidaycottages.demon.co.uk Website: www.holidaycottages.demon.co.uk

Hunter Holiday Cottages offer a range of cottages in beautiful countryside only eight miles from Edinburgh city centre. These superior cottages are recently renovated, have all modern facilities and sleep six to eight plus. They provide the ideal base for the perfect Scottish holiday from their location in Midlothian's historic countryside. There is easy access to Scotland's capital and the major routes to the rest of Scotland. For more information visit our website. Also B&B, £20-£25 per night.

See also Colour Advertisement on page 40

Edinburgh

Scotland's capital with magnificent castle overlooking "The Athens of the North".

MRS GARVIE, THE JOPPA ROCKS GUEST HOUSE, 99 JOPPA ROAD, EDINBURGH EH15 2HB (0131 669 8695). Joppa Rocks Guest House is a small family-run guest house. ideally situated to visit Edinburgh and surrounding countryside. Situated toward the east of the city, accessed by road from the A1 and the city bypass. Excellent bus service to the city.

Haddington

Historic town on River Tyne 16 miles east of Edinburgh. Birthplace of John Knox, 1505. Renovated Church of St Mary, 14c-15c; St Martin's Church, AM.

THE MONKS' MUIR, HADDINGTON EH41 3SB (01620 860340; Fax: 01620 861770). Secluded and tranquil amidst beautiful countryside, only 15 minutes from Edinburgh. Tourers, tents and luxury hire caravans. Award winning, lovely facilities, totally 'green', very friendly. Open all year. ✓✓✓✓ EXCELLENT. STB ★★★★★ . [🐾]

Musselburgh

Town to the east of Edinburgh famous for golf.

MRS GARVIE, ARDEN HOUSE, 26 LINKFIELD ROAD, MUSSELBURGH EH21 (Tel & Fax: 0131 665 0663). AA ★★★★. Family run guest house five miles from Edinburgh, opposite race track. [Pets £2 per night.]

Rosewell

Village four miles south west of Dalkeith, to the south east of Edinburgh.

HUNTER HOLIDAY COTTAGES, DUNCAN HUNTER (Tel: 0131 448 0888 Fax: 0131 440 2082). Superior cottages, recently renovated with modern facilities, sleeping six to eight plus, in beautiful countryside only eight miles from Edinburgh. The ideal base for the perfect Scottish holiday. Also B&B, £20-£25 per night. [🐕 🏠]
E–mail: hunter@holidaycottages.demon.co.uk
Website: www.holidaycottages.demon.co.uk

FIFE

FIFE *St Andrews*

ST ANDREWS COUNTRY COTTAGES
Self catering

Idyllic Country Cottages and Farmhouses on a beautiful Country Estate. Perfect for golf, exploring or relaxing. Enclosed gardens, log fires, private walking. Sleeps 4 to 14. Brochure:- **Mountquhanie Estate, FREEPOST Cupar, Fife KY15 4BR Tel 01382 330 318 Fax 01382 330480**

E-mail: enquiries@standrews-cottages.com   Website: www.standrews-cottages.com

St Andrews

Home of golf – British Golf Museum has memorabilia dating back to the origins of the game. Remains of castle and cathedral. Sealife Centre and beach Leisure Centre. Excellent sands. Ideal base for exploring the picturesque East Neuk of Fife.

MR & MRS WEDDERBURN, ST ANDREWS COUNTRY COTTAGES, MOUN-TQUHANIE ESTATE, FREEPOST, CUPAR KY15 4BR (Tel: 01382 330318; Mobile: 07966 373007; Fax: 01382 330480). Quality self-catering houses and cottages on tranquil Country Estate. Central heating, colour TV, telephone. Enclosed gardens. STB ★★★ to ★★★★★ Self Catering. [pw! Pets £10 per week].
E–mail: enquiries@standrews-cottages.com
Website: www.standrews-cottages.com

Key to Tourist Board Ratings Scotland and Wales

The Scottish Tourist Board Star Grading System. This easy-to-understand system tells you at a glance the quality standard you can expect. The gradings range from ★ (Fair and acceptable) to ★★★★★ (Exceptional, world-class) and will also include the type of accommodation eg ★★★ Self-catering or ★★ Hotel.

The Wales Tourist Board also operates the above system for serviced accommodation only. Self-catering properties will continue to show the **Dragon Award Grading** from **One** to **Five** depending on quality and facilities.

HIGHLANDS

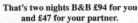

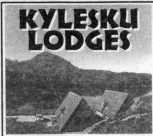

Mansfield House Hotel *Scotsburn Road, Tain, Ross-shire IV19 1PR*

Heather and Beth are two Golden Retrievers/Head Receptionists and look forward to welcoming you and your pets to their lovely Scottish Mansion. The hotel is rated STB 4 Stars following independent Lab. tests. Its pedigree includes Merit Awards for Hospitality, Comfort and Cuisine, and the Restaurant is accredited by Taste of Scotland (i.e Top Eaters recommend it) and has 2 AA Rosettes. All well-trained pets and owners welcome. **Telephone 01862 892052**   **AA ★★★ RAC**

 11 DIABAIG, TORRIDON MRS CHRISTINE DUNCAN, HAZELBANK. DIABAIG, TORRIDON IV2 2HE   *Tel: 01445 790259*

Holiday cottage in quiet location overlooking Diabaig Bay with glorious views out to Skye. The cottage sleeps six in two doubles and one twin, kitchen with electric cooker, washing machine, fridge, etc; livingroom has electric fire and colour TV. All linen supplied. Pets welcome. Ideal for fishing and hill walking. Car parking beside house. Open January to December. Price from £160 to £220 per week.

MILTON HOTELS & LEISURE CLUBS. Discover a warm Traditional Scottish Welcome, in the West Highland Shopping Towns of Fort William, Inverness, Oban and Stirling. PETS STAY FOR FREE! Call us today free on 0800 731 8191 and when you quote Reference FHGP1, your partner can stay for half price.

Aultbea

Village on east shore of Loch Ewe, 5 miles north of Poolewe.

AULTBEA LODGES, AULTBEA, ROSS-SHIRE IV22 2HU (Tel/Fax: 01445 731268). Tranquil hillside location with spectacular views over Loch Ewe and beyond to the Hebrides. Local amenities within walking distance. Ideal for birdwatching, fishing, walking or just relaxing. [pw! Pets £2 per night, £10 per week]
E–mail: AultbeaLodge@ukgateway.net
Website: www.aultbea-lodges.co.uk

COVE VIEW, 36 MELLON CHARLES, AULTBEA IV22 2JL (01445 731351). Wester Ross is ideal for hill walking or a quiet restful holiday. Detached chalet with two small bedrooms, sitting room, bathroom and mini kitchen. From £180 per week. A warm welcome awaits you and your pet. [🐾]

Aviemore

Scotland's leading ski resort in Spey valley with superb sport and entertainment facilities. All-weather holiday centre with accommodation to suit all pockets. Excellent fishing. Centre for exploring Cairngorms. Edinburgh 129 miles, Grantown-on-Spey 14, Kingussie 12, Carr-Bridge 7.

PREMIER VACATIONS, 5 ST PETERS BUILDINGS, EDINBURGH EH3 9PG (0131 221 9001). Cosy lodges and superbly appointed villas. Open all year. Free Brochure. Sky TV, video, payphone, barbecue. Pets Welcome. Many activities available. [Pets £20 per week].

PINE BANK CHALETS, DALFABER ROAD, AVIEMORE PH22 1PX (01479 810000; Fax: 01479 811469). Cosy Log Cabins and Quality Chalets, situated in a secluded area near the River Spey. Superb Family/Activity Holidays by mountains. Ideal skiing, walking, fishing and golf. Sky TV, mountain bikes. Short breaks available. Pets welcome. Open all year. ASSC Member. Brochure. [Pets £2.50 per night, £20 per week.]

Beauly

Town at head of Beauly Firth, 11 miles west of Inverness.

GILL KIRKPATRICK, KERROW HOUSE, CANNICH, BY BEAULY IV4 7NA (01456 415243; Fax: 01456 415425). Country house accommodation and five self-catering cottages in own grounds with private trout fishing. B&B with optional dinner. A haven for animal lovers.
E–mail: Gill@kerrow-house.demon.co.uk

Carr-bridge

Village on River Dulnain, 7 miles north of Aviemore. Landmark Visitor Centre has exhibition explaining history of local enviroment.

LIZ AND IAN BISHOP, SLOCHD COTTAGES, BY CARR-BRIDGE PH23 3AY (Tel & Fax 01479 841 666). Country Cottage, sleeps 6. Wonderful forest and mountain trails. Ideally placed for touring. Close to golfing, fishing, skiing etc. From £100 per week. SAE for details. [🐎]

LYNN & DAVE BENGE, THE PINES COUNTRY HOUSE, DUTHIL, CARR-BRIDGE PH23 3ND (01479 841220). STB ★★ Guest House. Relax and enjoy our Highland hospitality, woodland setting; all rooms en suite. Traditional or vegetarian home cooking. Children and pets welcome. B&B from £19 daily; DB&B from £183 weekly. [🐎]
Website: www.dbenge.freeserve.co.uk

Contin

Village in Ross and Cromarty district two miles south-west of Strathpeffer.

COUL HOUSE HOTEL, CONTIN, BY STRATHPEFFER IV14 9EY (01997 421487; Fax: 01997 421945). Hamish and Angus, our lovable labradors look forward to welcoming you. "Taste of Scotland" food, log fires, well-equipped bedrooms. Miles of wonderful walks. STB ★★★★ Hotel. [🐎 pw!]

Daviot

Village 5 miles south-east of Inverness, the Highland "capital".

TORGUISH HOUSE & HOLIDAY HOMES, DAVIOT, INVERNESS IV2 5XQ (01463 772208; Fax: 01463 772308). Homely Guest House with generous rooms, some en suite, all with TV, tea/coffee. Large garden. Also, The Steading (self catering cottages sleeping 2–4). Fully equipped kitchen and bathroom. [🐎]
E–mail: Torguish@Torguish.com
Website: www.Torguish.com/

SYMBOLS

🐎   Indicates that pets are welcome free of charge.

£   Indicates that a charge is made for pets: nightly or weekly.

pw!   Shows some special provision for pets; exercise facility, feeding or accommodation arrangement.

⌂   Indicates separate pets accommodation.

Dornoch

Broad tree-lined streets and one of the best golf courses in Britain.

MRS E. A. DUNLOP, CLUAINE, EVELIX, DORNOCH, SUTHERLAND IV25 3RD (01862 810276). Modern bungalow, set in owner's garden, woods around. Sleeps four, non-smoking only please. Quiet, one-and-a-half miles from Dornoch, lovely walks by sea, golf courses.

Drumnadrochit

Village on the shores of Loch Ness with monster visitors centre. Sonar scanning cruises.

CAROL HUGHES, GLENURQUHART LODGES, BY DRUMNADROCHIT, INVER-NESS-SHIRE. IV3 6TJ (01456 476234; Fax: 01456 476286). Situated between Loch Ness and Glen Affric in a spectacular setting ideal for walking, touring or just relaxing in this tranquil location. Four spacious chalets all fully equipped for six people, set in wooded grounds. Owners hotel adjacent where guests are most welcome in the restaurant and bar. [Pets £10 per week.]

Dulnain Bridge

Village to the south west of Grantown-and-Spey

RICHARD & ANGELA ROULSON, ROSEGROVE GUESTHOUSE, SKYE OF CURR, DULNAIN BRIDGE, GRANTOWN-ON-SPEY, INVERNESS-SHIRE (0147 9851335). Situated in the heart of the Scottish Highlands. Comfortable centrally heated rooms and good home cooked food. Evening meals available. Golf, fishing and skiing available. [🐾]
E–mail: rosegroveguesthouse@tesco.net

Fort William

Small town at foot of Ben Nevis, ideal base for climbers and hillwalkers. .

MRS MARY MACDONALD, AONACH-MOR HOUSE, TORLUNDY, FORT WILLIAM PH33 6SW (01397 704525). Bungalow overlooking Ben Nevis set in quiet location on edge of forest. Ideal for doggie walking. 3 miles north of Fort William. 2 family/1 double room, en suite. TV, teamakers, Scottish breakfast. From £13 p.p.p.n., reductions for children.

THE CLAN MACDUFF HOTEL, ACHINTORE, FORT WILLIAM PH33 6RW (01397 702341; Fax: 01397 706174). This family-run hotel overlooks Loch Linnhe, two miles south of Fort William, excellent for touring the rugged mountains of the West Highlands. All rooms have TV, hairdryer and hospitality tray; all with private facilities. 3 nights DB&B from £87.50pppn. STB ★★ Hotel. Phone or write for colour brochure and tariff. [🐾]

LINNHE CARAVAN & CHALET PARK, DEPT PW, CORPACH, FORT WILLIAM PH33 7NL (01397 772376). One of the best and most beautiful lochside parks in Scotland. Thistle Award caravans for hire. "Best park in Scotland 1999 Award". Private beach, free fishing. Prices from £180. [pw! £2 per night, £14 per week],
E–mail: holidays@linnhe.demon.co.uk,
Website: www.lochaber.com/linnhe

NETHER LOCHABER HOTEL, ONICH, FORT WILLIAM PH33 6SE (01855 821235; 01855 821545). Traditional home cooking goes hand in hand with homely service, comfortable accommodation and private facilities on the shores of beautiful Loch Linnhe. B&B from £20-£35 per person. [🐕]

MRS M. MATHESON, THISTLE COTTAGE, TORLUNDY, FORT WILLIAM (01397 702428). Central for touring the Highlands - 31/2 miles from Fort William. Double and family rooms with TV, tea/coffee making facilities. En suite available. Ample parking. B&B from £13 per night. STB ★★ B&B [🐕]

Invergarry

Village south of Fort Augustus on the shore of Loch Oich

INVERGARRY HOTEL, INVERGARRY, INVERNESS-SHIRE PH35 4HJ (Tel: 01809 501206 Fax: 01809 501400). STB ★★★ Hotel. Fine Scottish produce and a well-stocked bar in a distinctive Victorian building, amidst the beautiful scenery of the Scottish Highlands. Ten comfortable en suite rooms. [🐕]
E–mail: hotel@invergarry.net
Website: www.invergarry.net/hotel

Kingussie

Tourist centre on the River Spey 28 miles south of Inverness.

COLUMBA HOUSE HOTEL & RESTAURANT, MANSE ROAD, KINGUSSIE PH21 1JF (01540 661402; Fax: 01540 661652). Nestling in large grounds. Restaurant, overlooking walled garden, offers superb Scottish cuisine. En suite bedrooms with mini-bar, TV, telephone, tea/coffee. Romantic four-posters and family suite. Parking. AA ★★. [pw! 🐕]
E–mail: reservations@columba-hotel.co.uk

Kylesku

Situated on Loch Cairnbawn across from Ullapool.

KYLESKU LODGES, KYLESKU IV27 4HW (Tel & Fax: 01971 502003). Self catering holiday lodges in secluded location, convenient for bird watching, hill walking and fishing. Open March to October. Colour brochure on request. [Pets £10 per week]

Lochcarron

Long inlet extending from Kyle of Lochalsh to foot of Glen Carron

KRISTINE MACKENZIE, "BLACKWOOD", ARINACKAIG, STRATHCARRON IV54 8YN (01520 722296). Three properties in tranquil, secluded surroundings. Abundance of wildlife on working croft. Equipped to high standard, light, spacious with panoramic views. £100 to £300 inclusive.

Loch Maree

Narrow, very deep loch running from Kinlochewe to near Poolewe in dramatic and unspoiled countryside.

THE SHEILING. Secluded Bungalow in wooded grounds, amidst spectacular scenery. Sleeps 5, with coal fire in lounge; equipped to high standard. All pets are welcome. Terms from £180 to £295; electricity by coin meter. APPLY: MR & MRS A. ALLAN, TORGUISH, DAVIOT, INVERNESS IV1 2XQ (01463 772208; Fax: 01463 772308). [🐕]

Loch Ness

Home of "Nessie", extending for 23 miles from Fort Augustus to south of Inverness.

Former croft situated 16 miles south of Inverness. Comfortable lounge, digital TV, video and open fireplace. Separate dining room. Fully equipped kitchen.Three bedrooms. Central heating. Pets welcome. For a colour brochure contact: ANDY AND ROSEMARY HOLT, ISLAND COTTAGE, INVERFARIGAIG, INVERNESS IV2 6XR (Tel/Fax: 01456 486631). [🐕 🏠]

DAVID AND PATRICIA ALLEN, WILDSIDE HIGHLAND LODGES, WILDSIDE, WHITEBRIDGE, INVERNESS IV2 6UN. (01456 486373). STB ★★★ and ★★★★. Self-Catering. Cosy studio units built for two. Well appointed stone and cedar lodges for up to six. Open all year round, with free central heating. Mini breaks available and pets welcome. See our colour brochure or visit our web site. [Pets £15 per week].
E–mail: patricia@wildside-lodges.demon.co.uk
Website: www.wildside-lodges.demon.co.uk

Mallaig

Busy port at the end of the West Highland Railway line. Ferry port for Skye.

JILL AND TOM SMITH, SPRINGBANK GUEST HOUSE, EAST BAY, MALLAIG PH41 4QF (TEL & FAX: 01687 462459). STB ★ GUEST HOUSE. Overlooking the harbour and the Sound of Sleat to Skye. The house is fully centrally heated and double glazed. B&B from £16 to £17 per night. Evening meal by arrangement. Children and pets welcome. Phone for brochure. [🐕]

Nethybridge

Popular Strathspey resort on River Nethy with extensive Abernethy Forest to the south. Impressive mountain scenery. Grantown-on-Spey 5 miles.

NETHYBRIDGE, STRATHSPEY. Choice of modern cottages or converted smithy. Linen and visitor laundry included. September to May storage heating included. Good walking and touring area. STB ★★★/★★★★. Write or phone for brochure. MR AND MRS P. W. PATRICK, CHAPELTON PLACE, FORRES, MORAY IV36 2NL (01309 672505). [One dog free, thereafter £20 per week.]
E–mail: speyside@enterprise.net
Website: www.nethybridge.com/speysidecottages.htm

Onich

On shores of Loch Linnhe. Good boating, fishing. Fort William 10 miles.

INCHREE CHALETS, ONICH, FORT WILLIAM PH33 6SD (01855 821287). STB ★★ Self-Catering. Comfortable chalets sleeping 4/6; all facilities. Restaurant and lounge bar. Forest walks from site. Midway between Ben Nevis and Glencoe. Discount for couples. [🐾]
E–mail: paddy@inchreecentre1.netlink.net

THE LODGE ON THE LOCH, CREAG DHU, ONICH, BY FORT WILLIAM PH33 6RY (01855 821582; Fax: 01855 821463). Enjoying one of the finest panoramas in Scotland, a spell-binding blend of gentle elegance and a delightful, informal atmosphere. Taste of Scotland cuisine. STB ★★★★, AA ★★★.
E–mail: reservations@freedomglen.co.uk

STRATHLINNHE HOLIDAY HOMES, ONICH, FORT WILLIAM PH33 6SD (01855 821264). Situated by shores of Loch Linnhe. Wonderful position overlooking the loch betwixt Glencoe and Ben Nevis. Telephone MRS MACLEAN (01855 821264) [🐾]

MRS K. A. McCALLUM, TIGH-A-RIGH GUEST HOUSE, ONICH PH33 6SE (01855 821255). STB ★★ Guest House. Dinner, Bed and Breakfast. TV available in rooms on request. Two TV lounges. Hot and cold water, some rooms en suite. Tea and coffee. Parking. Dogs welcome. [🐾]

Poolewe

Village lying between Lochs Ewe and Maree with the River Ewe flowing through.

MR A. URQUHART, CROFTERS COTTAGES, 15 CROFT, POOLEWE, ROSS-SHIRE IV22 2JY (Tel: 01445 781 268; 01445 781 704). Three traditional cottages situated in a scenic and tranquil area, ideal for a "get away from it all" holiday. Comfortably furnished with all mod cons.

Roy Bridge

Located in Glen Spean at foot of Glen Roy in Lochaber, 3 miles east of Spean Bridge.

BUNROY HOLIDAY PARK, ROY BRIDGE PH31 4AG (01397 712332). In a quiet woodland setting, modern insulated chalets, double glazed and fully equipped. Camping and caravans welcome. Ideal base for touring. Short Breaks available October to Easter. [Pets £10 per week in lodges, maximum two pets]
E–mail: bunroy@btinternet.com

Fully equipped bungalows (sleep 2-6) £160-£360, and chalets (sleep 8) £250-£510. Set amid heath and birch in Glen Spean; shops and hotels nearby. Discounts for couples and Senior Citizens. Fort William 12 miles. Colour brochure available. STB 2/3 Stars Self-Catering. IAN MATHESON, THE LITTLE HOUSES, EAST PARK, ROY BRIDGE PH31 4AG (01397 712370; Fax: 01397 712831). [1st pet free, additional pet £15]

STRONLOSSIT HOTEL, ROY BRIDGE PH31 4AG (01397 712253; Fax:01397 712641). Ideal centre for touring Highlands. 11 fully appointed bedrooms with en suite facilities. Lounge bar with log fire, meals service. Excellent food. Discounts available for three nights or more. AA ★★. [Pets £3 per night]

Spean Bridge

Village on River Spean at foot of Loch Lochy. Site of WWII Commando Memorial.

Animal friendly holidays in the heart of the Scottish Highlands. EARENDIL, MUCOMIR, BY SPEAN BRIDGE PH34 4EQ (Tel & Fax 01397 712548). E–mail: helen@dreamweavers.co.uk

MRS M. H. CAIRNS, INVERGLOY HOUSE, SPEAN BRIDGE PH34 4DY (01397 712681). Two spacious 4-5-berth luxury caravans, highest standard (fridge, shower, TV). 50 acre wooded estate, beautifully secluded overlooking Loch Lochy; beach, fishing, rowing boats, bird watching, lovely walks. Free gas and electricity. Discounts for two occupancy and two-week bookings. Controlled dog welcome. £180-£275 per week. Fort William & Lochaber Tourist Board, British Graded Holiday Parks inspected. SAE for details [🐕]

Tain

Small town in Ross & Cromarty district on south shore of Dornoch Firth. Invergordon 10 miles.

MANSFIELD HOUSE HOTEL, SCOTSBURN ROAD, TAIN IV19 1PR (01862 892052). STB 4 Star Hotel. Excellent restaurant accredited by Taste of Scotland with AA 2 Rosettes. Well-trained pets and owners welcome. [🐕]

Torridon

National Trust owned with visitor centre giving advice on the area. Wildlife and walking country.

11 DIABAIG, TORRIDON. Well-equipped holiday cottage in quiet location over-looking Diabaig Bay with glorious views out to Skye. Pets welcome. Ideal for fishing and hill walking. Open January to December. £160 to £220 per week. Contact: MRS CHRISTINE DUNCAN, HAZELBANK, DIABAIG, TORRIDON IV2 2HE (01445 790259)

Key to Tourist Board Ratings Scotland and Wales

The Scottish Tourist Board Star Grading System. This easy-to-understand system tells you at a glance the quality standard you can expect. The gradings range from ★ (Fair and acceptable) to ★★★★★ (Exceptional, world-class) and will also include the type of accommodation eg ★★★ Self-catering or ★★ Hotel.

The Wales Tourist Board also operates the above system for serviced accommodation only. Self-catering properties will continue to show the **Dragon Award Grading** from **One** to **Five** depending on quality and facilities.

CARMICHAEL COUNTRY COTTAGES ★★ – ★★★★ *SELF-CATERING*
CARMICHAEL ESTATE, BY BIGGAR, LANARKSHIRE ML12 6PG Tel: 01899 308336
Fax: 01899 308481 http://www.carmichael.co.uk/cottages   e-mail: chiefcarm@aol.com

Our stone cottages nestle in the woods and fields of our historic family-run estate. Ideal homes for families, pets and particularly dogs. Walking trails, private tennis, fishing, restaurant/farm shop. Pony trekking. Off-road racing. 15 cottages, 32 bedrooms. Open all year. Central location. £180 to £480 per week.

Blair Mains Farm, Harthill ML7 5TJ   Tel: 01501 751278
Attractive farmhouse on small farm of 72 acres. Immediately adjacent to Junction 5 of M8 motorway. Ideal centre for touring, with Edinburgh, Glasgow, Stirling 30 minutes' drive. Fishing (trout and coarse) and golf nearby. One family, two double, two twin and two single bedrooms; bathroom; sittingroom, diningroom; sun porch. Central heating. Children welcome, babysitting offered. Pets welcome. Car essential – parking. Bed and Breakfast from £16; weekly rates available. Reduced rates for children. Open all year.

Farmhouse in glorious countryside, leather couches, log fire. Bedrooms with colour TV, tea and coffee facilities. Ground floor en suite available. B & B from £14. Dinner £7. Full breakfast and table d'hôte menu available on request. Own organic produce. Pets and children welcome. Great food, great value. Great atmosphere.

Todcastle Farm, Strathaven, Lanarkshire ML10 6QD   Tel: 01357 440259

Biggar

Small town set round broad main street. Gasworks museum, puppet theatre seating 100, street museum displaying old shopfronts and interiors. Peebles 13 miles.

CARMICHAEL COUNTRY COTTAGES, CARMICHAEL ESTATE, BY BIGGAR ML12 6PG (01899 308336; Fax: 01899 308481). Our stone cottages nestle in the woods and fields of our historic family-run estate. Ideal homes for families, pets and dogs. 15 cottages, 32 bedrooms. STB ★★/★★★★ Self catering. Open all year. £180 to £480 per week. [pw! 🐾]
E–mail: chiefcarm@aol.com
Website: www.carmichael.co.uk/cottages

Harthill

Village 5 miles south-west of Bathgate.

MRS STEPHENS, BLAIR MAINS FARM, HARTHILL ML7 5TJ (01501 751278). Attractive farmhouse on small farm. Ideal for touring. Children welcome, babysitting offered. Bed and Breakfast from £16; weekly rates available. Reduced rates for children. Open all year. [pw! 🐾],

Skirling

Village two miles east of Biggar. Easy access for Glasgow and Edinburgh

MRS MARION MCINTYRE, FOREST EDGE, MUIRBURN FARM, SKIRLING, NEAR BIGGAR ML12 6HL (01899 860284). Beautiful surroundings and good dog walking country. Convenient for Glasgow and Edinburgh. Lounge with log fire. Ample parking. B&B £15 double/family room, single £13; Children five to 11 years half-price, under five years FREE. Three-course Evening Meal £7, Two courses £6.

Strathaven

Small town 7 miles south of Hamilton.

MRS ANNE WHITE, TODCASTLE FARM, STRATHAVEN ML10 6QD (01357 440259). Farmhouse in glorious countryside. Bedrooms with colour TV, tea and coffee facilities. Ground floor en suite available. B & B from £14. Dinner £7. Organic produce. Great food, great value. Great atmosphere. [🐾]

PERTH & KINROSS

PERTH & KINROSS *Aberfeldy, Blairgowrie*

Aberfeldy

Small town standing on both sides of Urlar Burn near its confluence with the River Tay. Pitlochry 8 miles.

LOCH TAY LODGES, REMONY, ACHARN, ABERFELDY PH15 2HR (01887 830209). STB 4 Crowns Highly Commended. Self catering in village close to Loch. Enjoy hill walking, golf, sailing or touring. Salmon and trout fishing available. Log fires. Pets welcome. Walks along loch shore from house. For brochure, contact MRS G. DUNCAN MILLAR at above address. [🐾]
E–mail: remony@btinternet.com

Blairgowrie

Town in picturesque situation near Ericht Gorge. Fine touring centre. Several castles in vicinity. Pitlochry 23 miles, Dundee 20, Forfar 20, Perth 15.

ALTAMOUNT CHALETS, COUPAR ANGUS ROAD, BLAIRGOWRIE PH10 6JN (Tel: 01250 873324; Fax: 01250 872464). Modern, fully equipped 1, 2 and 3 bedroom Scandinavian-style Chalets. Colour television. Centrally situated for touring Highlands. Children's amenities on site. Pets welcome. [Pets £1.50 per night.]

BALNAKILLY, KIRKMICHAEL, BLAIRGOWRIE, PERTHSHIRE PH10 7NB (Tel & Fax: 01250 881281). Four log cabins, two houses and two cottages. Facilities include washing machine, microwave and colour TV. Pets welcome. Open January to December. Terms from £140 to £440. [£10 per dog]

GLENSHIELING HOUSE HOTEL, HATTON ROAD, RATTRAY, BLAIRGOWRIE PH10 7HZ (01250 874605). Located in two acres of garden and woodland. Licensed, relaxed atmosphere. Special short breaks and group party rates available. Self-catering lodge also available.

EASTER DRIMMIE. STB ★★. Two adjoining cottages, fully furnished and equipped. Sleeps five/six Golf, tennis court, riding, fishing, water skiing. Weekly terms from £170 low season, £210 high season. Controlled pets permitted. SAE, please, for details to MRS E. D. CHURCH, RANNAGULZION HOUSE, BRIDGE OF CALLY, NR. BLAIRGOWRIE PH10 7JR (01250 886359).

Bridge of Cally

Village 5 miles north-west of Blairgowrie.

MRS JOSEPHINE MACLAREN, BLACKCRAIG CASTLE, BRIDGE OF CALLY PH10 7PX (01250 886251 or 0131–551 1863). Beautiful castle of architectural interest situated in spacious grounds. Ideal centre for touring, walking, golf. Free fishing. Dogs most welcome. B&B £23.50 pppn, reductions for children. Open for guests from 1st July and close 7th September. [🐾]

Callander

Good base for walks and drives around the Trossachs and Loch Katrine. Stirling 14 miles.

LORNA AND ROBERT LECKIE, THE HIGHLAND HOUSE HOTEL, SOUTH CHURCH STREET, CALLANDER FK17 8BN (Tel: 01877 330269; Fax: 01877 339004). Georgian town house built around 1790. Nine en suite bedrooms with colour TV, hospitality trays and full central heating. Comfortable lounge, evening dinners, bar meals. B&B £20-£25 pp; Room only £17-£20 pp.
E-mail: highland.house.hotel@lineone.net

LYNNE AND ALISTAIR FERGUSON, ROSLIN COTTAGE GUEST HOUSE, LAGRANNOCH, CALLANDER FK17 8LE (Tel: 01877 330638; Fax: 01877 331448). Bed and good Scottish Breakfast from £15.50 per person. Evening Meal optional. Comfortable accommodation in 18th century Cottage, historic features. Good "walkies" area – dogs are especially welcome. [🐾 pw!]
E-mail: alifer@msn.com

Crieff

Town at the beginning of the Central Highlands, with craft factories open to visitors.

THE MURRAYPARK HOTEL, CONNAUGHT TERRACE, CRIEFF PH7 3DJ (01764 653731; Fax: 01764 655311). Ideal base for some of Scotland's finest golf, fishing, shooting and walking. And who better to enjoy it with than man's best friend, as dogs are warmly welcomed. A bonus for active guests is the option to take day tickets for Crieff Hydro's extensive leisure complex. ★★. [🐾]

Glenisla

On the River Isla 12 miles north of Alyth

GLENISLA HOTEL, KIRKTON OF GLENISLA, BY ALYTH, PERTHSHIRE PH11 8PH (01575 582223; Fax: 01575 582202). Six en suite/private rooms. Ample parking. Tea and coffee facilities. No smoking. Pets welcome. Disabled access. Open January to Febuary. ★★.

Lochearnhead

Popular little touring centre on wooded Loch Earn, dominated by Ben Vorlich (3,244 ft). Edinburgh 65 miles, Glasgow 50, Aberfeldy 30, Crieff 19, Crianlarich 16, Callander 14.

FOUR SEASONS HOTEL, ST FILLANS PH6 2NF (Tel & Fax: 01764 685333). Ideal holiday venue for pets and their owners. Spectacular Highland scenery, walking, fishing, watersports. Wonderful food. Full details on request. STB ★★★ Hotel, AA ★★★ and 2 Red Rosettes, RAC ★★★ , Egon Ronay, Taste of Scotland.

MR ANGUS CAMERON, LOCHEARNHEAD HOTEL, LOCHEARNHEAD FK19 8PU (01567 830229). Small family-run ★★ hotel, restaurant and self-catering chalets at the west end of Loch Earn with lovely views across the loch. Excellent golf and touring centre with water ski-ing, sailing and windsurfing on our doorstep. Ample hill walking. AA ★. [Pets £1 per night, £7 per week]

Loch Tay

Scenic area, ideal for outdoor activities

BEN LAWERS HOTEL, LAWERS, BY ABERFELDY PH15 2PA (Tel & Fax: 01567 820436). Small family owned hotel. Good reputation for food, licensed bar. Fishing available. Perfect base for hill walking. Water sports and horse riding centres nearby. Well behaved dogs welcome in rooms and bar. [🐕]

Pitlochry

Popular resort on River Tummel in beautiful Perthshire Highlands. Excellent golf, loch and river fishing. Famous for summer Festival Theatre; distillery, Highland Games.

BALROBIN HOTEL, HIGHER OAKFIELD, PITLOCHRY PH16 5HT (01796 472901; Fax: 01796 474200). Scottish Country House Hotel. 15 en suite rooms, most with panoramic views, yet close to the town centre. Owned and run by the Hohman family at value-for-money prices. [🐕]

BONSKEID HOUSE, PITLOCHRY PH16 5NP (01796 473208; Fax: 01796 473310). Secure dog exercise area in walled garden. The house is ideally suited for families, individuals, and canine companions of all ages. A brochure is only a phone call away. Special weekend, weekly and Senior Citizen rates. Ring for details. [pw! 🐕]

MRS BARBARA M. BRIGHT, CRAIG DUBH COTTAGE, MANSE ROAD, MOULIN, PITLOCHRY PH16 5EP (01796 472058). Pets and guests are welcomed to our family home in a rural setting, one mile from Pitlochry. B&B accommodation, one twin en suite, one double, two singles. All tea/coffee, electric blankets. £14/£15. [🐕]

THE DUNALASTAIR HOTEL, KINLOCH RANNOCH, BY PITLOCHRY PH16 5PW (01882 632323; Fax: 01882 632371). Area of outstanding natural beauty. Hotel Fishing on Loch Rannoch and Dunalastair water. Great for outdoor pursuits including rafting and abseiling. Ideal touring base, yet far from the madding crowd. Friendly and professional staff. Hotel of unrivalled character with baronial dining room, elegant lounges, a sun lounge and delightful bar. All the good things Scotland has to offer in one great hotel!
E-mail: kids@dunalastair
Website: www.dunalastair.co.uk

KILLIECRANKIE HOTEL, KILLIECRANKIE, BY PITLOCHRY PH16 5LG (01796 473220; Fax: 01796 472451). Charming small Hotel set in 4 acres. Wonderful views. Superb food, high standard of comfort. Open Christmas and New Year. STB ★★★★ Hotel. AA ★★ Rosette. [🐕 pw!]

JACKY & MALCOLM CATTERALL, "TULLOCH", ENOCHDHU, BY KIRKMICHAEL, STRATHARDLE PH10 7PW (01250 881404). STB Listed Commended. Former farmhouse offers comfortable accommodation and good food. One family room with washbasin, one twin with washbasin; one en suite double room. All have tea/coffee facilities and face open country to mountains beyond. Peace and quiet guaranteed. Haven for wildlife and dogs. B&B £16; Dinner if required £9.

Stanley

Pretty village on River Tay 8 miles south-east of Dunkeld and 6 miles north of Perth.

MRS A. GUTHRIE, NEWMILL FARM, STANLEY PH1 4QD (01738 828281). On A9 six miles north of Perth. Lounge, sitting room. Twin, double, family rooms, most en suite. Bed and Breakfast from £18. Evening meal on request. Reductions for children. Ideal for touring, fishing, golf. STB ★★★ B&B.
E–mail: guthrienewmill@sol.co.uk

South LochTayside

Scenic area, ideal for outdoor activities

ARDEONAIG HOTEL, SOUTH LOCH TAY SIDE FK21 8SU (Tel: 01567 820400; Fax: 01567 820282). Very comfortable three star Inn. Impressive scenery. First class cuisine. Eight acres of grounds. Fishing, stalking, walking and relaxation. Dogs most welcome. No charge. [🐴]
E–mail: ardeonaighotel@btinternet.com

Strathyre

Village set in middle of Strathyre Forest, just off A84 north of Callander. Information centre and picnic area to south of village.

ARDOCH LODGE, STRATHYRE (01877 384666). Log cabins and cottage in wonderful mountain scenery. Comfortably furnished and fully equipped. Country house accommodation also available. Phone for brochure. Open all year. Pets most welcome. STB ★★★★. [🐴]

STIRLING & DISTRICT

Thornhill

Centrally situated for touring

MRS A. AGNEW, BRAES OF BOQUHAPPLE FARM, THORNHILL, NEAR STIRLING FK8 3QH (01786 850484). This farm is situated on B822 between Thornhill and Callander. It has splendid panoramic views. There are two en suite family rooms. Evening Meals provided by arrangement. Grazing and stabling available for horses, and all well-behaved pets are welcome.

Readers are requested to mention this guidebook
when seeking accommodation
(and please enclose a stamped addressed envelope).

SCOTTISH ISLANDS

ISLE OF COLL

Isle of Coll

Small island in Inner Hebrides with lochs noted for trout fishing.

ACHAMORE GUEST HOUSE, ISLE OF COLL PA78 6TE (01879 230430). A comfortable guest house where you and your pet will receive a warm welcome. Within easy walking distance of beaches; ideal for hikers, fishermen and birdwatchers. Self catering available. STB ★★★. [pets £1 per night.]

JOHN BRACKENBURY, COALAS HOUSE ISLE OF COLL, ARGYLL. PA78 6TB (01879 230438). Remote shoreline farmhouse. Lots of clean white beaches all within easy walking. Home grown organic vegetables. Fishing. Baby sitting available. Pets are welcome. One Double en suite. One Twin. Cot. Self-catering available.

ISLE OF MULL *Dervaig*

Dervaig(Mull)

Village 5 miles west of Tobermory.

DRUIMARD COUNTRY HOUSE AND RESTAURANT, DERVAIG, TOBERMORY, ISLE OF MULL PA75 6QW (TEL & FAX: 01688 400345/400291). Victorian Country House with widely acclaimed restaurant using top quality Scottish Produce. Boat trips and wildlife visits arranged. "Mull Little Theatre" is situated within the hotel grounds. AA 2 Rosettes STB ★★★★ Hotel. [🐾]]

ISLE OF SKYE

Dunvegan

Village at head of loch on north-west coast of Skye. Castle is ancient stronghold of the MacLeods.

Well equipped detached house offering superb views overlooking Loch Bracadale. Two bedrooms, lounge, dining room, fully equipped kitchen. Heating throughout, TV. Enclosed garden. Prices from £120 weekly. Contact MR & MRS MACDIARMID, 21 DUNROBIN AVENUE, ELDERSLIE, RENFREWSHIRE PA5 9NW (01505 324460). [🐴 pwl (maximum 2 pets)]

Staffin

Crofting and fishing village on rocky coast around Staffin bay, 12 miles north of Portree.

C. M. BOOTH, GLENVIEW INN & RESTAURANT, CULNACNOC, STAFFIN IV51 9JH (01470 562248; Fax: 01470 562211). STB ★★ HOTEL, Taste of Scotland, WHICH? Best B&B. Traditional island house, ideally situated for exploring north east Skye. Comfortable en suite bedrooms. Restaurant renowned for traditional seafood, ethnic and vegetarian specialities. Dogs most welcome. [🐴] E-mail: valtos@lineone.net

ISLE OF ORKNEY

Westray

Part hilly, part low lying island.

MOUNT PLEASANT, WESTRAY KW17 2DH (01857 677229). Relax on this beautiful island. Lovely sandy beach only 5 minutes' walk from caravans. Ideal for children. Indoor swimming pool. Bicycles and cars for hire. 3 caravans for hire. All linen provided. From £80-£85 per week. [🐴

Our World by the Sea

Map Ref. H8

FOR INEXPENSIVE QUALITY

FEATURED BY **BBC**

DOLPHIN QUALITY — VERY GOOD

BEACH MODERN LUXURY HOLIDAY HOME *or Caravan*

With the beach moments from your door. An Award winning Park, in an area of outstanding natural beauty. This is a quiet secluded cove and Park with sub-tropical plants confirming Gulf Stream mild climate. Safe bathing, water sports, sea & river fishing. Ramble along the flat coastal strip. The local post office & shop is only 3 min. walk. Nearby restaurants, Bar Snacks, Take Aways, golf, pony trekking, three modern leisure centres, Nature Trails in the Historic Glynllifon Country Park. Tour **beautiful Snowdonia** and the famous Llŷn peninsula, beaches & Portmeirion. Featured by the BBC, Wales Tourist Board & British Holiday Home Parks. Families return to us year after year with the new Dual expressway making the journey so easy. Come & view anytime. All our Accommodation comprises Shower, W/basin & Toilet, 2 or 3 Bedrooms, Remote Control Colour TV, Well Heated, **Free Electric & Gas**, Fridge/Freezer, Cooker, Electric Blanket, Kettle, Hoover, Blankets, Pillows, Crockery, Cutlery, Cooking Utensils. Bring your own sheets, pillow cases & towels or own duvet. All have **Heated Bedroom**, Microwave & Toaster. **Full Central Heating to 65°** on Request. Some are double glazed. Try a **"Super 12"** Home which is 20% more spacious. Park next to your Accommodation. Try a £12 Minibreak Special. Holiday Home Caravans for sale on Park. Phone for our detailed Brochure.

SUPER 12 20% more spacious	2000	Model Type	Sleeps	Bad rooms	MAR 25	APRIL 1/8 GF	15 BH	22	29 BH	MAY 6	13	20 BH	27	JUNE 3	10	17	24	JULY 1	8	15	22	29	AUGUST 5/12	19 BH	26	SEPTEMBER 2	9	16	23	30	OCTOBER 7/14	21	Model Type
	Week Commencing																																
	Economy Standard Caravan	C	4-6	3	59	65	79	99	79	59	59	69	159	95	99	129	139	149	149	209	239	249	249	189	129	99	89	69	69	69	79	C
	Budget Holiday Home	D	4-7	2	69	75	95	139	99	85	95	99	199	139	149	159	169	179	189	209	289	299	299	299	249	169	149	119	99	89	79	119	D
	Budget Holiday Home	E	4-8	2	69	79	99	149	109	95	99	109	229	149	159	179	179	199	199	239	299	319	329	329	259	179	149	125	99	89	85	129	E
	Super Holiday Home	F	4-7	2	69	79	99	149	115	89	109	109	219	149	159	169	179	189	199	239	299	319	329	329	259	179	149	105	89	85	125	F
	Super Holiday Home	G	4-8	3	79	85	119	169	129	109	119	119	249	159	169	189	199	209	229	249	329	359	359	359	279	189	159	129	109	95	89	139	G
	UP MARKET PLUS Holiday Home	H	4-6	2	75	85	119	169	119	109	129	129	249	169	179	189	219	239	239	259	319	339	359	359	279	189	159	129	119	99	89	129	H
	Superior Holiday Home	I	4-8	2	75	85	119	169	129	109	129	129	249	169	179	199	219	239	239	259	319	359	359	359	269	179	159	129	119	99	89	129	I
	Superior Holiday Home	L	6-10	3	89	105	169	239	169	139	169	169	289	229	239	249	259	279	289	329	349	389	399	399	319	229	189	169	149	129	119	179	L

SUPER SHORT BREAKS – ANYTIME
3 nights weekend. 4/3 nights midweek,
HALF weekly price to next £ and add →
Other dates/nights by arrangement.
Phone for quotation.
ANY DATES TO SUIT YOU

10	15/20	25	40	25	40	25	15	20	20	45	25	25	25	30	30	40	45	45	50	40	40	30	25	20	15	35

NO HIDDEN EXTRAS. COME AND INSPECT ANYTIME & CHOOSE

Deposit £33 P.W., and Insurance £1 Nightly per Holiday Home. Cots & High Chairs £2 Nightly each.
Some Double Glazed. Over £6 persons £5 per night each. Full Central Heating to 65°
£5 Nightly Request. All prices inc. electric, piped gas & VAT @ 17½%.
Recent Model £5 Nightly. Dogs £3 Nightly.

INSTANT HOLIDAYS – ANYTIME

Should you be able to take a last minute break, please ring **01286 660400**, and we will do our best to accommodate you – the same day if you wish.

MINIBREAK – A few days, week-end or mid-week
4-5 Berth — FROM £10 per night per Holiday Home, Caravan
4-8 Berth — FROM £12 per night per Holiday Home, Caravan
6-10 Berth — FROM £14 per night per Holiday Home, Caravan

ANY 4 DAYS – BEACH MODERN LUXURY HOLIDAY HOME, ANY 3 NIGHTS, Extra nights available. FROM

EASTER WEEK-END
19th April to 26th April
From 4-6 / 4-6 / 6-10 Berth / Berth / Berth
2 nights £49 £79 £99
3 nights £89 £109 £115
4 nights £118 £145 £149
Also "Super 12" 20% more spacious. Villa chalets & Executive Bungalows.

MAY DAY BANK HOLIDAY WEEK-END
28 APRIL-4 MAY 4-6 Berth / 4-6 Berth / 6-10 Berth

WHIT BANK HOLIDAY WEEK-END
26 MAY-1 JUNE 4-6 Berth / 4-6 Berth / 6-10 Berth
Any 2 nights FROM £124 £144 £159

AUGUST BANK HOLIDAY WEEK-END
24 AUG-31 SEPT 4-6 Berth / 4-6 Berth / 6-10 Berth
Any 3 nights FROM £144 £174 £179
Also "Super 12" 20% more spacious. Villa chalets & Executive Bungalows.

ALSO VILLA CHALET

Also FOR SALE
New & one owner Villa Chalets, Holiday Homes & Caravans for sale on the Park.
Come and inspect anytime

HOW TO FIND US

So easy to get to on new A55 Expressway

BEACH HOLIDAY, WEST POINT, THE BEACH, PONTLLYFNI, CAERNARFON, NORTH WALES, LL54 5ET

PERSONAL ATTENTION, BROCHURE
& RESERVATIONS – TEL. 01286 660400

WALES

ANGLESEY & GWYNEDD

ANGLESEY & GWYNEDD *Abersoch, Bala, Blaenau Ffestiniog*

*Q*UALITY COTTAGES

AROUND THE MAGNIFICENT WELSH COAST

Away from the madding crowd
Near safe sandy beaches

A small specialist agency with over 37 years' experience
of providing quality self-catering, offers privacy, peace
and unashamed luxury.
The first WTB self-catering award winners
Highest residential standards.
Dishwashers, microwaves, washing machines
Central heating NO Slot Meters
Log Fires
Linen Provided

PETS WELCOME FREE

All in coastal areas famed for scenery, walks,
wild flowers, birds, badgers and foxes

Free colour brochure:

P. W. REES
"Quality Cottages"
Cerbid, Solva, Haverfordwest,
Pembrokeshire SA62 6YE
Tel: (01348) 837871

SEASIDE COTTAGES. MANN'S, SHAW'S AND SNOWDONIA TOURIST SER-VICES (01758 701702). Large selection of self-catering seaside and country cottages, bungalows, farmhouses, caravans etc. offering superb, reasonably priced accommodation for owners and their pets. Please telephone for brochure

Abersoch

Dinghy sailing and windsurfing centre with safe sandy beaches. Pony trekking, golf, fishing and sea trips.

DEUCOCH HOTEL, ABERSOCH, PWLLHELI LL53 7LD (01758 712680; Fax: 01758 712670). Stuart & Barbara White invite you to their comfortable, informal, family-run hotel. Spacious gardens with magnificent views across Cardigan Bay to Snowdonia. Open all year. [🐕].

MR P. W. REES, "QUALITY COTTAGES", CERBID, SOLVA, HAVERFORDWEST, PEMBROKESHIRE SA62 6YE (01348 837871). Cottages set in all coastal areas, unashamed luxury, highest residential standards. Dishwashers, microwaves, washing machines. Log fires. Linen supplied. Pets welcome. [pw!]

Bala

Natural touring centre for Snowdonia. Narrow-gauge railway runs along side of Bala lake, the largest natural lake in Wales. Golf, sailing, fishing, canoeing.

MR & MRS LOOKE, RAFEL, PARC, BALA LL23 7YU (01678 540369). Delightful, cosy, well equipped cottage. Situated in tranquil, picturesque setting. £160 – £290 weekly inclusive of electricity, logs, bed linen. Open all year, short breaks available. [🐕]

TALYBONT ISA, Self-catering annexe. Twin bedded studio type with shower/bathroom, colour TV. Situated just two miles from Bala in beautiful country area. Ideal for walking, sailing, canoeing and fishing. Contact MRS G. SKINNER, TALYBONT ISA. RHYDUCHAF, BALA (01678 520234). [🐕]

MRS ANN SKINNER, TY GWYN BUNGALOW, RHYDUCHAF, BALA LL23 7SD (01678 521267). WTB ★★★. Bed and Breakfast, twin room and double room, ground floor situated in beautiful country area just near Bala Lake. Ideal area for walking, sailing, canoeing, fishing. Also six berth caravan with all mod cons to let self-catering. [🐕]

Barmouth

Modern seaside resort with two miles of sandy beaches. Surrounding hills full of interesting archaeological remains.

LAWRENNY LODGE HOTEL, BARMOUTH LL42 1SU (01341 280466). Quiet, family-run hotel overlooking harbour and estuary but only 5 minutes from town. Most rooms en suite, all with TV, tea/coffee making facilities and clock radio alarms. Restaurant menu includes vegetarian dishes. Residential licence. Large car park. Two Star Hotel. [🐾]

Beaumaris

Elegant little town dominated by castle built by Edward I in 13th century. Museum of Childhood has Victorian toys and music boxes.

MR P. W. REES, "QUALITY COTTAGES", CERBID, SOLVA, HAVERFORDWEST, PEMBROKESHIRE SA62 6YE (01348 837871). Cottages set in all coastal areas, unashamed luxury, highest residential standards. Dishwashers, microwaves, washing machines. Log fires. Linen supplied. Pets welcome. [pw!]

Beddgelert

Delightfully picturesque village in scenic landscape 4 miles south of Snowdonia.

COLWYN, BEDDGELERT, GWYNEDD LL55 4UY (01766 890276). WTB ★★. Small, friendly 18th century cottage guest house with beams and original stone fireplace. Most rooms en suite, white linen, central heating. Overlooking river in picturesque village centre, at foot of Snowdon, surrounded by wooded mountains, lakes and streams. Bed and Breakfast from £19 to £23. (Also small cottage, sleeps two £180, sleeps four £340. Wet pets and muddy boots welcome. Early booking advised. Tel: 01766 890 652)

Blaenau Ffestiniog

Good touring centre amidst dramatic scenery. Well-known slate quarries. Betws-y-Coed 12 miles. Ffestiniog 3.

OFFEREN COTTAGE, BLAENAU FFESTINIOG. Fully equipped 3-bedroomed centrally heated cottage. Sleeps 6 adults plus small child. 2 bathrooms. £89 to £270 per week. Brochure on request from: MR E.H. PRESTON, 3 BANKS MOUNT, PONTEFRACT WF8 4DN (Tel/Fax: 01977 703092 or Tel: 01766 830982). [🐾]

Bodorgan

Town on the west side of the River Cefni estuary.

MRS J. GUNDRY, FARMYARD LODGE, BODORGAN, ANGLESEY LL62 5LW (01407 840977). Comfortable three-bedroomed house, WTB graded 4 Dragons. Enclosed garden. Near beaches, common, forest. Dogs and children welcome. Fully equipped, bedding and electricity inclusive. Colour TV, microwave. [🐾]

Caernarfon

Historic walled town and resort, ideal for touring Snowdonia. Museums, Segontium Roman Fort, magnificent 13th century castle. Old harbour, sailing trips.

BEACH HOLIDAY HOMES, WEST POINT, THE BEACH, PONTLLYFNI, CAERNARVON LL54 5ET (01286 660400). ✓✓✓✓ and ✓✓✓✓✓ Beach Holiday offers bungalow, chalet and caravan accommodation in areas of outstanding natural beauty with sea views. Nearby restaurants, bar snacks and take aways. Most leisure activities close by.

THE STABLES HOTEL, LLANWNDA, CAERNARFON LL54 5SD (Tel: 01286 830711; Fax: 01286 830413). Set in 15 acres of beautiful countryside in Snowdonia. 18 en suite bedrooms, all ground floor, with colour TV, intercom, direct dial telephone and tea/coffee making facilities. Holiday Cottages. Idyllic rural location. Very popular with walkers. Ideal for Pet owners.

Conwy

One of the best preserved medieval fortified towns in Britain on dramatic estuary setting. Telford Suspension Bridge, many historic buildings, lively quayside (site of smallest house in Britain). Golf, pony trekking, pleasure cruises.

NORTH WALES HOLIDAY COTTAGES AND FARMHOUSES, STATION ROAD, DEGANWY, CONWY LL31 9DF (01492 582492). Brochure available for relaxing or activity holidays in selected Snowdonia and coastal properties. Website: www.northwalesholidaycottages.co.uk

Criccieth

Popular family resort with safe beaches divided by ruins of 13th century castle. Salmon and sea trout fishing; Festival of Music & Arts in summer.

ABEREISTEDD HOTEL, WEST PARADE, CRICCIETH LL52 0EN (01766 522710; Fax 01766 523526). Sea front position. En suite rooms with colour TV, telephone, tea/coffee. Residents' lounge and licensed bar. Private parking.WTB ★★★ Hotel, AA QQQQ. Taste of Wales Award. [🐾]

MRS A. M. JONES, BETWS-BACH, YNYS, CRICCIETH LL52 0PB (Tel and Fax: 01758 720047/01766 810295). Quality self-catering, traditional cosy cottages in an idyllic setting with oak beams, inglenook fireplace, log fires, antiques and lovely country furnishings. Some have four poster beds, own snooker table, sauna or jacuzzi. [🐾]
E–mail: cottages@rhos.freeserve.co.uk
Website: www.criccieth.co.uk/rhos

MRS M. WILLIAMS, GAERWEN FARM, YNYS, CRICCIETH LL52 0NU (01766 810324). Enjoy a break on a working farm in homely self-catering accommodation. Easy access by car to beaches, inns, golfing etc./ Short Breaks available. Pets Welcome. [🐾]

MR P. W. REES, "QUALITY COTTAGES", CERBID, SOLVA, HAVERFORDWEST, PEMBROKESHIRE SA62 6YE (01348 837871). Cottages set in all coastal areas, unashamed luxury, highest residential standards. Dishwashers, microwaves, washing machines. Log fires. Linen supplied. Pets welcome. [pw!]

MRS LENA HUGHES JONES, TYDDYN HEILYN, CHWILOG, CRICCIETH LL53 6SW (01766 810441). Cosy and comfortable renovated Welshstone country cottage. Parking and spacious mowed garden. Beautiful river walks amid wildlife, with public tree-lined walks. Also Norwegian home to let furnished. [🐾]

WERNOL CARAVAN & CHALET PARK, CHWILOG, PWLLHELI, GWYNEDD LL53 6SW (Tel & Fax: 01766 810506). Family-run park adjacent to farm. Cycle route, horse riding and golf courses nearby. Two or three bedroom chalets, and luxury caravans. Playing area, games room, pay-phone and laundry room. Colour brochure. WTB Grade 4. [Pets £10 per week.]

MRS V. WILLIAMS, YNYS GRAIANOG, YNYS, CRICCIETH LL52 0NT (01766 530234). Two stone cottages, sleep 12 and six, set on a smallholding in a quiet rural area. Convenient for the lofty mountains of Snowdonia and the Lleyn Peninsula, renowned for its beautiful coastline and sandy beaches. Plenty of parking space.

Dulas Bay

On north-east coast of Anglesey, between Amlwch and Moelfre.

MRS G. McCREADIE, DERI ISAF, DULAS BAY LL70 9DX (01248 410536; Mobile: 077 21 374471). Beautiful Victorian country house standing in 20 acres of woodland, gardens and fields. High standard of accommodation in two family rooms and one double all en suite. Pets welcome; stabling available. ★★★. [🐾]

Dwyran

Village on Anglesey 2 miles east of Newborough.

JUDY HUTCHINGS, TALY-Y-FOEL STUD FARM AND RIDING CENTRE, DWYRAN, ANGLESEY LL61 6LQ (01248 430377; Fax: 01248 430977) Waterfront location with spectacular views of Caernarfon Castle and Snowdonia. Three Star Wales Tourist Board en suite Bed and Breakfast. Private caravan. Riding and horse livery. Brochures and prices on application. [🐾].
Website: www.nwi.co.uk/talyfoelriding

Fairbourne

Bright little resort facing Barmouth across the Mawddach estuary. Safe spacious sands. A short distance inland is Cader Idris. Dolgellau 9 miles.

THE FAIRBOURNE HOTEL, FAIRBOURNE LL38 2HQ (01341 250203; Fax: 01341 250587). Views of Cardigan Bay from own grounds. Licensed. Private bathrooms. Bowls green. Games room. Car park. Open all year. Pets welcome. [🐾]

Harlech

Small stone-built town dominated by remains of 13th century castle. Golf, theatre, swimming pool, fine stretch of sands.

FRON DEG GUEST HOUSE, LLANFAIR, HARLECH LL46 2RE (01766 780448). Small Georgian cottage overlooking beach at Harlech. Pretty bedrooms. Central for unspoiled beaches and countryside, yet within easy reach of Porthmadog. Reasonable terms for Bed and Breakfast, also Dinner. [🐴]

MR P. W. REES, "QUALITY COTTAGES", CERBID, SOLVA, HAVERFORDWEST, PEMBROKESHIRE SA62 6YE (01348 837871). Cottages set in all coastal areas, unashamed luxury, highest residential standards. Dishwashers, microwaves, washing machines. Log fires. Linen supplied. Pets welcome. [pw!]

Holyhead

Principal town on Holy Island. Passenger ferry terminal for Ireland

DAVID AND BARBARA PRICE, "OROTAVIA" GUEST HOUSE, 66 WALTHEW AVENUE, HOLYHEAD LL65 1AG (Tel and Fax: 01407 760259). A warm welcome to you and your pets in our guest house situated adjacent to park, beach and ferries to Ireland. Comfortable accommodation with first-class facilities. Welcome trays, colour TV and central heating in all rooms. Colour brochure available. WTB 3 Star Guest House, Welcome Host Gold Award. [🐴]

WAVECREST, 93 NEWRY STREET, HOLYHEAD LL65 1HU (Tel: 01407 763637; Fax: 01407 764862). WTB/AA ◆◆◆. Ideal for break of journey to/from Ireland. Close to ferry and town centre. Nearby South Stack, lovely beachs and country walks.

Llanddaniel

Village just off the A5, Menai Bridge 5 miles E.

MRS M. E. WILLIAMS, TYDDYN GOBLET, BRYNSIENCYN, ANGLESEY LL61 6TZ (01248 430296). WTB 3 STARS. Secluded farmhouse, uninterrupted views Snowdonia. 3 bedrooms, bathroom, kitchen, living and sitting rooms. Telephone. Modern 34ft 3 bedroomed caravan very pleasantly and privately situated on smallholding. Shower etc. Also en suite B&B. Ground floor bedrooms. [🐴]

Llanddona

Village on Anglesey 3 miles north west of Beaumaris.

MR P. W. REES, "QUALITY COTTAGES", CERBID, SOLVA, HAVERFORDWEST, PEMBROKESHIRE SA62 6YE (01348 837871). Cottages set in all coastal areas, unashamed luxury, highest residential standards. Dishwashers, microwaves, washing machines. Log fires. Linen supplied. Pets welcome. [pw!]

Llanfairfechan

Small resort on Conway Bay midway between Bangor and Conway.

YENTON, PROMENADE, LLANFAIRFECHAN LL33 0BY (01248 680075). Self-contained, seafront family apartments situated between the mountains and the sea. Fully-equipped, sleep two to six, sandy beach, scenic views, easy seaside or mountain walks. Good touring position. Relax in our beautiful, fragrant, award-winning garden. Tourist Board Grade Four. Pets Welcome. Ring Barbara Allix for brochure. [Pets £10 per week]
E–mail: yenton@llan-holidays.freeserve.co.uk

Morfa Nefyn

Picturesque village 2 miles west of Nefyn.

MR P. W. REES, "QUALITY COTTAGES", CERBID, SOLVA, HAVERFORDWEST, PEMBROKESHIRE SA62 6YE (01348 837871). Cottages set in all coastal areas, unashamed luxury, highest residential standards. Dishwashers, microwaves, washing machines. Log fires. Linen supplied. Pets welcome. [pw!]

Porthmadog

Harbour town with mile-long Cob embankment, along which runs Ffestiniog Narrow Gauge Steam Railway to Blaenau Ffestiniog. Pottery, maritime museum, car museum. Good beaches nearby.

BLACK ROCK SANDS, PORTHMADOG. Private site, beach 150 yards.14 Caravans only. Fully equipped 6 berths. Own flush toilets. Showers and TVs. Shop and tavern near. APPLY: M. HUMPHRIES, 251 HEDNESFORD ROAD, NORTON CANES, CANNOCK, STAFFORDSHIRE WS11 3RZ (01543 279583).

MR P. W. REES, "QUALITY COTTAGES", CERBID, SOLVA, HAVERFORDWEST, PEMBROKESHIRE SA62 6YE (01348 837871). Cottages set in all coastal areas, unashamed luxury, highest residential standards. Dishwashers, microwaves, washing machines. Log fires. Linen supplied. Pets welcome. [pw!]

MRS P. W. WILLIAMS, TYDDYN DU FARM, GELLILYDAN, NEAR FFESTINIOG, PORTHMADOG LL41 4RB (Tel & Fax: 01766 590281). WTB ★★★★. Beautiful historic 17th century farmhouse situated in the heart of Snowdonia National Park. Cosy farmhouse bedrooms or superb stable and barn suites. [Pets £2 per night, £10 per week]
E–mail: info@tyddyndu.co.uk
Website: www.tyddyndu.co.uk

Porth Neigel

Bay on south side of Lleyn peninsula, also known as Hell's Mouth.

Attractive cottage set in meadow near beach, quiet rural area. Sleeps 6, open fire, all comforts. Local carer. Near Abersoch. Details from MRS E.M. COOPER, 18 ST MARY'S LANE, LOUTH, LINCOLNSHIRE LN11 0DT (01507 604408).

Pwllheli

Popular sailing centre with harbour and long sandy beach. Golf, leisure centre, river and sea fishing.

MRS M. PARRY ROBERTS, "TY FRY", ABERDARON, PWLLHELI LL53 8BY (01758 760274). Modernised, fully furnished cottage with views over Aberdaron Bay. Two bedrooms sleeping five, cot, bathroom; large lounge, TV; kitchen/diner, cooker, fridge; metered electricity. Ample parking. Sandy beaches and coves, mountain walks nearby. Pets welcome. Booking March – October. SAE please.

Red Wharf Bay

Deep curving bay with vast expanse of sand, very popular for sailing and swimming.

BRYN TIRION HOTEL, RED WHARF BAY, ANGLESEY LL75 8RZ (01248 852366; Fax: 01248 852013). WTB 3 Star Hotel. Family-run hotel with magnificent views. All bedrooms en suite. Large garden. Excellent restaurant. 20 minutes from Snowdonia, ideal for touring North Wales. [Pets £3 per night].

MR P. W. REES, "QUALITY COTTAGES", CERBID, SOLVA, HAVERFORDWEST, PEMBROKESHIRE SA62 6YE (01348 837871). Cottages set in all coastal areas, unashamed luxury, highest residential standards. Dishwashers, microwaves, washing machines. Log fires. Linen supplied. Pets welcome. [pw!]

Trearddur Bay

Attractive holiday spot set amongst low cliffs on Holy Island, near Holyhead. Golf, sailing, fishing, swimming.

CLIFF COTTAGES AND PLAS DARIEN APARTMENTS, TREARDDUR BAY LL65 2TZ (01407 860789). Fully equipped holiday cottages, sleeping 4/8 plus cot. Near sea. Children's playground. Indoor and outdoor heated pools. Colour television. Choice of centrally heated apartments or stone-built cottages. Own private leisure complex with bowls, sauna, snooker, table tennis etc. Also tennis, croquet. Adjacent golf course. [🐾]

Tywyn

Pleasant seaside resort, start of Talyllyn Narrow Gauge Railway. Sea and river fishing, golf.

Fully equipped coastal house, close to sandy beach. 3 bedrooms, sleeps five. Gardens; garage. Pets welcome free of charge. APPLY – MR IAN WESTON, 18 ELIZABETH ROAD, BASINGSTOKE, HAMPSHIRE RG22 6AX (01256 352364; 01256 412233 evenings).

GWESTY MINFFORDD HOTEL TALYLLYN LL36 9AJ (Tel: 01654 761665 Fax: 01654 761517). Small 17th century Drover's Inn at the base of Cader Idris, ideal for 'walkies' or as a centre for touring. Residential and restaurant licence; seven en suite bedrooms. WTB ★★★ AA ★★ Founder Member Taste of Wales, Good Food Guide 2000. [pw! 🐾]

Sunnydowns Hotel

WTB ★★★ *Luxury Hotel*

**66 Abbey Road, Rhos-on-Sea,
Conway LL28 4NU
Tel: 01492 544256
Fax: 01492 543223**

(Proprietors: Mr & Mrs Mike Willington)

A warm, friendly welcome awaits you at the Sunnydowns, just a two minute stroll from the sea front. A perfect base for touring Snowdonia, the Isle of Anglesey and the famous Castles of North Wales, or to enjoy golf, bowling, tennis, boat trips, fishing and water sports nearby. There are also lovely walks for you and your dog to enjoy and Llandudno and Colwyn Bay are only five minutes' drive away. The hotel has a lounge, bar, games room, sauna and car park. Enjoy excellent cooking in our non-smoking restaurant (Thai cuisine a speciality) or, by arrangement, eat in the Bar with your dog. Special diets can be catered for. All bedrooms are en suite, with colour TV (video & satellite), tea/coffee making facilities, hairdyer, mini-bar, refrigerator, direct dial telephone and baby listening service. Dog sitting also available. We are open all year.

For further information, please phone or write for our colour brochure.

Betws y Coed

Popular mountain resort in picturesque setting where three rivers meet. Trout fishing, craft shops, golf, railway and motor museums, Snowdonia National Park Visitor Centre. Nearby Swallow Falls are famous beauty spot.

HAFOD COUNTRY HOTEL, TREFRIW, CONWY LL27 0RQ (Tel: 01492 640029; Fax: 01492 641351). WTB ★★★ Country Hotel. Small informal hotel. Over two acres of grounds. Excellent food in restaurant (Les Routiers Silver Award). Short breaks from £32 per night low season; from £43.50 high season. Website: http://ukweb4.cableinet.co.uk/headcase/

SUMMER HILL NON-SMOKERS' GUEST HOUSE, BETWS-Y-COED LL24 0BL (01690 710306). Quiet location, overlooking river. 150 yards from main road, shops. En suite and standard rooms, tea-making. Residents' lounge. TV. Singles, children welcome. EM available. B&B from £16.50. [Pets £1.50 per night.]

MRS MORRIS, TY COCH FARM-TREKKING CENTRE, PENMACHNO, BETWS-Y-COED LL25 0HJ (01690 760248). Hill farm in Wales. TV, teamaking, en suite. Set in National Park/Snowdonia. Very quiet and off the beaten track. A great welcome and good food. Many return visits. [🐾]

Colwyn Bay

Lively seaside resort with promenade amusements. Attractions include Mountain Zoo, Eirias Park; golf, tennis, riding and other sports. Good touring centre for Snowdonia. The quieter resort of Rhos-on-Sea lies at the western end of the bay.

MRS L.J. DENT, BRON-Y-WENDON HOLIDAY COTTAGES, WERN ROAD, LLAND-DULAS, COLWYN BAY LL22 8HG (01492 512903). The ultimate in self-catering accommodation. Luxurious, centrally heated cottages with sea views. Facilities include satellite TV, dishwasher, microwave and games room. Beach just a short walk away. Pets welcome. Colour brochure. [🐕]

EDELWEISS HOTEL, OFF LAWSON ROAD, COLWYN BAY LL29 8HD (01492 532314). Comfortable Country House Hotel set in own wooded grounds close to open parkland; ideal for dog owners. All rooms with en suite facilities. Well-behaved dogs welcome. [🐕]

NANT-Y-GLYN HOLIDAY PARK, THE LODGE, NANT-Y-GLYN ROAD, COLWYN BAY LL29 7RD (01492 512282). Set in a peaceful, sheltered valley, Nant-y-Glyn offers cedarwood chalets, garden cottages and a coach house. 15 minutes' walk to the beach and town centre. Colour brochure available. [Pets £8 per week]

Conwy

One of the best preserved medieval fortified towns in Britain on dramatic estuary setting. Telford Suspension Bridge, many historic buildings, lively quayside (site of smallest house in Britain). Golf, pony trekking, pleasure cruises.

THE LODGE, TAL-Y-BONT, CONWY LL32 8YX (01492 660766; Fax: 01492 660534). Family-run Hotel with lovely en suite bedrooms. Enjoy peace and quiet, superb food and attention from friendly and efficient staff. B&B from £25 to £35; two days DB&B from £75 to £87.50. Pets welcome. [Pets £2 per night]

SYCHNANT PASS HOUSE, SYCHNANT PASS ROAD, CONWY LL32 8BJ (01492 596868). Sychnant Pass House is a lovely Victorian House set in two acres with a little pond and stream running through it. Step out of our garden and straight onto Snowdonia National Park land where you can walk for miles with your dogs. All rooms en suite. [🐕]

Conwy Valley

Scenic area with many places of interest.

"Saronfa", an attractive self-catering cottage in the beautiful Conwy Valley. Sleeps 4. Pets taken. Well equipped. Cosy log fire. Owner supervised. Snowdonia National Park, mountains, river, lakes. Terms £110 to £235. Winter Breaks from £16 per night. Free logs. MRS M.C. WADDINGHAM, "CEFN", TYN-Y-GROES, CONWY LL32 8TA (01492 650233; mobile: 077 74 860233). [🐕]

Secluded cottages with log fire and beams. Dogs will love it. Plenty of walks around mountains and lakes. For up to 5/7 people plus their pet(s). MRS WILLIAMS, LOW RISBY HOUSE, LOW RISBY, SCUNTHORPE, North Lincolnshire DN15 0BX (01724 733990 or 077 11 217 448). [🐕]

Llandudno

Premier holiday resort of North Wales coast flanked by Great Orme and Little Orme headlands. Wide promenade, pier, two beaches; water ski-ing, sailing, fishing trips from jetty. Excellent sports facilities: golf, indoor pool, tennis, pony trekking, Leisure Centre. Summer variety shows, Alice In Wonderland Visitor Centre.

BRYN Y BIA LODGE, CRAIGSIDE, LLANDUDNO, NORTH WALES LL30 3AS (Tel & Fax: 01492 549644). WTB ★★★ AA ◆◆◆◆◆ Premier SelectedVictorian house overlooking Llandudno and the sea, set in a large walled garden. Ideally situated for exploring the Snowdonia National Park. Good pubs, restaurants and bistros nearby.
E–mail: carol@brynybia.demon.co.uk

MR AND MRS J. WILLIAMS, "DEVA", 34 TRINITY AVENUE, LLANDUDNO LL30 2TQ (01492 879518). Three top grade self-contained holiday apartments for 2/3/4 adults. Central location. Car parking on premises. Well behaved dogs welcome. Short breaks early and late season. Highly recommended Telephone for brochure. [🐕]

MR AND MRS C. WATTS, HEN DY HOTEL, 10 NORTH PARADE, LLANDUDNO LL30 2LP (01492 876184). Experience the warm welcome extended by the proprietors of this charming Hotel, set opposite the Pier, with panoramic views. All rooms with central heating, TV, radio, teamakers; some en suite. Good food. Cosy bar. From £18.50 per night. WTB ★★ Hotel. [🐕]

WARWICK HOTEL, 56 CHURCH WALKS, LLANDUDNO LL30 2HL (01492 876823). Friendly family-run hotel, all rooms en suite. Colour TV, hospitality trays. Superb discounts throughout the year. Private garden. 5 minutes' walk to town centre and pier. Pets welcome free of charge. [🐕]

Llangollen

Famous for International Music Eisteddfod held in July. Plas Newydd, Valle Crucis Abbey nearby. Standard gauge steam railway; canal cruises; ideal for golf and walking.

BRYN DERWEN HOTEL, ABBEY ROAD, LLANGOLLEN LL20 8EF (01978 860583). Warm, friendly welcome for your pet in well-appointed hotel in picturesque Dee Valley. Super walking country, many tourist attractions including Llangollen Steam Railway. Special discounts for Pets Welcome! readers.
Website: www.city2000.com/tl/bryn-derwen-hotel.html [🐕]

GOLDEN PHEASANT COUNTRY HOTEL, GLYN CEIRIOG, NEAR LLANGOLLEN LL20 7BB (01691 718281; Fax: 01691 718479). AA 3 Star, 4 Crowns Highly Commended. Situated in the beautiful Ceiriog Valley. All 19 rooms en suite, colour TV and tea/coffee making facilities. Dogs welcome in all rooms (except restaurant). 2 nights Dinner, Bed and Breakfast from only £85.00 p.p. [🐴]

PEN-Y-DYFFRYN COUNTRY HOUSE HOTEL, NEAR RHYDYCROESAU, OSWESTRY SY10 7JD (01691 653700). Picturesque Georgian Rectory quietly set in Shropshire/ Welsh Hills. Ten en suite bedrooms, two with private patios. 5-acre grounds. No passing traffic. Johansens recommended. Dinner, Bed and Breakfast from £53.00 per person per day. ETC ★★★. [🐴 pw!]

Rhos-on-Sea

Popular resort at east end of Penrhyn Bay, adjoining Colwyn Bay to the north-west.

SUNNYDOWNS HOTEL, 66 ABBEY ROAD, RHOS-ON-SEA, CONWY LL28 4NU (01492 544256; Fax: 01492 543223). A WTB ★★★ luxury family hotel just 2 minutes' walk to beach & shops. All rooms en suite with colour TV, video & satellite channels, tea/coffee facilities and central heating. Hotel has bar, pool room and car park. [🐴 pw!]

Trefriw

Hillside village, popular as spa in Victorian times. Local beauty spots at Llyn Crafnant and Llyn Geironnydd. Woollen mill demonstrating traditional techniques.

MRS B. COLE, GLANDWR, TREFRIW, NEAR LLANRWST LL27 0JP (01492 640431). Large country house on outskirts of Trefriw village. Good touring area with Llanrwst, Betws-y-Coed and Swallow Falls five miles away. Fishing, walking, golf, pony trekking close by. Comfortable bedrooms, lounge with TV, dining room. Good home cooking. Parking. Bed and Breakfast from £16

Key to Tourist Board Ratings Scotland and Wales

The Scottish Tourist Board Star Grading System. This easy-to-understand system tells you at a glance the quality standard you can expect. The gradings range from ★ (Fair and acceptable) to ★★★★★ (Exceptional, world-class) and will also include the type of accommodation eg ★★★ Self-catering or ★★ Hotel.

The Wales Tourist Board also operates the above system for serviced accommodation only. Self-catering properties will continue to show the **Dragon Award Grading** from **One** to **Five** depending on quality and facilities.

Aberaeron

Attractive little town on Cardigan Bay, good touring centre for coast and inland. The Aeron Express Aerial ferry offers an exciting trip across the harbour. Marine aquarium; Aberarth Leisure Park nearby.

GILFACH HOLIDAY VILLAGE, LLWYNCELYN, NEAR ABERAERON SA46 ONN (01545 580288). Choice of modern Bungalows (4 persons) or luxury 2/3 person apartments. Fully equipped, linen, colour TV. Horse and pony riding. Tennis. Write or phone for brochure pack to the Manager. [Pets £15 per week.]

Aberporth

Popular seaside village offering safe swimming and good sea fishing. Good base for exploring Cardigan Bay coastline.

MRS JANN TUCKER, PENFFYNNON, ABERPORTH, CARDIGAN SA34 2DA (Tel: 01239 810387; Fax: 01239 811401). Comfortable, self-contained, fully-equipped cottages adjacent to safe and sandy beaches. Dogs welcome by arrangement. Local attractions include water sports, Cardigan Bay dolphins and walking in the Hills. £150-£700 per week. [🐾]
E–mail: tt@lineone.net

MISS M. ALLEN, YR YSGUBOR, PANTYFFWRN, ABERPORTH, CARDIGAN SA43 2DT (01239 810509). Delightful stone cottage on beautiful, unspoilt West Wales coast. Quiet, comfortable; all amenities. Sleeps 2. Large dog-friendly garden. Ample parking. From £70 plus electricity. [🐾]

MR P. W. REES, "QUALITY COTTAGES", CERBID, SOLVA, HAVERFORDWEST, PEMBROKESHIRE SA62 6YE (01348 837871). Cottages set in all coastal areas, unashamed luxury, highest residential standards. Dishwashers, microwaves, washing machines. Log fires. Linen supplied. Pets welcome. [pw!]

HIGHCLIFFE HOTEL, SCHOOL ROAD, ABERPORTH SA43 2DA (Tel&Fax: 01239 810534). DOLPHINS 'N' DAFFODILS beside our clean, safe sandy beach where dolphins cruise the bay. Olde worlde restaurant, en suite rooms, superb food and special diets. Beach 100 yards, free daily dog chew. [pw! Pets £3 per night, £20 per week]

Ciliau Aeron

Village in undulating country just inland from the charming Cardigan Bay resorts of New Quay and Aberaeron. New Quay 12 miles, Aberaeron 6.

MR P. W. REES, "QUALITY COTTAGES", CERBID, SOLVA, HAVERFORDWEST, PEMBROKESHIRE SA62 6YE (01348 837871). Cottages set in all coastal areas, unashamed luxury, highest residential standards. Dishwashers, microwaves, washing machines. Log fires. Linen supplied. Pets welcome. [pw!]

Lampeter

Small market town on River Teifi 20 miles from Carmarthen.

TYGLYN HOLIDAY ESTATE, CILIAU AERON, NEAR LAMPETER SA48 8DD (Tel & Fax: 01570 470684). In the heart of rural Wales and only four miles from the seaside town of Aberaeron. Twenty award-winning brick-built semi-detached two-bedroom Bungalows with all modern facilities and colour TV. Range of outdoor activities locally. [pw!]

Llangrannog

Pretty little seaside village overlooking a sandy beach. Superb cliff walk to NT Ynys Lochtyn, a secluded promontory.

MR P. W. REES, "QUALITY COTTAGES", CERBID, SOLVA, HAVERFORDWEST, PEMBROKESHIRE SA62 6YE (01348 837871). Cottages set in all coastal areas, unashamed luxury, highest residential standards. Dishwashers, microwaves, washing machines. Log fires. Linen supplied. Pets welcome. [pw!]

FOR THE MUTUAL GUIDANCE OF GUEST AND HOST

Every year literally thousands of holidays, short breaks and overnight stops are arranged through our guides, the vast majority without any problems at all. In a handful of cases, however, difficulties do arise about bookings, which often could have been prevented from the outset.

It is important to remember that when accommodation has been booked, both parties – guests and hosts – have entered into a form of contract. We hope that the following points will provide helpful guidance.

GUESTS: When enquiring about accommodation, be as precise as possible. Give exact dates, numbers in your party and the ages of any children. State the number and type of rooms wanted and also what catering you require – bed and breakfast, full board etc. Make sure that the position about evening meals is clear – and about pets, reductions for children or any other special points.

Read our reviews carefully to ensure that the proprietors you are going to contact can supply what you want. Ask for a letter confirming all arrangements, if possible.

If you have to cancel, do so as soon as possible. Proprietors do have the right to retain deposits and under certain circumstances to charge for cancelled holidays if adequate notice is not given and they cannot re-let the accommodation.

HOSTS: Give details about your facilities and about any special conditions. Explain your deposit system clearly and arrangements for cancellations, charges etc. and whether or not your terms include VAT.

If for any reason you are unable to fulfil an agreed booking without adequate notice, you may be under an obligation to arrange suitable alternative accommodation or to make some form of compensation.

While every effort is made to ensure accuracy, we regret that FHG Publications cannot accept responsibility for errors, omissions or misrepresentations in our entries or any consequences thereof.

Prices in particular should be checked because we go to press early. We will follow up complaints but cannot act as arbiters or agents for either party.

QUALITY COTTAGES

AROUND THE MAGNIFICENT WELSH COAST

Away from the madding crowd
Near safe sandy beaches

A small specialist agency with over 37 years' experience
of providing quality self-catering, offers privacy, peace
and unashamed luxury.
The first WTB self-catering award winners
Highest residential standards.
Dishwashers, microwaves, washing machines
Central heating NO Slot Meters
Log Fires
Linen Provided

PETS WELCOME FREE

All in coastal areas famed for scenery, walks,
wild flowers, birds, badgers and foxes

Free colour brochure:

P. W. REES
"Quality Cottages"
Cerbid, Solva, Haverfordwest,
Pembrokeshire SA62 6YE

Tel: (01348) 837871

PEMBROKESHIRE

PEMBROKESHIRE *Broad Haven, Croes Goch, Croft*

Bosherston

Village 4 miles south of Pembroke, bordered by 3 man-made lakes, a haven for wildlife and covered in water lilies in early summer.

MR P. W. REES, "QUALITY COTTAGES", CERBID, SOLVA, HAVERFORDWEST, PEMBROKESHIRE SA62 6YE (01348 837871). Cottages set in all coastal areas, unashamed luxury, highest residential standards. Dishwashers, microwaves, washing machines. Log fires. Linen supplied. Pets welcome. [pw!]

Broad Haven

Attractive little resort on St Bride's Bay in the Pembrokeshire Coast National Park. Superb sandy beach; National Park Information Centre.

MILLMOOR FARM COTTAGES AND ROCKSDRIFT APARTMENTS. Enjoy a relaxing and peaceful holiday only yards from safe sandy beaches and woodland walks. Personal supervision. Microwaves, fridge freezers, colour TV. Full central heating. Children's play areas, cots, high chairs. Brochure from HELEN MOCK (REF: PW00), MILLMOOR, BROAD HAVEN, HAVERFORDWEST SA62 3JH (01437 781507; Fax 01437 781002; FREEPHONE 0800 019 9930). [Pets £12 per week.]

PEMBROKESHIRE NATIONAL PARK. Three-bedroom fully furnished holiday house, sleeps 6. Walking distance sandy beaches and coastal footpath. £100 to £275 per week. MRS L.P. ASHTON, 10 ST LEONARDS ROAD, THAMES DITTON, SURREY KT7 0RJ (020-8398 6349). [🐕]
E–mail: lejash@aol.com

Croes Goch

Hamlet 6 miles north east of St Davids.

MRS M. REES, 'CROFTY', CROES GOCH, HAVERFORDWEST SA62 5JT (01348 831441). We offer comfortable beds and a hearty breakfast. Three bedrooms share bathroom, separate toilet, one large ensuite room. All with tea/coffee and TV. From £15 per person. [🐕]

MR P. W. REES, "QUALITY COTTAGES", CERBID, SOLVA, HAVERFORDWEST, PEMBROKESHIRE SA62 6YE (01348 837871). Cottages set in all coastal areas, unashamed luxury, highest residential standards. Dishwashers, microwaves, washing machines. Log fires. Linen supplied. Pets welcome. [pw!]

Croft

Village to the south-west of Cardigan.

CROFT FARM & CELTIC COTTAGES, CROFT NEAR CARDIGAN SA43 3NT (01239 615179). Luxury accommodation in thoughtfully furnished stone cottages, indoor heated pool, jacuzzi, sauna and recreation/fitness room. Orchard, colourful gardens, patio, BBQ and play area. Pets welcome. WTB 5 Dragons Award. [Pets £15 per week]

Haverfordwest

Administrative and shopping centre for the area; ideal base for exploring National Park Historic town of narrow streets; museum in castle grounds; many fine buildings.

CASTLE FARM CARAVAN PARK, MRS WENDY EVANS, CASTLE FARM, KEESTON, HAVERFORDWEST SA62 6ED (01437 710988). Enjoy a peaceful holiday on our working dairy farm. Fully-equipped six-berth caravans with colour TV etc. Pets most welcome with well behaved owners! Farmhouse B&B also available. [🐕]

MRS C. REES, DUDWELL, CAMROSE, HAVERFORDWEST, PEMBROKESHIRE. SA62 6HJ (01437 710324). Large house and stables in own grounds fully equipped, sleeps 10, close to beaches and pubs. Excellent riding country. Bring your own horse or hire nearby.

MRS TUSON, GREENWAYS GUEST HOUSE, SHOALS HOOK LANE, HAVER-
FORDWEST SA61 2XN (Tel & Fax: 01437 762345; mobile: 0378 136578; Fax:
01437 762345). A home from home in peaceful setting. Year round touring in
Pembrokeshire. Golf course, ferry, Oakwood Park, islands. Ground floor bed-
rooms, colour TV, en suite available.
Website: http:freespace.virgin.net/jeff.sutton/index.htm

PHILIP & HELEN THOMAS, NOLTON CROSS CARAVAN PARK, NOLTON, HAVER-
FORDWEST SA62 3NP (01437 710701). Small, quiet, family park set in open
countryside overlooking St Brides Bay. Ideal for touring. Luxury caravans for
hire; short breaks available. Open March to November. [🐕]

JEAN AND MAURICE GOULD, SCAMFORD CARAVAN PARK, KEESTON,
HAVERFORDWEST SA62 6HN (Tel and Fax: 01437 710304). 25 luxurious caravans (shower, fridge, microwave, colour TV). Peaceful park near lovely sandy
beaches. Super playground. Launderette. Five touring pitches, hook-ups.
Modern shower block. [Pets £5 per week]

Lawrenny

Village near River Cresswell estuary, 8 miles south-west of Narberth

MRS VIRGINIA LORT PHILLIPS, KNOWLES FARM, LAWRENNY SA68 0PX (01834
891221; Fax: 01834 891344). Come and relax with us, be spoilt and enjoy the
delights of hidden Pembrokeshire. Walk your dog along the shores of the estuary
which surrounds us. Stunning coast 15 minutes away. Bed and Breakfast £17 to
£23. Dinner on request. WTB ★★★ Farm. [🐕 One pet free, more on request]
E–mail: owenlp@globalnet.co.uk

Little Haven

Village on St Bride's Bay ,10 miles from Haverfordwest.

**HAVEN COTTAGES, WHITEGATES, LITTLE HAVEN, HAVERFORDWEST, PEM-
BROKESHIRE SA62 3LA (01437 781552). Cottages sleep two to twelve. On
Coastal Path, 200 yards beach. Organic chicken and ostrich farm. Linen pro-
vided. B&B in fishing village. AA QQQQ. [Pets £12 per week]**

Manorbier

Unspoiled village on South Pembrokeshire coast near Tenby. Sandy bay and fine coastal walks.

AQUARIUM COTTAGE, THE LOBSTER POT AND ORCHARD END, MANOR-
BIER. Three pleasant country properties. Detached cottage (sleeps 6). Ground
floor flat (sleeps 4). Detached bungalow (sleeps 6). All properties half-a-mile
from the sea. Pets Welcome. Ample parking. Electricity, heating, bed linen and
towels inclusive. Brochure from: MRS J. HUGHES, ROSE COTTAGE, MANOR-
BIER, PEMBROKESHIRE SA70 7ST (01834 871408). [🐕]

Newgale

*On St Bride's Bay 3 miles east of Solva. Long beach where at exceptionally low tide the stumps
of a submerged forest may be seen.*

MR P. W. REES, "QUALITY COTTAGES", CERBID, SOLVA, HAVERFORDWEST,
PEMBROKESHIRE SA62 6YE (01348 837871). Cottages set in all coastal areas,
unashamed luxury, highest residential standards. Dishwashers, microwaves,
washing machines. Log fires. Linen supplied. Pets welcome. [pw!]

Newport

Small town at mouth of the River Nyfer, 9 miles south west of Cardigan. Remains of 13th-century castle.

MR P. W. REES, "QUALITY COTTAGES", CERBID, SOLVA, HAVERFORDWEST, PEMBROKESHIRE SA62 6YE (01348 837871). Cottages set in all coastal areas, unashamed luxury, highest residential standards. Dishwashers, microwaves, washing machines. Log fires. Linen supplied. Pets welcome. [pw!]

Nolton Haven

Hamlet at head of inlet on St Bride's Bay. Fine coastal views.

Quality beachfront Cottages 30 yards from Nolton Haven's sandy beach. Fully equipped, sleeping 4/6. Also nearby Farm Guest House offering Bed and Breakfast. APPLY – J. CANTON, NOLTON HAVEN FARM, NOLTON HAVEN, HAVERFORDWEST SA62 6NH (01437 710263).

FOLKESTON HILL HOLIDAY BUNGALOWS. A small group of bungalows in a sheltered valley which winds down to the sea. WTB Graded. Pets welcome – no charge. Brochure from JOHN & CERI PRICE, ST BRIDES BAY COTTAGES, NINE WELLS, SOLVA, HAVERFORDWEST, PEMBROKESHIRE SA62 6UH (01437 720027). [🐾]

St David's

Smallest cathedral city in Britain, shrine of Wales' patron saint. Magnificent ruins of Bishop's Palace. Craft shops, farm parks and museums; boat trips to Ramsey Island.

LOWER MOOR COTTAGES, ST DAVID'S. Beautifully restored stone and slate cottages. panoramic views over coast and open countryside. Near coastal path and sandy beaches. Dishwashers, TV, games room, log fire, gas fired central heating. Open all year. Two to seven bedrooms; sleep four to sixteen. WTB Graded Five Dragons. Correspondence: T.M. HARDMAN. 140 CHURCH ROAD, EARLEY, READING RG6 1HR. Telephone LILIAN MARLOW (0118 9266094).

RAMSEY HOUSE, LOWER MOOR, ST DAVID'S SA62 6RP (01437 720321). Mac and Sandra Thompson offer quiet relaxation exclusively for non-smoking adults. Superior en suite rooms with central heating, TV and tea makers. Traditional Welsh cuisine. Licensed bar. Parking. Open all year. Superb beaches and walks nearby – DOGS' PARADISE! WTB ★★★★ Guest House, RAC ◆◆◆◆, AA ◆◆◆. DB&B £41 – £46. [🐾]

MR P. W. REES, "QUALITY COTTAGES", CERBID, SOLVA, HAVERFORDWEST, PEMBROKESHIRE SA62 6YE (01348 837871). Cottages set in all coastal areas, unashamed luxury, highest residential standards. Dishwashers, microwaves, washing machines. Log fires. Linen supplied. Pets welcome. [pw!]

FELINDRE COTTAGES, PORTHGAIN, ST. DAVIDS, HAVERFORDWEST, PEM-BROKESHIRE SA62 5BH (01348 831220). Well-equipped self catering cottages set in peaceful 8 acre location. Sea views. Away from main roads, safe for children and pets. WTB graded. Near sandy beaches, spectacular cliff walks and pub. [pw! Pets £10 per week]

Saundersfoot

Popular resort and sailing centre with picturesque harbour and sandy beach. Tenby 3 miles.

MRS JOY HOLGATE, CARNE MOUNTAIN FARM, REYNALTON, KILGETTY SA68 0PD (01834 860 546). A warm welcome awaits you at our lovely 200-year-old farmhouse set amidst the peace and tranquillity of the beautiful Pembrokeshire countryside. Bedrooms have colour TV and all facilities. B&B from £16. [One dog free, second pet £1.00 per night.]

VINE FARM, THE RIDGEWAY, SAUNDERSFOOT SA69 9LA (01834 813543). Former Farmhouse close to village and beaches. Central heating, log fires. All rooms en suite. Pets welcome – garden and paddock. AA Listed ◆◆◆◆. [pw! Pets £1-£2 per night.] Also available, one-bedroomed self -catering flat for 2.

Solva

Picturesque coastal village with sheltered harbour and excellent craft shops. Sailing and watersports; sea fishing, long sandy beach.

MRS M. JONES, LOCHMEYLER FARM GUEST HOUSE, PEN-Y-CWM, NEAR SOLVA, ST DAVID'S SA62 6LL (Tel: 01348 837724; Fax: 01348 837622). WTB ★★★★ Farm, RAC ◆◆◆◆◆, Welcome Host Gold Award. 16 en suite luxury bedrooms, eight in the cottage suites adjacent to the house. All bedrooms non-smoking, with TV, video and refreshment facilities. Children Welcome. [pw! 🐕]

MR P. W. REES, "QUALITY COTTAGES", CERBID, SOLVA, HAVERFORDWEST, PEMBROKESHIRE SA62 6YE (01348 837871). Cottages set in all coastal areas, unashamed luxury, highest residential standards. Dishwashers, microwaves, washing machines. Log fires. Linen supplied. Pets welcome. [pw!]

Tenby

Popular resort with two wide beaches. Fishing trips, craft shops, museum. Medieval castle ruins, 13th-century church. Golf, fishing and watersports; boat trips to nearby Caldy Island with monastery and medieval church.

MR P. W. REES, "QUALITY COTTAGES", CERBID, SOLVA, HAVERFORDWEST, PEMBROKESHIRE SA62 6YE (01348 837871). Cottages set in all coastal areas, unashamed luxury, highest residential standards. Dishwashers, microwaves, washing machines. Log fires. Linen supplied. Pets welcome. [pw!]

Whitland

Village 6 miles east of Narberth. Scanty ruins of 12th century Cistercian house remain.

MARGARET & PETER GILDER, LLANGWM HOUSE, WHITLAND SA34 0RB (Tel & Fax 01994 240621). Fully modernised farmhouse set in its own 15 acres. En suite bedrooms with colour TV and tea/coffee making facilities. Licensed bar. No children under five. [🐕]
E–mail: llangwm.house@tesco.net

The Park Motel
Crossgates
Llandrindod Wells
Powys LD1 6RF
Tel: (01597) 851201
WTB ★★ *Country Hotel*

Set in 3 acres, amidst beautiful Mid-Wales countryside, near the famous Elan Valley reservoirs and centrally situated for touring. Accommodation in modern luxury self-contained centrally heated Chalets, each with twin-bedded room and shower room with WC, tea/coffee-making facilities. Colour TV, kitchenette for self-catering option. Licensed restaurant open all day for meals and bar snacks. Lounge bar. Swimming pool. Children's play area. Ample parking. Pets welcome. Resident proprietors. Games room. Brochure available.

Mrs Ann Reed, Madog's Wells, Llanfair Caereinion, Welshpool SY21 0DE Tel: 01938 810446. WTB 4 Dragons.

Tastefully furnished bungalow designed for wheelchair access (criteria 2) on a small hill farm in beautiful secluded valley. Also two six berth caravans (self contained, WC, Shower, fridge, cooker). Free gas/electricity and linen. Picnic benches, games room and children's play area. Farmhouse B&B also available from £16 per person. Astronomy Breaks: view the night sky through superb 16" Dobsonian telescope. Ideal base for touring mid-Wales. Weekly rates: Bungalow £125 to £270, open all year; Caravans £125 to £210, Open April to November. No hidden extras, daily rates available out of main holiday season.

 **OAK WOOD LODGES**

Self-catering Log Cabins

Luxurious Norwegian log cabins situated at approximately 1000ft above sea level with spectacular views of the Elan Valley and Cambrian Mountains. Enjoy pursuits such as walking, pony trekking, mountain biking, fishing, and bird watching in the most idyllic of surroundings. Excellent touring centre. Dogs welcome. Short breaks as well as full weeks. Open all year round. **For more information call 01597 811422**

FOREST CABIN BARGAIN BREAKS (02920 754887). Arguably as like the Canadian Rockies as you'll find in this country. As low as £59 for 3 nights. Includes cabin, breakfast and dinner. Pets welcome.

Brecon

Main touring centre for National Park. Busy market; Jazz Festival in summer. Brecknock Museum, ruined castle, cathedral of interest. Golf, walking, fishing, canal cruising, pony trekking.

THE BEACONS, RESTAURANT AND ACCOMMODATION, 16 BRIDGE STREET, BRECON LD3 8AH (Tel/Fax: 01874 623339). WTB 3 STARS Guest House, AA QQQ, RAC Highly Acclaimed. In the heart of the National Park surrounded by magnificent scenery, an elegant Georgian house with well equipped rooms (mostly en suite). Luxury 4 poster and king size coronet rooms also available. Candlelit restaurant offering fine food and wines. [Pets £2 per night]
E–mail: beacons@brecon.co.uk
Website: www.beacons.brecon.co.uk

MRS ANN PHILLIPS, TYLEBRYTHOS FARM, CANTREF, BRECON LD3 8LR (01874 665329). Quality self-catering accommodation with beautiful rural views in the Brecon Beacons National Park. Perfect setting for a peaceful relaxing holiday. Superb walking from the doorstep and ideal for all outdoor pursuits or as a base for touring. Well maintained lawns and childrens play area. Ample parking. Short breaks. Guests comfort my priority. Pets by prior arrangement. WTB Grade 4/5. Brochure on request. [pw! £15 per week]

SYMBOLS

🐾	Indicates that pets are welcome free of charge.
£	Indicates that a charge is made for pets: nightly or weekly.
pw!	Shows some special provision for pets; exercise facility, feeding or accommodation arrangement.
⌂	Indicates separate pets accommodation.

Builth Wells

Old country town in lovely setting on River Wye amid beautiful hills. Lively sheep and cattle markets; host to Royal Welsh Agricultural Show.

MRS KATHERINE SMITH, CAER BERIS MANOR, BUILTH WELLS LD2 3NP (01982 552601; Fax: 01982 552586). Family owned country house hotel set in 27 acres of parkland. Free salmon and trout fishing; golf nearby, superb walking and touring. All rooms en suite. WTB ★★★, AA ★★★. [Pets £3.50] Website: www.caerberis.co.uk

MRS LINDA WILLIAMS, OLD VICARAGE, ERWOOD, BUILTH WELLS LD2 3SZ (01982 560680). Beautiful situation just off A470 near Erwood in secluded grounds. Lovely views from attractive, spacious rooms with double aspects, drinks tray, washbasins, TV in bedrooms, central heating, private lounge with literature etc. Bathroom, separate WC. Produce from our vegetable garden for evening meals. B&B £15.50 – £16.50. WTB ★★★ rating.

Corris

Peaceful village 4 miles north of Machynlleth.

BRAICH GOCH INN & RESTAURANT, CORRIS, NEAR MACHYNLLETH, POWYS SY20 9RD (Tel/Fax: 01654 761229). Set in beautiful surroundings in the foothills of Snowdonia. Bedrooms en suite or with private facilities; licensed restaurant with extensive menu; cheerful beamed bar. Pets most welcome.

Crickhowell

Pleasant village in the Usk Valley at foot of Black Mountains. Fine Georgian houses, fragments of a castle, gateway of a long-vanished manor house, and 14th-cent church with elaborate tombs.

MRS P. LLEWELYN, WHITE HALL, GLANGRWYNEY, CRICKHOWELL NP8 1EW (01873 811155/840267). Comfortably furnished and well placed for exploring Black Mountains, Brecon Beacons, Big Pit Mine, Abergavenny and Hay-on-Wye. Double and twin-bedded en suite rooms with TV and tea-making. Terms from £15. WTB 2 Crowns. [🐾]

Garthmyl

Situated on A483 between Welshpool and Newtown in unspoilt countryside.

Self-catering log cabins set in 30 acres of unspoilt woodland teeming with wildlife. Central heating, colour TV, microwave etc. Pets Welcome. From £185 – £605 per cabin per week breaks. Apply PENLLWYN LODGES, GARTHMYL, POWYS SY15 6SB or Tel/Fax 01686 640269 for colour brochure. [Pets £10 per week/breaks]

Hay-on-Wye

Small market town at north end of Black Mountains, 15 miles north-east of Brecon.

PETER & OLWEN ROBERTS, YORK HOUSE, CUSOP, HAY-ON-WYE HR3 5QX (01497 820705). AA ◆◆◆◆. Enjoy a relaxing holiday in this elegant Victorian guest house quietly situated on the edge of Hay, "Town of Books". Excellent walking country for pets. [Pets £4.00 per visit.] Website: www.hay-on-wye.co.uk/yorkhouse/welcome.html

Llandrindod Wells

Popular inland resort, Victorian spa town, excellent touring centre. Golf, fishing, bowling, boating and tennis. Visitors can still take the waters at Rock Park Gardens.

THE PARK MOTEL, CROSSGATES, LLANDRINDOD WELLS LD1 6RF (01597 851201). In three acres, amidst beautiful countryside near Elan Valley. Luxury, self-contained, centrally heated Chalets. Licensed restaurant open all day. Swimming pool. Children's play area. Pets welcome. [Pets £1 per night, £5 per week]

Llanfair Caereinion

Small town on River Banwy, 8 miles west of Welshpool.

MRS ANN REED, MADOG'S WELLS, LLANFAIR CAEREINION, WELSHPOOL SY21 0DE (01938 810446). WTB 4 Dragons. Furnished bungalow designed for wheelchair access. Open all year. Also two six berth caravans, available April to November. Farmhouse B&B from £16 per person. [🐾]

Llangurig

Village on River Wye, 4 miles south-west of Llanidloes. Ideal walking countryside.

MRS J. BAILEY, GLANGWY, LLANGURIG, LLANIDLOES SY18 6RS (01686 440697). Bed, breakfast and evening meals in the countryside. Plenty of walking locally. Prices on request.

A. Hine, Wye View Cottages, Cilgwrgan Fach, Llangurig, Powys SY18 6RX (01686 440205; Fax: 01686 412200). WTB 4 Dragons. Nestled into a hillside with breathtaking views over River Wye Valley and mountains beyond. Very comfortable accommodation, four poster bed, oakbeams. Inns/restaurants walking distance. Wonderful walks from our grounds, kids love feeding our affectionate sheep. Beautiful and peaceful. [£7.50 per week. pw!]

Presteigne

An attractive old town with half-timbered houses. Ideal for hillside rambles and pony trekking.

MRS R. L. JONES, UPPER HOUSE, KINNERTON, NEAR PRESTEIGNE LD8 2PE (01547 560207). Charming Tudor cottage in lovely Border countryside. 2 miles from Offa's Dyke. Children and pets welcome. Storage heaters, washing machine, microwave, colour TV, woodburner. Linen hire optional. Sleeps 5 plus 2 cots. Ample parking. Sun trap garden. On working farm in peaceful hamlet. WTB Grade 4. [🐾]

Rhayader

Small market town on River Wye north of Builth Wells. Popular for angling and pony trekking.

OAK WOOD LODGES – SELF-CATERING LOG CABINS. Luxurious Norwegian log cabins with spectacular views of the Elan Valley and Cambrian Mountains. Walking, pony trekking, mountain biking, fishing, and bird watching in idyllic surroundings. (01597 811422)

SOUTH WALES

Abergavenny

Historic market town at south-eastern gateway to Brecon Beacons National Park. Pony trekking, leisure centre; excellent touring base for Vale of Usk.

CHRISTINE SMITH, THE HALF MOON, LLANTHONY, NEAR ABERGAVENNY NP7 7NN (01873 890611). Friendly 17th-century inn. Serves good food and real ale. Enjoy wonderful scenery of Black Mountains. Good base. Walking, pony trekking. Dogs welcome. [🐾]

Gower

Britain's first designated Area of Outstanding Natural Beauty with numerous sandy beaches and lovely countryside to explore.

CULVER HOUSE HOTEL, PORT EYNON, GOWER SA3 1NN (01792 390755). Small, friendly hotel with fabulous food and quality service. Peacefully situated, with superb coast and countryside. En suite, sea views. WTB ★★ Hotel, AA ★★. [Pets £2 per night.]

Llanmadoc

Village on Gower Peninsula, a secluded area with unspoilt beaches and many bird reserves.

MRS A. MAIN, TALLIZMAND, LLANMADOC, GOWER SA3 1DE (01792 386373). Located near the splendid Gower coastline, surrounded by beautiful countryside. Tallizmand has tastefully furnished en suite bedrooms with tea/coffee facilities. Home cooking, packed lunches. Pets by arrangement. WTB 3 Stars Guest House [🐾]

Mumbles

Seaside resort of Swansea to west and north west of Mumbles Head

MUMBLES & SWANSEA holiday homes, some with sea views. Flat locations. Well equipped, modern conveniences – carpets throughout. Convenient for beaches, countryside and town's amenities. Personally supervised. WTB Graded Three and Four Dragons. Cottage, flat and town house available. MRS JEAN GRIERSON, 112 MUMBLES ROAD, BLACKPILL, SWANSEA SA3 5AS (01792 402278). [🐾]

Pontypool

Town 8 miles north of Newport. Valley Inheritance exhibition centre in former Georgian stable of Pontypool Park House tells story of the valleys.

MRS S. ARMITAGE, TY'RYWEN FARM, TREVETHIN, PONTYPOOL NP4 8TT (Tel & Fax: 01495 785200). A very remote 16th Century Longhouse high in the Brecon Beacons National Park. Spacious en suite rooms, colour TV and beverage tray. Some four-posters. One room with jacuzzi. No smoking. No children. Light supper available. B&B from £20.00. We can also take horses. Stabling for two horses. Hill farm grazing, miles of unfenced riding. [🐾]

Wye Valley

Scenic area, ideal for relaxation.

MR & MRS J. LLEWELLYN, CWRT-Y-GAER, WOLVESNEWTON, CHEPSTOW NP16 6PR (01291 650700). 1, 4 or more dogs welcome free. Self-catering, attractively converted stone buildings of Welsh Longhouse. 20 acres, super views of Usk Vale. Brochure. Three units (one suitable for disabled). Four Dragons Award. [🐾 pw!]

SPECIAL SUPPLEMENTS:

Kennels & Catteries and *Holidays with Horses*

If you are having difficulty in locating a kennel or cattery in an area other than your own, then we hope that the special *Kennels and Catteries Supplement* will prove useful. And for the horse lover, the *Holidays with Horses Supplement* provides a selection of accommodation where horse and owner/rider can be put up at the same address – if not actually under the same roof!

We would be grateful if readers making enquiries and/or bookings from these Supplements would mention *Pets Welcome!*.

KENNELS AND CATTERIES

Cambridgeshire

NOBLES FARM CATTERY,
RUSSET LODGE, NOBLES LANE, BLUNTISHAM,
HUNTINGDON PE17 3LG (Tel/Fax: 01487 841327)

Cats only. 27 pens, all different – heated, with play areas. Special diets catered for. All cats must be vaccinated; 24 hr emergency veterinary service plus comprehensive insurance inclusive. Long stay boarding; special care for elderly or infirm cats. Inspection welcome.

FIELDSVIEW KENNELS AND CATTERY,
FENSTANTON ROAD, HILTON, HUNTINGDON PE18 9JA
(Tel: 01480 830215)

Dogs, cats and small animals. All have individual kennels and runs. Full current inoculation required. Pampered pets section and grooming parlour for all breeds – Member of Pet Groomers Association. Pets with special diets catered for. Collection and delivery service available. All staff qualified to NVQ level 2.

Derbyshire

UPPERWOOD COUNTRY BOARDING ESTABLISHMENT
TOP OF SYDNOPE HILL, TWO DALES, MATLOCK DE4 5LP
(Tel: 01629 733268: Fax: 01629 733571)

40 dogs, 14 cats. Dogs with individual heated accommodation with six outside paddocks and runs, aces of space, organised playtimes, proper walks. Cats individual pens. Require full vaccination certificate including "Intrac" nasal drops for canine coughs. Grooming parlour. One to one obedience training. Microchipping, pet tagging, worming service.

Essex

KAHN-ROHAN KENNELS,
TUDWICK ROAD, LITTLE TOTHAM, NEAR MALDON CM9 8LR
(Tel: 01621 815344)

54 dogs, 40 cats; both have large sleeping quarters and individual outside runs with grass paddocks for dogs and 6' outside runs for cats. Full up-to-date vaccination certificates required. Animal rescue unit.

Hertfordshire

NATIONAL ANIMAL WELFARE TRUST (AWT TRADING LTD)
TYLER'S WAY, WATFORD BY-PASS, WATFORD WD2 8HQ
(Tel: 0181 950 1320)

Dogs (36) cats (36) and small domestic pets. Concrete kennels with runs for dogs and cats, heated in winter. All dogs must be fully inoculated; cats must be inoculated against feline enteritis and cat flu. Inspection welcomed. Bathing and grooming available.

Kent

PARK HOUSE ANIMAL SANCTUARY,
PARK HOUSE, STELLING MINNIS, NEAR CANTERBURY CT4 6AN
(Tel: 01303 862622; Fax: 01303 863007)

Dogs, cats, birds and small animals. Viewing welcome by appointment. Individual housing, runs heated, dogs lead walked. Full inoculations for dogs, cats and rabbits essential. Veterinary clinic for those on limited income. Grooming. Sanctuary.

THE ANIMAL INN,
DOVER ROAD, RINGWOULD, NEAR DEAL CT14 8HH
(Tel: 01304 373597; Fax 01304 380305)
E-mail: jrmeshaw@animalin.demon.co.uk

Dogs (110), cats (40). Daily vet visit as also quarantine. Dogs in individual kennels, all with own covered runs; cats in individual pens; kennels and pens have optional heating. Require proof of vaccination within previous 12 months. Open all year. £1 Trial Day available. Day boarding for those trips to France. Individual diets fed.

DENELAND BOARDING KENNELS AND CATTERY,
TURNAGAIN LODGE, HOOK GREEN, WILMINGTON DA2 7AJ
(Tel: 01322 225191)

Dogs and cats. Individual kennels and cat pens, each with own exercise area. Must have current full inoculation certificate. We specialise in small breeds.

THE OTFORD BOARDING KENNELS
PILGRIMS WAY WEST, OTFORD, SEVENOAKS, TN14 5JN
(Tel: 01959 525880)
E-mail: hmosaic@aol.com

50 dogs. Licensed kennels. Open all year. 24 hour vet cover. Luxury heated individual kennels with attached covered runs. Free individual exercise in three grassed paddocks. Individual diets. Vaccination certificates must be produced. Pampered pets only!

Lincolnshire

GLEBE CATTERY,
GLEBE FARMHOUSE, GLENTHAM, MARKET RASEN LN8 2AQ
(Tel: 01673 878269)

Licensed for 30 cats. Large indoor heated runs. Full vaccination essential. Collection and delivery service. Special diets catered for. Open all year. Highly recommended throughout the area.

Merseyside

KENNOTELS
GRINTON LODGE FARM, CHURCH ROAD, ROBY L36 9TN
(Tel & Fax: 0151 489 4645)

110 dogs, 108 cats. Dogs individual kennels. Cats individual pens. Veterinary insurance while boarding is included. Full vaccination and boosters up to date (card must be shown). Local collection and delivery service. Open all year.

Nottinghamshire

HILLBANKS KENNELS AND CATTERY,
COMMONSIDE, SELSTON NG16 6FL
(Tel: 01773 860586; Fax: 01773 860586)

36 dogs, 20 cats, up to two paddocks (ponies, llamas, goats). Small pets boarded. Large kennels with covered runs. Cats have 8' indoor cubicles and heated chalets with outdoor runs. Vet on call. Up-to-date vaccination and boosters required (at least two weeks in advance). Grooming and show preparation. Daily rates.

Warwickshire

**TUDOR KENNELS AND CATTERY,
CAMPDEN ROAD, WILLICOTE, STRATFORD-UPON-AVON CV37 8LL
(Tel: 01789 205016)**

Dogs (36), cats (12). Double and single kennels with individual runs; double and single cat accommodation. Current inoculation certificates should be produced. Dogs lead walked daily. Special diets catered for; bathing and grooming available. Cuddles guaranteed!

West Yorkshire

**CARLTON BOARDING KENNELS,
CHURCH HOUSE, CARLTON, YEADON, NEAR LEEDS LS19 7BG
(Tel: 0113 250 5113)**

Dogs (40), cats (20). Concrete individual accommodation with outside runs; heated kennels and cat palaces. Dogs walked on lead twice daily in farm land. Full vaccination required. Trimming by qualified staff.

Carmarthenshire

**THE LINKS BOARDING KENNELS,
PEMBREY SA16 0HT
(Tel: 01554 832409)**

Dogs and cats. Individual heated kennels with large runs; two enclosed grass runs for dogs to run free; heated cattery with covered run. All animals must be inoculated. Other small domestic animals catered for.

Are you having difficulty locating a boarding kennel/cattery in an area other than your own? Have you words of praise (or criticism) for a kennel/cattery you have used? The Boarding Kennels Advisory Bureau is a free service for the general public and monitors progress within the industry. Please write with your enquiry (enclosing SAE) or comments:

The Boarding Kennels Advisory Bureau, c/o Blue Grass Animal Hotel,

Little Leigh, Near Northwich, Cheshire CW8 4RJ (Tel: 01606 891303)

FHG PUBLICATIONS LIMITED publish a large range of well-known accommodation guides. We will be happy to send you details or you can use the order form at the back of this book.

HOLIDAYS WITH HORSES

Cornwall/Otterham Station

**JOHN AND ANGIE LAPHAM,
SEA VIEW FARM, OTTERHAM STATION, CAMELFORD PL32 9SW
(Tel: 01840 261355).**

Comfy guest house in 10 acres, beaches nearby. Walking, fishing, riding, Bodmin Moor 3 miles. Rooms, tea/coffee, H&C, B&B, EM optional. Dogs welcome free.

Devon/Dartmoor

**MRS J.COLTON
PEEK HILL FARM, DOUSLAND, YELVERTON PL20 6PD
(Tel/Fax: 01822 854808)**

The gateway to dartmoor. Sunny, en suite rooms. The biggest breakfast. Packed lunches. Evening meal. Spectacular views. All pets welcomed. 2 Crowns Commended

Devon/Exmoor

**JAYE JONES & HELEN ASHER,
TWITCHEN FARM,
CHALLACOMBE, BARNSTAPLE EX31 4TT
(Telephone 01598 763568;
E-mail: holidays@twitchen.co.uk; Website: www.twitchen.co.uk)**

Exmoor has 400 miles of bridlepaths! Explore heather moorland and wooded valleys. We offer excellent stabling, rider guide, route planning. good food and a hot bath!

Durham/Castleside

**LIZ LAWSON,
BEE COTTAGE FARM, CASTLESIDE, CONSETT DH8 9HW
(Tel: 01207 508224)**

Working farm in lovely surroundings. Ideal for touring. Bed & Breakfast; Evening meal available.

Durham/Waterhouses

**MRS P. A. BOOTH,
IVESLEY EQUESTRIAN CENTRE, WATERHOUSES, DURHAM DH7 9HB
0191 373 4324; Fax: 0191 373 4757)**

Elegantly furnished comfortable country house set in 220 acres. Near Durham but quiet and rural. En suite bedrooms. Excellent food. Licensed. Equestrian facilities available.

Hampshire/Bramshaw

**BRAMBLE HILL HOTEL,
BRAMSHAW, NEAR LYNDHURST S043 7JG
(01703 813165).**

Fully licensed country house hotel with own livery stables. Unique seclusion amidst glorious surroundings. Unlimited riding and walking territory. Dogs welcome. DIY livery for horses.

Hampshire/Ringwood

**JENNY MONGER,
LITTLE HORSESHOES, SOUTH GORLEY, RINGWOOD BH24 3NL
(Tel: 01425 479340
E-mail: jenny@littlehorseshoes.freeserve.co.uk)**

ETC ♔♔♔ Commended. Give your horse a holiday. Excellent DIY stabling and grazing, direct forest/heath access. Cosy, superior modern bungalow, enclosed garden and patio. Well behaved dogs and owners welcome.

Lancashire/Pilling

**BELL FARM,
BRADSHAW LANE, SCRONKEY, PILLING, PRESTON PR3 6SN
(01253 790324).**

18th century farmhouse with one family room with en suite facilities, one double and one twin with private bathroom. All centrally heated. Full English breakfast is served. Open all year except Christmas and New Year. B&B from £20.

Shropshire/Church Stretton

**MRS C.F. BRANDON-LODGE,
NORTH HILL FARM, CARDINGTON, CHURCH STRETTON SY6 7LL
(01694 771532)**

Rooms with a view! B&B in beautiful Shropshire hills. TV in rooms, tea etc. Ideal walking country. Children, dogs and horses welcome.

Somerset/Exford

**BRYAN & JANE JACKSON,
HUNTERS MOON, EXFORD, NEAR MINEHEAD TA24 7PP
(Tel: 01643 831695).**

Cosy bungalow smallholding in the heart of Exmoor. Good food (optional Evening Meal), glorious views, friendly atmosphere. Pets welcome free, stabling available. Open all year.

North Yorkshire/Helmsley

**MRS ELIZABETH EASTON,
LOCKTON HOUSE FARM, BILSDALE, HELMSLEY YO6 5NE
(Tel: 01439 798303)**

Bring your horse and stay on a farm. Wonderful riding over moorland and woodland; many bridleways. Horses stabled or at grass.

North Yorkshire/Leyburn

**PARK GRANGE HOLIDAY FARM
PAM SHEPPARD, LOW GILL FARM, AGGLETHORPE, LEYBURN DL8 4TN
(Tel: 01969 640258)**

A working farm close to Leyburn, Wensleydale. Children, dogs and horses welcome. Ample parking. Grazing/stabling for horses and ponies. We cater for special occasions – Yorkshire Welcome Pack for every booking.

North Yorkshire/Whitby

**MRS TYERMAN,
PARTRIDGE NEST FARM, ESKDALESIDE, SLEIGHTS,
WHITBY YO22 5ES
(Tel: 01947 810450).**

Six caravans on secluded site, five miles from Whitby and sea. Ideal touring centre. All have mains electricity, colour TV, fridge, gas cooker.

North Yorkshire/York

**HIGH BELTHORPE
MEG ABU HAMDAN, BISHOP WILTON, YORK YO4 1SB
(Tel: 01759 368238; Mobile: 078 89 270970)**

BHS Approved Livery yard in lovely surroundings. Bring your horse to enjoy the most fabulous hacking over the Yorkshire Wolds, still unspoilt and quiet. Farmhouse B&B.

Dumfries & Galloway/Dumfries

**BARNSOUL FARM,
IRONGRAY, SHAWHEAD, DUMFRIES DG2 9SQ
(Tel/Fax 01387 730249).
Website: BarnsoulDG@aol.com**

Barnsoul, one of Galloway's scenic working farms. Birdwatching, walking, fishing on your doorstep. Spot the dog awaits your arrival. Open Easter-October.

Dumfries & Galloway/Dumfries

**DAVID & GILL STEWART,
GUBHILL FARM, AE, DUMFRIES DG1 1RL
(01387 860648)
E-mail: stewart@creaturefeature.freeserve.co.uk**

Listed farm steading flats in peaceful pastoral valley surrounded by wooded hills and forest lanes. Nature-friendly management. Lower flat wheelchair compatible. Riding, fishing, mountain biking and hillwalking all nearby.

Dumfries & Galloway/Castle Douglas

**RUSKO HOLIDAYS,
RUSKO, GATEHOUSE OF FLEET, CASTLE DOUGLAS. DG7 2BS
(01557 814215; Fax: 01557 814679)**

Lovely spacious farmhouse and cosy, comfortable cottages near beaches, hills and forests. Use of tennis court. loch and river fishing with tuition given, stabling and grazing available for your own horse, beautiful walking and riding country. Rates £150-£600. 2-3 Stars

Edinburgh & Lothians/Rosewell

**DUNCAN HUNTER
HUNTER HOLIDAY COTTAGES, ROSEWELL, EDINBURGH
(Tel: 0131 448 0888 Fax: 0131 440 2082).
E-mail: hunter@holidaycottages.demon.co.uk
Website: www.holidaycottages.demon.co.uk**

Superior cottages, recently renovated with modern facilities, sleeping six to eight plus, in beautiful countryside only eight miles from Edinburgh. The ideal base for the perfect Scottish holiday. Also B&B, £20-£25 per night.

Anglesey and Gwynedd/Dwyran

**JUDY HUTCHINGS,
TAL-Y-FOEL STUD FARM AND RIDING CENTRE,
DWYRAN, ANGLESEY LL61 6LQ
(Tel: 01248 430377; Fax: 01248 430977)**

Comfortable waterfront WTB three star bed and breakfast and private caravan. Stabled livery. Open all year. Several miles of grass tracks and beach track riding, outdoor menage and cross country training course. Lessons.

FHG PUBLICATIONS

publish a large range of well-known accommodation guides. We will be happy to send you details or you can use the order form at the back of this book.

Caernarfon/ Llanwnda

**THE STABLES HOTEL
LLANWNDA, CAERNARFON LL54 5SD
(Tel: 01286 830711; Fax: 01286 830413)**

Set in 15 acres of beautiful countryside amid the magnificent backdrop of Snowdonia. 18 en suite bedrooms, all ground floor, with colour television, intercom, direct dial telephone and tea/coffee making facilities. Holiday Cottages, Carvery Restaurant, idyllic rural location, Very popular with walkers. Ideal for Pet owners.

Pembrokeshire/Haverfordwest

**MRS C. REES,
DUDWELL, CAMROSE, HAVERFORDWEST. SA62 6HJ
(Tel: 01437 710324)**

Large house and stables in own grounds fully equipped, sleeps 10, close to beaches and pubs. Excellent riding country. Bring your own horse or hire nearby.

Visit the website
www.holidayguides.com
for details of the wide choice of
accommodation featured in the full
range of FHG titles

THE FHG DIPLOMA

HELP IMPROVE
BRITISH TOURIST STANDARDS

You are choosing holiday accommodation from our very popular FHG Publications. Whether it be a hotel, guest house, farmhouse or self-catering accommodation, we think you will find it hospitable, comfortable and clean, and your host and hostess friendly and helpful.

Why not write and tell us about it?

As a recognition of the generally well-run and excellent holiday accommodation reviewed in our publications, we at FHG Publications Ltd. present a diploma to proprietors who receive the highest recommendation from their guests who are also readers of our Guides. If you care to write to us praising the holiday you have booked through FHG Publications Ltd. – whether this be board, self-catering accommodation, a sporting or a caravan holiday, what you say will be evaluated and the proprietors who reach our final list will be contacted.

The winning proprietor will receive an attractive framed diploma to display on his premises as recognition of a high standard of comfort, amenity and hospitality. FHG Publications Ltd. offer this diploma as a contribution towards the improvement of standards in tourist accommodation in Britain. Help your excellent host or hostess to win it!

FHG DIPLOMA

We nominate ....

....

Because

Name ....

Address ....

....Telephone No ....

The Beta Guide to
Pet-Friendly Pubs

Whenever you visit one of the public houses or hotels in the BETA Guide To Pet Friendly Pubs, you can be sure your four legged friends will be more than welcome. He will find a fresh bowl of water provided by the landlord to quench his thirst and it's more than likely he will meet other canine visitors.

BETA Complete BIOplus – the best nutritional care for your dog at home and on holiday...

Beta, from Friskies, has revolutionised canine nutrition with the launch of new **Beta Complete BIOplus**. The No 1 Complete Lifestage range of nutritionally balanced, highly digestible dog food now includes chicory - a natural pre-biotic ingredient - proven to aid a dog's digestion.

In the same way that healthy nutrition helps us combat the stresses and strains of everyday life, new **Beta Complete BIOplus** will ensure, through enhanced digestion, a dog receives the maximum benefit from his diet for optimum health and vitality!

Chicory - contains a natural fibre, 'Inulin', which increases the number of good bacteria, 'bifidobacteria', in the intestine, which in turn inhibits the build up of bad bacteria. The benefits of boosting good bacteria are numerous: they assist maximum absorption of beneficial nutrients, essential vitamins and minerals, enhance a dogís immune system helping him to resist illness even when under stress, while contributing positively to his overall well being - whatever his age, breed or lifestyle.

BETA Complete BIOplus INCREASES THE NUMBER OF GOOD BACTERIA BY A FACTOR OF 100 WHEN FED OVER A CONTINUOUS PERIOD OF 30 DAYS.

Help Your Dog Beat the Heat on the Road

Follow these three tips from John Foster B.VSc., Cert.V.Ophthal., M.R.C.V.S., consultant vet to Beta Petfoods, and you could make your dog's life in the car considerably more comfortable during the summer months.

When travelling with your dog carry plenty of fresh water and a drinking bowl. An average 20kg dog will drink about 1½ pints per day. In the heat this can increase by 200-300%.

Always ensure that your dog has plenty of fresh air. Placing a dog in the back of an estate car without an open rear window is undesirable, probably cruel, and may be fatal.

When you leave your car parked in the shade, remember how quickly the sun moves. As the shade disappears, the inside of the car can quickly reach oven hot temperatures – up to 140 degrees. Heat stroke can happen within minutes.

Beta Complete BIOplus, expertly prepared and developed by the Friskies team of vets and nutritionists uses the finest ingredients with no added colourants, to provide exactly what a dog needs through every lifestage:

- ***Beta Puppy*** – higher in energy and protein to meet the demands of growth and play up to 6 months.
- ***Beta Junior*** – balanced to suit young growing dogs from 6 months to maturity.
- ***Beta Pet*** – Chicken Recipe or with Fish and Rice - provides all the nourishment an adult family dog needs.
- ***Beta Field*** – for working and sporting dogs.
- ***Beta Sensitive*** – for dogs with dietary intolerances.
- ***Beta Light*** for less active dogs or those with a tendency to put on weight
- ***NEW Beta Senior*** for older dogs
- ***Beta Treats*** – a lifestage range of delicious chews and biscuits

If you would like further advice on caring for your pet, or ***BETA Complete BIOplus*** call ***Friskies Pet Care Line, Freephone: 0800 21 21 61***

The Beta Guide to Pet-Friendly Pubs
ENGLAND

BERKSHIRE

THE GREYHOUND (known locally as 'The Dog')
The Walk, Eton Wick, Berkshire (01753 863925).
Dogs allowed throughout the pub.
Pet Regulars: Harvey (Retreiver), retreives anything, including Beer mats. KIA - German Shepherd.

THE SWAN
9 Mill Lane, Clewer, Windsor, Berkshire (01753 862069).
Dogs allowed throughout the pub.
Pet Regulars: Ziggy and her family, Simba, Thumper and Cassy (Bichon Prise) – useful for keeping your lap warm; Taffy, who has a very waggy tail and who curls up and sleeps under a chair until closing time; Ben, a very friendly Alsatian who enjoys a drop or two of London Pride; Rupert, another Bichon, who calls in after his walks; Ben, the latest addition, a playful Springer Spaniel puppy.

THE TWO BREWERS
Park Street, Windsor, Berkshire (01753 855426).
Dogs allowed, public and saloon bars.
Pet Regulars: Jack (Labrador), Chef feeds him sausages. Harry (Perranean) and his mate Molly (Newfoundland) take up the whole bar. Newcomer - 'Bear' - Black Labrador.

BUCKINGHAMSHIRE

WHITE HORSE
Village Lane, Hedgerley, Buckinghamshire SL2 3UY (01753 643225).
Dogs allowed at tables on pub frontage, beer garden (on leads), public bar.

CAMBRIDGESHIRE

YE OLD WHITE HART
Main Street, Ufford, Peterborough, Cambridgeshire (01780 740250).
Dogs allowed in non-food areas.

> **NOTE**
> A few abbreviations and 'pet' descriptions have been used In this section which deserve mention and, where necessary, explanation as follows: **GSD:** German Shepherd Dog. **...** **-cross:** a cross-breed where one breed appears identifiable. **57:** richly varied origin. You will also encounter **'mongrel'**, **'Bitsa'** and **'???!'** which are self evident and generally affectionate.

CHESHIRE

JACKSONS BOAT
Rifle Road, Sale, Cheshire (0161 973 3208).
Dogs allowed throughout on lead with the exception of the dining area.

CORNWALL

DRIFTWOOD SPARS HOTEL
Trevaunance Cove, St Agnes, Cornwall (01872 552428).
Dogs allowed everywhere except the restaurant.
Pet Regulars: Buster (Cornish Labrador cross) - devours anything.

JUBILEE INN
Pelynt, Near Looe, Cornwall PL13 2JZ (01503 220312).
Dogs allowed in all areas except restaurant; accommodation for guests with dogs.

THE MILL HOUSE INN
Trebarwith Strand, Tintagel, Cornwall PL34 0HD (01840 770200).
Pet Friendly.

THE MOLESWORTH ARMS HOTEL
Molesworth Street, Wadebridge, Cornwall PL27 7DP (01208 812055).
Dogs allowed in all public areas and in hotel rooms.
Pet Regulars: Thomson Cassidy (Black Lab) and his mate Ozzie who is partial to a bit of cheese on a Sunday.

THE WHITE HART
Chilsworthy, Near Gunnislake, Cornwall (01822 832307).
Dogs allowed in non-food bar, car park tables, beer garden.
Pet Regulars: Kai, Ben and Lawson (German Shepherds).

WELLINGTON HOTEL,
The Harbour, Boscastle, Cornwall (01840 250202).
Dogs allowed in bedrooms and on lead in pub.
Own private 10-acre woodland walk. Dogs welcome free of charge.

CUMBRIA

THE BRITANNIA INN
Elterwater, Ambleside, Cumbria LA22 9HP (015394 37210).
Dogs allowed in all areas except dining room.
Pet Regulars: Bonnie (Collie cross) meat-only scrounger with his own chair.

THE MORTAL MAN HOTEL
Troutbeck, Windermere, Cumbria LA23 lPL (015394 33193).
Dogs allowed throughout and in guest rooms.

STAG INN

Dufton, Appleby, Cumbria (017683 51608).
Dogs allowed in non-food bar, beer garden, village green plus B&B.
Pet Regulars: Kirk (Dachshund), carries out tour of inspection unaccompanied – but wearing lead; Kim (Weimaraner), best bitter drinker; Buster (Jack Russell), enjoys a quiet evening.

WATERMILL INN

School Lane, Ings, Near Staveley, Kendal, Cumbria (01539 821309).
Dogs allowed in beer garden, Wrynose bottom bar.
Pet Regulars: Smudge (sheepdog); Gowan (Westie) and Scruffy (mongrel). All enjoy a range of crisps and snacks. Scruffy regularly drinks Blacksheep special. Pub dogs Misty (Beardie). Owners cannot walk dogs past pub, without being dragged in!

DERBYSHIRE

JINGLERS/FOX & HOUNDS

(A517) Belper Road, Bradley, Ashbourne, Derbyshire (01335 370855).
Dogs allowed in non-food bars, beer garden, accommodation for guests with dogs.
Pet Regulars: Benson (Springer), Hamlet (Pointer/Lab) – pedigree drinkers and Walkers crisps crunchers.

THE GEORGE HOTEL

Commercial Road, Tideswell, Near Buxton, Derbyshire SK17 8NU (01298 871382).
Dogs allowed in snug and around the bar, water bowls provided.

DOG AND PARTRIDGE COUNTRY INN & MOTEL

Swinscoe, Ashbourne, Derbyshire (01335 343183).
Dogs allowed throughout, except restaurant.
Pet Regulars: Include Mitsy (57); Rusty (Cairn); Spider (Collie/GSD) and Rex (GSD).

DEVONSHIRE ARMS

Peak Forest, Near Buxton, Derbyshire SK17 8EJ (01298 23875)
Dogs allowed in bar.
Pet Regulars: Fergie (Collie-cross), known as "The Fireguard".

WHITE HART

Station Road, West Hallam, Derbyshire DE7 6GW (0115 932 6069).
Dogs allowed in all non-food areas.
Pet Regulars: Archie, Chester and Brewser. Four cats: Itsy, Bitsy, Jasper and Bertie.

DEVON

THE SHIP INN

Axmouth, Devon EX12 4AF (01297 21838).

A predominantly catering pub, so dogs on a lead and on the floor please.

Pet Regulars: Cassie, Charlie, Digby and Beamish. Also resident Tawny Owls.

BRENDON HOUSE HOTEL

Brendon, Lynton, North Devon EX35 6PS (01598 741206).

Dogs very welcome and allowed in tea gardens, guest bedrooms by arrangement.

Pet Regulars: Jasmine (cat), self appointed cream tea receptionist. Years of practice have perfected dirty looks at visiting dogs.

THE BULLERS ARMS

Chagford, Newton Abbot, Devon (01647 432348).

Dogs allowed throughout pub, except dining room/kitchen. "More than welcome".

CROWN AND SCEPTRE

2 Petitor Road, Torquay, Devon TQ1 4QA (01803 328290).

Dogs allowed in non-food bar, family room, lounge.

Pet Regulars: Samantha (Labrador), opens, consumes and returns empties when offered crisp packets; Max (Collie), Bar dancer; Buddy & Jessie (Collies), beer-mat frisbee experts; Cassie (Collie), scrounging.

THE DEVONSHIRE INN

Sticklepath, Near Okehampton, Devon EX20 2NW (01837 840626).

Dogs allowed in non-food bar, car park, beer garden, family room, guest rooms.

Pet Regulars: Bess (Labrador), 'minds' owner; Annie (Shihtzu), snoring a speciality; Daisy (Collie), accompanies folk singers.

THE JOURNEY'S END INN

Ringmore, Near Kingsbridge, South Devon TQ7 4HL (01548 810205).

Dogs allowed throughout the pub except in the dining room.

PALK ARMS INN

Hennock, Bovey Tracey, Devon TQ13 9QS (01626 836584).

Pets welcome.

THE ROYAL OAK INN

Dunsford, Near Exeter, Devon EX6 7DA (01647 252256).

Dogs allowed in non-food bars, beer garden, accommodation for guests with dogs.

Pet Regulars: Cleo

THE SEA TROUT INN

Staverton, Near Totnes, Devon TQ9 6PA (01803 762274).
Dogs allowed in lounge and public bar, car park tables, beer garden, owners' rooms (but not on beds).

Pet Regulars: Billy (Labrador-cross), partial to drip trays; Curnow (Poodle), brings a blanket.

THE WHITE HART HOTEL

Moretonhampstead, Newton Abbot, Devon TQ13 8NF (01647 440406).
Dogs allowed throughout, except restaurant.

Pet Regulars: Twiggers and Demi.

DORSET

THE ANVIL HOTEL

Sailsbury Road, Pimperne, Blandford, Dorset DT11 8UQ (01258 453431).
Pets allowed in bar, lounge and bedrooms.

DURHAM

MOORCOCK INN

Hill Top, Eggleston, Teesdale, County Durham DL12 9AU (01833 650395).
Pet Regulars: Thor, the in-house hound dog, and Raymond, the resident hack, welcome all equine travellers.

TAP AND SPILE

27 Front Street, Framwellgate Moor, Durham DH1 5EE (0191 386 5451).
Dogs allowed throughout the pub.

ESSEX

THE OLD SHIP

Heybridge Basin, Heybridge, Maldon, Essex (01621 854150).
Dogs allowed throughout pub.

GLOUCESTERSHIRE

THE CROWN INN

Frampton Mansell, Stroud, Gloucestershire GL6 8JG (01285 760601).
Well behaved pooches welcome in our comfortable hotel.

Pet Regulars: Buster (Sheepdog) rounds up all the beer-mats and gathers then in a pile in the corner.

THE OLD STOCKS HOTEL

The Square, Stow on the Wold, Gloucestershire GL54 1AF (01451 830666).
Dogs allowed in the beer garden, accommodation for dogs and their owners also available.

Pet Regulars: Ben (Labrador) enjoys bitter from the drip trays and Oscar (Doberman) often gets carried out as he refuses to leave.

Beta Complete Dog Food –
the best nutritional care at home and on holiday.

GREATER LONDON

THE PHOENIX

28 Thames Street, Sunbury on Thames, Middlesex (01932 789163).
Dogs allowed in non-food bar, beer garden, family room.
Pet Regulars: "Olly" (57 variety).

THE TIDE END COTTAGE

Ferry Road, Teddington, Middlesex (0181 977 7762).
Dogs allowed throughout the pub.
Pet Regulars: Chester, Golder Retriever – eats anything.

HAMPSHIRE

HIGH CORNER INN

Linwood, Near Ringwood, Hampshire BH24 3QY (01425 473973).
Dogs, horses and even goats are catered for here.

THE CHEQUERS

Ridgeway Lane, Lower Pennington, Lymington, Hants (01590 673415).
Dogs allowed in non-food bar, outdoor barbecue area (away from food).
Pet Regulars: Otto (Hungarian Vizsla), eats beer-mats and paper napkins. Likes beer but not often indulged.

THE VICTORY

High Street, Hamble-le-Rice, Southampton, Hampshire (01703 453105).
Dogs allowed.
Pet Regulars: Sefton (Labrador), his 'usual' chew bars are kept especially.

HEREFORDSHIRE

THE GREEN MAN INN

Fownhope, Hereford, Herefordshire HR1 4PE (01432 860243).
Dogs welcome, but not in the restaurant.

HERTFORDSHIRE

THE BLACK HORSE

Chorly Wood Common, Dog Kennel Lane, Rickmansworth, Herts (01923 282252).
Dogs very welcome and allowed throughout the pub.

THE ROBIN HOOD AND LITTLE JOHN

Rabley Heath, near Codicote, Hertfordshire (01438 812361).
Dogs allowed in non-food bar, car park tables, beer garden.

Pet Regulars: Bonnie (Labrador), beer-mat catcher. The locals of the pub have close to 50 dogs between them, most of which visit from time to time. The team includes a two Labrador search squad dispatched by one regular's wife to indicate time's up. When they arrive he has five minutes' drinking up time before all three leave together.

KENT

KENTISH HORSE
Cow Lane, Mark Beech, Edenbridge, Kent (01342 850493).
Dogs allowed.

THE OLD NEPTUNE
Marine Terrace, Whitstable, Kent CT5 lEJ (01227 272262).
Dogs allowed in non-food bar and beach frontage.

Pet Regulars: Josh (mongrel), solo visits, serves himself from pub water-bowl. Poppy and Fred (mongrel and GSD), soft touch and dedicated vocalist – barks at anything that runs away.

PRINCE ALBERT
38 High Street, Broadstairs, Kent CT10 ILH (01843 861937).
Dogs allowed in non-food bar.

THE SWANN INN
Little Chart, Kent TN27 OQB (01233 840702).
Dogs allowed - everywhere except restaurant.

Pet Regulars: Tramp – cross Lurcher – chases rabbits; Duster (Retriever?), places his order – for crisps – with one soft bark for the landlady.

UNCLE TOM'S CABIN
Lavender Hill, Tonbridge, Kent (01628 483339).
Dogs allowed throughout.

Pet Regulars: Flossie, Pipa, Rusty. 10pm is dog biscuit time!

LANCASHIRE

ABBEYLEE
Abbeyhills Road, Oldham, Lancashire (0161 678 8795).
Dogs allowed throughout.

Pet Regulars: Include Susie (Boxer), so fond of pork scratchings they are now used by her owners as a reward in the show ring.

MALT'N HOPS
50 Friday Street, Chorley, Lancashire PR6 0AH (01257 260967).
Dogs allowed throughout pub.

Pet Regulars: Abbie (GSD), under-seat sleeper; Brandy (Rhodesian Ridgeback), at the sound of a bag of crisps opening will lean on eater until guest's legs go numb or he is offered a share; Toby (Labrador), valued customer in his own right, due to amount of crisps he eats, also retrieves empty bags; Mork – says please for bag of crisps.

Abbreviations in this section include: **GSD**: German Shepherd Dog. **Cross:** a cross-breed where one breed appears identifiable. **57**: richly varied origin. You will also encounter **"mongrel"**. **"bitsa"** and **"???!"**: which are self-evident and generally affectionate.

LEICESTERSHIRE

CHEQUERS INN

1 Gilmorton Road, Ashby Magna, Near Lutterworth, Leicestershire (01455 209523).

Dogs allowed in bar.

Pet Regulars: Suki – talking Samoyed.

LINCOLNSHIRE

THE HAVEN INN

Ferry Road, Barrow Haven, North Lincolnshire DN19 7EX (01469 530247).

Dogs allowed in the public bar, beer garden, and bedrooms on their own bed/blanket.

Pet Regulars: Moby, the one-eyed Jack Russell, and Jester the Collie.

THE BLUE DOG INN

Main Street, Sewstern, Grantham, Lincs NG33 5QR (01476 860097).

Dogs allowed in bar.

Pet Regulars: The Guv'nor (Great Dane), best draught-excluder in history; Jenny (Westie) shares biscuits with pub cats; Jemma (98% Collie), atmosphere lapper-upper. Spud and Nelson – Terriers.

MERSEYSIDE

AMBASSADOR PRIVATE HOTEL

13 Bath Street, Southport, Merseyside PR9 0DP (01704 543998).

Dogs allowed in non-food bar, lounge, guest bedrooms.

THE SCOTCH PIPER

Southport Road, Lydiate, Merseyside (0151 526 0503).

Dogs allowed throughout the pub.

MIDLANDS

AWENTSBURY HOTEL

21 Serpentine Road, Selly Park, Birmingham B29 7HU (0121 472 1258).

Dogs allowed.

Pet Regulars: Well-behaved dogs welcome.

NORFOLK

THE SPREAD EAGLE COUNTRY INN

Barton Bendish, Norfolk PE33 9DP (01366 347295).

Pet Regulars: Dirty Gertie and Little Urn.

MARINE HOTEL

10 St Edmunds Terrace, Hunstanton, Norfolk PE36 5EH (01485 533310).

Dogs allowed throughout, except dining room.

Pet Regulars: Many dogs have returned with their owners year after year to stay at The Marine Bar.

THE OLD RAILWAY TAVERN

Eccles Road, Quidenham, Norwich, Norfolk NR16 2JG (01953 888223).

Dogs allowed in non-food bar, beer garden.

Pet Regulars: Maggie (Clumber Spaniel); Soshie (GSD); Annie (Labrador); and pub dogs Elsa (GSD). Elsa is so fond of sitting, motionless, on her own window ledge that new customers often think she's stuffed!

THE ROSE AND CROWN

Nethergate Street, Harpley, King's Lynn, Norfolk (01485 520577).

Dogs allowed in non-food bar, car park tables.

Pet Regulars: A merry bunch with shared interests – Duffy (mongrel); Tammy (Airedale); Bertie & Pru (Standard Poodles), all enjoy pub garden romps during summer and fireside seats in winter.

OXFORDSHIRE

THE BELL INN

High Street, Adderbury, Oxon (01295 810338).

Dogs allowed throughout the pub.

Owner's dogs; Bess and Elsa (Black Labradors).

SHROPSHIRE

THE TRAVELLERS REST INN

Church Stretton, Shropshire (01694 781275).

Well-mannered pets welcome - but beware of the cats!

LONGMYND HOTEL

Cunnery Road, Church Stretton, Shropshire SY6 6AG (01694 722244).

Dogs allowed in owners' hotel bedrooms but not in public areas.

Pet Regulars: Sox (Collie/Labrador), occasional drinker and regular customer greeter; Sadie (Retriever), self appointed fire-guard; and owner's dogs, Sam and Sailor.

REDFERN HOTEL

Cleobury Mortimer, Shropshire SY14 8AA (01299 270395).

Dogs allowed in reception area and in guests' bedrooms.

SOMERSET

CASTLE OF COMFORT HOTEL

Dodington, Nether Stowey, Bridgwater, Somerset TA5 1LE (01278 741264).

Pet Friendly.

THE SPARKFORD INN

High Street, Sparkford, Somerset BA22 7JN (01963 440218).

Dogs allowed in bar areas but not in restaurant; safe garden and car park.

Pet Regulars: Holly (Jack Russell) and Stoner (Grizzly Bear)!

THE BUTCHERS ARMS

Carhampton, Somerset (01643 821333).
Dogs allowed in bar.
Pet Regulars: Lobo and Chera (Samoyeds), eating ice cubes and drinking; Emma (Spaniel), a whisky drinker; Benji (Spaniel-cross), self-appointed rug. Jimmy, a pony, also occasionally drops in for a drink.

HALFWAY HOUSE

Pitney, Langport, Somerset TA10 9AB (01458 252513).
Dogs allowed.
Pet Regulars: Sam (Collie), Barnaby (Retriever), Joe (Cocker Spaniel).

HOOD ARMS

Kilve, Somerset TA5 1EA (01278 741210)
Pets welcome.

THE SHIP INN

High Street, Porlock, Somerset (01643 862507).
Dogs allowed throughout and in guests' rooms.
Pet Regulars: Include Buster, Hardy and Crackers (Jack Russells), terrorists from London; Bijoux (Peke), while on holiday at The Ship enjoys Chicken Supreme cooked to order every evening.

SUFFOLK

SIX BELLS AT BARDWELL

The Green, Bardwell, Bury St Edmunds IP31 1AW (01359 250820).
Dogs allowed in guest bedrooms and garden but not allowed in bar and restaurant.

THE COMPASSES INN

Wenhaston, Near Southwold, Suffolk IP19 9EF (01502 478319).
Dogs allowed throughout the pub and B&B (but not on the beds!). Bar open evenings only Monday to Saturday, and Sunday lunchtimes.
Pet Regulars: Raffles (ex racing Greyhound) who loves all visiting dogs and crisps; Penny (Collie) and Cisco (young Doberman) who like to stand up at the bar.

SURREY

THE CRICKETERS

12 Oxenden Road, Tongham, Farnham, Surrey (01252 333262).
Dogs allowed in beer garden.

SUSSEX

CHARCOAL BURNER

Weald Drive, Furnace Green, Crawley, West Sussex RH10 6NY (01293 653981).
Dogs allowed in non-food bar areas and front and back patios.
Pet Regulars: Lucy (Irish Setter), dedicated to cheese snips.

THE FORESTERS ARMS

High Street, Fairwarp, Near Uckfield, East Sussex TN22 3BP (01825 712808).
Dogs allowed in the beer garden and at car park tables, also inside.
Owner's Dogs: Rascal and Sophie (Springer Spaniels).

THE INN IN THE PARK (CHEF & BREWER)

Tilgate Park, Tilgate, Crawley, West Sussex RH10 5PQ (01293 545324).
Dogs allowed in Patio area.
Owner's dogs; "Mia".

THE PLOUGH

Crowhurst, Near Battle, East Sussex TN33 9AY (01424 830310).
Dogs allowed in non-food bar, car park tables, beer garden.
Pet Regulars: Kai (Belgian Shepherd), drinks halves of Websters; Poppy and Cassie (Springer Spaniels), divided between the lure of crisps and fireside.

THE PRESTONVILLE ARMS

64 Hamilton Road, Brighton, East Sussex (01273 701007).
Dogs allowed in beer garden, throughout the pub (Pet Friendly).

QUEENS HEAD

Village Green, Sedlescombe, East Sussex (01424 870228).
Dogs allowed throughout the pub.

THE SLOOP INN

Freshfield Lock, Haywards Heath, West Sussex RH17 7NP (01444 831219).
Dogs allowed in public bar and garden.

THE SMUGGLERS' ROOST

125 Sea Lane, Rustington, West Sussex BN16 2SG (01903 785714).
Dogs allowed in non-food bar, at car park tables, in beer garden, family room.
Pet Regulars: Moffat (Border Terrier), beer makes him sneeze; Leo (Border Terrier), forms instant affections with anyone who notices him; Tim (King Charles Spaniel), quite prepared to guard his corner when food appears. The landlord owns a Great Dane and an Alsatian.

THE SPORTSMAN'S ARMS

Rackham Road, Amberley, Near Arundel, West Sussex BN18 9NR (01798 831787).
Dogs allowed throughout the pub.
Pet Regulars: Pippin, Spud Mollie, Nell; Tess, the Landlord's dog will not venture into the cellar which is haunted by the ghost of a young girl.

WELLDIGGERS ARMS

Lowheath, Petworth, West Sussex GU28 0HG (01798 342287).
Dogs allowed throughout the pub.

WILTSHIRE

THE HORSE AND GROOM

The Street, Charlton, Near Malmesbury, Wiltshire (01666 823904).
Pet Regulars: P.D. (Pub Dog – Labrador).

THE PETERBOROUGH ARMS

Dauntsey Lock, Near Chippenham, Wiltshire SN15 4HD (01249 890409).
Dogs allowed in non-food bar, at car park tables, in beer garden, family room (when non-food).
Pet Regulars: Include Winston (Jack Russell), will wait for command before eating a biscuit placed on his nose; Waddi (GSD), can grab a bowling ball before it hits the skittle pins.

THE THREE HORSESHOES

High Street, Chapmanslade, Near Westbury, Wiltshire (01373 832280).
Dogs allowed in non-food bar and beer garden.
Pet Regulars: Include Clieo (Golden Retriever), possibly the youngest 'regular' in the land - his first trip to the pub was at eight weeks. Westbury and District Canine Society repair to the Three Horseshoes after training nights (Monday/Wednesday). Six cats and two dogs in residence.

WAGGON AND HORSES

High Street, Wootton Bassett, Swindon, Wiltshire (01793 850617).
Dogs allowed throughout.
Pet Regulars: Include Gemma, a very irregular Whippet/Border collie cross. She likes to balance beer-mats on her nose, then flip them over and catch them, opens and shuts doors on command, walks on her hind legs and returns empty crisp bags. She is limited to one glass of Guinness a night.

YORKSHIRE

BARNES WALLIS INN

North Howden, Howden, East Yorkshire (01430 430639).
Guide dogs only
Pet Regulars: A healthy cross-section of mongrels, Collies and Labradors. One of the most popular pastimes is giving the pub cat a bit of a run for his money.

KINGS HEAD INN

Barmby on the Marsh, East Yorkshire DN14 7HL (01757 638357).
Dogs allowed in non-food bar.
Pet Regulars: Many and varied!

THE FORESTERS ARMS

Kilburn, North Yorkshire YO6 4AH (01347 868386).
Dogs allowed throughout, except restaurant.
Pet Regulars: Ainsley (Black Labrador)..

THE GREENE DRAGON INN

Hardraw, Hawes, North Yorkshire DL8 3LZ (01969 667392).
Dogs allowed in bar, at car park tables, in beer garden, family room but not dining room or restaurant.

NEW INN HOTEL

Clapham, Near Settle, North Yorkshire LA2 8HH (015242 51203).

Dogs allowed in non-food bar, beer garden, family room.

Owner's dog: Time, (Rhodesian Ridgeback).

PREMIER HOTEL

66 Esplanade, South Cliff, Scarborough, North Yorkshire YO11 2UZ (01723 501062).

Dogs allowed throughout in non-food areas of hotel.

SIMONSTONE HALL

Hawes, North Yorkshire DL8 3LY (01969 667255).

Dogs allowed except dining area.

Pet Regulars: account for 2,000 nights per annum. More than 50% of guests are accompanied by their dogs, from Pekes to an Anatolian Shepherd (the size of a small Shetland pony!) Two dogs have stayed, with their owners, on 23 separate occasions.

THE SPINNEY

Forest Rise, Balby, Doncaster, South Yorkshire DN4 9HQ (01302 852033).

Dogs allowed throughout the pub.

Pet Regulars: Shamus (Irish Setter), pub thief. Fair game includes pool balls, beer mats, crisps, beer, coats, hats. Recently jumped 15 feet off pub roof with no ill effect. Josh; (Labrador) a guide dog. Indi and Jacques.

THE ROCKINGHAM ARMS

8 Main Street, Wentworth, Rotherham, South Yorkshire S62 7LO (01226 742075).

Dogs allowed throughout pub.

Pet Regulars: Sheeba (Springer Spaniel), Charlie and Gypsy (Black Labradors). Kate and Rags (Airedale and cross-breed), prefer lager to coffee; Holly (terrier and pub dog), dubbed 'the flying squirrel', likes everyone, whather they like it or not!

THE GOLDEN FLEECE

Lindley Road, Blackley, near Huddersfield, West Yorkshire (01422 372704).

Dogs allowed in non-food bar, at outside tables.

Pet Regulars: "Holly", (Border Collie).

If you require any further advice on caring for your dog, or on the Beta dog food range, **please call the**

Friskies Petcare Freephone
0800 738 2273

WALES

ANGLESEY & GWYNEDD

THE GRAPES HOTEL

Maentwrog, Blaenau Ffestiniog, Gwynedd LL41 4HN (01766 590365).
Pet Friendly.

PLAS YR EIFL HOTEL

Trefor, Caernarfon, Gwynedd LL54 5NA (01286 660781).
Pet Regulars: We have both dogs and cats

THE BUCKLEY HOTEL

Castle Street, Beaumaris, Isle of Anglesey LL58 8AW (01248 810415).
Dogs allowed throughout the pub, except in the dining room and bistro.

Pet Regulars: Cassie (Springer Spaniel) and Rex (mongrel), dedicated 'companion' dogs, also Charlie (Spaniel).

NORTH WALES

THE WEST ARMS HOTEL

Llanarmon Dyffryn Ceiriog, Llangollen, North Wales LL20 7LD (01691 600665).
Welcome Pets.

POWYS

SEVERN ARMS HOTEL

Penybont, Llandrindod Wells, Powys LD1 5UA (01597 851224).
Dogs allowed in the bar, but not the restaurant, and in the rooms - but not on the beds.

SCOTLAND

ABERDEEN, BANFF & MORAY

THE CLIFTON BAR

Clifton Road, Lossiemouth, Moray (01343 812100).
Dogs allowed throughout pub.

Pet Regulars: Include Zoe (Westie), has her own seat and is served coffee with two lumps; Milo (Jack Russel) and Bob (Collie).

ROYAL OAK

Station Road, Urquhart, Elgin, Moray (01343 842607).
Dogs allowed throughout pub.

Pet Regulars: Mollie (Staffordshire Bull Terrier) – food bin. Biscuits (from the landlady), Maltesers (from the landlord), sausages and burgers (from the barbecue).

ARGYLL & BUTE

CAIRNDOW STAGECOACH INN
Cairndow, Argyll PA26 8BN (01499 600286).
Pet Regulars: Our own dog Rocky is a Golden Labrador.

THE BALLACHULISH HOTEL
Ballachulish, Argyll PA39 4JY (01855 811606).
Dogs allowed in the lounge, beer garden and guests' bedrooms, excluding food areas.
Pet Regulars: Thumper (Border Collie/GSD-cross), devoted to his owner and follows him everywhere.

BORDERS

CULGRUFF HOUSE HOTEL
Crossmichael, Castle Douglas, Kirkcudbrightshire DG7 3BB (01556 670230).
Dogs allowed in family room, guest bedrooms, but must be kept on leads outside.
Pet Regulars: A cross-section of canine visitors.

HIGHLANDS

ARISAIG HOTEL
Arisaig, Inverness-shire (01687 450210).
Dogs welcome.
Pet Regulars. Regulars in the public bar include Luar (Lurcher), Cindy (Collie), Whisky (Terrier).

PERTH & KINROSS

FOUR SEASONS HOTEL
St Fillans, Perthshire (01764 685333)
Dogs allowed in all non-food areas.
Pet Regulars: Regulars are few but passing trade frequent and welcome. Previous owner's dog was a renowned water-skier.

CHANNEL ISLANDS

JERSEY

LA PULENTE INN
La Pulente, St Brelade, Jersey (01534 44487).
Dogs allowed in public bar..
Pet Regulars: Dusty (Old English Sheepdog).

ONE FOR YOUR FRIEND 2000

FHG Publications have a large range of attractive holiday accommodation guides for all kinds of holiday opportunities throughout Britain. They also make useful gifts at any time of year. Our guides are available in most bookshops and larger newsagents but we will be happy to post you a copy direct if you have any difficulty. We will also post abroad but have to charge separately for post or freight. The inclusive cost of posting and packing the guides to you or your friends in the UK is as follows:

Farm Holiday Guide
ENGLAND, SCOTLAND, WALES and IRELAND
Board, Self-catering, Caravans/Camping, Activity Holidays.   **£5.60**

SELF-CATERING HOLIDAYS IN BRITAIN
Over 1000 addresses throughout for Self-catering and caravans in Britain.   **£5.00**

BRITAIN'S BEST HOLIDAYS
A quick-reference general guide for all kinds of holidays.   **£4.20**

The FHG Guide to CARAVAN & CAMPING HOLIDAYS
Caravans for hire, sites and holiday parks and centres.   **£4.30**

BED AND BREAKFAST STOPS
Over 1000 friendly and comfortable overnight stops. Non-smoking, The Disabled and Special Diets Supplements.   **£5.60**

CHILDREN WELCOME! FAMILY HOLIDAY & ATTRACTIONS GUIDE
Family holidays with details of amenities for children and babies.   **£5.00**

Recommended SHORT BREAK HOLIDAYS IN BRITAIN
'Approved' accommodation for quality bargain breaks.
Introduced by John Carter.   **£5.00**

Recommended COUNTRY HOTELS OF BRITAIN
Including Country Houses, for the discriminating.   **£5.00**

Recommended WAYSIDE AND COUNTRY INNS OF BRITAIN
Pubs, Inns and small hotels.
Includes guide to pet-friendly pubs   **£5.00**

GOLF GUIDE
Where to play. Where to stay
Over 2000 golf courses in Britain with convenient accommodation.
In association with Golf Monthly.
Holiday Golf in France, Portugal, Spain, Thailand, Dubai and USA.   **£10.50**

PETS WELCOME!
The unique guide to holidays for pet owners and their pets.   **£5.60**

BED AND BREAKFAST IN BRITAIN
Over 1000 choices for touring and holidays throughout Britain.
Airports and Ferries Supplement.   **£4.20**

Tick your choice and send your order and payment to FHG PUBLICATIONS, ABBEY MILL BUSINESS CENTRE, SEEDHILL, PAISLEY PA1 1TJ (TEL: 0141-887 0428; FAX: 0141-889 7204). **Deduct** 10% for 2/3 titles or copies; 20% for 4 or more.

Send to: NAME ....

ADDRESS ....

....

POST CODE ....

I enclose Cheque/Postal Order for £..

SIGNATURE ....DATE ....

Please complete the following to help us improve the service we provide. How did you find out about our guides:

❑ Press   ❑ Magazines   ❑ TV/Radio   ❑ Family/Friend   ❑ Other.